£23.10

# Wills, Administration and Taxation:
# A Practical Guide

AUSTRALIA
The Law Book Company Ltd.
Sydney : Melbourne : Brisbane : Perth

CANADA
The Carswell Company Ltd.
Toronto : Calgary : Vancouver : Ottawa

INDIA
N. M. Tripathi Private Ltd.
Bombay
*and*
Eastern Law House Private Ltd.
Calcutta
M.P.P. House
Bangalore

ISRAEL
Steimatzky's Agency Ltd.
Jerusalem : Tel Aviv : Haifa

PAKISTAN
Pakistan Law House
Karachi

# Wills, Administration and Taxation: A Practical Guide

by

## J. S. Barlow, M.A. (Cantab.) LL.M. (London)
*Solicitor; Principal Lecturer, College of Law, York*

## L. C. King, LL.B. (Bristol), Dip. Crim. (Cantab.)
*Solicitor (hons); Principal Lecturer, College of Law, Lancaster Gate*

## A. G. King, M.A. *Solicitor (hons); Director of Education Clifford Chance, London; formerly Senior Lecturer, College of Law, Lancaster Gate*

FOURTH EDITION

LONDON ● SWEET & MAXWELL ● 1990

*First edition 1983*
*Second edition 1986*
*Third edition 1988*
*Fourth edition 1990*


Published by Sweet & Maxwell Ltd.
South Quay Plaza, 183 Marsh Wall, London E14 9FT
Laserset by P.B. Computer Typesetting, N. Yorks.
Printed in Great Britain by
Richard Clay Ltd., Bungay, Suffolk.


**British Library Cataloguing in Publication Data**

Barlow, J. S. (John S.)
    Wills, administration and taxation: a practical guide.—
4th ed.
    1. England. Succession. Law
    I. Title    II. King, L. C. (Lesley C.)    III. King, A. G.
(Anthony G.)
    344.2065

    ISBN 0–121–43100–8

# Preface

This book is intended principally for students studying for the Law Society's Final Examination but it is hoped that practitioners will also find it useful. It is, we believe, the only book which covers the whole syllabus for the Wills, Probate and Administration course of the examination. We have tried to keep the text reasonably concise while covering all the important points.

We have tried to ensure the book accurately states the law as at May 15, 1990. However, at the time when we delivered the manuscript the Finance Bill 1990 was still before Parliament and, therefore, there may be changes introduced at a late stage in the passage of that Bill which we have not been able to include in this edition.

J. S. Barlow                                              MAY 1990
L. C. King
A. G. King

# Acknowledgments

The publishers and authors wish to thank the following bodies for permission to reprint material from the following sources:

Butterworth & Co. (Publishers) Ltd.: *Encyclopaedia of Forms and Precedents* (4th ed.).

Capital Taxes Office: *IHT Forms 200* and *202*. Crown copyright. Reproduced with the permission of the Controller of Her Majesty's Stationery Office.

Longman Professional Publishing: Pettitt's *Will Draftsman's Handbook* (4th ed.).

Oyez: *Probate Forms* (4, 8, 11). Reproduced by kind permission of the Solicitors' Law Stationery Society Ltd.

# Contents

# Table of Cases

# Table of Statutes

NB: With the passing of the Finance Act 1986, the Capital Transfer Tax Act 1984 is now known as the Inheritance Tax Act 1984. References in this table are to the name of the Act as it appears in the text.

# Table of Statutory Instruments

# 1. Introduction: What to do After Death

When a person dies there are a number of practical steps that must be taken. For example, the death must be registered, the funeral arranged and the property of the deceased must be made safe. These matters are usually dealt with by members of the deceased's family or by friends.

The question then arises "Who is to be entitled to the deceased's assets?" It is at this point that a solicitor is most likely to be consulted. It is often assumed that the disposition of property depends entirely on whether or not a deceased made a valid will but in fact the disposition of many substantial assets is not affected by the presence or absence of a will. For example, if a deceased owned a house as a joint tenant with another person that property will pass automatically to the survivor as a result of the right of survivorship; if the deceased had taken out insurance policies for the benefit of other people the proceeds of such policies will frequently be paid directly to those people; if the terms of the deceased's employment provide for payment of a lump sum on death it is usual for the trustees of the scheme to be given a discretion to pay the lump sum to the person or persons they consider appropriate (the employee is entitled to inform the trustees of his or her wishes as to the destination of the lump sum but the trustees have an overriding discretion). These matters are discussed in Chapter 21.

The disposition of other assets does, however, depend on whether or not there is a valid will. If there is no valid will the disposition of property will be determined by the intestacy rules (explained in Chapter 3). If there is a will it is necessary to discover whether or not it is valid. This requires a consideration of whether or not the testator had sufficient mental capacity at the time the will was made and whether the appropriate formalities were complied with (see Chapter 2). It is quite possible for a will successfully to dispose of some but not all of

1

the deceased's assets. This may be because the will does not deal with all of the deceased's property or because some of the gifts fail (see Chapters 16 & 17). In such cases the disposition of the property is governed partly by the will and partly by the intestacy rules.

It may be difficult to discover whether or not a will exists. If one cannot be found amongst the deceased's papers it is advisable to contact any solicitors consulted by the deceased to discover whether or not a will was deposited with them and to contact the deceased's bank to discover whether or not the deceased had a safe deposit box which might contain it. There is a procedure whereby wills can be deposited during a person's lifetime at the Principal Registry of the Family Division but this is little used. However, it would obviously be worth contacting the Registry if a will is proving difficult to find (there are similar provisions for Scotland and Northern Ireland).

It is necessary for someone to undertake the task of finding the will and checking whether or not it is valid. It is also necessary for someone to collect in the assets of the deceased, pay the debts and other liabilities of the deceased and then transfer the remaining assets to the persons entitled. In order to collect in the assets a person dealing with the estate will often have to *prove* that he or she has authority to deal with the deceased's assets. This is done by producing a grant of representation obtained from the Probate Registry by the person(s) entitled to administer the estate.

Similarly there may be problems when it comes to transferring property of the deceased to the persons entitled. In the case of chattels it will often be sufficient to hand them to the person entitled; many assets (for example, land) are, however, held in the name of the deceased and must somehow be transferred into the name of the new owner if the new owner is to be able to deal with them. A grant of representation enables the person entitled to act on behalf of the estate of the deceased person to transfer property into the name of the new owner.

If the deceased by will appointed someone to administer his estate, that person is called an executor and obtains a grant of representation called a grant of probate which merely *confirms* that person's authority to act in connection with the estate. If no executor was appointed or if the appointed executor is not willing or able to act the Non-Contentious Probate Rules 1987 set out an order for determining who is entitled to act; such a person is called an administrator and must obtain a grant of letters of administration which *confers* authority to act.

Executors and administrators can both be referred to as "the personal representatives" of the deceased.

It will often be necessary to obtain a grant of representation in connection with the administration before assets can be collected in or transferred to beneficiaries. The procedure is explained in Chapter 10.

Acting as executor or administrator is a time consuming task. It is also one that carries with it duties and obligations and if those duties are not properly carried out there may be personal liability (this is discussed in Chapter 11). Readers may wonder why anyone is ever willing to act as a personal representative. There are a variety of reasons. Solicitors, banks and trust corporations will be willing to act as executors provided the will authorises them to charge for their services; beneficiaries will usually be willing to act since until someone accepts office it may be impossible to distribute the assets; friends or relatives of the deceased appointed as executors may be willing to accept office as a mark of their respect for the deceased and as a way of helping the bereaved.

# 2. Is There a Valid Will?

## A. Formalities

### 1. INTRODUCTION

The formalities required for a valid will are set out in Wills Act **2.1**
1837, s.9, as substituted by Administration of Justice Act 1982,
s.17. A will which fails to comply with these formalities is
invalid and cannot be admitted to probate.

The substituted section 9 provides that:

"No will shall be valid unless—
- (a) it is in writing, and signed by the testator, or by some other person in his presence and by his direction; and
- (b) it appears that the testator intended by his signature to give effect to the will; and
- (c) the signature is made or acknowledged by the testator in the presence of two or more witnesses present at the same time; and
- (d) each witness either—
  - (i) attests and signs the will; or
  - (ii) acknowledges his signature,
  in the presence of the testator (but not necessarily in the presence of any other witness), but no form of attestation shall be necessary."

Different formalities are required in the case of a statutory will
of a mental patient and a privileged testator may make a valid
will informally (see paragraphs 2.11–2.12 below).

### 2. "IN WRITING"

A will must be "in writing." The writing may be the **2.2**
handwriting of the testator or any other person or it may be
typewriting or any form of printing or (presumably) produced
by a photographic process. The writing may be in ink, pencil or
produced by any other means which make it visible. However,

using a combination of ink and pencil writing raises a rebuttable presumption that the parts in pencil are deliberative only and they will be excluded from probate in the absence of evidence that the testator intended them to be final.

A will may be made on any material and may be written in any language (or even in code provided that evidence is available from which the code may be deciphered).

In practice most wills are either prepared by a solicitor and typed on paper or are handwritten by the testator on a will form which contains printed clauses for the standard parts of the will.

## 3. THE SIGNATURE

*Signature of the testator*

**2.3** Any mark made by the testator is a valid signature provided the testator *intended* it to be his signature. Testators should be encouraged to sign with their usual signatures so as to avoid any doubt as to the validity of the signature.

The following have been held to be signatures:

(i) a mark made by a rubber stamp with the testator's name on it (*In the Goods of Jenkins* (1863));
(ii) the thumb print of an illiterate (*In the Estate of Finn* (1935));
(iii) a set of initials (*In the Goods of Savory* (1851)).

The signature need not consist of a name at all. Thus in *In the Estate of Cook* (1960) a document ending with the words "your loving mother" was admitted to probate on the basis that the testatrix in writing them had intended to refer back to her name which appeared earlier in the document.

The mark relied on as a signature must be complete in the sense that the testator completed as much as he *intended* to be his signature. For example, in *Re Colling* (1972) the testator started to sign his name in the presence of two witnesses one of whom left before he had finished writing. The will was held not to be properly executed since the signature was not completed in the presence of two witnesses. In *In the Goods of Chalcraft* (1948) the testatrix started to sign her name and wrote "E. Chal" before she became too weak to continue. This was held to be a valid signature on the basis that she had decided to end the signature at that point and so the signature was complete.

*Signature by another person*

**2.4** The signature of some person other than the testator is valid provided it is made "in his presence and by his direction." The testator must be present both mentally and physically when the signature is made (see paragraph 2.6 below for the meaning of "presence").

The person signing at the testator's direction may be any person including one of the witnesses and may sign either with his own name or with the testator's name. (It is best for the person signing to sign his own name and write that he is signing on behalf of the testator, in his presence and by his direction).

## 4. THE TESTATOR INTENDED BY HIS SIGNATURE TO GIVE EFFECT TO HIS WILL

The original section 9 required that the signature should be "at **2.5** the foot or end" of the will. This led to a number of cases where probate was refused because the position of the signature did not comply exactly with this description. The Wills Act Amendment Act 1852 was then passed to extend the meaning of "foot or end." However, the excessively complicated wording of that Act forced the courts to make some very narrow distinctions. The substituted section 9 now no longer requires that the signature should be at the foot or end of the will. It is sufficient that "it appears that the testator intended by his signature to give effect to the will."

The exact scope of this requirement will have to be decided upon by the court. A signature in the margin of a will would probably satisfy the requirement and so probably would a signature on a separate page attached to the beginning or end of the will. A handwritten will which happened to include the testator's name (for example by starting with words such as "This is the will of me John Smith ... ") might, however, still be refused probate on the basis that the words were not intended as a validating *signature* at all but merely as a description of the testator.

The practice (resulting from the wording of the Wills Act Amendment Act 1852) of admitting part of a document to probate but of refusing to admit the parts which appear physically after the signature in certain circumstances, would seem no longer to be possible. This is because the substituted section contemplates that the signature validates all or none of the will.

A signature on an envelope containing an otherwise unsigned will is valid if it was intended to give effect to the will. However, if the signature was written for some other reason (for example, to *identify* the will) the will is not validly signed.

5. SIGNATURE MADE OR ACKNOWLEDGED IN THE PRESENCE OF
AT LEAST TWO WITNESSES

**2.6**   The substituted section 9 (like its predecessor) requires that the
testator's signature is "made or acknowledged by the testator in
the presence of two or more witnesses present at the same
time." A signature is made in the presence of witnesses if they
see the testator in the act of signing. The witnesses are not
required to look at the signature itself nor need they know that
the document is a will. It is not necessary to prove that the
witnesses actually saw the act of signing; it is sufficient to show
they were in such a position that they *could* have seen.

An acknowledgment of signature can be made by words or by
conduct. There is an acknowledgement if the testator, or
someone else in his presence, asks the witnesses to sign a
document and they see his signature on it. The witnesses need
not know that the document is a will. However, they must see
the signature or at least have an opportunity of doing so. If the
*signature* is covered up there is, therefore, no valid acknowledgment (however, the fact that the rest of the will is covered up
does not prevent the acknowledgment being valid). The
acknowledgment must be made to two or more witnesses
present *at the same time*. A will is not, therefore, valid if an
acknowledgment is made by the testator to each witness in the
absence of the other.

6. WITNESSES

*Attestation*

**2.7**   The substituted section 9 requires that each witness must attest
and sign the will or acknowledge his signature in the presence of
the testator. It is not essential that they should sign in each
other's presence although, as we have already seen, they must
both be present when the testator signs or acknowledges his
signature. The signatures of the witnesses must "attest" the will,
that is the signature must be placed on the will with the
intention of validating the testator's signature and not, for
example, for the purpose of merely identifying the will. The
signatures may appear anywhere on the will and need not be
next to or after the testator's signature.

The testator must be mentally and physically present when
the witnesses sign. The testator is not mentally present if, for
example, he lapses into a coma before the witnesses have
finished signing. The testator need not have actually seen the
witnesses sign: he is regarded as physically present if he could

have seen them had he chosen to look. Thus, in *Casson* v. *Dade* (1781) the testatrix signed in her solicitor's office in the presence of two witnesses and then retired to her carriage which was waiting in the street outside. There was no evidence that she saw the witnesses sign but if she had turned her head she could have seen them through the windows of the carriage and the office. The will was admitted to probate.

*Capacity of witnesses*
No particular rules are laid down as to who may act as a **2.8** witness. The sole test is whether the witnesses were capable of attesting at the time when they signed. A minor may therefore witness a will although a very young child may not since he would not be capable of understanding the significance of what he was doing. A blind person cannot act as a witness since he cannot have the opportunity to see the signature, similarly a person who is very drunk or of unsound mind would be incapable of attesting.

In choosing witnesses a solicitor should bear in mind that they may be required to give evidence as to due execution. The persons chosen should therefore not be very old or likely to be hard to trace. A beneficiary of the will or a beneficiary's spouse should not be chosen since, although his signature is perfectly valid, he will usually lose his legacy if he witnesses (Wills Act 1837, s.15, see Chapter 16 below). A charging clause is a legacy for these purposes and so the solicitor should not witness the will himself if it contains a professional charging clause and appoints him or a firm in which he is a partner as executor.

## 7. ATTESTATION CLAUSES

An attestation clause recites that the proper formalities have **2.9** been complied with. A simple clause might read "signed by the said [Testator] in our joint presence and then by us in his presence" and would be written next to the testator's signature and immediately above the witnesses' signatures. The value of such a clause is that it raises a presumption of due execution.

If there is no attestation clause the registrar, before admitting the will to probate, must require an affidavit of due execution from a witness or if this is not convenient from any other person who was present at execution (Non-Contentious Probate Rules 1987, rule 12(1)). If such an affidavit cannot be obtained, other evidence (such as an affidavit to show that the signature on the will is in the handwriting of the deceased) will be required (rule 12(2)). Rule 12(3) of the Non-Contentious Probate Rules provides that a registrar may accept a will for proof without evidence if he is satisfied that the distribution of the estate is not thereby affected. In other cases where there is no evidence the court may apply the maxim *omnia praesumuntur rite ac solemniter esse acta* and admit the will to probate if it appears to have been signed and witnessed but this will usually require a hearing before a judge and will, therefore, lead to delay and added expense.

Where the will has been signed by another person at the direction of the testator or where the testator is blind or illiterate special forms of attestation clauses are desirable. The clause should make it clear that the testator had knowledge of the contents of the will at the time of execution.

### 8. ARRANGEMENTS FOR EXECUTION

**2.10**   When a solicitor is asked to prepare a will for a client it is best, in order to avoid problems, to adopt the following procedure wherever possible:

(a)   The will is prepared by the solicitor from the client's instructions and explained to him.

(b)   A number of cases have held that, where a will is written on more than one piece of paper, there must be physical contact between the pages at the time of attestation if the will is to be valid. It is doubtful whether this rule survives the enactment of the substituted section 9. However, for the avoidance of doubt as to what has been attested and to prevent accidental loss of parts of the will, all the pages should be securely fastened together.

(c)   The client attends at the solicitor's office and, in the presence of two witnesses, places his signature at the end of the will next to a suitable attestation clause.

(i)   The witnesses must not be beneficiaries or spouses of beneficiaries.

(ii)   The solicitor must not be a witness if there is a charging clause in favour of him or his firm.

(iii)   Even if the solicitor is not a witness he should be present to ensure that the correct procedure is adopted.

(d)   The witnesses sign in the presence of the testator (as required by law) and of each other (not required, but useful so that either witness can give evidence as to the other's signature if necessary).

(e) It is good office practice to keep an attendance note explaining what was done and referring to the addresses of the witnesses so that they can be contacted if necessary to prove due execution.

(f) A copy of the will should be kept and the solicitor should insert on it the names of the testator and witnesses and date of execution. (Such a copy may be admissible to probate if the original is lost, see paragraph 2.31).

If a will is sent to a client for execution it should be accompanied by very clear instructions. (In particular the client should be warned not to allow anyone who is or whose spouse is a beneficiary to witness, should be told where to sign, should be told to sign his usual signature in ink and should be told to sign in the presence of the witnesses and before they sign).

If a will is to be executed in hospital the solicitor should bear in mind that in some hospitals medical staff are prohibited from witnessing wills by the hospital authorities. If this rule applies it is safer to take witnesses to the hospital than to rely on finding witnesses there (other patients are not suitable since there may be doubt about their capacity and they are likely to be hard to trace if needed to give evidence).

If there is any possibility that the capacity of the testator to make a will may be challenged at a later date it is advisable to try to get a doctor to witness the will and/or to make a written statement as to the testator's mental state on the relevant day. (See paragraph 2.23.)

## 9. PRIVILEGED WILLS

*The form of the will*
A will can be made informally by a testator who has privileged **2.11** status. The will can be made in any form including a mere oral statement. Such a will is known as a nuncupative will. The only requirement is that the statement made should show an intention to dispose of property in the event of death even if the person making it does not know that he is making a will. Such a will is valid even though made by a minor provided he has privileged status.

*Privileged status*
The right to make a privileged will extends to any soldier on **2.12** actual military service or mariner or seaman being at sea.

"Soldier" includes a member of the R.A.F. and naval or marine personnel serving on land. The exact extent of "actual military service" is open to some doubt and a detailed discussion of the cases decided by the courts is beyond the scope of this book. Broadly speaking the term may be said to include activities closely connected with warfare, whether or not war has been declared and whether or not the testator has actually arrived at the scene of the fighting. In *Re Jones* (1976) a soldier serving in Northern Ireland was held to have privileged status. Similarly the term "being at sea" cannot be defined precisely but a mariner is treated as being at sea for this purpose when he is still on land but under orders to join his ship.

It is the circumstances in which the will was made which are relevant in deciding whether a person had privileged status not the circumstances in which death occurred.

### 10. INCORPORATION OF DOCUMENTS

**2.13**   A properly-drawn will should be contained in one document so as to avoid doubt as to its contents. If changes are to be made later they may be included in a codicil (see paragraphs 2.32–2.34 below). However, if desired an unexecuted document can be incorporated into a will by referring to it in the will. The document is then admitted to probate as part of the will.

An unexecuted document is incorporated if:

  (i)   it is in existence at the time of execution of the will (or of a codicil republishing the will); and

 (ii)   it is *referred to* in the will as being in existence at the time of execution; and

(iii)   it is clearly identified in the will.

*Document in existence*
**2.14**   Whether a document is in existence at the time of execution is a question of fact. The person who seeks to have it admitted to probate must prove its existence at that time.

*Referred to as in existence*
**2.15**   The document must be referred to in the will as in existence at the time of execution. Thus a will which says "I leave £100 to each of the persons named in the list *now* to be found in my desk" satisfies this condition (and the list will be validly incorporated provided it can be shown that it was in fact in existence when the will or confirming codicil was executed.) A will which says "I leave £100 to each of the persons named in a

list which *I will write* before my death" does not satisfy this condition. Even if the list was made before execution it will not be admitted to probate as the will refers to its coming into existence at a later date. There are some marginal cases where the wording of the will does not make it clear whether or not the document is extant at the time of execution. In such cases the court will refuse to incorporate the unexecuted document. For example, in *University College of North Wales* v. *Taylor* (1908) probate was refused where the will referred to "any memorandum amongst my papers."

If the will is republished by a codicil an unexecuted document will be incorporated if it is in existence at the time of execution of the codicil and is referred to as being in existence in either the will (which is republished and so speaks from the date of the codicil) or the codicil. *In the Goods of Smart* (1902) demonstrates that this is so but on the facts of that case probate of the unexecuted document was refused because the will referred to its coming into existence in the future.

*The document must be identified*
The unexecuted document is only incorporated if it is identified **2.16** by the will. The identification must be sufficient to indicate what document is referred to.

*Practical considerations*
Incorporation of documents by reference should be avoided **2.17** unless absolutely necessary both because of the danger of drafting the will in a way which does not properly incorporate them and because of the danger that the document referred to might be lost before the testator dies.

A properly-drafted will should not refer to other documents unless it is intended that they be incorporated. If it does so refer, the registrar is likely to require any such document to be produced and may call for affidavit evidence as to whether or not the document is incorporated (Non-Contentious Probate Rules 1987, rule 14(3)).

Once a document has been incorporated into a will it is treated as an ordinary part of the will and must be filed at the probate registry with the rest of the will. Wills are a matter of public record so that the whole of the will, including the unexecuted document incorporated by reference, is available to the public. There is no point, therefore, in putting sensitive information into a document to be incorporated into the will, with the intention of keeping that information secret.

# B. Capacity

## 1. AGE

**2.18**   Persons under the age of 18 cannot make a valid will (Wills Act 1837, s.7 as amended by the Family Law Reform Act 1969, s.3(1)(*a*)) unless they have privileged status. Privileged status is enjoyed by soldiers on actual military service and mariners and seamen at sea (Wills Act 1837, s.11).

On the death of an infant (other than one who has made a privileged will) his estate will be administered under the intestacy rules.

Persons aged 16 and over can, however, make a valid statutory nomination of certain assets provided the nomination is in writing and witnessed by at least one person. For a fuller discussion of nominations see Chapter 21.

## 2. THE MENTAL STATE OF THE TESTATOR

*Testamentary capacity*

**2.19**   According to *Banks* v. *Goodfellow* (1870) a testator only has testamentary capacity if he has "a sound and disposing mind and memory." This requires the testator to understand three things:

(a) *The nature of the act and its effects.* It is not necessary for the testator to understand the precise legal machinery involved in the will so long as he understands its broad effects.

(b) *The extent of the property of which he is disposing.* The testator is not expected to be able to produce a detailed list of every item of property owned. It is sufficient if he has a broad recollection of its extent.

(c) *The claims to which he ought to give effect.* This means that the testator must be able to bring to mind the persons who are "fitting objects of the testator's bounty" (*Per* Sir J. Hannen in *Boughton* v. *Knight* (1873)). It does not of course mean that having done so he must dispose of his property to those people. It is sufficient that he is capable of considering them. In *Battan Singh* v. *Armirchand* (1948) a testator who was very ill in the last stages of consumption left his property to certain creditors stating that he had no living relatives. In fact he had three nephews of whom, the evidence showed, he was very fond. The court said that he clearly lacked testamentary capacity having forgotten the moral claims of his nephews.

*The time at which testamentary capacity is to be judged*
The general rule is that the testator must have the testamentary **2.20**
capacity at the time the will is signed and witnessed. However,
under the rule in *Parker* v. *Felgate* a will may be valid even
though the testator has lost testamentary capacity by the time
the will is executed provided:

(a) the testator had testamentary capacity at the time he
gave a solicitor instructions to prepare a will; and

(b) the will is prepared in accordance with those instructions; and

(c) at the time the will is executed the testator remembers
having given instructions for a will to be prepared and
believes that the will has been prepared in accordance
with those instructions. It is immaterial that the
testator does not remember precisely what the
instructions were or cannot understand the will if it is
read to him.

This principle has been extended to a will prepared by a
solicitor on the basis of his client's own draft (*In the Estate of
Wallace, Solicitor of the Duchy of Cornwall* v. *Batten* (1952)).
However, because of the possibility of abuse, this principle will
be applied with caution, if at all, where instructions are relayed
to a solicitor through an intermediary (*Battan Singh* v.
*Armirchand*).

*The burden of proof*
Just as the person propounding a will must *prove* that it was **2.21**
properly signed and witnessed so must he prove that at the time
of execution the testator had testamentary capacity. If the
burden of proof is not discharged the will is not admitted to
probate. There are, however, two presumptions which must be
considered:

(a) *Will rational.* If the will appears rational on the face of it
there is a presumption that the testator had testamentary
capacity; the will is therefore admitted to probate unless anyone
attacking it can produce sufficient evidence to rebut the
presumption. If the presumption is rebutted it is then up to the
propounder to prove testamentary capacity.

(b) *Mental states continue.* Mental states are presumed to
continue; thus, if a person who normally suffers from mental
illness makes a will it is presumed that he lacked testamentary

capacity. It is then up to the propounder of the will to rebut the presumption by proving that the will was made in a lucid interval.

### Insane delusions

**2.22** An insane delusion is a belief in the existence of something in which no rational person could believe and which could not be eradicated from the testator's mind by reasoned argument (*Dew* v. *Clark and Clark* (1826)). A person suffering from such a delusion can make a valid will provided the delusion is on a subject in no way connected with the will (for example, a delusion that the testator is pursued by evil spirits). However, if the delusion affects the testator's judgment, either generally or on one point which affects the dispositions made, the testator does not have testamentary capacity. If the delusion affects the whole will (as in *Dew* v. *Clark and Clark* where the testator had an irrational dislike of his daughter as a result of which he left her nothing in his will) probate will be refused to the whole will. If the delusion affects only part of the will then only that part will be excluded from probate (as in *In the Estate of Bohrmann* (1938) where one clause of a codicil was omitted from probate).

### Practical precautions

**2.23** A solicitor who has any doubts as to the capacity of a client proposing to make a will or any suspicion that lack of capacity may later be alleged, should try to avoid future problems by obtaining medical advice. It is desirable that a medical practitioner examine the testator, preferably at the time the will is signed since the severity of certain mental conditions, for example, senility, vary markedly over relatively short periods of time. The medical practitioner should be asked to witness the will but hospitals and similar institutions sometimes have regulations forbidding staff to witness wills. In such a case the medical practitioner should be asked to make a statement as to the mental condition of the testator. It may be advisable to consult an external medical practitioner and to ask that person to witness the will. A full and careful attendance note should be made by the solicitor or member of his staff who is present.

### Statutory wills

**2.24** Section 96(1)(*e*) of the Mental Health Act 1983 (replacing the Mental Health Act 1959, s.103A as amended) gives the Court of Protection power to make a will on behalf of an adult mental patient. The will is made by an "authorised person" who signs the patient's name and his own name; it is witnessed in the usual way and then sealed with the official seal of the Court of Protection.

A mental patient is a person who is incapable by reason of mental disorder of managing and administering his property and affairs (section 94). It is not necessary for the person to have been committed to an institution.

A statutory will can make any provision which could be made by the patient if he had capacity except that it cannot dispose of immovable property situate outside England and Wales. The Court seeks to make the will which the patient would have made, acting reasonably and on competent legal advice, had he or she enjoyed a brief lucid interval.

An example of the use of the procedure was *Re D.(J.)* (1982). The testatrix made a will leaving her house to one of her daughters (who lived with her) and residue to be divided between her other children. The daughter then remarried, the testatrix sold her house, bought a house near her daughter but in fact moved in with the daughter and never used the new house as her home. (The sale of the original house caused the gift of it to her daughter to fail (see "ademption," paragraphs 16.14–16.19)). The daughter and her husband paid for the testatrix's maintenance out of their own pockets for a considerable time until the Court of Protection ordered a payment to them out of the mother's property. The daughter applied to the Court of Protection for the execution of a codicil to her mother's will on the ground that the mother had become senile. The deputy master ordered a legacy of £10,000 to the daughter. The daughter appealed contending that she was entitled to more. The High Court held that the test to be applied was what provision this patient would have made in her will had she not been suffering from mental disorder. A judge has a complete discretion in reviewing the master's order (that is, a judge can vary an order without finding that the master has erred in principle) and on the facts of this case ordered a legacy of £15,000 to the daughter with a substitutional gift to the daughter's husband if the daughter predeceased her mother.

## C. Knowledge and Approval

1. PRESUMPTION

A testator must know and approve the contents of the will. **2.25** (This does not apply to an adult mental patient who need not know and approve the contents of a statutory will). If a testator signs a will having no knowledge of the contents, the will is invalid. The time at which knowledge and approval is required is the time of execution of the will. However, knowledge and approval (like testamentary capacity) is established if the testator knew and approved of instructions given to a solicitor to draw up a will (*Parker* v. *Felgate* above).

The burden of proof of knowledge and approval lies on the person propounding the will; however, there is normally a rebuttable presumption that a testator who executes a will (particularly if he has read the will or has had the will read over to him) does so with knowledge and approval of the contents. This presumption does not arise:

(a) *In the case of a blind or illiterate testator or where another person signs on behalf of the testator.* In such cases the registrar will require evidence that the testator had actual knowledge of the contents (Non-Contentious Probate Rules 1987, rule 13). It is advisable in such a case that the attestation clause should include a statement that the will was read over to and approved by the testator. If it does not, affidavit evidence will be required from the witnesses or from some other person present.
*or*

(b) *Where there are suspicious circumstances.* If there is evidence of suspicious circumstances there is no presumption of knowledge and approval and the will is not admitted to probate unless the propounder can prove that the testator did know and approve the contents. The most obvious example of a suspicious circumstance is where the will is prepared by a major beneficiary or close relative of a major beneficiary. In *Wintle* v. *Nye* (1959) the House of Lords expressed the view that: "It is not the law that in no circumstances can a solicitor or other person who has prepared a will for a testator take a benefit under it. But that fact creates a suspicion that must be removed by the person propounding the will. In all cases the court must be vigilant and jealous. The degree of suspicion will vary with the circumstances of the case. It may be slight and easily dispelled. It may, on the other hand, be so grave that it can hardly be removed." *per* Viscount Simmonds. In *Wintle* v. *Nye* it was held that the gift to the draftsman was not admissible to probate for want of knowledge and approval but that the rest of the will could stand. (Solicitors are subject to special rules of professional conduct in relation to receiving legacies from clients; these are dealt with in paragraph 2.27).

## 2. MISTAKE

A mistake may mean that the testator had no knowledge or **2.26** approval of the will as a whole (for example, where he executes the wrong will) or of part only of the will (as in *Wintle* v. *Nye*). If a testator includes words in his will having intended to write other words, the words mistakenly included will be omitted from probate; similarly if a testator includes words in his will but does not know or approve them those words will be omitted from probate. An example of the latter type of mistake occurred in *Re Phelan* (1972). The testator bought three printed will forms and, thinking that every holding of shares had to be dealt with in a separate will, executed three wills in favour of X, each will disposing of a separate shareholding. Each will was executed on the same day and each contained a printed revocation clause. Stirling J. held that as the words of revocation were clearly included in the wills by inadvertence and misunderstanding they could be omitted from probate.

The probate court will not interfere, however, where a testator deliberately selects certain words and includes them in the will, even if it is clearly shown that the testator was mistaken as to their legal effect. Thus in *Collins* v. *Elstone* (1893) a testatrix deliberately included a revocation clause under the misapprehension that it would revoke only a small part of her earlier will. The court held that the revocation clause could not be omitted from the will. The rule is the same where a draftsman prepares a will on behalf of a testator and deliberately selects words being mistaken as to their legal effect; those words will be admitted to probate (*Re Horrocks* (1939)).

The probate court has always had power to omit words from probate. Prior to the Administration of Justice Act 1982 it did not have any power to insert words even where it was obvious that words had been omitted accidentally. However, section 20 of that Act alters this rule to a limited extent. It provides that if a court is satisfied that a will is so expressed that it fails to carry out the testator's intentions in consequence of:

(a)   a clerical error, or

(b)   a failure to understand his instructions,

it may order that the will be rectified so as to carry out his intentions. After the expiry of six months from the date of the grant of representation an application for rectification cannot be made except with leave from the court. Personal representatives who distribute after that date will not be liable on the ground that they should have taken into account the possibility of an out-of-time application being made.

If, therefore, a typing error is made in a will the probate court can order that words included by mistake be omitted and that words omitted by mistake be inserted. Similarly if a solicitor misunderstands his instructions the court can order that the mistake be rectified. However, it would appear that the Act has not altered the rule that if the testator or draftsman is mistaken as to the legal effect of words deliberately selected for inclusion in the will the court cannot interfere.

An application for rectification may be made to a registrar, unless a probate action has been commenced.

The application must be supported by an affidavit, setting out the grounds of the application, together with such evidence as can be adduced as to the testator's intentions and as to whichever of the following matters are in issue:

    (a)    the respects in which the testator's intentions were not understood, or

    (b)    the nature of any alleged clerical error.

Unless otherwise directed, notice of the application shall be given to every person having an interest under the will whose interest might be prejudiced by the rectification applied for and any comments in writing by any such person shall be exhibited to the affidavit in support of the application (Non-Contentious Probate Rules 1987, rule 55).

### 3. SPECIAL RULES RELATING TO SOLICITORS

**2.27**    As we saw in paragraph 2.25 above if a will is prepared by a major beneficiary or close relative of a major beneficiary the propounder of the will must prove that the testator knew and approved the contents of the will. If the propounder can do this then, unless there is evidence of fraud or undue influence (see paragraph 4) the will is admitted to probate. However, solicitors are subject to special rules of conduct laid down by the Council of the Law Society as a result of a case in 1973. In that case two solicitors in partnership were struck off the roll on the grounds, *inter alia*, that they or their respective families had been given substantial benefits under two wills prepared in their office, neither client having received independent advice. The Law Society's ruling is as follows:

"Where a client intends to make a gift *inter vivos* or by will to his solicitor, or to the solicitor's partner, or a member of staff or to the families of any of them and the gift is of a significant amount, either in itself or having regard to the size of the client's estate and the reasonable expectations of prospective beneficiaries, the solicitor must advise the client to be independently advised as to that gift and if the client declines, must refuse to act.

The following points should be noted:

(1) If the client declines to be independently advised, the solicitor must refuse to act for him in drawing the will, or any other document by which the gift is to be made. It is not sufficient merely to have the will or other document witnessed by an independent solicitor.

(2) A solicitor must also ensure that members of his staff do not embody in any will or document a gift to themselves without the approval of the solicitor. If the member of staff seeks the solicitor's approval, the same rule as to independent advice applies.

(3) Where a client wishes to leave a legacy which is not of a significant amount to his solicitor, there is no need for independent advice. However, the solicitor should satisfy himself that the client does not feel obliged to make such a gift.

(4) Occasionally, a testator may wish to leave all or a substantial part of his estate to a solicitor to be dealt with in accordance with the testator's wishes as communicated to the solicitor either orally or in a document, or as a secret trust. The Council consider that where a solicitor in such circumstances will not benefit personally and financially, there is no need to ensure the testator receives independent advice. However, solicitors should preserve the instructions from which the will was drawn and should also see that the terms of such secret trust are embodied in a written document signed or initialled by the testator.

(5) Where the donor or testator is a relative of the solicitor and wishes to make a gift or leave a legacy to the solicitor, the solicitor must consider whether in these circumstances independent advice is essential. The same principle will apply if the intended recipient is a partner of the solicitor, or a member of his staff and the donor or testator is a relative of the intended recipient."

# D. Force, Fear, Fraud or Undue Influence

### 1. INTRODUCTION

**2.28** If a will is made as a result of force, fear, fraud or undue influence it will not be regarded as the act of the testator and will be refused probate. A person who alleges that a will was made as a result of one of these factors must *prove* it. There are no presumptions to assist in discharging the burden of proof.

### 2. FORCE OR FEAR

**2.29** There is little authority on this but obviously if it can be shown that a testator made a will only because he was being injured or threatened with injury the will cannot be admitted to probate.

### 3. FRAUD AND UNDUE INFLUENCE

**2.30** Fraud is something which misleads a testator. Examples of fraud are making false representations as to the character of others to induce the testator to make or to revoke gifts or to exclude persons from a proposed will. Another example would be obtaining a gift from a testator as a result of pretending to be lawfully married to him. As Lord Langdale said in *Giles* v. *Giles* (1836) it is clear that "a legacy given to a person in a character which the legatee does not fill, and by the fraudulent assumption of which character the testator has been deceived, will not take effect." See also *In the Estate of Posner* (1953).

Undue influence is something which overpowers the volition of the testator without convincing the judgment; a testator may be persuaded but not coerced. It is often difficult to draw the line between zealous persuasion and undue influence; so long as the testator retained real freedom of choice a court will not interfere but if it can be shown that the testator merely surrendered to intolerable pressure this will amount to undue influence. The court will more readily find undue influence where a testator was weak (whether mentally or physically). In the case of *inter vivos* gifts there is a presumption of undue influence where a donee stands in a fiduciary relationship to a donor, for example, father and child, doctor and patient, solicitor and client, but there is no such presumption in the case of testamentary gifts. This is because many of the relationships which give rise to the presumption *inter vivos* are precisely the relationships which would lead a testator to want to make a gift by will. Thus, if there is no positive evidence of undue influence there is no question of refusing probate (*Parfitt* v. *Lawless* (1872)).

The action which the court will take if fraud or undue influence is proved depends on the effect that the fraud or undue influence produced. If it resulted in the entire will being made in a particular way the entire will is refused probate; if it resulted in a legacy being given to a beneficiary that legacy will fail (*Giles* v. *Giles* (1836); *Kennell* v. *Abbott* (1799)). If a testator was prevented from revoking a will in favour of X and making one in favour of Y the court may allow Y to claim that the property should be held by X on trust for him (*Betts* v. *Doughty* (1879)).

## E. Lost Wills

If a will has been lost or accidentally destroyed it is possible to obtain probate of a copy or reconstruction provided an order is first obtained. If, however, a will which was known to have been in the testator's possession cannot be found after his death there is a presumption that it was destroyed by the testator with the intention of revoking it (*Eckersley* v. *Platt* (1866)). This presumption will have to be rebutted if an order for the proof of a copy or reconstruction is to be obtained.   **2.31**

The procedure for obtaining an order is set out in the Non-Contentious Probate Rules 1987, rule 54. The same procedure is used where probate of an oral will is sought. The order can be made by a registrar but he can require that the matter be referred to a judge. The application must be supported by an affidavit setting out the grounds of the application, and by such evidence on affidavit as the applicant can adduce as to:

(a)   the will's existence after the death of the testator or, where there is no such evidence, the facts on which the applicant relies to rebut the presumption that the will has been revoked by destruction;

(b)   in respect of an oral will, the contents of that will; and

(c)   in respect of a reconstruction of a will, the accuracy of that reconstruction.

The registrar may require additional evidence in the circumstances of a particular case as to due execution of the will or as to the accuracy of the copy will, and may direct that notice be given to persons who would be prejudiced by the application.

# F. Codicils

## 1. DEFINITION

**2.32** A testamentary instrument which is executed in the same way as a will and which supplements the terms of an existing will (either by adding to it, by amending it or by revoking it in part) is usually referred to as a codicil. A codicil must comply with the same requirements as a will if it is to be admitted to probate.

## 2. REPUBLICATION

**2.33** The execution of a codicil to a will "republishes" the will provided there is some indication of an intention to republish. Any reference to the earlier will in the codicil is sufficient to amount to an indication of an intention to republish. When a will is republished it takes effect as if executed at the date of the codicil but with the incorporation of any changes made by the codicil.

Republication may affect the construction of a will both in respect of persons and property. In *Re Hardyman, Teesdale* v. *McClintock* (1925) a will made in 1898 gave a legacy to the "wife of my cousin." The wife died with the result that the gift to her lapsed. The testatrix later executed a codicil to her will (which did not refer specifically to the legacy). This republished the will at the date of the codicil. Since the cousin had no wife living at that date the gift in the will took effect as a gift to the first person the cousin married after the date of the codicil.

In *Re Reeves, Reeves* v. *Pawson* (1928) the testator gave his daughter "my present lease" in certain named property. At the time the will was executed the testator owned a short lease of the property. He later took a longer lease of the same property and then executed a codicil which referred to the will. The daughter was held entitled to the new (long) lease which the deceased owned at the date of the codicil.

If a will is altered before its republication and the alteration is not executed the republication has the effect of validating the alteration. However, there is a presumption that unexecuted alterations were made after the execution of the codicil so that evidence will be required to rebut the presumption.

The republication of a will by a codicil executed by independent witnesses has the effect of saving a gift to a witness of the original will (who would otherwise be deprived of the gift under Wills Act 1837, s.15). This remains so even if the beneficiary witnesses a later codicil.

## 3. REVIVAL

A *revoked* will can be revived by re-execution of the will or by **2.34**
execution of a codicil to the will showing an intention to revive.
A mere reference to the earlier instrument is not sufficient to
revive it; there must be words which make it clear that the
effect of that document is being confirmed. A will cannot be
revived unless it is still in existence. The effect of revival is the
same as republication.

The revocation of a will by a codicil is not sufficient to revive
an earlier revoked will. Once revoked a will stays revoked
unless there is a formal act of revival. For example, a testator
makes a will in 1980 and then makes a will in 1981 which
revokes the 1980 will. The testator then executes a codicil which
revokes the 1981 will. The 1980 will is not thereby revived. The
codicil is the only document admissible to probate.

## 4. REVOCATION

A codicil may expressly revoke an earlier will or codicil in
whole or in part. If no express revocation clause is included it
will impliedly revoke an earlier instrument to the extent that it
is inconsistent with it. Revocation is dealt with in the next
section.

# G. Revocation

## 1. INTRODUCTION

A will is always revocable during the lifetime of the testator **2.35**
(unless he loses testamentary capacity). A will cannot be made
irrevocable. If a testator contracts not to revoke he is still free
to do so. However, in that case revocation would be a breach of
contract and the testator's estate would be liable to pay
damages.

Equity may intervene under the doctrine of mutual wills
to impose a trust on a testator's property. This occurs where
two or more people make wills in agreed terms and agree
that neither will revoke without the consent of the other.
If the first to die carries out his part of the agreement equity
will regard it as unconscionable for the survivor to deviate
from the agreed terms. Therefore, equity will impose a trust

on the survivor's property. The survivor remains free to revoke his will but because of the existence of the trust the new dispositions of the property will be ineffective.

The various ways in which wills can be revoked are dealt with in the following paragraphs.

### 2. MARRIAGE

**2.36** Section 18 of the Wills Act 1837 deals with the effect of marriage on a will. A new section 18 was substituted by the Administration of Justice Act 1982. The new section applies to wills executed after December 31, 1982. The somewhat different rules which apply to earlier wills are not considered in this book. The new section provides that the marriage of the testator automatically revokes any will made before marriage. There are, however, three exceptions to this rule:

(1) Section 18(3) provides that:
"Where it appears from a will that at the time it was made the testator was expecting to be married to a particular person and that he intended that the will should not be revoked by the marriage, the will shall not be revoked by his marriage to that person."

This subsection saves a will from being revoked by marriage provided that two conditions are satisfied.

(i) The testator must have been expecting to be married to a *particular* person at the time of execution. A will made by a testator who expected to marry someone soon after making the will but who had not decided whom to marry would, therefore, be revoked by the subsequent marriage of the testator. It is not, however, required that the testator should be engaged to marry at the time when the will is made.

It must "appear from the will" that the testator is expecting to marry a particular person so that an express statement to that effect should be included. It is probable that in the absence of such a statement a reference to "my fiancée" or "my future wife" in the will would satisfy this requirement.

(ii) It must also "appear from the will" that the testator intended that the will should not be revoked by the marriage. There is no guidance in the Act as to how such an intention is to be shown. It is possible that if the will gives substantially all of the testator's estate to the expected spouse this condition might be satisfied. However, it is preferable to include an express statement as to the testator's intention in a professionally drawn will. A suitable clause would be: "I declare that I make this will expecting to be married to [insert name of expected spouse] and that I intend that this will shall not be revoked by my marriage to the said [expected spouse]."

Marriage to any person other than the person whom the testator expected to marry at the time of execution will revoke the will.

(2) Section 18(4) provides that:
"Where it appears from a will that at the time it was made the testator was expecting to be married to a particular person and that he intended that *a disposition in the will* should not be revoked by his marriage to that person:–
(a) that disposition shall take effect notwithstanding the marriage; and
(b) any other disposition in the will shall take effect also, unless it appears from the will that the testator intended the disposition to be revoked by the marriage."

In a professionally drawn will the testator's intention should be made clear by the use of a suitable declaration. For example, the testator may wish to give £10,000 to X notwithstanding his marriage. A suitable declaration would be "I give £10,000 to X and declare that this gift is to take effect notwithstanding the celebration of my forthcoming marriage with Y."

If the testator wishes any other dispositions to be revoked by the marriage it must "appear from the will" that this is his intention (section 18(4)(*b*)). If the testator includes a declaration that one disposition is not to be revoked by a marriage and does not make any such declaration in relation to other dispositions, it is arguable that he has shown an intention that those other dispositions *are* to be revoked by marriage. An express declaration to that effect should be included in the will for the sake of certainty. For example: "I declare that all the gifts contained in this will other than the gift to X are to be revoked by the celebration of my forthcoming marriage with Y."

An appointment of executors is not a "disposition" nor are administrative provisions (such as an extension to the statutory power of insurance). Such clauses will, therefore, be revoked by marriage even though the dispositive parts of the will are saved from revocation in whole or in part by section 18(4). However, if the entire will is saved from revocation by section 18(3) it is clear that the non-dispositive clauses remain effective.

(3) Section 18(2) provides that the exercise of a power of appointment by will remains effective notwithstanding subsequent marriage. In this case the appointment is saved from revocation whether or not the will is expressed to be made in expectation of marriage and whether or not the testator was expecting to be married when the will was made. The exercise of a power of appointment is not, however, saved from revocation by section 18(2) where the property appointed would pass to the personal representatives of the testator in default of appointment.

### 3. DIVORCE

2.37    The Administration of Justice Act 1982 inserts a new section 18A into the Wills Act 1837. This provides that if a marriage is dissolved or annulled by the decree of a court the will is to take effect as if any appointment of the former spouse as executor or executor and trustee of the will were omitted. This will usually mean that the deceased will die without an executor so that letters of administration with the will annexed will be required but if any person has been appointed co-executor with the former spouse that person will remain entitled to take a grant of probate.

The new section also provides that on dissolution or annulment of a marriage any devise or bequest to the former spouse lapses. If the will contains no substitutional gift the property given to the former spouse will, therefore, fall into residue or if itself a gift of residue will pass on intestacy.

In *Re Sinclair (Deceased), Lloyds Bank* v. *Imperial Cancer Research Fund* (1985) a testator had left property to his wife provided she survived by one month. There was then a gift to the Cancer Research Fund which was expressed to take effect "if my said wife shall predecease me or fail to survive me for one month. ... " The testator and his wife were divorced and the gift to her, therefore, "lapsed." The testator then died and his former wife survived by more than one month. Clearly the wife could not take but the question arose as to whether the gift to the Fund would take effect or whether there was an intestacy. The Fund argued that the primary meaning of the word lapse is "failure by reason of the death of a beneficiary in the testator's lifetime" and therefore the spouse should be *deemed* to have predeceased so that the condition on the gift to the Fund would be deemed satisfied. The Court of Appeal unanimously rejected this argument (although it had been accepted by the High Court in an earlier case). They said that the word lapse means no more than "fail" so that the divorced beneficiary is not deemed to have died before the testator. The conditional gift to the Fund, therefore, could not take effect. The residuary gift having failed, the property therefore passed under the intestacy rules to the testator's brother. The decision in *Re Sinclair* should be borne in mind by the draftsman of any will in which there is a gift to a spouse. It is preferable to state that the substitutional gift is to take effect "If the gift to my said spouse shall fail *for any reason* ... " The conditional gift can then take effect.

Section 18A(3) provides that if the gift to the spouse is a gift of a life interest the interest of the remainderman is accelerated so that he takes an immediate interest even if his interest was expressed to be contingent on surviving the life tenant.

The provisions of section 18A are subject to any contrary intention expressed in the will and the lapse of gifts to the former spouse is expressly stated to be without prejudice to any claim under the Inheritance (Provision for Family and Dependants) Act 1975 (as to which see Chapter 20).

It should be noted that section 18A applies only to dissolution or annulment decreed by a court. A separation does not, therefore, in any way change the effect of a married person's will. A person contemplating separation should always consider making a new will. Furthermore, even when a dissolution or annulment is decreed the only effect is to cause gifts to the former spouse to lapse; the will should therefore be reviewed at such time to ensure that it disposes of the property as the testator wishes in view of the changed circumstances.


4. DESTRUCTION

A will may be revoked by "burning tearing or otherwise **2.38** destroying the same by the testator or by some person in his presence and by his direction with the intention of revoking the same." (Wills Act 1837, s.20). Both an act of destruction and an intention to revoke are required for this type of revocation. Neither alone is sufficient.

*"Burning tearing or otherwise destroying"*

**2.39** A physical act of destruction is required so that crossing out the wording of the will or the signature of the testator or writing words such as "cancelled" or "revoked" across the will is insufficient to revoke. For example, in *Cheese* v. *Lovejoy* (1877) the testator wrote "all these are cancelled" on the will and crossed out part of it. He then threw the will away but it was found by a servant who preserved it until the testator's death. The will was held to be valid. Although the testator intended to revoke the will he had done nothing which could be regarded as "burning tearing or otherwise destroying" it.

If the testator destroys part of a will this may amount to revocation of the will as a whole if the part destroyed is sufficiently substantial or important (for example, the attestation clause). However, destruction of part may be treated as revocation of only part where the part destroyed is less important. Thus, in *Re Everest* (1975) the testator cut off certain parts of the will containing trusts of residue. It was held that the rest of the will remained valid. In *Hobbs* v. *Knight* (1838) the testator cut out his signature from the will. This was held to be a revocation of the whole will. In deciding how far the revocation extends the court will hear evidence of the testator's intention. In the absence of such evidence the court will decide on the basis of the state of the will after the destruction. If a testator wishes to revoke a will by destruction he should ensure that the will is totally destroyed. However, since doubts may arise after death as to the testator's true intention at the time of destruction it is usually preferable to effect the revocation by means of a further testamentary instrument.

Revocation by destruction is only effective if the testator has completed the intended act of destruction. This is illustrated by the curious case of *Doe d. Perkes* v. *Perkes* (1820) where the testator tore a will into four pieces in the presence of a beneficiary with whom he was angry. He was then restrained from further destruction by a third party and, when his anger had subsided, was heard to say "It is a good job it is no worse"; from this the court inferred that the testator had intended more tearing so the act of destruction was incomplete and the will still valid.

If the destruction is carried out by some person other than the testator it is only effective if done in his presence and by his direction. A destruction in the absence of the testator or without his direction cannot be ratified by the testator so that his only course is to revoke by a further testamentary instrument.

*Intention*

The testator must *intend* to revoke the will at the time of the destruction. Accidental destruction does not, therefore, revoke a will nor does destruction by a testator who thinks the will is invalid (since then his intention is merely to destroy an apparently useless piece of paper). **2.40**

If a will known to have been in the testator's possession is not found after his death it is presumed that he destroyed it with intention to revoke it. Similarly if a will is known to have been in the testator's possession and is found torn or otherwise destroyed at his death there is a presumption that the testator destroyed it with the intention of revoking it. Either of these presumptions may be rebutted (for example, by evidence that the testator referred to his will shortly before death in such a way as to indicate that he regarded it as valid).

If a will is destroyed but not revoked (because of lack of intention to revoke or because the destruction was done in the absence of the testator), it remains valid. Probate may be obtained of a copy or reconstruction if the terms can be proved with sufficient certainty (see paragraph 2.31).

*Conditional revocation*

Where a will is destroyed with an intention to revoke, it is a question of fact whether the revocation is absolute (and therefore immediately effective) or conditional (and therefore only effective if the condition is satisfied). Extrinsic evidence is admissible to prove whether the revocation was conditional. **2.41**

A common reason for revoking a will is that the testator wishes to make a new will disposing of his property in a different way. If the testator has left the bulk of his property to X he may decide to revoke his will so as to make a new will leaving it to Y. If this is done primarily so as to exclude X from benefit the court will infer that the revocation of the original will was absolute. If on the other hand it can be shown that the testator wanted to benefit Y but would have preferred X to take rather than those entitled on intestacy the court will infer that the revocation was conditional on the execution of a valid will leaving the property to Y so that X will take unless a new will has been made. This is often referred to as "the doctrine of dependent relative revocation" since the revocation is dependent on the making of the new will. However, there must be some evidence that the testator's intention to revoke was conditional. For example, in *Re Jones* (1976) the testatrix made a will leaving a smallholding to certain beneficiaries. She later told her bank manager that she wished to leave the smallholding to her nephew because of the beneficiaries' attitude to her and because they had acquired their own property. The testatrix died soon after this conversation and the will was found mutilated after her death (the signatures and the gift of the smallholding having been cut out). The court held that the will was not saved from revocation since the testatrix's intention was to revoke whether or not she was able to make a new will.

The fact that a new will is intended is only one of many things which may lead to the inference that revocation was conditional. For example, in *In the Estate of Southerden* (1925) the testator made a will in favour of his wife. He thought that his wife would take all his property on intestacy and so destroyed the will by burning it. Because of the size of the estate the wife was entitled to only part of the testator's property on intestacy; the court held that the will was destroyed conditionally on the wife taking the whole estate. It therefore remained valid as the condition would not be satisfied by revocation of the will.

### 5. A TESTAMENTARY INSTRUMENT

**2.42**   A will may be revoked in whole or in part by a later will or codicil or by "some writing declaring an intention to revoke the same and executed in the manner in which a will is ... executed" (Wills Act 1837, s.20).

The clearest way in which a later will may revoke an earlier one is where it contains an express revocation clause. Such a clause should always be included in a new will which deals with the whole of the testator's property. A common form of wording is "I hereby revoke all former wills and testamentary dispositions heretofore made by me." If a codicil is drawn up great care should be taken with the wording of any revocation clause to ensure that it revokes only those parts of the earlier will which the testator intends to revoke or replace.

Even without express words of revocation a will or codicil revokes an earlier will or codicil to the extent that it is inconsistent with it.

The doctrine of dependent relative revocation may apply to save a will (or part of it) from revocation by a later will or codicil. This applies where the revocation (express or implied) in the later instrument is conditional on the effectiveness of that instrument. If the later will starts with a revocation clause but then disposes of the property in a way which is ineffective (for example, because of ambiguity as to the identity of the beneficiary) the court may construe the revocation clause as conditional so that it will not be admitted to probate. In this case, as the court is required to construe the later will or codicil, it will not hear extrinsic evidence as to the testator's intention.

### 6. REVOCATION BY PRIVILEGED TESTATOR

A testator who enjoys privileged status may revoke a will **2.43** informally whether the will was made informally or not. A testator who makes a privileged will while an infant may revoke it while still an infant even if he has lost the privileged status before revoking (Family Law Reform Act 1969, s.3). However, it seems that the revocation cannot then be made by an informal document but only by destruction (if there is a written will capable of destruction) or by a formal, attested document.

### 7. ALTERATIONS AND OBLITERATIONS

Section 21 of the Wills Act 1837 provides that "No obliteration, **2.44** interlineation or other alteration made in any will after the execution thereof shall be valid ... except so far as the words or effect of the will before such alteration shall not be apparent, unless the alteration shall be executed in like manner as hereinbefore is required for the execution of a will ... "

An alteration made before execution with the knowledge and approval of the testator is valid. However, an alteration in a will is presumed to have been made after execution except that an alteration which completes a blank space in the will is presumed to have been made before execution. Either of these presumptions may be rebutted by internal evidence from the will itself or by extrinsic evidence (for example, a sworn statement from the draftsman or a witness). Once an alteration is shown to have been made before execution it is admissible to probate as part of the will.

An alteration made after execution of the will which is itself signed by the testator and by at least two witnesses is admitted to probate as it complies with the formalities required by the Wills Act 1837. For the avoidance of doubt, any alteration to a will, even if made before execution, should be attested. It is sufficient if the testator and witnesses of the will put their initials in the margin next to the alteration.

A slightly different problem arises where words are crossed out or otherwise made more difficult to read without the alteration being attested. If the original wording is "apparent" it is admitted to probate, the crossing out being ignored. Wording is regarded as apparent if it can be read by ordinary means such as close inspection through a magnifying glass or by holding the document up to the light.

Where the original wording is not apparent because it has been scratched out, covered over or otherwise obliterated it is excluded from probate if the obliteration was made by the testator with an intention to revoke. The effect of obliterating words in this way is that they are revoked.

If the obliteration was made by someone other than the testator or by the testator but without intention to revoke, extrinsic evidence (such as evidence from drafts or copies, infra-red photographs or removal of paper stuck over the words) is permitted to prove the original wording.

Where the testator made the obliteration with a conditional intention to revoke, the court will allow the original wording to be proved by extrinsic evidence and admitted to probate if the condition has not been satisfied. The most likely example of such a conditional intention is that the original wording should only be revoked if the substituted wording is admissible to probate. (For example, the will originally says "I give to X the sum of £1,000," the testator obliterates "£1,000" and writes "£1,500" instead—clearly the court can infer that X is to get £1,000 if the substitution of £1,500 is not effective). If the substitution is ineffective because it has not been executed the court will admit extrinsic evidence to prove the original wording. This is really another example of dependent relative revocation and the same considerations apply as in the case of conditional destruction (see paragraph 2.41 above).

# 3. Intestacy

## A. Introduction

**3.1** There are many advantages to be gained by making a will, but the majority of people die without having made one, either out of ignorance of the courses of action open to them, or out of a reluctance to comtemplate their own deaths, or from a mistaken belief that, for them, a will is pointless.

The devolution of certain assets is fixed irrespective of whether there is a will. Thus, property held as joint tenants passes by the right of survivorship and nominated property passes to the nominee. (See Chapter 21.)

The problem where there is no will is to determine who is to share in the other assets of the deceased's estate. The answer is to be found in Part IV of the Administration of Estates Act 1925, as amended, which lays down who is entitled to an intestate's residuary estate (that is, the deceased's assets after the payment of debts and expenses). The Act specifies the entitlements of the deceased's immediate family; the provisions were based on "the average will" filed with the Probate Registry in the years before 1925, although they have been amended since. While the provisions ensure that the "next-of-kin" share in the estate the proportions are arbitrary and therefore often unsuitable; inevitably they give no rights to friends or charities who might have benefited had the deceased made a will. (If a relative or dependant feels the intestacy rules do not make adequate financial provision for him, he may be able to bring a claim under the Inheritance (Provisions for Family and Dependants) Act 1975, s.1(1) which provides that the court is not bound to assume that the intestacy rules make reasonable provision for the next-of-kin—see Chapter 20).

## B. Total or Partial Intestacy

**3.2** For the rules to apply, the deceased must have died either totally or partially intestate.

The deceased dies totally intestate if he has either made no will at all, has made an invalid will, has revoked any wills that he has made or has made a will which does not effectively dispose of any property.

The deceased dies partially intestate if he has left a valid will which disposes of only part of his estate. This can happen in two ways:

(a) The deceased may have made a valid will which fails to dispose of the whole estate (for example, because it contains no residuary gift). An example of such a will is one leaving money in a building society account to X but not dealing with the rest of the estate; *or*

(b) The deceased may have made a valid will which dealt with the whole of his estate but the residuary gift may fail in whole or in part (for example, because a residuary beneficiary predeceases the testator and no substitutional gift is included in the will).

In general the same rules apply whether the deceased died totally or partially intestate. Where there are differences these will be indicated later.

## C. The Statutory Trust for Sale

### 1. THE GENERAL RULE

**3.3** The Administration of Estates Act 1925, s.33(1) provides:

"on the death of a person intestate as to any real or personal estate, such estate shall be held by his personal representatives:
(a) as to the real estate upon trust to sell the same; and
(b) as to the personal estate upon trust to call in, sell and convert into money such part thereof as may not consist of money,
with power to postpone such sale and conversion for such a period as the personal representatives, without being liable to account, may think proper ... "

(In many cases this power of sale is never exercised and the personal representatives simply vest the assets in the beneficiaries).

Section 33(1) goes on to provide that:

(a) any reversionary interests must not be sold before they fall into possession unless there is a "special reason" for selling; and

(b) personal chattels (see paragraph 3.8 for definition) must not be sold unless required for the purposes of the administration because of the lack of other assets, or unless there is a special reason.

The personal representatives must pay the funeral, testamentary and administration expenses as well as any other debts and liabilities of the deceased. After such liabilities have been paid the personal representatives must set aside a fund to meet pecuniary legacies left by the deceased in the will (if any). The balance remaining is the residuary estate of the deceased which is shared among the beneficiaries in accordance with their entitlement under the 1925 Act.

## 2. PARTIAL INTESTACY

The statutory trust for sale imposed by section 33 applies to a **3.4** partial intestacy as well as to a total intestacy. The provisions of the will take precedence over the intestacy rules. Thus if the undisposed-of property was left on an *express* trust for sale (for example, T leaves "residue on trust for sale to A and B in equal shares" and A predeceases T) the express trust for sale prevails over the statutory trust. This may appear to be a minor point but will be important if the *terms* of the express trust differ from section 33 (for example, by removing the power to postpone the sale).

# D. Order of Entitlement Under the Intestacy Rules

Before considering the detailed rules relating to the entitlements **3.5** of the beneficiaries it is useful to set out the basic structure of the Administration of Estates Act provisions.

First, where there is a surviving spouse he or she takes everything unless the intestate also left certain relatives.

(a) If the intestate also left issue (that is children, grandchildren and remoter lineal descendants) the spouse and issue share the estate provided the issue satisfy the requirements of the statutory trusts.

(b) If the intestate left no surviving issue, but left a surviving parent or parents, the parent(s) and the spouse share the estate. The parent(s) take(s) the property absolutely or in equal shares. If no parent survives, but the intestate left a living brother or sister of the whole blood (or their issue) they share the assets with the spouse, provided that they satisfy the requirements of the statutory trusts.

(The 'statutory trusts" are defined in paragraph 3.14 below.)

If the intestate left no surviving spouse, the estate is distributed as follows:

(a) to issue on the statutory trusts but if none, then to
(b) parents absolutely (and equally if both are alive), but if none, then to
(c) brothers and sisters of the whole blood (*i.e.* the children of the same parents as the deceased) on the statutory trusts, but if none, then to
(d) brothers and sisters of the half blood (*i.e.* those who share one parent with the deceased) on the statutory trusts, but if none, then to
(e) grandparents absolutely and equally if more than one, but if none, then to
(f) uncles and aunts of the whole blood (*i.e.* brothers and sisters of the whole blood of one of the parents of the deceased) on the statutory trusts, but if none, then to
(g) uncles and aunts of the half blood (*i.e.* those with one parent in common with one of the parents of the deceased) on the statutory trusts, but if none, then to
(h) the Crown, Duchy of Lancaster or the Duke of Cornwall as "*bona vacantia*."

Section 46(1)(vi) of the Administration of Estates Act 1925 gives the Crown a discretion to make provision for dependants of the intestate whether they are related to the deceased or not. Similarly the Crown may provide for "other persons for whom the intestate might reasonably have been expected to make provision."

If the intestate died resident within the Duchy of Lancaster or in Cornwall, the Duchy or the Duke of Cornwall respectively take the assets as *bona vacantia* subject to the same discretions.

It should be noted that each category must be considered in the order listed above and only if there is *no one* in a particular category is it necessary to consider the next category. Furthermore, since a blood relationship is vital under the intestacy rules, the *spouse* of a person within one of these categories has no right to share in the estate. Matters relevant to the particular categories are considered below.

# E. The Rights of a Surviving Spouse

### 1. THE SPOUSE'S ENTITLEMENT

The spouse's precise entitlement to the deceased's undisposed-of **3.6** "residuary estate" depends on whether any other close relatives survived the intestate.

For these purposes, a divorced spouse has no rights in the deceased's estate and for deaths occurring on or after January 1, 1970, neither has a *judicially* separated spouse, since he or she is treated as already being dead provided the separation is still continuing (Matrimonial Causes Act 1973, s.18(2)). This is not the case, however, if there is a magistrates' court separation order in effect (*ibid.* section 18(3)) although no such separation orders may be made after the Domestic Proceedings and Magistrates' Courts Act 1978.

A client who consults a solicitor with a view to obtaining a divorce or judicial separation should be asked whether or not he has made a will. If he has not, he should be advised to consider making one since if he dies intestate before the date of the decree absolute, his property will pass to the surviving spouse. If he has made a will, he should be advised to review it in the light of the changed circumstances.

*Spouse alone surviving*
If the intestate left a surviving spouse but no issue, parents or **3.7** brothers or sisters of the whole blood (or their issue), the personal representatives hold *the whole of the estate* on trust for sale for the spouse *absolutely*. Remoter relatives such as grandparents or uncles and aunts have no rights to share in the estate.

*Spouse and issue surviving*
The estate of an intestate who leaves a surviving spouse and **3.8** issue is divided between the spouse and the issue. The spouse receives:

(a) The deceased's "personal chattels" absolutely. "Personal chattels" are defined in Administration of Estates Act 1925, s.55(1)(x). They are "carriages, horses, stable furniture and effects (not used for business purposes), motor cars and accessories (not used for business purposes), garden effects, domestic animals, plate, plated articles, linen, china, glass, books, pictures, prints, furniture, jewellery, articles of household or personal use or ornament, musical and scientific instruments and apparatus, wines, liquors and consumable stores, but do not include any chattels used at the death of the intestate for business purposes nor money or securities for money." To summarise this long definition, personal chattels are items of personal and domestic use and ornament. This has been held to cover a yacht (*Re Chaplin* (1950)) and a collection of watches (*Re Crispins' Will Trusts* (1975)). In the latter case Russell L.J. said that "cherishing . . . by eye and hand [could bring the watches] within the definition of articles of personal use."

(b) A "statutory legacy" of £75,000 where death occurs on or after June 1, 1987. The legacy is payable free of tax and costs, together with interest at 6 per cent. per annum from death until payment. The costs and interest come from the residue of the estate. In the case of deaths occurring prior to June 1, 1987 lower levels of statutory legacy are payable.

(c) If there is anything left in the estate after (a) and (b), the spouse receives a life interest (*i.e.* a right to the income until death) in one-half of the residue.

The other half of the residue and the interest in remainder in the trust created for the spouse go to the issue on the statutory trusts.

*Spouse and parent or brother and sister (or their issue) surviving*

**3.9** Where the intestate leaves a spouse but no issue, the estate is divided as follows if one or more parents of the intestate (or brothers and sisters or their issue) also survive. The spouse receives:

(a) The "personal chattels" (defined above) absolutely.

(b) A statutory legacy of £125,000 where death occurs on or after June 1, 1987. Again the legacy is payable free of tax and costs plus 6 per cent. per annum interest. In the case of deaths occurring prior to June 1, 1987 lower levels of statutory legacy are payable.

(c) One-half of the residue *absolutely*. In contrast to paragraph 3.8 above, the spouse in this case receives the capital and not merely the income from this part of the estate.

The rest of the estate (that is, the other half of any residue) goes to the parent or parents in equal shares absolutely or, if none, to the brothers and sisters of the whole blood or their issue on the statutory trusts (see below).

## 2. THE SPECIAL RULES APPLYING TO SPOUSES

*Redemption of life interest*

Where the intestate is survived by a spouse and issue, the spouse is entitled to a life interest in one-half of the residue of the estate. This means the spouse will receive the income from the trust for sale for life. However, a spouse may prefer to receive a capital sum (particularly if the residue is small and so capable of producing only a small income).

**3.10**

Section 47A of the Administration of Estates Act 1925 allows the spouse to elect to convert the life interest into a capital sum. The election must be made within 12 months of the grant of representation (the time limit may be extended at the discretion of the court) in writing to the personal representatives (section 47A(6)). If the sole personal representative is the surviving spouse, the election is made to the Senior Registrar of the Family Division of the High Court. A complex formula for determining the capital value of the interest is laid down in statutory instruments made under the Administration of Justice Act 1977. Provided the issue are *sui juris* the life interest can be valued by agreement between the spouse and issue, thus removing the necessity of complying with the statutory provisions.

The effect of the provision can be seen in the following example. The residue of the intestate's estate, after taking personal chattels and the statutory legacy, is £50,000, and the spouse is entitled to a life interest in £25,000. Instead of receiving the income from this, the spouse can capitalise the interest using the formula and receive, say, £10,000 in cash. The rest of the estate, after deducting the costs of the capitalisation is held on the statutory trusts for the issue.

If the spouse makes this election, no "transfer of value" is made for the purposes of inheritance tax. However, since less of the deceased's estate is treated as passing to the spouse, less of the estate attracts the spouse exemption so more inheritance tax may become payable on the deceased's estate (see Chapter 4).

### Acquiring the matrimonial home

**3.11** If the intestate and the surviving spouse were joint beneficial tenants of the dwelling-house in which the surviving spouse was resident at the deceased's death, the *jus accrescendi* will automatically vest it in the spouse. If, however, the intestate was the sole owner or held as tenant-in-common, the house or his interest as tenant-in-common in the house will be part of the undisposed-of property. The surviving spouse may wish to acquire the house. This can be achieved in a number of ways.

The Second Schedule to the Intestates Estate Act 1952 gives a surviving spouse the right to *require* the personal representatives to appropriate "any dwelling-house in which the surviving spouse was resident at the time of the intestate's death" in total or partial satisfaction of an absolute and/or capitalised interest in the estate.

If the dwelling-house is worth more than the spouse's absolute entitlement, the personal representative can still be required to appropriate the dwelling-house but the spouse must then pay "equality money" from his or her own resources to make up the difference (Sched. 2, para. 5(2)). The house is valued at the value at the date of appropriation, not death (*Re Collins* (1975)). If it is a time of rising property values it is important to advise a client to make such an election quickly.

As with capitalising a life interest, the spouse must exercise the right within 12 months of the grant of representation (again subject to the court's power to extend the time limit) by notice in writing to the personal representatives.

The spouse will frequently be a personal representative of the deceased. If the spouse is one of two or more personal representatives notice must be given to the others. The Schedule does not mention the giving of notice where the spouse is the sole personal representative.

A personal representative is in a fiduciary position as regards the estate and like a trustee must not profit from that fiduciary position. The Schedule provides that where the spouse is one of two or more personal representatives the rule that a trustee should not purchase trust property is not to prevent the purchase of a dwelling-house from the estate. The Schedule says nothing of the position where a spouse is a sole personal representative. Presumably, a spouse who is a sole personal representative and who wishes to exercise the right to take a dwelling-house ought to do one of the following:

(a) secure the appointment of a second personal representative; or

(b) obtain the consent of the other beneficiaries (but this is only appropriate if they are of full age and capacity); or

(c) obtain the consent of the court.

During the 12-month period the personal representatives need to obtain the spouse's written consent if they wish to dispose of the house, unless they have to sell it to raise money for the administration when there is no other asset available.

When a spouse chooses to exercise this right, it does not matter whether the deceased held the freehold or merely a leasehold interest in the house (except where the lease has less than two years to run). However, in four circumstances set out in Schedule 2, paragraphs 2 and 4(2) to the 1952 Act, the consent of the court is required before the spouse can exercise the right. The consent is required if the house:

(a) forms part of a building, the whole of which is comprised in the residuary estate; or

(b) is held with agricultural land similarly comprised; or

(c) as to the whole or part was used as a hotel or lodging house at the death of the intestate; or

(d) as to part was used for non-domestic purposes at the death of the intestate (which would be the case if part of the house was used as a shop).

In these circumstances, the court must be satisfied that the exercise of the right will not diminish the value of the other residuary assets nor make them more difficult to sell.

If a spouse wishes to avoid an application to the court or if the right of election is unavailable for any other reason (for example, expiry of the 12 months' time limit) it is possible to make use of the ordinary power of appropriation contained in section 41 of the Administration of Estates Act 1925. This power allows personal representatives to appropriate assets in or towards satisfaction of pecuniary legacies or entitlement under the intestacy rules provided the legatee or next-of-kin consents and provided no specific legatees are prejudiced. The power is freely available and the court's consent is never required. However, the spouse has no right to insist on such an appropriation and so must seek the agreement of the personal representatives.

*Hotchpot*

**3.12**   Where there is a partial intestacy, section 49(1)(*aa*) of the Administration of Estates Act 1925 provides that if a surviving spouse has benefited under the terms of the will, this benefit must be brought into account against the statutory legacy; the spouse's rights to the personal chattels or to share in the residue of the estate are unaffected.

*Example*

W makes a will leaving £15,000 to her husband, H. The rest of her property is undisposed of. W leaves her husband and issue surviving her. H would *normally* receive on intestacy the personal chattels, a £75,000 statutory legacy plus interest and a life interest in one-half of the residue. However, the statutory legacy must be reduced by the £15,000 legacy left in the will, *i.e.* leaving £60,000. Had the legacy in the will been of £80,000, it would have extinguished the right to receive a statutory legacy but H's entitlement to the personal chattels and a life interest in half the residue of the undisposed-of property would have remained unaffected.

# F. The Rights of Issue

## 1. GENERAL

**3.13**   As we saw in paragraph 3.5 above, after the surviving spouse the next category of next-of-kin who share in the deceased's estate are the issue. The issue take the appropriate share of the estate on the statutory trusts. If a spouse survives, the issue take one-half of the residuary estate after the statutory legacy has been deducted as well as the interest in remainder in the spouse's one-half. If there is no surviving spouse the issue take the whole residuary estate.

## 2. THE STATUTORY TRUSTS

**3.14**   The "statutory trusts" are set out in the Administration of Estates Act 1925, s.47. Under this section the property is held equally for the children of the intestate who are either alive or *en ventre sa mère* at the date of the intestate's death. The children who satisfy this requirement have a mere contingent interest unless and until they reach 18 or marry under that age. If an infant child dies unmarried the property is dealt with as if that child had never existed.

Thus far, references have been made only to "children" since it is children who are the primary beneficiaries under this heading. However, if a child predeceases the intestate and that child leaves issue at the date of death, those grandchildren or their issue take *per stirpes* the share which their parent would have taken provided those issue reach 18 or marry under that age.

*Example 1*

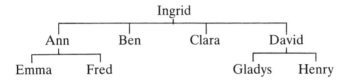

Clara and David predeceased Ingrid who died intestate. Ann, Ben and all the grandchildren are over 18. The estate will be divided into three parts. Ann and Ben each have vested interests in one-third of the estate. Clara has predeceased the intestate without leaving issue and has no entitlement. David has predeceased the intestate but has left issue. David's issue divide his share equally between them so that Gladys and Henry take one-sixth of the estate each. If Henry had also predeceased Ingrid but was survived by children, they would have shared the property to which he was entitled, provided they satisfied the statutory trusts.

*Example 2*

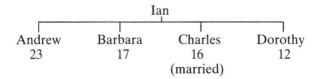

Ian died intestate; all the children survived Ian. Andrew and Charles have vested interests immediately on the death of the intestate. If they die before receiving their share of the deceased's property, their share will pass to their estates. Barbara and Dorothy have only contingent interests and therefore if either dies without attaining the age of 18 or marrying, her share of the estate will be divided amongst Ian's other children.

*Example 3*

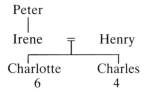

Peter
|
Irene  =  Henry

Charlotte      Charles
6            4

Irene dies intestate, survived by her husband Henry, her two children and her father Peter. Henry, therefore, receives the personal chattels, the £75,000 statutory legacy (plus interest) and a life interest in one-half of the residue. The other half of the residue is held on the statutory trusts for the two children. If either dies unmarried and before reaching the age of 18, the property will be held for the other on the statutory trusts. If both die unmarried and before reaching 18 the estate is dealt with as if they had never existed. Henry will be entitled to a statutory legacy of £125,000 (plus interest) and the residue of the estate will be shared equally by him with Peter, Irene's father.

The fact that persons who fail to reach the age of 18 or marry earlier are dealt with as if they had never existed means that property may pass to someone (Peter, in this example) who appeared to have no entitlement at the moment of death. Furthermore if Henry and Peter had survived Irene but both died before Charlotte and Charles, Henry's and Peter's estates could both have benefited. This is because the property is distributed as it would have been at the date of Irene's death had neither Charlotte nor Charles existed.

## 3. HOTCHPOT

*General*

**3.15** There are two hotchpot provisions. The idea behind them is that a parent is presumed to want to treat his children equally.

Under section 47(1)(iii) of Administration of Estates Act 1925:

(a)   on a *total* or *partial* intestacy
(b)   *inter vivos advancements*
(c)   to a *child* of the deceased

must be brought into account by the child when assessing his entitlement.
   Under section 49(1)(*a*):

(a)   on a *partial* intestacy
(b)   gifts by *will*
(c)   to the deceased's *issue*

must be brought into account.

*Section 47(1)(iii) of the Administration of Estates Act 1925*
Whenever a total or partial intestacy arises, any *child* of the   **3.16**
deceased who received an *inter vivos* "advancement" has his or
her share on the intestacy reduced by the amount of the
advance unless the intestate showed a contrary intention. The
test is subjective and it is that "looking at all the circumstances,
do they require an inference that (the intestate's) intention was
that the gift should not be brought into hotchpot" (*per* Goff J.
in *Hardy* v. *Shaw* (1976)). The party alleging contrary intention
must prove it.
   The gift that must be brought into account is "any money or
property which, by way of advancement or on the marriage of a
child of the intestate, has been paid to such child by the
intestate or settled by the intestate for the benefit of such child
including any life or less interest, and including property
covenanted to be paid or settled." This covers both cash
received and assets transferred provided they amount to
"advancement."
   An advancement is a substantial payment to set a child up in
life. Thus, it would cover a lump sum to enable a child to buy
into a firm of solicitors but not a lump sum to help a child with
living expenses while training to be a solicitor. There is a
presumption of "advancement" if the payment is of such a
substantial amount as to represent permanent provision for the
child (*Re Hayward* (1957)) and the person alleging "advancement" must prove it (*Re Grover's Will Trusts* (1971)).
   The advancement is valued at the date of death which causes
no problems if *cash* was given since the value taken into account
is always the actual amount of the gift. However, if an *asset* was
given, its value may have changed dramatically since the gift
was made. Thus, if a parent made a cash advance to a child of

£10,000 to buy a house the child must bring £10,000 into account on his parent's intestacy. However, if the parent gave the child a house, worth £10,000 at the time of the gift, on the parent's intestacy the child would have to bring into account the value of the house at the date of death. This may have risen substantially in the intervening period.

The advancement reduces the child's share under the intestacy and will similarly reduce the share of his own issue if he predeceases the intestate leaving issue who are entitled to take the share he would have taken.

When bringing an advancement into account, to calculate the child's share, these steps must be followed:

(a) Calculate the "notional estate." This is undisposed-of property plus the value at death of any advancements.

(b) Divide the "notional estate" between the children (or issue of a deceased child).

(c) Deduct the amount of the advancement from the share of the child, or children, in question.

(d) Distribute the "residuary estate" accordingly.

*Example*

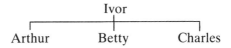

Ivor

Arthur      Betty      Charles

Ivor dies intestate leaving undisposed-of residue of £16,000, and is survived only by three adult children, Arthur, Betty and Charles. He has made an "advancement" of £2,000 to Arthur. The entitlement of each will be calculated as follows.

(a) The "notional estate" is £18,000 (£16,000 + £2,000).

(b) Each child is entitled to a one-third share, *i.e.* £6,000.

(c) However, Arthur has already received £2,000 of his entitlement so his share is reduced by this amount.

(d) The undisposed-of property is divided so that Arthur receives £4,000 and Betty and Charles receive £6,000 each.

If the advancement to Arthur had been £11,000, the "notional estate" would have been £27,000 so that each child would have been entitled to £9,000. However, Arthur would not be required to return anything to the estate; the undisposed-of property would simply be divided equally between Betty and Charles.

*Section 49(a) of the Administration of Estates Act 1925*
The hotchpot rules in section 49 apply whenever, on a *partial*   **3.17**
intestacy, the *issue* of the deceased received beneficial interests
under the will. The wording of s.49(*a*) is not clear. It provides
that:

> "(a) The requirements [of s.47] as to bringing property into
> account shall apply to any beneficial interests acquired by
> any issue of the deceased under the will of the deceased,
> but not to beneficial interests so acquired by any other
> persons."

There are conflicting academic views on how the section
should be interpreted but Harman J. said, in *Re Young* (1951),
that "issue must mean children or remoter issue and any
member of the family belonging to a certain branch must bring
in everything that has been taken or acquired under the will by
that branch." This view has been followed in *Re Morton* (1956)
and in *Re Grover's Will Trusts* (1971).

*Example*
The operation of section 49 can be illustrated as follows:

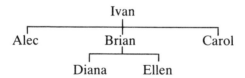

Ivan died partially intestate having given by will £5,000 each
to Diana and Ellen. His undisposed-of property amounts to
£50,000. The entitlements of the various members of the family
are calculated following the steps set out in paragraph 3.16
above except that the gifts in the will are substituted for the
advancements.

   (a)   The "notional estate" is £60,000 (£50,000 + £5,000 +
£5,000).
   (b)   Each child is entitled to a one-third share, *i.e.* £20,000.
   (c)   However, since Diana and Ellen have already received
between them £10,000, Brian's share is reduced by
that amount.
   (d)   The undisposed-of property is divided so that Alec and
Carol receive £20,000 each, Brian receiving only
£10,000.

*Valuation.* The interest is valued at the date of the intestate's death. Difficulties have arisen when a testator has given a life interest to a child, remainder to the child's issue. The method of valuation apparently depends on the circumstances and the one most likely to achieve equality and fairness will be adopted.

In *Re Morton* (1956), the deceased gave a share in the residue to a son for life and thereafter to the son's child for life. The court had to decide whether the value to be brought into account was the capital value of the trust fund or the actuarial values of the interests given by the will. Adopting the latter method of valuation, Danckwerts J. said "To value the interest as being equivalent to a gift of capital in a case where a person takes no more than a life interest seems to me contrary to fairness, commonsense and everything else."

*Contrary intention.* Section 49(1)(iii) provides that these provisions can be prevented from applying where the deceased shows a contrary intention expressed or appearing from the circumstances of the case. The testator can thus exclude section 49 by a term in the will.

*The inter-relation between sections 47 and 49*

**3.18** The differences between the two sections have already been set out in paragraph 3.15 but both sets of rules could come into play on the death of an intestate. The following example illustrates this.

*Example*

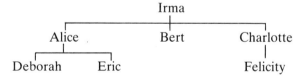

Irma died intestate and during her lifetime made advancements of £10,000 each to her daughter Alice and her granddaughter Felicity. By will she left Bert and Felicity £15,000 each and £5,000 to Eric. She was intestate as to the rest of her estate, her undisposed-of residuary estate amounting to £90,000.

   (a)   The "notional estate" is £135,000 which is made up as follows:

         (i)   Undisposed of property           £90,000

        (ii)   Advancement to Alice inter vivos
              (advancement to *grandchild* is ignored)  £10,000

      (iii)   Gifts by will (to Bert, Eric and Felicity) £35,000

(b)   Each child is entitled to a one-third share, *i.e.* £45,000.

(c)   However, from this must be deducted the amounts brought into account under the two hotchpot rules:
> (i)   Alice must deduct the advancement to her of £10,000 and the gift in the will of £5,000 to Eric (£45,000 − £15,000 = £30,000).
> (ii)   Bert must deduct the gift in the will to him of £15,000 (£45,000 − £15,000 = £30,000).
> (iii)   Charlotte must deduct the gift in the will of £15,000 to her daughter Felicity (£45,000 − £15,000 = £30,000).

## 4. ADOPTED, LEGITIMATE AND ILLEGITIMATE CHILDREN

### Adopted children

For the purposes of entitlement under an intestacy arising on or after January 1, 1976, sections 39 and 46(4) of the Children Act 1975 provide that an adopted child is the legitimate child of its adoptive parent or parents. (This rule applies if the adoption order was made by a court in the United Kingdom, the Isle of Man or the Channel Islands. The same rule applies to certain foreign adoptions). The child is thus debarred from claiming on the intestacy of its natural parents and is treated as a child of the adopting parents. Such a child is therefore entitled to take on the intestacy of adoptive grandparents and brothers and sisters.    **3.19**

### Legitimated children

Sections 5(1)–(4) and 10(1) of the Legitimacy Act 1976 provide that a legitimated child is entitled to share in a deceased's intestacy as if it had been born legitimate.    **3.20**

### Children whose parents were not married at the time of their birth

In the case of deaths occurring before the coming into force of the Family Law Reform Act 1987, an illegitimate relationship was not recognised for the purposes of distribution of property on intestacy subject to two limited exceptions. Thus, (in respect of deaths occurring on or after January 1, 1970) an illegitimate child (and his legitimate issue) could take on his parents' intestacy as if he had been born legitimate and his parents could take on the child's intestacy on the same footing. No other relationships were recognised. For example, an illegitimate child could not take on the intestacy of brothers and sisters or    **3.21** grandparents nor could such people take on the intestacy of the illegitimate.

In respect of deaths occurring after April 4, 1988, the distribution of assets on intestacy (and otherwise) is to be determined without regard to whether or not the parents of a particular person were married to each other.

Section 20 of the 1987 Act removes the protection which existed under the old law for personal representatives who distributed property in ignorance of the existence of illegitimate claimants. Prima facie it appears, therefore, that personal representatives should undertake investigations to discover whether or not there are hitherto unknown relatives of the deceased alive whose parents were not married. Presumably, however, the protection against claimants of the estate available generally to personal representatives under the Trustee Act 1925, s.27 and the Benjamin Order procedure (see Chapter 14) extends to cover the claims of persons whose parents were not married. Moreover, section 18(2) of the Family Law Reform Act makes special provision for the administration of an intestate's estate. It provides that where the parents of a child who dies intestate were not married to each other at the time of that child's birth there is a presumption that the child has not been survived by *his father or by any person related to him only through his father*. Thus, personal representatives will be able in the absence of evidence to the contrary to distribute on the basis that no such persons are alive.

*Example*

(1) X, whose parents have not married, dies intestate without a spouse or issue. He is known to be survived by his mother but nothing is known of his father or of his father's relatives.

X's mother will take the whole estate since the personal representatives are entitled to presume that the father and the father's relatives have predeceased X.

(2) As above, X, whose parents did not marry, has died intestate without a spouse or issue. However, his mother is dead and the only relative on his mother's side still living is her brother of the whole blood (X's maternal uncle). Nothing is known of X's father or of any of the father's relatives except that the father's brother of the whole blood is known to be alive (X's paternal uncle). X's estate will be divided between the two uncles. X's personal representatives are entitled to presume that the father and father's relatives other than the brother have predeceased X.

# G. The Rights of Others

It should be noted that the other relatives who take on the **3.22** statutory trusts (that is brothers and sisters of the whole and half blood and uncles and aunts of the whole or half blood) must fulfil the same requirements as issue; that is, they must be living at the intestate's death and reach 18 or marry earlier. A person who predeceases the intestate can be replaced *per stirpes* by his own issue provided they reach the age of 18 or marry earlier. Other relatives are not subject to the hotchpot rules.

# 4. Inheritance Tax

## A. Introduction

### 1. DEFINITIONS

Inheritance tax is, prima facie, payable where there is a **4.1**
*chargeable transfer*. A chargeable transfer is defined as "any
*transfer of value* which is made to an individual but is not ... an
exempt transfer" (Inheritance Tax Act 1984, s.2(1)). A transfer
of value is defined as "a *disposition* made by a person ... as a
result of which the value of his estate immediately after the
transfer is less than it would be but for the disposition. ... "
The amount by which the value of the transferor's estate is less
as a result of the disposition is the *value transferred* on which
inheritance tax is prima facie payable.

Transfers of value occur *inter vivos* as a result of gifts of
property or sales at an undervalue. Section 4 of the Inheritance
Tax Act 1984 provides that a deceased person is to be treated as
if he had made a transfer of value immediately before his death
the value of which is equal to the value of his whole estate
immediately before death. The "estate" is the aggregate of all
the property to which a deceased person was beneficially
entitled immediately before death (section 5). In fact the charge
on death is by far the most important type of charge as most
*inter vivos* transfers are exempt or potentially exempt (in the
latter case they become exempt if the donor survives seven
years).

The structure of inheritance tax is rather complicated as the
outline above will show. This is largely because the tax is a
modification of capital transfer tax. Capital transfer tax was a
tax on death estates and on *inter vivos* transfers (with far less
extensive exemptions than apply to inheritance tax). The Act
which is now called the Inheritance Tax Act 1984 was formerly
the Capital Transfer Tax Act 1984. That Act in its unamended
form continues to apply to certain transactions entered into
before March 18, 1986. References in documents (for example,

wills) made before that date to capital transfer tax are now to be taken as references to inheritance tax.

## 2. OCCASIONS OF CHARGE TO INHERITANCE TAX

**4.2** There are three categories of transfer which can give rise to inheritance tax (exemptions or reliefs may be available to extinguish or reduce a charge—these are dealt with later.)

(a) *A transfer on death.* Such a transfer is taxed at the full rates of tax.

(b) *A potentially exempt transfer.* This is an *inter vivos* transfer of value made on or after March 18, 1986 made by an individual whereby property becomes comprised in the estate of another individual or in an accumulation and maintenance settlement or a disabled trust (the taxation of settlements and trusts is dealt with in Chapter 7). In addition a transfer of value made on or after March 17, 1987 by an individual into a settlement with an interest in possession (that is, broadly speaking, where an individual creates a life interest in property by making an *inter vivos* gift—see Chapter 7) is a potentially exempt transfer as is the surrender or sale of an interest in possession in such a settlement.

A potentially exempt transfer becomes fully exempt if the transferor survives seven years after the transfer. If he dies within seven years the transfer becomes chargeable at the rates in force at the date of death (see below for the calculation of tax and the reduction where the transferor survives more than three years).

(c) *A chargeable transfer* made before death. This type of transfer is immediately taxable but at only half the rates which apply on death. If the transferor dies within seven years the transferee becomes taxable at the full rates in force at the date of the death.

Most transfers made *inter vivos* are now potentially exempt so that few transfers are immediately taxable as chargeable transfers. The main categories of chargeable transfers made before death are:

(i) Transfers to settlements without an interest in possession (see Chapter 7—a "settlement without an interest in possession" is a discretionary trust or an accumulation trust other than one which satisfies the definition of an accumulation and maintenance settlement).

(ii) Chargeable events within settlements without an interest in possession (see Chapter 7).

(iii) Transfers under which no property becomes comprised in the estate of another by virtue of the transfer. This occurs where one person buys a service for another. One of the commonest examples is where a grandparent pays school fees for his grandchild. The grandparent's estate is reduced in value so (assuming no exemption is available) there is a transfer of value. However, as the grandchild's estate is not increased it is not within the definition of a potentially exempt transfer.

## B. Excluded Property

Excluded property does not form part of the owner's estate on death for inheritance tax purposes so that, in effect, it is exempt from tax. As far as lifetime transfers are concerned the position is slightly more complicated. A transfer of excluded property *inter vivos* is not a chargeable or potentially exempt transfer unless the transfer causes a reduction in value of non-excluded property in which case there is, to the extent of that reduction, a chargeable or potentially exempt transfer as the case may be. **4.3**

Excluded property is:

(a) reversionary interests in settled property unless:
    (i) acquired for money or money's worth, or
    (ii) vested in the settlor or settlor's spouse, or
    (iii) expectant on a lease for life at a nominal rent;

(b) most types of property situate outside the United Kingdom and owned by a person domiciled outside the United Kingdom and some types of property situate in the United Kingdom but owned by a person not domiciled in the United Kingdom;

(c) settled property situate outside the United Kingdom provided the settlor was domiciled outside the United Kingdom when the settlement was made.

## C. The Calculation of Tax

### 1. TWO RATES OF TAX

In respect of transfers made before March 15, 1988 the rates of tax were "progressive," that is to say, the rate of tax increased **4.4** as the total of taxable gifts made by the transferor increased. However, in respect of transfers made on or after that date there are only two rates of tax. There is a nil rate band of £128,000 and, once that has been exhausted, tax is charged at the rate of 40 per cent.

### 2. CUMULATION

**4.5**  In order to establish whether or not the nil rate band has been exhausted in respect of a particular chargeable transfer it is necessary to take into account all previous chargeable transfers made by the transferor within the seven years before the present transfer (Inheritance Tax Act 1984, s.7(1)). This is called the principle of cumulation. The present transfer is added to all the previous transfers in the last seven years and the tax is then calculated as if the present transfer is the highest part of a single transfer equal to all the transfers (including the present one) made within the last seven years. It is therefore taxed at 40 per cent. to the extent that it exceeds £128,000.

The full rate of 40 per cent. applies where the transfer is made on death or was made before death but death follows within *three* years. If the transfer is a chargeable transfer made before death the tax charged at the time of the transfer is at half the full rates (Inheritance Tax Act 1984, s.7(2)). If the transfer is a potentially exempt transfer or a chargeable transfer and death occurs within seven years (but not less than three years) of the transfer the tax is charged on the value of the transfer (at the date it was made) at the following percentage of the full rates in force at the time of death:

  (a)  where the transfer is made more than three years but not more than four years before the death, 80 per cent.;

  (b)  where the transfer is made more than four years but not more than five years before the death, 60 per cent.;

  (c)  where the transfer is made more than five but not more than six years before the death, 40 per cent.;

  (d)  where the transfer is made more than six but not more than seven years before the death, 20 per cent.; (Inheritance Tax Act 1984, s.7(4)).

In the case of a *chargeable* transfer made before death the reduction in the rates mentioned above will be available only to the extent that it does not reduce the amount of tax due on that transfer below the amount originally paid on the *inter vivos* transfer. Thus, no refund of tax is allowed.

*Examples*

(1) A makes a potentially exempt transfer to B, an individual, of £158,000. A has made no previous chargeable transfers. The potentially exempt transfer is treated initially as one which will prove to be exempt. No inheritance tax is payable at the time of the transfer. (For the purposes of this illustration and the following ones in this section exemptions and reliefs are ignored.)

If A dies within three years of the transfer, the potentially exempt transfer becomes chargeable and tax will become payable at the full rates in force at the date of death. Thus, assuming that the 1990/91 rates are still in force at the time of the transferor's death the first £128,000 will be taxed at nil per cent. and the remaining £30,000 will be taxed at 40 per cent.; a total of £12,000 will be payable.

If A dies more than three years after but within seven years of the transfer, the potentially exempt transfer becomes chargeable but at only a percentage of the full rate in force at the date of the death. Thus, assuming that the 1990/91 rates are still in force at the time of the transferor's death and A's death was within four years of the transfer, tax will be charged at 80 per cent. of the full rate, that is:

$$\frac{80}{100} \times £12,000 = £9,600$$

(2) Before death A makes a chargeable transfer to a settlement with no interest in possession of £158,000. A has made no other chargeable transfers. As explained in the previous example tax calculated at the full rate on such a transfer would be £12,000. Since this is a transfer made before death tax is payable at half that rate so £6,000 will be payable.

(3) Having made the chargeable transfer of £158,000 referred to in the previous example, A dies three years six months later when the table of rates provides for (say) £138,000 to be taxed at a nil rate and the balance at 40 per cent. The recalculation of tax on the transfer will give a tax figure of:

|  £ |   |  £ | Rate % |   | Amount £ |
|---|---|---|---|---|---|
| 0 | – | 138,000 | 0 | = | Nil |
| 138 | – | 158,000 | 40 | = | 8,000 |

Only 80 per cent. of that tax figure of £8,000 is payable since death occurred more than three years after the transfer. Thus,

$$\text{Tax payable on death } \frac{80}{100} \times £8,000 = £6,400$$

Credit must be given for any tax already paid. Thus,

|   | £ |
|---|---|
| Tax payable on death | 6,400 |
| *Less*: Lifetime tax paid | (6,000) |
| Extra tax now payable | 400 |

If the table of rates on A's death provides for (say) £148,000 to be taxed at a nil rate and the balance at 40 per cent. the recalculation would give a tax figure of:

|  £ |   |  £ | Rate % |   | £ |
|---|---|---|---|---|---|
| 0 | – | 148,000 | 0 | = | Nil |
| 148 | – | 158,000 | 40 | = | 4,000 |

Only 80 per cent. of that tax figure of £4,000 is payable since death occurred more than 3 years after the transfer. Thus,

$$\text{Tax payable on death } \frac{80}{100} \times £4,000 = £3,200$$

More than £3,200 in tax was paid *inter vivos*. No reclaim is, however, permitted so there will simply be no extra tax payable on death.

As we explained briefly above when deciding which rates of tax are to be charged on a particular chargeable transfer it is necessary to take into account all previous chargeable transfers made within seven years before the present transfer. An illustration may be helpful. For the purposes of this illustration exemptions and reliefs have been ignored.

*Example*
A has made no previous chargeable transfers.

| | |
|---|---|
| March 20, 1990 | A transfers £100,000 to X, an individual |
| March 20, 1991 | A transfers £138,000 to Y, a discretionary trust |
| March 20, 1996 | A transfers £120,000 to X, an individual |
| January 20, 1998 | A dies, owning £120,000 of assets |

Since the 1990 transfer is potentially exempt, it is assumed that it will prove to be an exempt transfer until either seven years expires or the transferor dies within that period. Therefore, no tax is payable in 1990 and the transfer is not cumulated with the chargeable transfer to Y made in 1991. On March 20, 1997 the 1990 transfer actually becomes exempt.

The transfer to Y in 1991 is a chargeable transfer made before death and as such is taxed at half the full rates of tax. Tax will be calculated as follows:

| Amount transferred £ | Full rate | Half rate | Tax payable at half rate £ |
|---|---|---|---|
| 0 — 128,000 | nil | nil | nil |
| 128 — 138,000 | 40% | 20% | 2,000 |
| | | | 2,000 |

Therefore £2,000 will be payable in 1991.

The 1996 transfer is potentially exempt and so no tax is paid at the time of the transfer.

On A's death in 1998 tax on the 1991 transfer will be recalculated at the full rates in force in tax year 1997/98. Since death has occurred more than six years after the transfer only 20 per cent. of the full rates of tax is payable. If this is less than the £2,000 already paid no refund is available.

As a result of A's death within seven years of the 1996 transfer it becomes chargeable. In fact death has occurred within three years of the transfer and so tax will be calculated at the full rates in force in tax year 1997/98. As £138,000 of chargeable transfers have already been made the rates appropriate to a transfer from £138,000 to £258,000 will be used. Finally the tax due on the transfer on death will be calculated at the full rates for tax year 1997/98. As £258,000 of chargeable transfers have already been made the rates appropriate to a transfer from £258,000 to £378,000 will be used.

### 3. GROSSING-UP

*The basic principle*

**4.6** Where inheritance tax is paid by the donor (as it may be in the case of a chargeable transfer made before death), the loss to the donor resulting from the transfer is the value of the gift *plus* the inheritance tax on it. It is on this gross figure that inheritance tax is payable. In such a case the value of the *net* gift is known but in order to calculate the gross loss to the estate it is necessary to "gross up" the net gift. Inheritance tax is then calculated on the gross loss to the donor.

*Example*

A has made chargeable transfers of £128,000 (so his nil rate band has been exhausted). He now makes a chargeable transfer to a discretionary trust of £10,000 and agrees to pay the inheritance tax attributable to the transfer.

The tax payable is calculated by "grossing up" the gift of £10,000, that is by treating the £10,000 as a net amount the tax on which has been notionally deducted. The whole transfer falls within the 40 per cent. tax band but as it is a transfer made *before* death tax will be charged at one-half the full rate, that is at 20 per cent. Thus, it can be seen that the gift is 80 per cent. of the gross amount transferred.

$$net = \frac{80}{100} \text{ x gross}$$

The gross figure can, therefore, be found by multiplying the net amount by 100 and dividing it by 80.

$$\text{gross} = \text{net} \times \frac{100}{80}$$

$$i.e. \ \pounds10,000 \times \frac{100}{80} = \pounds12,500$$

The difference between the gross and net amounts is the amount of the tax, *i.e.* £12,500 − £10,000 = £2,500.

Where inheritance tax is paid by the donee the gross loss to the donor is known and no grossing-up calculation is necessary.

*Example*
A has made chargeable transfers of £128,000 (so his nil rate band has been exhausted). He now makes a chargeable transfer to a discretionary trust of £10,000; the donee is to pay the inheritance tax attributable to the transfer.

The gross loss to the donor is £10,000. The transfer falls within the 40 per cent. band but as it is a transfer made before death, the tax will be charged at one-half the full rate, that is at 20 per cent. The inheritance tax is, therefore:

$$\pounds10,000 \times \frac{20}{100} = \pounds2,000$$

It will be observed that in the first example the donee receives £10,000 and the donor loses £12,500 whereas in the second example the donee receives £8,000 and the donor loses £10,000. In the case of *inter vivos* transfers it is, therefore, important for the donor to consider carefully the amount he can afford to transfer and the amount he wishes the donee to receive. Where the gift consists of an asset rather than cash, the problem may be particularly serious as neither donor nor donee may have sufficient cash available to pay the inheritance tax. However, if the *donee* is paying the tax it is possible in respect of certain types of property to elect to pay the tax by instalments (see paragraph 4.42 below) and this will mitigate the problem.

Grossing-up is required on an *inter vivos* gift whenever the *donor* pays the tax. The parties may agree that the donee will pay but if the donee fails to do so and the donor in fact pays, grossing-up is required.

Grossing-up is not normally required on the transfer of property forming part of the estate on death. The reason for this is that the tax on death is on the full value of the estate (subject to exemptions) not on the loss to the donor's estate. In very limited circumstances grossing-up is required to calculate the tax on death (see paragraphs 4.43–4.46 below).

Where a potentially exempt or a chargeable transfer has been made and death occurs within seven years, tax may be payable as a result of the death. This is primarily the liability of the donee. As the donee will be paying the tax the gift to the donee is a gross gift and no grossing-up is required.

*Gifts involving more than one tax band*

**4.7** If a transferor makes a transfer of value part of which is taxed at nil per cent. and part of which is taxed at 40 per cent., only the part falling within the 40 per cent. tax band needs to be grossed up. (In respect of transfers made before March 15, 1988 when there were several different rates of tax the calculation is more complicated).

4. GIFTS WITHIN SEVEN YEARS OF DEATH—CHANGES IN VALUE

**4.8** The object of charging the full rates or a proportion of the full rates of tax on death within seven years of a transfer is to prevent donors who know they are about to die from saving tax by making *inter vivos* transfers. It is, therefore, considered appropriate that relief from the extra tax should be given in certain cases where the value of the property transferred has declined between the transfer and the death. The rules which provide this relief are, in detail, very complex but their broad effect is to allow a decline in value of an asset to be deducted from the amount liable to the extra tax where the donee still owns the asset at the donor's death. Where the asset has been sold before the donor's death by the donee (or his spouse) at a loss in a qualifying sale (which broadly means in a genuine commercial transaction) the decline in value between the date of the gift and the date of sale may be deducted from the amount liable to extra tax. Special rules apply to certain types of property (including land and shares) and no relief is given where the asset was tangible movable property which had a predictable useful life of 50 years or less immediately before the transfer to the donee.

5. GIFTS WITH A RESERVATION

**4.9** The Finance Act 1986 contains special provisions in respect of property subject to a reservation. Property is regarded as subject to a reservation where an individual transfers property by way of gift and *either* the donee does not bona fide assume possession and enjoyment within the relevant period *or* at any time in the relevant period the property is not enjoyed to the entire, or virtually the entire, exclusion of the donor. The relevant period is the period ending with the date of death of the deceased and beginning seven years earlier or at the date of the gift if it was made within seven years of the death.

If a donor dies and there is property which is regarded as subject to a reservation at the date of his death, the property is treated for the purpose of inheritance tax as if it was part of his estate on death.

If property ceases to be subject to a reservation within the "relevant period" the donor is treated as making a potentially exempt transfer at that date. This means that tax will be payable on the property which was subject to a reservation if the donor dies within seven years of the property ceasing to be subject to a reservation.

# D. Valuation of Property

## 1. GENERAL RULES

On a lifetime transfer the loss to the donor or on death the value of the estate will depend on the valuation of particular items of property. **4.10**

Section 160 of the Inheritance Tax Act 1984 provides that "... the value at any time of any property shall for the purposes of inheritance tax be the price which the property might reasonably be expected to fetch if sold in the open market at that time; but that price shall not be assumed to be reduced on the grounds that the whole property is to be placed on the market at one and the same time." The market value of any property is a question of fact. If property is actually sold within a short period after death on the open market the price received will be evidence (though not conclusive evidence) of the market value at the date of death.

The qualification which prohibits the assumption that all the property is to be sold at the same time will not affect valuation in most cases but would be relevant in valuing a large holding of shares in a private company (or even in a public company if the holding was a significant proportion of the share capital).

2. VALUATION ON DEATH

**4.11**    The transfer of value on death is a transfer of all property owned by the deceased *immediately before his death.* However, the Inheritance Tax Act 1984, s.171(1) provides that "changes in the value of [the] estate which have occurred by reason of the death ... shall be taken into account as if they had occurred before the death." The effect of this provision is to take into account changes in the market value of property which *result* from the death. Sometimes this will lead to an increase in the value of the estate, sometimes to a decrease.

For example, if the deceased is the managing director of a private company and owns a majority shareholding in it the value of the shares may well decline because of his death. Such a decline is likely to occur wherever the goodwill of the company is dependent on the personal ability of the deceased and is particularly likely in cases where the deceased has no successor able and willing to continue to run the company's business.

An example of an increase in the value of property resulting from the death of the owner is where the deceased owned a life insurance policy on his own life payable to his estate. Clearly, the value of the policy will increase as a result of the death from the surrender value of the policy to its capital value.

It is important to remember that the transfer on death is a transfer of the deceased's "estate," that is property to which the deceased was beneficially entitled (Inheritance Tax Act, s.5). Thus, any item not in the deceased's beneficial enjoyment will not be part of the estate and will not attract inheritance tax. Insurance policies must be looked at closely to see whether or not they are part of the estate. Where a policy on the deceased's life is owned beneficially by a third party it does not form part of the deceased's estate and so no inheritance tax is payable on the proceeds of the policy on his death. Examples of policies not beneficially owned by the deceased are policies taken out under the Married Women's Property Act or written in trust for a third party.

Section 171 only allows changes in the *market* value of property to be taken into account, it does not allow changes in the value of the property *to the deceased* to be taken into account. For this reason the deceased's share in joint property (which passes to the remaining joint tenant by survivorship) is fully taxable. Although it is true that the value to the deceased's *estate* of the joint property is nil once the deceased is dead, this does not affect the market value of the *property*.

## 3. SPECIAL VALUATION RULES

*Quoted shares*
Quoted stocks and shares are normally valued by taking the lower of the two prices quoted in the Stock Exchange Daily Official List for the relevant day and adding to it one-quarter of the difference between the lower and higher prices there quoted (for example, if the Daily List shows 200p/205p the value will be 201.25p for inheritance tax purposes) or if it produces a lower figure by taking a figure halfway between the lowest and highest prices at which bargains were struck on the relevant day. The "relevant day" is the day of death or the last or next trading day before or after death. "Quoted" means quoted on a recognised stock exchange or dealt in on the Unlisted Securities Market, Inheritance Tax Act 1984, s.272.

**4.12**

*Unquoted shares*
Unquoted shares are valued according to the normal market value principle. The valuation of unquoted shares is factually very difficult but will take into account: the dividend record of the company, the retained earnings (especially where earnings have been retained with a view to increasing the share value), the profitability of the company even if profits have not been used to pay dividends (this is especially relevant where profits have been used to pay high director's fees to a controlling shareholder) and the value of the assets owned by the company (this is especially relevant where the company is likely to be wound up).

**4.13**

Three special rules apply to the valuation of unquoted shares:

(a) A reduction in value resulting from the death cannot be taken into account if it arises from the fact that the rights attached to the shares are varied as a result of the death (for example, because the articles of the company provide that the shares are then to lose their right to dividend or to vote). (Inheritance Tax Act 1984, s.171(2)).

(b) If the shares are subject to pre-emption rights the market value is to be assessed on the basis that the pre-emption rights do not apply to the hypothetical sale on the open market at the time of death but that they will apply to the hypothetical purchaser (in other

words the value is the price that a purchaser would
pay knowing that he would be subject to the pre-
emption rights in the future). This was established in
*I.R.C.* v. *Crossman* (1937) an estate duty case decided
on legislation which was in this respect similar to the
inheritance tax legislation.

(c)   The value on death is calculated on the assumption
that a prospective purchaser would have all the
information which a prudent prospective purchaser
might reasonably require if he were purchasing from a
willing vendor by private treaty and at arm's length
(Inheritance Tax Act 1984, s.168(1)).

*Sale within one or three years of death*

**4.14**   If quoted shares are sold within one year of death or an interest
in land within three years of death for less than the value at
death a reduction of the tax may be claimed in certain
circumstances. (See paragraph 12.13).

*Commorientes*

**4.15**   Section 184 of the Law of Property Act 1925 provides that
where two or more people die in circumstances such that it is
uncertain which of them survived, for the purposes of succession
to property the deaths are deemed to occur in the order of
seniority so that the elder is deemed to die first. Consequently if
the elder has left property to the younger, the younger will
inherit that property which will then pass under the terms of the
will or intestacy of the younger. (For a detailed discussion of
this rule and a limited exception to it, see Chapter 16).

However, for inheritance tax purposes, section 4(2) of the
Inheritance Tax Act 1984 provides that "where it cannot be
known which of two or more persons who have died survived
the other or others they shall be assumed to have died at the
same instant." Therefore, where two or more persons die and
the order of deaths cannot be known a double charge to tax is
avoided. If the elder person has left property to the younger it
will be taxed as part of the elder's estate (unless an exemption is
available) but the younger will not be deemed to have survived
for tax purposes and so the property will not be taxed as part of
his estate.

*Example*

A and her son B are killed in a car accident. A's will leaves
everything to B. B's will leaves everything to X. It is uncertain
whether A or B died first; therefore for the purposes of

succession to property the deaths are deemed to occur in order of seniority and A's property passes to B. B's property (including that which has been inherited from A) then passes to X. For the purposes of inheritance tax, A and B are deemed to die at the same instant. Thus, when calculating inheritance tax payable on B's estate, B's estate is deemed not to include the property received from A.

## 4. RELATED PROPERTY

Certain assets are more valuable when owned in conjunction with other assets of the same type than when owned individually. For example, a share in a company owned as part of a majority shareholding in the company will be more valuable than a share owned as part of a minority shareholding. There is a possibility that spouses might try to avoid inheritance tax by using the spouse exemption to split the ownership of such items between themselves. In order to prevent this special rules applying to the valuation of "related property" exist. Section 161(2) of the Inheritance Tax Act 1984 provides that property is related to other property owned by the transferor's spouse at the time of the transfer. Property is also related to property which was transferred by the transferor by an exempt transfer to a charity, political party or certain national bodies (as defined by Inheritance Tax Act 1984, Schedule 3), and is owned by the charity, etc. at the time of the transfer or has been owned by it within five years before the transfer. This provision is designed to prevent abuse where a person makes an exempt transfer to a charity of property from which he can benefit or which he controls.

**4.16**

On a transfer of related property the transferred property and the property related to it are valued as one asset. Tax is then paid on the proportion of the total which is transferred.

*Example*
A owns 40 per cent. of the shares in a private company and A's spouse owns another 30 per cent. If A dies and makes a chargeable transfer of the shares his estate will be taxed not on a 40 per cent. holding but on four-sevenths of a 70 per cent. holding. This figure is likely to be considerably higher than the value of a 40 per cent. holding since a 70 per cent. holding gives control of the company.

*All* property held by spouses is related but in most cases the value will not be affected (for example, if each spouse owns a motor car neither car will be more highly valued as the values of the two properties are factually entirely independent). Apart from shares in private companies, the most likely types of property which may be more highly valued because of the related property rule are collections of chattels and joint property.

When property is valued as related property on death, it is that value which is taxed (unless an exemption applies). However, if that property is sold within three years of death by the personal representatives or a person in whom the property concerned vested immediately after the death in an arm's length sale it can be revalued as if there had been no related property (Inheritance Tax Act 1984, s.176). This may result in a repayment of tax. Such a revaluation is not permitted where the sale is made in conjunction with a sale of the related property.

5. APPORTIONMENT OF INCOME ATTRIBUTABLE TO A PERIOD FALLING PARTLY BEFORE AND PARTLY AFTER DEATH

**4.17**  In order to calculate the value of the estate for inheritance tax purposes it is necessary to include any income which accrued prior to death even if it is not paid until after death. The pre-death portion of such income is chargeable to inheritance tax and must be shown on the Inland Revenue Account (if one is required) while the post-death portion is not chargeable to inheritance tax and will not be shown on an Inland Revenue Account. Income which is *paid* before death and which relates to a period falling wholly or partly *after* death is not apportioned. It is all treated as a capital asset of the estate. A direction in the will that no apportionments of income should be made, while relevant for the purposes of distribution amongst beneficiaries, is entirely irrelevant for the purposes of inheritance tax.

The following examples illustrate the way in which types of income may have to be apportioned when calculating the value of the estate for inheritance tax.

*Examples*

(a) *Interest.* Interest which has accrued *up to* the date of death on assets such as money in a building society account or deposit bank account is treated as capital and is chargeable to inheritance tax. Interest on such assets which accrues *from* the date of death is treated as income and is not chargeable to inheritance tax.

(b) *Rent.* If rent is payable in advance and the due date for payment falls *before* death the whole of the rent is treated as capital irrespective of when it is paid. Thus, even if it is paid after death the whole amount due must be included as an asset on the Inland Revenue Account and is chargeable to inheritance tax.

If the rent is payable in arrear for a period which falls partly before and partly after death it is necessary to apportion the rent. The pre-death portion is included as an asset on the Inland Revenue Account and is chargeable to inheritance tax, the post-death portion is not.

(c) *Dividends.* Shares may be valued "cum div." or "ex div." If they are valued "cum div." this means that the share price has been calculated on the basis that a purchaser buying the stocks or shares would be entitled to the *whole* of the next dividend. The share price is, therefore, increased to compensate the vendor for the loss of that part of the year's interest or dividend that has already accrued. For inheritance tax purposes if the probate valuation is made "cum div." that value is entered on the Inland Revenue Account and no further reference need be made to the dividend, since the value of the dividend or interest is included in the share price.

As the date for payment of interest or of a dividend approaches companies close their transfer books. This means that if shares are sold after that date the next interest payment or dividend will be sent to the *old* registered owner. If shares are valued after this date they will be valued "ex div." This means that the basic share price is reduced to compensate the purchaser for the fact that if he buys he will receive no benefit from the next dividend payment. For inheritance tax purposes if the probate valuation is made "ex div." the ex div. price is entered on the Inland Revenue Account but so is the whole of the dividend payment which will be paid to the estate by the company.

We will see in Chapter 6 that for income tax purposes if a dividend is declared after death or interest paid after death for a period which falls partly before and partly after death the whole of such a receipt will be treated as income and will, therefore, be liable to income tax. This could lead to an element of double taxation since the receipt would already have been apportioned and a part of it made chargeable to inheritance tax. There is, therefore, a limited income tax relief (Income and Corporation Taxes Act 1988, s.699 as amended) whereby residuary income is treated as reduced, for the purposes of income tax liability in excess of the basic rate only, by an amount equal to the inheritance tax liability on that income, grossed up at the basic rate.

(d) *Government securities.* A holder of securities receives interest rather than dividends. Just as the price of company shares can be quoted "cum" or "ex div." so the price of securities can be quoted "cum interest" (that is with the right to receive accrued interest) or "ex interest" (that is without the right to receive any of the next interest payment). For inheritance tax purposes if the valuation is "cum interest" that value is entered on the Inland Revenue Account and no further reference is made to the interest. If the valuation is "ex interest" the capital value of the security and the whole of the next interest payment payable to the estate are included as separate items.

### 6. LIABILITIES

**4.18** Liabilities are taken into account in valuing a transferor's estate to the extent that they were incurred for consideration in money or money's worth or imposed by law (Inheritance Tax Act 1984, s.5) and provided there is no right to reimbursement (Inheritance Tax Act 1984, s.162(1)). In the case of death, the value of the estate for tax purposes is the net amount after deducting debts (and other liabilities incurred for consideration) and liabilities imposed by law (such as a liability to pay the community charge and a liability to pay damages in tort). Reasonable funeral expenses may also be deducted (Inheritance Tax Act 1984, s.172).

A mortgage or other liability which is an incumbrance on particular property is taken as reducing the value of that property (rather than the estate generally) so far as that is possible. At first sight this rule might seem unimportant since the whole net value of the estate is taxable anyway but it is relevant where exemptions, such as the spouse exemption (see paragraph 4.20 below), are available.

For example, an estate consists of a house worth £100,000 and £100,000 cash. The house is subject to a mortgage of £10,000. The value of the estate on death is, therefore, £190,000 for tax purposes. If the house is given to the spouse of the deceased and the cash to children an asset worth £90,000 will pass to the spouse and will be exempt (since the mortgage reduces the value of the property given to the spouse). The remaining £100,000 will be regarded as passing to non-exempt beneficiaries and, therefore, chargeable to inheritance tax. If the mortgage reduced the value of the estate generally, an asset worth £100,000 would have passed to the spouse (and been exempt) leaving £90,000 to be regarded as passing to the non-exempt beneficiaries (and chargeable to inheritance tax).

Incidental costs of transferring assets are ignored in calculating the value transferred unless they are incurred by the transferee in which case they reduce the value transferred. This rule has no application to transfers on death because the transfer on death (which takes place for tax purposes the moment before death) is an automatic transfer on which no incidental costs can arise.

Where an estate includes property situated outside the United Kingdom, an allowance is made against that property for any expense incurred in administering or realising the property which is shown to be attributable to the situation of the property. The allowance cannot exceed 5 per cent. of the value of the property.

The Finance Act 1986 introduced special provisions to prevent deduction being made for a debt where consideration has been provided directly or indirectly by the deceased; a liability to pay an insurance company a sum from the death estate in return for a payment from the company is not deductible unless the policy proceeds form part of the death estate.

# E. Exemptions

## 1. INTRODUCTION

Certain transfers are exempt from inheritance tax as a result of the Inheritance Tax Act 1984, ss.18–29 and other parts of the inheritance tax legislation. An exempt transfer is not liable to tax nor is it included in the cumulative total of the transferor (so that it does not affect the rate of tax on later transfers). All the exemptions will be considered in this chapter although they are not all relevant on death. The exemptions which are relevant only to transfers made *before* death are included since lifetime

**4.19**

gifts are sometimes a suitable (and from the tax point of view beneficial) alternative to disposing of property by will.

## 2. THE SPOUSE EXEMPTION

**4.20** This exemption is available *inter vivos* and on death. Inheritance Tax Act 1984, s.18 provides that a transfer of value is exempt "to the extent that the value transferred is attributable to property which becomes comprised in the estate of the transferor's spouse. ... " This means that gifts to the transferor's spouse, before death or on death, are completely exempt. The exemption is lost if the gift does not take effect immediately so that a gift by a testator "to A for life, remainder to my spouse" is not an exempt transfer. However, the spouse exemption is not lost if the gift is conditional and the condition is satisfied within 12 months of the transfer. Thus, if property is left to a spouse, provided he survives for a period of up to 12 months, the spouse exemption will be available provided that the spouse survives the specified period. However, there are other considerations which make a survivorship period exceeding six months inadvisable. Such a gift will be treated as creating a settlement without an interest in possession (see Chapter 7) and will result in an immediate chargeable transfer from the deceased to the settlement.

The spouse exemption is available even though the gift to the spouse is not absolute, provided the spouse takes an immediate interest. The exemption applies, therefore, if T makes a gift "to my spouse for life remainder to X."

For inheritance tax purposes (unlike income tax and capital gains tax) "spouse" has a normal meaning so that the exemption is available even though the parties are separated.

The spouse exemption is only available in full if the spouse is domiciled in the United Kingdom. If the spouse is domiciled elsewhere only the first £55,000 of transfers to him or her are exempt.

## 3. GIFTS TO CHARITIES, ETC.

**4.21** Transfers of value are exempt "to the extent that the values transferred ... are attributable to property which is given to charities." (Inheritance Tax Act 1984, s.23). There is now no limit to the amount which is exempt under this provision. As with the spouse exemption the gift must be immediate and, if conditional, any condition must be satisfied within 12 months. In addition a gift to a charity must normally be absolute if the exemption is to be available.

Transfers of value to exempt political parties are entitled to relief in the same way as transfers to charity. A political party qualifies for exemption if it had two members elected to the House of Commons at the last general election or one member if the party's candidates generally got at least 150,000 votes.

Transfers of value to certain national bodies are entitled to relief in the same way as transfers to charities. The Inheritance Tax Act 1984, Sched. 13 contains a list of the national bodies to which this rule applies; they include, for example, national museums and art galleries, universities and their libraries, local authorities and government departments.

Transfers of value to non-profit-making bodies (other than charities, political parties and national bodies) are also exempt if the property transferred is within certain specified categories (which may broadly be described as covering scenic, historic or scientifically important land, buildings, books, papers or objects) and the Treasury direct that an exemption is to be available.

Transfers to charities, etc., are only exempt if the money or other property given is to be used exclusively for the purposes of a charity, political party, national or non-profit-making body. The exemptions are not available if "the property or any part of it *may* become applicable for (other) purposes. ... " (Inheritance Tax Act 1984, ss.24(3), 25(2), 26(7)).

4. THE "ANNUAL" EXEMPTIONS

These exemptions are only available on transfers made *before* **4.22** death. Section 19 of the Inheritance Tax Act 1984 provides for an annual exemption of £3,000. This exemption applies to the first £3,000 of transfers in each tax year (April 6 to April 5 inclusive). This exemption is available in addition to other exemptions so that a transferor can give as much property as he likes to his spouse and still have the annual exemption available for gifts to others.

To the extent that the annual exemption is not used in a particular year the unused part may be carried forward for one year but no longer. For example, a transferor who made no transfer last year will be entitled to a £6,000 exemption this year. To ensure that the carry forward is limited to one year the exemption of the current year must be used first and only after the whole of that exemption is exhausted can anything brought forward from the previous year be used.

For example, if A transfers nothing in year one, £6,000 of relief will be available in year two. If only £4,000 is transferred in year two this will use up the whole of year two's exemption and £1,000 from year one. Thus, in year three only an exemption of £3,000 will be available.

In addition to the annual exemption, outright *inter vivos* gifts worth up to £250 per donee are exempt (Inheritance Tax Act 1984, s.20). This exemption does not apply to the first part of a gift which exceeds £250. (For example, a donor who gives three people £250 each does not pay any tax and does not use up any of the £3,000 exemption but if £600 is given to one donee £600 of the £3,000 exemption is used up).

### 5. NORMAL EXPENDITURE OUT OF INCOME

**4.23** The relief for normal expenditure is only available *inter vivos*. The Inheritance Tax Act 1984, s.21 provides that a transfer of value is exempt to the extent that:

(a) It is made as part of the normal expenditure of the transferor. (It is a question of fact whether this requirement is satisfied. The Revenue will treat expenditure as normal if it is made under a legal obligation (for example, a deed of covenant) or if similar expenditure is in fact incurred on a regular basis).

(b) It is (taking one year with another) made out of income; and

(c) It is such that the transferor's usual standard of living is not affected by it.

### 6. GIFTS IN CONSIDERATION OF MARRIAGE

**4.24** This exemption is only available *inter vivos*. The Inheritance Tax Act 1984, s.22 provides that a gift in consideration of marriage is exempt to the extent of:

(a) £5,000 if made by a parent of one of the parties to the marriage

(b) £2,500 if made by a remoter ancestor of one of the parties,

(c) £1,000 in any other case.

The limits apply to each marriage, not to each donee (so that a parent cannot give £5,000 to his child and £1,000 to his future child-in-law and obtain exemption for £6,000).

## 7. FAMILY MAINTENANCE

This exemption is only available *inter vivos*. The Inheritance **4.25**
Tax Act 1984, s.11 provides that a disposition is not a transfer
of value (and so is exempt) if it is made by one party to a
marriage in favour of the other party or of a child of either
party and is for the maintenance of the other party or for the
maintenance, education or training of the child. In the case of a
disposition in favour of a spouse there would usually be an
exemption anyway (see paragraph 4.20 above) but the family
maintenance exemption applies to ex-spouses and to spouses
domiciled outside the United Kingdom whereas the normal
spouse exemption does not. The exemption for maintenance,
etc., of children is normally available only to the parents
(including adoptive and step-parents) but where the child is not
in the care of its parents it extends to others maintaining the
children in certain circumstances.

The Inheritance Tax Act 1984, s.11(3) provides that dispositions in favour of dependent relatives other than spouses and
children are exempt to the extent that they are "reasonable
provision for care or maintenance."

## 7. CUMULATIVE EFFECT OF EXEMPTIONS

The exemptions referred to above (other than the small gifts **4.26**
exemption) are cumulative with each other. After the exemptions have been claimed the transferor is entitled to £128,000
taxed at a nil rate. For example, a transferor who has made no
previous gifts and who wishes to benefit his child who is about
to be married as much as possible without a potential liability to
inheritance tax if he dies within seven years could give the
following:

|  | £ |
|---|---|
| Annual exemption from last year | 3,000 |
| Annual exemption for this year | 3,000 |
| Marriage exemption | 5,000 |
| Nil rate | 128,000 |
|  | 139,000 |

The transferor's spouse could make similar provision immediately and both could give further sums of £3,000 annually.
Seven years after these gifts the potentially exempt transfer of

£128,000 will prove to be exempt and the transferor will be free to make further transfers up to the limit of the nil rate band without any liability to inheritance tax.

## 9. MISCELLANEOUS

**4.27** An exemption is available for the whole value of the estate of a person who dies as a result of active or other warlike service and who is a member of the armed forces or a civilian accompanying armed forces (Inheritance Tax Act 1984, s.154).

"Conditional" exemption is available on death and on certain *inter vivos* transfers in respect of assets designated by the Treasury as being of national, scientific, historic or artistic interest (Inheritance Tax Act 1984, ss.33–35 as amended by Finance Act 1985, s.26). The exemption is only available if suitable undertakings are given (usually including undertakings to preserve the assets, keep them permanently in the United Kingdom, and make them available for research). The exemption is "conditional" on these undertakings. Tax becomes payable if an undertaking is broken or if there is a disposal and similar undertakings are not given. Tax will normally become payable in any event if the asset is sold.

# F. Reliefs

## 1. INTRODUCTION

**4.28** A relief does not give complete exemption from inheritance tax but does lead to a reduction in the inheritance tax payable.

A variety of reliefs are available such as quick succession relief under section 161 of the Inheritance Tax Act 1984 (where a *death* occurs within five years of a chargeable transfer), relief on the value of growing timber under the Inheritance Tax Act 1984, ss.125–130 (where within two years of a death an election claiming relief is made) and most importantly reliefs for business and agricultural property under Inheritance Tax Act 1984, ss.103–114 and ss.115–124A.

Quick succession relief and timber relief are only available on death, not on transfers made before death.

The reliefs on business and on agricultural property are available on transfers *inter vivos* and on death. They take effect by means of a percentage reduction in the value transferred. A reduction in the value transferred will have the effect of reducing the tax payable. For example, the tax on a transfer on death of £250,000 at the 1990/91 rates (with no cumulative total and no other exemptions available) is £48,800; if the transfer is reduced by £100,000 by business or agricultural relief the tax is only £8,800. The relief will prevent a charge to tax arising at all, where it brings the value transferred within the nil rate band.

The object of these reliefs is to ease the burden of taxation on businesses and agricultural land. To ensure that taxpayers cannot take unfair advantage of them there are rules requiring a minimum period of ownership before the relief becomes available. Further mitigation of the hardship of paying tax out of business and agricultural property (which might otherwise lead to the forced sale of such property) is provided by the instalment option (as to which see paragraph 4.42).

## 2. AGRICULTURAL RELIEF

Agricultural relief is available in respect of "agricultural property." Agricultural property is defined by the Inheritance Tax Act 1984, s.115(2) and includes agricultural land and pasture and certain land and buildings occupied in association with it including farm-houses, farm buildings and cottages.

**4.29**

The relief takes the form of a percentage reduction in the "agricultural value" of the property which is defined as "the value of the property if the property were subject to a perpetual covenant prohibiting its use otherwise than as agricultural property" (section 115(3)). The effect of this definition is that relief is available to the extent of the value of a farm or other agricultural property *as a farm* but any other value attached to it, such as development value, is not relieved (although business property relief may be available on that value—see below).

The percentage reduction in the agricultural value of the property is 50 per cent. where the transferor had the right to vacant possession immediately before the transfer or the right to obtain it within 12 months after the transfer (section 116(2)). (50 per cent. relief is also available in certain other cases where the transferor has been beneficially entitled to the property since before March 10, 1981 but in this case there is an upper limit of £250,000 on the value which can be reduced by 50 per cent.)

Where the transferor did not have a right to vacant possession immediately before or within 12 months of the transfer the relief is 30 per cent. (section 116(2)). Where land is owned by joint tenants or tenants in common each of them is deemed to have a right to vacant possession if the interests of all of them together carry that right (section 116(6)).

The right to agricultural relief only applies if certain requirements are satisfied. First, the transferor must have *occupied* the land for the purposes of agriculture "throughout the period of two years ending with the date of the transfer" or it must have been *owned* by him throughout the period of seven years ending with the date of the transfer and was occupied by him *or another* for the purposes of agriculture throughout that period (section 117). This means that a farmer who buys his own farm qualifies for relief (at 50 per cent.) after two years if he continues to occupy it up to the time of transfer. A person who buys a farm and puts in a tenant qualifies for relief (at 30 per cent.) only after seven years. A tenant who purchases his farm qualifies for relief (at 50 per cent.) immediately if he has been in occupation for two years.

Special rules apply in relation to the occupation requirement where a farmer moves from one farm to another (section 118), where a farm is owned by the spouse of a former owner or where there is a transfer within two years of a previous transfer provided one transfer is on death (section 120).

A transfer of shares in a company which owns agricultural property is eligible for relief to the extent that the value of the shares reflects the agricultural value of land and provided the shareholder is in control of the company. Occupation by the company is deemed to be occupation by the controlling shareholder (section 119).

In addition, where a transfer is made before death, whether chargeable or potentially exempt, and the transferor dies within seven years the relief is available only if the property originally given or qualifying property representing it has remained as agricultural property in the ownership of the transferee from the date of transfer to the date of death of the transferor. If the transferee dies before the transferor within the seven-year period, relief is only available on the death of the transferee if the same conditions are satisfied.

If only a proportion of the property originally given or qualifying property representing it remains in the ownership of the transferee at the date of death relief is available on the proportion of the property owned at that date (section 124A).

## 3. BUSINESS PROPERTY RELIEF

**4.30**  This relief is available in respect of "relevant business property." The relief is a reduction in the value transferred by a particular percentage depending on what type of property is being transferred (Inheritance Tax Act 1984, s.104)). Section 105(1) defines relevant business property as:

(i) property consisting of a business or an interest in a business (this includes the interest of a sole proprietor or of a partner in a business);

(ii) shares which alone or with other shares gave the transferor control of a company immediately before transfer;

(iii) minority shareholdings which alone or with related property (*e.g.* shares owned by the taxpayer's spouse) carry 25 per cent. of the votes in the company.

*In the three cases above the relief is 50 per cent.*

(iv) land or buildings, machinery or plant used immediately before the transfer wholly or mainly for the purposes of a company controlled by the transferor or of a partnership of which he was a member;

(v) land or buildings, machinery or plant used immediately before the transfer for the purposes of a business carried on by the transferor and which was settled property in which the transferor had an interest in possession;

(vi) shares in a company which did not give the transferor control and do not fall within paragraph (iii) above provided that they are not quoted on a recognised stock exchange.

*In the three cases above relief is 30 per cent.*

The term "business' includes a profession or vocation but does not include a business carried on otherwise than for gain (section 103(3)). Agriculture is regarded as a type of business so that business property relief may be available to the extent that agricultural relief cannot be claimed (that is business property relief is available for any non-agricultural value of agricultural property). Businesses which consist of dealing in securities, stocks, shares, land or buildings or of holding investments are specifically excluded from relief (section 105(3)).

Business property relief is given on the net value of business property (section 110). This is the value after deducting liabilities incurred for the purposes of the business (for other inheritance tax purposes in the case of death liabilities are deducted from *the whole estate* unless charged on particular property).

In order to qualify for relief certain requirements must be satisfied. First, the transferor must have owned the relevant business property throughout the period of two years before the transfer (section 107(1)). Except in the case of minority shareholdings property which replaces other relevant business property qualifies for relief even though not owned for two years provided that the aggregate period of ownership exceeds two years in the five years before the transfer. Until the new property has been owned for two years the relief is limited to the value of the original property (section 107(2)).

Where a transfer of value of relevant business property is followed by another transfer of the same property, the second owner need not own the property for two years before becoming entitled to the relief provided that the relief was available on the first transfer and one of the transfers was a transfer on death (section 109(1)). A person who received property on the death of his *spouse* may aggregate the spouse's period of ownership with his own so as to make up a two-year period of ownership (section 108).

When a business (or other relevant business property) has been owned for two years business property relief is available on its full value at the time of the transfer (at the appropriate percentage). It is not, therefore, necessary to show that particular assets of the business have been owned for two years. However, the value of an asset is excluded from relief if it has not been used wholly or mainly for the purpose of the business throughout the two years before the transfer or throughout the period since it was acquired if later.

In addition, as with agricultural relief, where a transfer is made before death, whether chargeable or potentially exempt, and the transferor dies within seven years the relief is available only if the property originally given or qualifying property representing it has remained as relevant business property in the ownership of the transferee from the date of the transfer to the date of death of the transferor. If the transferee dies before the transferor within the seven-year period, relief is only available on the death of the transferee if the same conditions are satisfied.

If only a proportion of the property originally given or qualifying property representing it remains in the ownership of the transferee at the date of death relief is available on the proportion of the property owned at that date (section 113A).

## 4. TIMBER

A relief is available on the value of growing timber for transfers **4.31** made on death but not for *inter vivos* transfers (Inheritance Act 1984, ss.125–130). The relief is only available if an election is made within two years of death. Where an election is made no tax is payable on the value of the timber provided that the deceased was either beneficially entitled to the land on which the timber is growing for five years before his death or acquired it otherwise than for consideration in money or money's worth within the five years. The relief for timber is merely a conditional relief since tax becomes payable on a later sale or *inter vivos* gift of the timber. The tax is payable at the deceased's death rate and treating the value as the highest part of the value of his estate. Tax is paid on the value of the timber at the date of the later disposal, not on its value at the date of death, and is payable by the person entitled to the proceeds of sale or who would be so entitled if the disposal had been a sale.

The effect of this relief is that no tax is payable on timber until it is sold or given away *inter vivos*; the tax payable is calculated by reference to the estate of the last person to die owning it.

## 5. QUICK SUCCESSION RELIEF

Where a person dies within five years of a transfer to him **4.32** (whether *inter vivos* or on death) a relief commonly called quick succession relief is available (Inheritance Tax Act 1984, s.141). The relief takes the form of a reduction in the amount of tax payable on death equal to a percentage of the tax paid on the *net* amount of the increase in the value of the deceased's estate caused by the transfer within five years.

The percentage relief is:

100 % if the death is within 1 year;
 80 % if more than one but not more than 2 years;
 60 % if more than two but not more than 3 years;
 40 % if more than three years but not more than 4 years; and
 20 % if more than four years but not more than 5 years.

*Example*
A dies and leaves B £10,000 worth of property. A's estate pays £2,500 in tax. B dies three years and three months later. The reduction of tax on B's death is 40 per cent. of the tax on the net amount of the increase in B's estate. This can be calculated in the following way:

$$\frac{\text{net amount}}{\text{gross amount}} \text{ x tax x } \% = \text{reduction}$$

*i.e.* in this case

$$\frac{£10,000}{£12,500} \text{ x } £2,500 \text{ x } \frac{40}{100} = £800$$

The reduction produced by quick succession relief is available whether or not the deceased still owned the property transferred to him within the five years before death. Where the amount of quick succession relief is more than the amount of tax to which the deceased would otherwise have been liable, no tax will be payable on the death (although no reclaim of the excess relief from the Revenue is possible—the excess may be carried forward to be set off against the liability of the deceased's beneficiary on his death if it is within five years of the original transfer to the deceased).

# G. Liability for Inheritance Tax on Death

### 1. INTRODUCTION

**4.33**   The inheritance tax legislation includes rules to determine who is liable to account to the Inland Revenue for inheritance tax due as a result of death.

Where inheritance tax is payable on an estate no grant of representation can be obtained until the amount due is paid to the Revenue. The Revenue is concerned with getting the money and section 200(1) sets out four categories of people who are concurrently "accountable" or "liable" to the Revenue for the inheritance tax due on death. The Revenue is not concerned with who actually bears the burden of inheritance tax and it may be that the person who is accountable to the Revenue for the tax (for example, the personal representative of the deceased) has a right to recover the money paid from individual beneficiaries. The question of where the burden of inheritance tax eventually falls will be dealt with at paragraphs 4.36–4.40 below.

Since inheritance tax must normally be paid before the grant of representation is obtained the persons accountable to the Revenue (for example, the personal representatives) frequently encounter difficulty in realising assets of the estate to raise cash to pay the amount due. (See Chapter 12). It is common for them to borrow money from a bank in order to discharge their liability.

2. THE FOUR CATEGORIES OF PERSONS ACCOUNTABLE FOR INHERITANCE TAX ON DEATH ARE SET OUT IN SECTION 200(1):

(a) The personal representatives of the deceased are **4.34** accountable for the inheritance tax attributable to any free estate of the deceased. Free estate includes property held by the deceased as co-owner (whether as joint tenant or tenant-in-common), property disposed of by *donatio mortis causa* and property disposed of by nomination.

The personal representatives are also accountable for the tax attributable to any land which was settled under the Settled Land Act 1925 immediately before the deceased's death *and which devolves on them.*

The question therefore arises of when settled land devolves on the personal representatives and when it devolves on others. Section 22 of the Administration of Estates Act 1925 provides that where land was comprised in a strict settlement immediately before death and the settlement continues after the death of the deceased the land devolves on the trustees of the settlement who must take out a special Settled Land Act Grant to deal with it (see Chapter 8). Thus the only occasions on which settled land will devolve on the ordinary personal representatives are:

(i) if the settlement comes to an end with the death of the deceased, for example, where land is settled on the deceased for life, remainder to X; *or*

(ii) if the land was not settled prior to the death of the testator but becomes so under a strict settlement created by the will.

Notice that with the exception of settled *land* devolving on them personal representatives are not liable for inheritance tax attributable to trust property.

A brief explanation of why land settled under the Settled Land Act 1925 is treated differently from other types of trust property may be helpful at this point. In the case of trusts other than Settled Land Act trusts, the legal title to trust assets is in the name of the trustees. When a beneficiary dies the trustees stop holding the assets for that beneficiary and start holding them for the benefit of the person next entitled. There is no need for any grant of representation to be obtained in respect of the trust assets. In the case of a Settled Land Act settlement the legal title is vested in the tenant for life (or statutory owner). When such a person dies the land must be transferred from that person's name into the name of the person next entitled and a grant of representation is required in order to accomplish this. Section 22 of the Administration of Estates Act 1925 determines whether the necessary grant is obtained by the trustees of the settlement or by the deceased's personal representatives.

The liability of ordinary personal representatives for inheritance tax is limited to the value of assets which they received or would have received but for their own neglect or default (section 204(1)).

The term personal representative includes an executor *de son tort, i.e.* a person who has made himself liable as executor by intermeddling in the estate (see Chapter 8). The liability for inheritance tax of such a person is limited to the value of assets that have come into his hands, *I.R.C.* v. *Stype Investments* (1982).

(b) The trustees of a settlement are accountable for inheritance tax attributable to property comprised in the settlement immediately before the death.

Their liability is limited to the value of assets which they received or disposed of or which they have become liable to account for to the beneficiaries and to the extent of any other property available in their hands for the payment of tax or which might have been available but for their own neglect or default (section 204(2)).

(c) Any person in whom property is vested (whether beneficially or not) or who is entitled to an interest in possession is accountable for the inheritance tax attributable to such property.

This category includes beneficiaries under a will, persons entitled to property under the intestacy rules, a beneficiary with an interest in possession in property settled after death and a purchaser. A purchaser for money or money's worth of property is not, however, liable where the property is not subject to an Inland Revenue charge (see below, paragraph 4.52).

Liability of such persons is limited to the value of the property (or any property which represents it) (section 204(3)).

(d) Where property was settled prior to death a beneficiary for whose benefit settled property or income therefrom is applied thereafter is accountable for the inheritance tax attributable to such property.

A beneficiary of a discretionary trust would be an example of such a person. Liability is limited to the amount of the property or income received (less any income tax) (section 204(5)).

Where a person makes a gift before death and reserves a benefit in the property, that property will be treated in certain circumstances as part of the donor's estate on death. Where it is so treated, the personal representatives of the deceased are liable for the tax on that property only if the tax remains unpaid 12 months after the end of the month of death. Their liability is limited to the value of assets which they received or would have received but for their own neglect or default.

### 3. LIABILITY FOR ADDITIONAL TAX ON LIFETIME GIFTS

Where death occurs within seven years of a potentially exempt transfer, inheritance tax may become payable. Where death occurs within seven years of a chargeable transfer extra tax may become payable. In such circumstances the following are liable for the tax or extra tax:  **4.35**

    (a)    The personal representatives of the transferor (but only to a limited extent—see below);

    (b)    Any person the value of whose estate is increased by the transfer;

    (c)    So far as the tax is attributable to the value of any property, any person in whom the property is vested (whether beneficially or otherwise) at any time after the transfer, or who at any such time is beneficially entitled to an interest in possession in the property;

    (d)    Where by the chargeable transfer any property becomes comprised in a settlement, any person for whose benefit any of the property or income from it is applied.

A person liable as a trustee is liable only to the extent of property which he has actually received or disposed of or has become liable to account for to the beneficiaries and to the extent of any other property available in his hands for the payment of tax or which might have been so available but for his own neglect or default.

A person liable for tax as a person in whom property is vested or as a person entitled to a beneficial interest in possession in property is liable only to the extent of that property.

A person liable for tax as a person for whose benefit property or income has been applied is liable only to the extent of that property or income (less any income tax).

The personal representatives of the transferor are liable only to the extent that as a result of the limitations of liability relevant to the other categories no one falling within any of the other categories is liable *or* the tax remains unpaid 12 months after the end of the month in which the death of the transferor occurred. In such a case their liability is limited to the value of assets which they received or would have received but for their own neglect or default.

In a case where potentially exempt or chargeable transfers were made within seven years of death and inheritance tax is due, personal representatives would be wise to refrain from completely distributing the assets of the estate until satisfied that the tax has been paid. If they do not they may find themselves personally liable for unpaid tax. (The same point applies where they may be liable for tax in respect of property given *inter vivos* subject to a reservation of benefit—see paragraph 4.34 above.) In cases where a solicitor acting as a personal representative incurs such a liability in the course of his private practice, the liability will be indemnified from the Solicitors' Indemnity Fund but only to the extent that funds are otherwise unavailable. See *Law Society's Gazette*, number 42, Wednesday November 22, 1989 (also see paragraph 14.6).

# H. Burden (or Incidence) of Inheritance Tax

1. INTRODUCTION

**4.36**   When inheritance tax is due on death the beneficiaries of the estate will be very concerned to discover on which part of the estate the burden of the tax will fall since this may affect the size of their entitlement. The following example illustrates this.

*Example*
T leaves a house to A, a pecuniary legacy to B, jewellery to C and the residue of the estate to D. There is substantial inheritance tax to pay. The personal representatives are liable for the inheritance tax and before obtaining a grant of representation must send a cheque for the amount due to the Capital Taxes Office. The personal representatives are likely to

borrow the money from the bank and the question then arises as to how the burden of repaying the loan is to be borne. If the entire burden falls on residue, D's benefit from the estate will be much reduced; whereas, if the burden is divided proportionately amongst the beneficiaries, D will receive rather more but the benefits received by A, B and C will be reduced.

A testator may include an express direction in the will as to whether or not assets are to bear their own tax. In the absence of such a direction there are statutory rules.

## 2. EXPRESS DIRECTION IN THE WILL AS TO BURDEN

The testator may state in the will that certain gifts are to be **4.37** "free of inheritance tax" while others are to bear their own; if such a direction is included it is conclusive and the inheritance tax payable on gifts made "free of tax" will be a testamentary expense paid from the property available to pay other debts of the estate (primarily undisposed-of property and residue). Any professionally drawn will should include an express direction as to the burden of inheritance tax since this not only avoids future disputes but leads the testator to consider whether the proposed disposition of property is satisfactory having regard to the burden of inheritance tax. (However, as we shall see in paragraph 4.45 a direction that an exempt share of residue is to bear inheritance tax attributable to a non-exempt share of residue must be disregarded).

## 3. NO EXPRESS DIRECTION IN WILL

In order to remove uncertainties which had arisen, Inheritance **4.38** Tax Act 1984, s.211 makes express provision for the burden of inheritance tax in relation to deaths occurring on or after July 25, 1983.

Section 211 provides that where personal representatives are liable for inheritance tax on the value transferred by a chargeable transfer made on death the tax shall be treated as part of the general testamentary and administration expenses of the estate but only so far as it is attributable to the value of property in the United Kingdom which:

(a)  vests in the deceased's personal representatives; and
(b)  was not, immediately before the death, comprised in a settlement.

The provision is subject to any contrary intention shown by the deceased in his will. As we shall see in Chapter 15—expenses of the estate (and debts) are paid primarily from undisposed-of property and, if none, from the residue of the estate. Thus, where under section 211(1) inheritance tax is to be treated as a general testamentary and administration expense the burden of it falls primarily on the undisposed-of property and on the residue. Section 211(3) provides that "where any amount of tax paid by personal representatives on the value transferred by a chargeable transfer made on death does not fall to to be borne as part of the general testamentary and administration expenses of the estate, that amount shall, where occasion requires, be repaid to them by the person in whom the property to the value of which the tax is attributable is vested."

The effect of section 211(3) is that whenever personal representatives are liable to pay inheritance tax (as they are on all of the deceased's free estate and on settled land which devolves on them) they have a right to recover it from the particular beneficiary taking the property to which it relates *unless* the tax is a general, testamentary and administration expense under section 211(1); (that is *unless* the property to which the inheritance tax is attributable was situate in the United Kingdom, vested in the personal representatives and was not comprised in a Settled Land Act settlement immediately before the death). As a result of section 211(3) the personal representatives can recover from the particular beneficiary concerned (subject to contrary intention) inheritance tax attributable to:

(a) non-United Kingdom property,
(b) property not vesting in the personal representatives (that is, joint property passing by survivorship, property subject to a nomination or to a *donatio mortis causa*),
(c) property which was immediately before the death comprised in a Settled Land Act settlement.

(The personal representatives will only have accounted for inheritance tax in respect of trust property where the property was settled land devolving on them. They are not *liable* for inheritance tax in respect of other types of trust property and so will not generally be involved in the payment or recovery of inheritance tax relating to it.)

4. PRACTICAL PROBLEMS

**4.39** In practice where personal representatives have accounted to the Inland Revenue for inheritance tax for which they were liable they may encounter difficulties in obtaining repayment for the residuary estate from the person in whom the property is vested. The personal representatives should take all possible steps to minimise such difficulties.

If a pecuniary legacy has been left to a beneficiary and the will declares that the legatee is to bear the burden of inheritance tax attributable to it the personal representatives should deduct an appropriate amount and pay the net legacy to the legatee. Obviously if an asset is left, rather than cash, no deduction can be made. However, the personal representatives should not vest the asset in the beneficiary until arrangements have been made for reimbursement of the amount due.

If the beneficiary has got possession of the asset (for example, because the property has passed by survivorship) there is nothing the personal representatives can do to prevent problems arising unless other assets due to the beneficiary under the will or intestacy rules are in the hands of the personal representatives. If the personal representatives have got possession of other assets due to the beneficiary they should ensure that all repayments of inheritance tax due to the residuary estate are made before they part with the assets.

## 5. APPORTIONING THE BURDEN OF INHERITANCE TAX

Where the burden of inheritance tax due is to be divided amongst different people, it is necessary to apportion the inheritance tax amongst the various assets comprised in the estate. This can be done in one of two ways. **4.40**

*Either* calculate an average rate of inheritance tax for the estate and apply that rate to the assets each beneficiary is to receive; *or* (more simply) allocate a proportionate part of the total inheritance tax to each beneficiary. The result of the two methods will be identical.

*Example*
A dies having made no chargeable *inter vivos* transfers. Her estate comprises:

|  |  |
|---|---|
| realty | £126,000 |
| personalty | £110,000 |
|  | £236,000 |

Her will directs that realty is to bear its own tax and is to pass to B, that a pecuniary legacy of £30,000 bearing its own tax is to pass to C, and that residue is to pass to D. No exemptions apply.

The tax on her estate is calculated as follows:

| Band | Rate | Tax |
|------|------|-----|
| £        £ | % | £ |
| 0 − 128,000 | nil | nil |
| 128 − 236,000 | 40 | 43,200 |

Total inheritance tax bill                          43,200

The tax must then be apportioned.

*Using method 1:*
Calculate estate rate
*i.e.*
$$\frac{\text{Total tax}}{\text{Value of estate}} \times 100$$

$$\frac{£43,200}{£236,000} \times 100 = 18.305\%$$

This rate can then be applied to the property bearing its own tax passing to each beneficiary:

*B's share of tax burden*    $\frac{18.305}{100} \times £126,000 = £23,064$

*C's share of tax burden*    $\frac{18.305}{100} \times £30,000 = £5,492$

The rate will also be applied to the residue passing to D. The residue amounts to £80,000 that is the personalty of £110,000 less the £30,000 legacy.

*D's share of tax burden*    $\frac{18.305}{100} \times £80,000 = £14,644$

The total tax payable on the whole estate is £43,200

*Using method 2:*
Allocate a proportion of the total inheritance tax to each beneficiary:

*i.e.* $\qquad$ total tax x $\dfrac{\text{beneficiary's share of estate}}{\text{total estate}}$

*B's share of tax burden*  £43,200 x $\dfrac{126,000}{236,000}$ = £23,064

*C's share of tax burden*  £43,200 x $\dfrac{30,000}{236,000}$ = £5,492

*D's share of tax burden*  £43,200 x $\dfrac{80,000}{236,000}$ = £14,644

The total tax payable on the whole estate is £43,200.

# I. Time for Payment

## 1. GENERAL POSITION

The tax on a transfer on death is payable six months after the **4.41** end of the month in which death occurred. The tax on a chargeable transfer made before death is payable six months after the end of the month in which the transfer is made or, if the transfer is made after April 5, and before October 1, at the end of April in the next year. Where tax or extra tax is payable on a lifetime transfer because of the death of the donor it is payable six months after the end of the month of death.

Where tax is paid after the date on which it should have been paid interest is chargeable on it. The rate of interest is prescribed by statutory instrument and is currently 11 per cent.

## 2. INSTALMENT OPTION

The inheritance tax on certain types of property may be paid by **4.42** instalments over a 10-year period in certain circumstances (Inheritance Tax Act, ss.227–228).

*Transfer on death*

(a) Land of any description (this term is not further defined but clearly freehold and leasehold interests are included).

(b) Shares or securities in a company giving the deceased control of the company immediately before death (whether or not quoted on a stock exchange or dealt in on the U.S.M.).

(c) Unquoted shares or securities which did not give the deceased control provided that the Revenue are satisfied that the payment of the tax in one sum would cause undue hardship.

(d) Unquoted shares or securities which did not give the deceased control where at least 20 per cent. of the tax payable on the death by the person paying the tax on those shares is either tax on those shares or on those shares and other instalment option property.

(e) Unquoted shares which did not give the deceased control and the value of which exceeds £20,000 at the time of death provided that either:
   (i) They are at least 10 per cent. (by nominal value) of all the shares in the company or
   (ii) they are ordinary shares and are at least 10 per cent. (by nominal value) of all the ordinary shares in the company.

(f) A business or an interest in a business including a profession or vocation. Liabilities incurred for the purposes of the business must be deducted in computing what is the value of the business for this purpose (normally liabilities are deducted from the whole rather than from particular assets unless the assets are charged with payment of the liabilities).

A person has control for this purpose if he (with the benefit of any shares or securities which are related property) has voting control on all questions affecting the company as a whole (Inheritance Tax Act 1984, s.269).

*Lifetime transfers*
Inheritance tax on chargeable transfers made before death may be paid by instalments in respect of the same types of property as in the case of transfers on death. However, this relief is only available where the inheritance tax is *paid by the donee.* In the case of tax payable on the value transferred by a potentially

exempt transfer which proves to be chargeable (or extra tax payable where the transferee dies within seven years of a chargeable transfer), the instalment option is available only to the extent that one of the following conditions is fulfilled:—

   (i)   the transferee owns the qualifying property throughout the period from transfer until the death of the transferor (or, if earlier, of the transferee); or,

  (ii)   in the case of property eligible for business or agricultural relief, the transferee has disposed of the original property but has applied the proceeds in acquiring replacement property; or

 (iii)   in the case of unquoted shares the shares must remain unquoted up to the date of death of the transferor (or, if earlier, of the transferee).

The instalment option is also available on transfers on the termination of an interest in possession in settled property and when tax becomes payable in the case of settlements without an interest in possession. In the case of woodlands tax can always be paid by instalments even if paid by the donor.

*Procedure for payment by instalments*
The payment of tax by instalments is only possible where the person paying the tax gives notice in writing to the Revenue that he wishes to pay in that way. (On death notice is given in the Inland Revenue Account—see paragraphs 10.34–10.53). Where the election is made tax is payable in 10 equal annual instalments. The first instalment is due on the date on which the tax would be due if not paid by instalments (in the case of death six months after the end of the month of death).

The taxpayer may pay off all remaining instalments at any time within the 10 years and must do so if the assets are sold. In the case of tax paid by instalments on non-agricultural land, not comprised in a business, interest on the whole of the outstanding tax is payable and is added to each instalment. In the case of tax paid by instalments on shares, business or interests in businesses interest is only payable to the extent that an instalment of tax is overdue.

It is common for personal representatives to choose to exercise the option initially even if they feel they may wish to pay off the outstanding amount in one lump sum at a later stage. The reason for considering a temporary exercise of the option is that it reduces the amount of inheritance tax falling due for payment six months after the end of the month of the death and so keeps to a minimum the amount of money which may have to be borrowed to pay the inheritance tax due. Once the personal representatives have obtained the grant of representation they are able to realise assets of the estate and may then decide (particularly if interest is payable on the amount outstanding) to use the money to pay off any outstanding inheritance tax.

## J. Partially Exempt Transfers

### 1. INTRODUCTION

**4.43** The transfer of value on death is for inheritance tax purposes one transfer of the whole of the deceased's estate. This transfer may be fully taxable, fully exempt or it may be partly taxable and partly exempt (for example, because part but not all of the property is given to a spouse, charity, political party or exempt body). If it is partly taxable and partly exempt Inheritance Tax Act 1984, s.38 contains rules for calculating the amount of inheritance tax and as to the burden of tax. These rules can give rise to rather complicated arithmetical computations. Details of the method of calculation vary according to the type of dispositions made. The two types of calculation are dealt with in the next two sub-paragraphs.

### 2. "SPECIFIC" GIFTS NOT BEARING THEIR OWN TAX TO NON-EXEMPT BENEFICIARY RESIDUE TO EXEMPT BENEFICIARY

**4.44** For this purpose any gift is "specific" if it is not a gift of residue. If a specific gift is not exempt, the tax in respect of it will normally be paid from residue (see paragraphs 4.33–4.35). The specific legatee is treated as having received an amount *net* of tax and, therefore, the net gift must be grossed up at the death rate to calculate the amount of the tax borne by residue.

*Example*
A has a cumulative total of £128,000 from lifetime transfers and an estate of £50,000. On his death he gives £12,000 to his son and *does not provide that this gift is subject to tax*; he gives the residue to his (*i.e.* A's) wife. Since the gift of £12,000 is not made to bear its own tax the tax will come out of exempt residue so grossing-up is required.

£12,000 grossed up at the death rates with a cumulative total of £128,000 is:

$$£12,000 \times \frac{100}{60} = £20,000$$

The tax is the difference between the gross and net gifts

$$£20,000 - £12,000 = £8,000.$$

The estate is therefore divided as follows:

|  | £ | £ |
|---|---|---|
| Tax |  | 8,000 |
| Gift to Son |  | 12,000 |
| Residue | 50,000 |  |
|  | (20,000) |  |
|  | ——— | 30,000 |
|  |  | 50,000 |

3. SPECIFIC GIFTS NOT BEARING THEIR OWN TAX TO NON-EXEMPT BENEFICIARIES RESIDUE PARTLY TO EXEMPT PARTLY TO NON-EXEMPT BENEFICIARIES

In this situation the tax on the "specific" gifts is borne by the **4.45** whole of the residue unless the will provides otherwise. The tax on the non-exempt part of residue *must* however be borne by that part of the residue only. This is because Inheritance Tax Act 1984, s.41 provides that exempt residue is not to bear the tax on any other part of *residue*.

To calculate the tax it is necessary to gross up the specific gift (or gifts) not bearing its own tax as if it were cumulated with any chargeable lifetime transfers but was the only taxable part of the estate on death. This figure is then added to any other parts of the estate which are in fact taxable (*i.e.* specific gifts bearing their own tax and non-exempt residue) to calculate an "assumed rate" of tax. The specific gift not bearing its own tax is then grossed up again at the assumed rate and the tax on the estate is tax on that figure plus tax on any other non-exempt parts of the estate (*e.g.* residue).

*Example*
A dies leaving an estate of £218,000. She has made no lifetime transfers and leaves £137,000 to her daughter, residue to be

divided between her husband and her sister. The will contains no directions as to the burden of inheritance tax.

(i)   Gross up the gift to the daughter as if it were the only taxable gift on death. On this assumption £128,000 is within the nil rate band so only £9,000 has to be grossed up at 40 per cent. £9,000 grossed up at 40 per cent is £15,000. The gross legacy is therefore £128,000 + £15,000 = £143,000

(ii)  Calculate the other taxable parts of the estate. Only half of the residue is taxable, the other half is going to the husband (and so is exempt):

(iii) Add the grossed-up legacy and the taxable half of residue to give the taxable estate:

|  | £ |
| --- | --- |
| Value of estate | 218,000 |
| *Less* grossed up legacy | (143,000) |
| "Residue" | 75,000 |
| Taxable half of residue | 37,500 |
| *Taxable estate* | |
| Taxable half of residue | 37,500 |
| Grossed up legacy | 143,000 |
| Taxable estate | 180,500 |

(iv)  Calculate an assumed rate. This is the rate of tax which would be charged on an estate of £180,500. The tax would be £21,000 and the assumed rate would therefore be:

$$\frac{£21,000}{£180,500} \times 100 = 11.63\%$$

(v)   Gross up the specific gift not bearing its own tax at the assumed rate:

$$£137,000 \times \frac{100}{100 - 11.63} = £155,029.98$$

(vi) Tax is now payable on the grossed-up specific gift and half the residue, *i.e.*:

|  | £ |
|---|---|
| Value of estate | 218,000 |
| *Less* legacy with tax thereon | (155,029.98) |
| "Residue" | 62,970.02 |
| Half residue | 31,485.01 |

Tax is therefore payable on:

|  | £ |
|---|---|
| Taxable half of residue | 31,485.01 |
| Legacy with tax thereon | 155,029.98 |
| Taxable estate | 186,514.99 |

Tax is therefore £23,405.

The portion of the £23,405 attributable to the specific legacy is borne by the residue as a whole. The balance of the residue is then split into two equal parts and the portion of the £23,405 attributable to the non-exempt residue is borne entirely from the non-exempt part of residue. In apportioning the inheritance tax bill either of the two methods explained in paragraph 4.40 can be used.

4. PARTLY EXEMPT TRANSFERS AND AGRICULTURAL AND BUSINESS PROPERTY RELIEF

**4.46** Prior to the Finance Act 1986 anomalous results sometimes arose where a partly exempt transfer included property qualifying for agricultural or business property relief. The Finance Act 1986 therefore includes provisions designed to ensure that the reliefs are available in a consistent manner. Where there is a specific gift of property qualifying for relief the relief attaches to that property irrespective of whether the specific beneficiary is an exempt or non-exempt beneficiary. In other cases, that is where such property is part of the residue of the estate, the relief is allocated *pro rata* between the exempt and the chargeable parts of the transfer.

## K. Some Particular Problems

### 1. INTER-RELATIONSHIP OF INHERITANCE TAX AND CAPITAL GAINS TAX

**4.47** Capital gains tax, like inheritance tax, is a tax charged on movements of capital assets. It is not payable on death (except in certain circumstances in respect of settled property). However, a lifetime transfer may give rise to capital gains tax liability, as well as to inheritance tax liability. Such liability must be taken into account when deciding between lifetime gifts and gifts on death. To ensure that one tax is not paid on the amount of the other tax two rules apply:

(1) Capital gains tax paid by the transferor is not treated as a loss to the transferor's estate for inheritance tax purposes.

(2) Capital gains tax paid by the transferee reduces the value transferred for inheritance tax purposes.

*Example*

A makes a chargeable *inter vivos* transfer to B of an asset acquired for £10,000; the current value of the asset is £20,000. It will be assumed that capital gains tax is £4,000 (*i.e.* 40 per cent. of the £10,000 gain—this will in fact be the amount of tax if there are no exemptions available and if A is a higher rate taxpayer). We will assume that the rate of inheritance tax is half of 40 per cent. This would be the appropriate rate if the transferor had used up his annual exemption and nil rate band. Remember that the value transferred is grossed up where the transferor pays the inheritance tax.

(a) If transferor pays both taxes:

(i) Capital gains tax (£4,000) is not a loss to the transferor's estate.

(ii) Inheritance tax is payable on the grossed-up gift.

Gross gift for inheritance tax purposes

$$£20,000 \times \frac{100}{80} = £25,000$$

$$\text{inheritance tax} = £5,000$$

(iii)  Total cost to transferor CGT  £4,000
                                       £20,000
                    IHT  £5,000
                                       ——— £29,000
      Amount added to cumulative total  £25,000
      Benefit to transferee  £20,000

(b) If transferee pays both taxes:

  (i)  Capital gains tax (£4,000) reduces value transferred to £16,000

  (ii)  Inheritance Tax is payable on gift (not grossed up) less £4,000 (the capital gains tax)
      Inheritance tax  £16,000 x 20% = £3,200

  (iii)  Total cost to transferor  £20,000
       Amount added to cumulative total  £16,000
       Net benefit to transferee  £12,800

(c) If transferor pays inheritance tax and transferee pays capital gains tax:

  (i)  Capital gains tax (£4,000) reduces value transferred.

  (ii)  Inheritance tax is payable on grossed up amount of gift less capital gains tax:

$$\text{£}16,000 \times \frac{100}{80} = \text{£}20,000$$

Inheritance tax:

$$\text{£}20,000 \times \frac{20}{100} = \text{£}4,000$$

  (iii)  Total cost to transferor  £20,000
                                     £4,000
                                       ——— £24,000
      Amount added to cumulative total  £20,000
      Benefit to transferee  £16,000

(d) If transferee pays inheritance tax and transferor pays capital gains tax:

   (i)   Capital gains tax (£4,000) not a loss to transferor's estate

   (ii)  Inheritance tax payable on gift (not grossed up)

   £20,000 x 20% = £4,000

   (iii) Total cost to transferor      £24,000

   Amount added to cumulative total      £20,000

   Benefit to transferee      £16,000

**Note:**
The amount added to the cumulative total (*i.e.* the amount on which inheritance tax is paid) is always less (by £4,000 in this example) than the real loss to transferor when capital gains tax is taken into account. This is because saying that capital gains tax is not a loss to the transferor's estate when he pays it and saying that capital gains tax paid by the transferee is treated as reducing the value transferred is really the same thing expressed in a different way.

Where capital gains tax hold-over relief is claimed on a gift (see paragraph 5.13) a different rule applies to deal with the overlap between the two taxes. The amount of inheritance tax paid on the transfer of value is deducted in computing the donee's chargeable gain on a later disposal by him. Where the donor dies within seven years of the gift the inheritance tax may have to be recalculated. In such a case the transferor's estate is entitled to a refund of capital gains tax paid, if appropriate. However, the deduction is only permitted to the extent that it will wipe out the chargeable gain and so cannot give rise to an allowable loss.

*Example*
A buys a business asset for £18,000 and makes a chargeable *inter vivos* transfer of it to B, when it is worth £20,000. Hold-over relief is claimed. We will assume that the rate of inheritance tax is half of 40 per cent. This would be the appropriate rate if the transferor had used up his annual exemption and the nil rate band. If A pays the inheritance tax it will be £5,000 (with grossing-up), if B pays it will be £4,000 (without grossing-up).

B then sells the business asset for £22,500. Assuming that there are no incidental costs of disposal and that no indexation relief is available, the gain according to normal capital gains tax principles would be £4,500 (£22,500 − £18,000 = £4,500) since B is allowed to deduct A's acquisition cost from his disposal consideration. However, as hold-over relief was claimed the amount of inheritance tax paid on the original transfer can be deducted in computing the gain for capital gains tax purposes.

(a) Chargeable gain where B (the donee) paid the inheritance tax:

|  | £ |
|---|---|
| Gain | 4,500 |
| Less | (4,000*) |
| Reduced gain | 500 |

\* **Note:**
The whole of the inheritance tax is deducted, thus leaving a chargeable gain of £500 on which capital gains tax will be payable unless there is an exemption available (for example the annual exemption).

(b) Chargeable gain where A (the donor) paid the inheritance tax:

|  | £ |
|---|---|
| Gain | 4,500 |
| Less | (5,000) |
| Reduced gain | Nil** |

\*\*   A deduction is permitted only to the extent that it is necessary to extinguish a gain. It is not allowed to produce a loss.

In the above example had the transfer been potentially exempt, no inheritance tax would have been payable at the time of the transfer. Therefore if B had sold the business asset for £22,500 before A's death capital gains tax would have been payable on the full gain of £4,500. If B was a higher rate taxpayer capital gains tax would be calculated as follows:

$$\frac{40}{100} \times £4,500 = £1,800$$

However, if A then died, say, four-and-a-half years after the transfer to B, inheritance tax would become payable at 60 per cent. of the full rate. Assuming that B paid the inheritance tax there would be no grossing-up and the inheritance tax would be 60 per cent. of the full rate of 40 per cent. (assuming the rates remain identical to the current rates):

$$\frac{60}{100} \times \frac{40}{100} \times £20,000 = £4,800$$

The £4,800 of inheritance tax now due would be deducted from the gain of £4,500 and would extinguish it. Thus the capital gains tax could be reclaimed.

## 2. ANTI-AVOIDANCE PROVISIONS

**4.48** Taxpayers are entitled to arrange their financial affairs so as to avoid paying tax unnecessarily. However, such arrangements may be attacked by the Inland Revenue either under the special inheritance tax provisions relating to "associated operations" rules or under general principles laid down by the House of Lords in *Furniss* v. *Dawson* (1984).

*Associated operations*

**4.49** Section 268 of the Inheritance Tax Act 1984 provides that where a transfer of value is made by "associated operations" carried out at different times it shall be treated as made at the time of the last of them. "Associated operations" are defined very widely as being "any two or more operations which affect the same property ... or any two operations of which one is effected with reference to the other or with a view to enabling or facilitating the other to be effected whether effected by the same or different people and whether or not they are simultaneous."

The object of these provisions is to prevent donors avoiding inheritance tax by making artificial arrangements; for example, by fragmenting transfers of value in order to get the benefit of successive annual exemptions.

There is uncertainty as to the circumstances in which the Revenue would seek to use these provisions. Obviously many individuals wish to arrange their financial affairs so as to provide the maximum benefit for members of their family and so as to avoid unnecessary tax; this may well involve arrangements which *could* be regarded as associated. In particular, it is common, where one spouse is much wealthier than the other, for the wealthier spouse to make use of the spouse exemption to transfer assets to the poorer spouse. This enables the poorer spouse to make transfers to the issue of the couple which will attract lifetime exemptions and/or prove to be fully exempt if the donor survives seven years. When the associated operations provisions were discussed in Parliament in 1975 the Chief

Secretary to the Treasury said that transfers between spouses would only be attacked in blatant cases where a transfer was made *on condition* that the recipient would at once use the money to make gifts to others. Thus, spouses appear to be free to equalise their estates but a certain amount of caution should be used.

*Furniss v. Dawson*

The House of Lords in *Furniss* v. *Dawson* stated that where a **4.50** taxpayer achieves a purpose either by using a preordained series of transactions or a single composite transaction and steps are inserted which have no commercial purpose apart from the avoidance of a liability to tax the inserted steps are to be disregarded for tax purposes.

The extent to which this principle will be applied in the area of personal taxation is uncertain but certainly taxpayers should be cautious about embarking on artificial schemes designed to achieve tax advantages.

In view of the House of Commons statement on the Revenue's approach to associated operations it is unlikely that transfers between spouses will be attacked under *Furniss* v. *Dawson*.

### 3. RELIEF FOR DOUBLE CHARGES

In some circumstances there could be two charges on property **4.51** as a result of a death. For example, A gives property to B; B dies two years later and leaves property to A; A dies one year later. The initial transfer from A to B was potentially exempt but, as A has died within seven years, it becomes a chargeable one. However, the property inherited from B by A will also be charged to tax as part of A's estate on death. Similarly a double charge may arise where A gives property to B but reserves a benefit (see paragraph 4.9). The property is potentially taxable as part of A's estate and as part of B's estate. The Inheritance Tax (Double Charge Relief) Regulations 1987 (S.I. 1987 No. 1130) provide for the avoidance of double charges in these and similar circumstances.

## L. Certificates of Discharge

If the Inland Revenue is satisfied that the tax attributable to a **4.52** chargeable transfer has been or will be paid they can (and, if the transfer is one made on death, must) give a certificate to that effect (section 239(1)). The effect is to discharge all persons (unless there was fraud or non-disclosure of material facts) from liability for any further claim for tax. It also extinguishes any Inland Revenue charge on property for that tax.

It is also possible to obtain a more limited certificate which extinguishes an Inland Revenue charge on property which is to be purchased but which does not discharge any accountable person.

An Inland Revenue charge for unpaid inheritance tax attaches to property other than United Kingdom personal property beneficially owned by the deceased before death which vests in the personal representatives.

Where property subject to an Inland Revenue charge is disposed of that property ceases to be subject to the charge (although the property representing it becomes subject to the charge) if:

(a)  in the case of land the charge was not registered; or
(b)  in the case of United Kingdom personalty the purchaser had no notice of the facts giving rise to the charge.

It frequently happens that adjustments have to be made to the value of the estate during the administration (for example, because estimated figures are finalised). In such a case the personal representatives must submit a corrective account to the Inland Revenue giving full information of all changes in value. Until the personal representatives have obtained a certificate of discharge they cannot safely complete the distribution of the assets comprised in the estate since further tax may become due as a result of adjustments to the value of the estate.

A certificate of discharge does not affect any further tax which becomes payable as a result of the discovery of additional assets or as a result of increases in the amount of property passing to non-exempt beneficiaries after a variation or disclaimer (see Chapter 19). In such a case the personal representatives should apply for a further certificate after the additional tax has been paid.

Where personal representatives have paid all the inheritance tax due other than that outstanding on instalment option property it is possible to obtain a limited certificate expressed to be a full discharge save and except the inheritance tax due on the instalment option property.

# 5. Capital Gains Tax

## A. Introduction

The *death* of an individual does not give rise to a liability to **5.1** capital gains tax (save in very limited circumstances where there is settled property). However, capital gains tax may have to be considered in connection with all or any of the following:

(a) disposals by the deceased made up to the date of death;

(b) disposals by the personal representatives realised after the date of death during the period of administration; and

(c) disposals by beneficiaries of assets they have received from the estate.

Before considering these three situations, a brief outline of the capital gains tax system contained in the Capital Gains Tax Act 1979, as amended, is necessary. All references are to that Act unless otherwise stated.

## B. Capital Gains Tax Generally

Capital gains tax is payable when a *taxable person* makes a **5.2** disposal of *chargeable assets* giving rise to a *chargeable gain* unless an *exemption or relief* applies. The tax is charged by reference to gains made in a "tax year," from April 6 to the following April 5 (officially called a "year of assessment").

### 1. TAXABLE PERSON

Every person who is resident or ordinarily resident in the **5.3** United Kingdom is potentially liable to capital gains tax. This includes the personal representatives of a deceased person, who are treated as a continuing body of persons with the same residence or ordinary residence as the deceased.

## 2. DISPOSALS

**5.4** The Act does not provide an exhaustive definition of the term but it is clear that a sale or gift amounts to a "disposal." Furthermore section 19(2) provides that the term "disposal" covers part disposals. Thus the sale of part of a plot of land is a disposal as is the grant of a lease or an easement.

In most situations the date of disposal is self-evident. However, if an asset is disposed of under a contract, the date of disposal is the date of the contract, not the date on which the asset is eventually transferred (section 27(1)). If a contract is conditional the operative date is the date on which the condition is satisfied (section 27(2)).

## 3. CHARGEABLE ASSETS

**5.5** The definition of *assets* for capital gains tax purposes is set out in section 19(1) which provides that:

"All forms of property shall be assets for the purposes of this Act, whether situated in the United Kingdom or not, including:

(a)  options, debts and incorporeal property generally, and

(b)  any currency other than sterling, and

(c)  any form of property created by the person disposing of it or otherwise coming to be owned without being acquired," (such as goodwill in a business).

All *assets* are *chargeable assets* subject to a few exceptions including sterling and motor cars.

## 4. CHARGEABLE GAINS

*The basic rule*

**5.6** A gain arises if the "consideration for disposal" exceeds the "allowable deductions" provided for in the Act.

The "consideration for disposal" is the sale price if the asset is sold in an arm's length transaction or the market value if there is a gift or a gift element. The market value is the price which the asset might reasonably be expected to fetch on a sale in the open market. Section 150(2) provides that no reduction in the value can be made by assuming that the assets would be placed on the market at the same time.

Once the "consideration for disposal" has been calculated, the allowable expenditure is deducted to calculate the chargeable gains. The allowable expenditure is defined by section 32(1) and falls into three categories:

(a)   Initial expenditure, which is the original purchase price (or market value if the asset was acquired by way of gift) plus incidental costs incurred in acquiring the asset, such as solicitors' fees and stamp duty. If the asset was not acquired by the taxpayer from anyone else (because, for example, it is the goodwill of a business he has set up) the initial expenditure is that wholly and exclusively incurred in providing the asset.

(b)   Subsequent expenditure, which is expenditure wholly and exclusively incurred for the purpose of enhancing the value of the asset (the expenditure being reflected in the state or nature of the asset at the time of disposal) and expenditure incurred in establishing preserving or defending title to, or a right over, the asset.

(c)   Incidental costs of disposal such as solicitors' fees, estate agents' fees, the cost of advertising, etc.

There must be excluded from the calculation any sum that is charged to income tax (such as portions of premiums on certain leases which are taxable under Income and Corporation Taxes Act 1970, Schedule A) or any expense that is deductible for income tax purposes (such as the cost of *repairs* to an asset as opposed to the cost of improvements).

With regard to the allowable deductions, special rules apply if part only of an asset is disposed of since it would clearly be unfair for the taxpayer to be able to deduct expenditure laid out on the whole asset against the sale price of only part. In these circumstances section 35(2) provides that the allowable expenditure to be deducted from the sale price (or market value if appropriate) of the part sold or given away is found by multiplying the total expenditure on the whole asset by:

$$\frac{A}{A + B}$$

where A is the consideration received for the part disposed of and B is the market value of the part retained.

*Example*
Terence buys a plot of land for £40,000 (his only allowable expenditure). He sells part for £45,000; the value of the remainder is £15,000. From the £45,000 sale proceeds he can deduct:

$$£40,000 \text{ x } \frac{£45,000}{£45,000 + £15,000}$$

i.e.                £40,000 x   $\dfrac{£45,000}{£60,000}$

$$= £30,000$$

He therefore has a gain of £15,000.

*The indexation allowance*
**5.7**   The system of capital gains taxation as originally enacted took no account of inflation, with the result that taxpayers suffered tax on the apparent gain arising as a result of inflation, rather than on the real increase in the asset's value.

Sections 86–89 of the Finance Act 1982, as amended by the Finance Act 1985, have partially remedied this defect by introducing provisions under which the initial and subsequent expenditure can be increased by an "indexation allowance."

In order to claim the allowance the taxpayer must show that the disposal took place on or after April 6, 1982.

To calculate the allowance each item of initial and subsequent expenditure is multiplied by a decimal fraction (rounded to three decimal places) produced from the following formula:

$$\frac{RD - RI}{RI}$$

where RD is the retail prices index for the month of the disposal and RI represents the retail prices index for March 1982 or, if later, the month in which the expenditure was incurred. If several items of expenditure were incurred at different times they must be indexed separately. If the figure for RD is smaller than that for RI, no allowance is available (so that gains are not increased if the Retail Prices Index goes down). Prior to the Finance Act 1985, an indexation allowance was only available where an asset had been owned for at least 12 months and the allowance was not permitted to create or increase a loss. In the case of disposals made on or after April 6, 1985, these limitations have been removed.

*Example*

Thelma buys a plot of land in August 1988 (when we will assume that the retail price index (RI) stood at 110) for £28,000 and sells it in August 1991 (when we will assume that the retail prices index (RD) stands at 130) for £44,000, a prima facie gain of £16,000. If we assume that the only allowable expenditure of Thelma was the purchase price, the indexation allowance will be:

$$£28,000 \text{ (Acquisition price)} \times \left( \frac{130 \text{ (RD)} - 110 \text{ (RI)}}{110 \text{ (RI)}} \right)$$

$$= 28,000 \times 0.182$$
$$= £5,096$$

The allowance together with the acquisition price is deducted from the sale price of £44,000 and reduces the gain to £10,904.

If the sale price had been £26,000, the indexation allowance of £5,096 would have increased the loss, as shown below:

|  | £ | £ |
|---|---|---|
| Sale Price |  | 26,000 |
| Less Acquisition price | 28,000 |  |
| Indexation allowance | 5,096 |  |
|  | —— | (33,096) |
| Loss |  | (7,096) |

Where a part disposal (see paragraph 5.6) takes place, the allowance is applied only to the apportioned expenditure.

Where an asset was acquired prior to April 1, 1982, and is disposed of after April 6, 1985, the indexation allowance can, if the taxpayer so elects, be calculated on the basis of the market value of the asset on March 31, 1982, rather than on the basis of the expenditure incurred prior to that date. A claim to this effect must be made within two years of the end of the tax year in which the disposal occurred.

*Special rules for assets held on April 6, 1965 and March 31, 1982*
**5.8** Capital gains tax came into force on April 6, 1965 and tax has never been levied on gains arising before that date. In March 1988 it was announced that the base date for capital gains tax would be altered. In respect of disposals made on or after April 6, 1988 no tax is levied on gains arising prior to March 31, 1982. Taxpayers are treated as having disposed of assets on March 31, 1982 and as having acquired them at market value at that date.

*Example*
A acquires an asset in 1980 for £2,000; on March 31, 1982 it is worth £8,000; on September 1, 1988 he disposes of the asset for £9,000. Ignoring exemptions and the availability of any indexation allowance for the purposes of this example he will be treated as making a chargeable gain of £1,000 (£9,000 − £8,000).

Special provisions ensure that the amount of a gain or loss is not increased by the new base date.

*Losses*
**5.9** If deducting the allowable expenditure from the sale proceeds or market value of the asset shows that the taxpayer has made a loss, it may be set off against all gains made during the current tax year. If this year's gains are insufficient to absorb the whole loss, it may be carried forward and set off against all future gains as they arise. The losses can be carried forward indefinitely until such gains arise (section 4(1) and section 5(4)).

It is important to note that in the tax year in which the loss arises, it must be set against that year's gains to reduce them as far as is possible. This is so even if the loss would reduce the gains below the annual exemption limit (currently £5,000—see paragraph 5.12). However, if there are unabsorbed losses which are carried forward, in the future years they are used only to the extent necessary to reduce the gains of those later years to the amount of the annual exemption (section 5(4)).

*Example*
During the tax year 1989/90, X sells two assets; one gives rise to a gain of £6,000 and the other disposal shows a loss of £8,000. The loss must be set against the gain reducing it to nil and leaving £2,000 unabsorbed loss that can be carried forward to 1990/91.

If X in this later year sells an asset making a gain of £5,200, only £200 of the loss brought forward is used to reduce the gain to £5,000, leaving £1,800 of the unabsorbed loss to be carried forward to 1991/92.

A loss is only allowable in circumstances where, if a gain had been made on the disposal of the asset it would have been a *chargeable* gain. Thus the sale of a private motor car at a loss does not give rise to an allowable loss.

## 5. EXEMPTIONS AND RELIEFS

Certain exemptions and reliefs are available. In some cases they extinguish, and in others they reduce, the taxpayer's liability.   **5.10**

*Exemptions*
The main exemptions are:   **5.11**

(a) The taxpayer's only or main residence together with gardens and grounds up to, normally, one acre (section 101). The property must normally have been the taxpayer's main residence throughout his period of ownership and not have been bought with a view to making a gain on the disposal (section 103(3)). Certain periods of absence are disregarded including:

    (i)   a period of absence not exceeding three years; and

    (ii)  any period of absence during which the taxpayer was employed, or held an office, all the duties of which were performed outside the United Kingdom; and

    (iii)  a period of absence, not exceeding four years, throughout which the taxpayer was prevented from residing as a result of the situation of his place of work or as a result of his employer requiring him to reside elsewhere, the condition being reasonably imposed to secure the effective performance of his duties.

(The last 24 months of ownership will be disregarded in any event; the taxpayer may still claim full relief whether or not the property was occupied as his main residence during that period—section 102(1)). If the taxpayer occupies more than one residence, he can choose which is to be treated as his main residence. By concession, "relief is also given where personal representatives dispose of a house which before and after the deceased's death has been used as their only or main residence by individuals who under the will or intestacy are entitled to the whole or substantially the whole of the proceeds of the house either absolutely or for life" (Inland Revenue Concession D5).

(b) Items of tangible movable property having a predictable useful life not exceeding 50 years (section 127), such as most yachts;

(c) Chattels where the *consideration* for disposal does not exceed £6,000 (section 128). Marginal relief exists if the consideration exceeds £6,000;

(d) National savings certificates and premium bonds (section 71).

Others include:

(a) Betting winnings (section 19(4));

(b) Interests under trusts, unless the interest was acquired for money or money's worth (section 58);

(c) Gains made on the disposal of certain government securities (section 67);

(d) Decorations for valour unless acquired for consideration in money or money's worth (section 131);

(e) Foreign currency purchased for personal use abroad (section 133);

(f) Life assurance policies and deferred annuity contracts (section 143);

(g) Works of art in certain circumstances (sections 147 and 148).

*Reliefs*

**5.12** If the assets disposed of do not come within any of the categories in paragraph 5.11, relief from liability to tax can be given in respect of the following:

(a) the first £5,000 of gains arising on the disposals made during the current tax year (section 5). As from April 6, 1990 married couples are taxed independently on their capital gains and have separate annual exemptions.

(b) Gains on disposal of business assets by a taxpayer who has attained the age of 60 or has retired on ill-health grounds below that age. Gains are wholly exempt up to £125,000; gains between £125,000 and £500,000 attract 50 per cent. relief. The maximum relief available can only be claimed where the taxpayer has owned the business for 10 years or more. (Where shares in a company are disposed of, certain special conditions must be satisfied if the relief is to be available).

*Deferments*

The final group of reliefs are those which have the effect of deferring the payment of tax. **5.13**

When a transfer is made by way of gift or sale at under-value, the donor and donee may in certain circumstances elect to "hold over" any gain so that the donee is treated as acquiring the asset at the donor's acquisition value. When an owner sells certain types of assets, he may elect to "roll over" any gain into new assets purchased so that the acquisition cost is reduced by the amount of the rolled-over gain. If an election is made either to hold over or roll over a gain, the whole of the gain must be held or rolled over. It is not possible to elect to hold or roll over a portion of a gain allowing the balance to be covered by the annual exemption.

While tax can eventually become payable on the "held-over" or "rolled-over" gain, it will not be payable until some time in the future. These reliefs may offer advantages beyond the mere postponement of the payment of tax but the possible advantages differ depending on whether the gain is "held over" on a gift or "rolled over" on a sale.

Considering "held-over" gains first, the advantages are that:

(a) when tax is paid by the donee in the future it will be paid with money that may have been reduced in value by inflation, and

(b) if the donee dies while owning the property the gain will be effectively extinguished (see paragraph 5.17).

There is, however, the disadvantage that the donor will lose the benefit of his annual exemption.

The circumstances in which the "hold-over" relief applies include:

(a) *Transfers between spouses.* If a gift is made from one spouse to the other, the asset is treated as having been acquired for a consideration giving rise to neither a gain nor a loss, so that any gain is *automatically* "held over" into the hands of the new owner (section 44).

(b) *Gifts to charities.* The donor is treated as having made the disposal for a consideration which gives rise to neither a gain nor a loss (section 146). Gains made by charities are normally exempt.

(c) *Business assets*. Where a taxpayer disposes (otherwise than under a bargain at arm's length) of "business assets" a joint election can be made by the transferor and transferee (or by the transferor alone if the disposal is to the trustees of a settlement) that any gain be held over. Business assets are, broadly, assets used for the purposes of a trade, profession or vocation carried on by the transferor or his family company. The term also covers shares, provided the shares are in an unquoted company or in the transferor's family company.

(d) *Transfers chargeable to inheritance tax*. Where a disposal is made which is chargeable to inheritance tax or would be but for the existence of the annual exemption, a joint election can be made by the transferor and transferee (or by the transferor alone if the disposal is to the trustees of a settlement) that any gain be held over. The relief is available only to disposals which are initially chargeable to inheritance tax, and not to those which are initially potentially exempt but which become chargeable as a result of the death of the transferor within the seven years. Chapter 7 deals more fully with chargeable transfers but they are broadly transfers to and from settlements without an interest in possession. Note that a transfer is technically chargeable to inheritance tax even though it is within the transferor's nil rate band.

(e) *Transfers exempt from inheritance tax*. Where a disposal is made which is exempt from inheritance tax because it is a transfer either to a political party, for the public benefit, to a maintenance fund for historic buildings or of property designated by the Treasury as of outstanding national interest, a joint election can be made by the transferor and transferee (or by the transferor alone if the transfer is to the trustees of a settlement) that the gain be held over.

(f) *Transfers from an accumulation and maintenance trust*. Where a beneficiary becomes absolutely entitled to assets from an accumulation and maintenance trust the trustees and beneficiary may jointly elect that any gain be held over. Chapter 7 deals more fully with accumulation and maintenance trusts. Hold-over relief is available only where the trust retains the status of an accumulation and maintenance trust at the time that the beneficiary becomes absolutely entitled to the assets.

**Note**
Prior to the Finance Act 1989 hold-over relief was available under Finance Act 1980, s.79 on all disposals made otherwise than under a bargain at arm's length.

Section 79 was repealed in Finance Act 1989 in respect of disposals made on or after March 14, 1989 and replaced by the more limited provisions set out in (c) to (f) above (section 124 and Schedule 14).

The roll-over relief which is available on the sale of assets offers the same advantages and suffers the same disadvantages as hold-over relief. It enjoys a further advantage in that when the tax becomes payable (because the asset has been sold in circumstances when the accrued gain cannot be rolled over) the taxpayer may be able to use a relief not previously available to him (such as "retirement relief") to reduce or cancel his gain.

The "roll-over" relief applies:

(a) *On the replacement of business assets.* When a trader sells certain business assets (including land, buildings, plant and machinery) and buys a replacement asset within certain time limits, any gain realised on the sale can be "rolled over" into the new asset. The effect of this is to reduce the trader's acquisition price of the asset by the "rolled-over" gain (sections 115–121).

(b) *On the incorporation of a business.* If the taxpayer transfers a business (and all assets other than cash) as a going concern to a company in exchange for shares, the gain realised on the disposal to the company can be "rolled over" into the newly acquired shares. The effect is that the shares (subject to certain conditions) are treated as having been acquired for the same value as the assets transferred instead of at market value at the date of the disposal (section 123).

## 6. THE RATES OF TAX

Once all relevant exemptions and reliefs have been deducted from the gain, tax is levied on the remaining chargeable gains. The rates of capital gains tax are equivalent to the rates of income tax which would apply if gains were treated as the top slice of income. Accordingly, and depending on the level of an individual's income a taxpayer is taxed at rates equivalent to either the basic rate of income tax (25 per cent.) or the higher rate of income tax (40 per cent.) or partly one and partly the other. **5.14**

*Example*
For tax year 1990/91 A has taxable income (after reliefs) of £15,000 and gains, after allowing for the annual exemption, of £11,000. The gains must be treated as the top slice of A's

income. The basic rate limit of £20,700 will be exceeded. Thus the first £5,700 of the gains will be taxed at 25 per cent. and the remaining £5,300 at 40 per cent.

### 7. THE DATE FOR PAYMENT OF TAX

**5.15**  Section 7 provides that tax in respect of chargeable gains in any tax year must be paid on or before December 1 following the end of the tax year or 30 days from the date of the assessment, whichever is the later.

If the sale price is paid by instalments over a period exceeding 18 months, the tax can be paid over a similar period (subject to a maximum of 10 years) if undue hardship would otherwise be caused (section 40(1)).

Where hold-over relief is not available on a disposal by way of gift (or deemed disposal under Capital Gains Tax Act 1979, s.54(1) or s.55—see Chapter 7) tax on certain assets can be paid in 10 equal yearly instalments. An election must be made in writing by the person paying the tax. Payment by instalments is possible only where hold-over relief is *not available* and not where it is available but the taxpayer chooses not to claim it.

The relevant assets are land or an interest in land, any shares or securities which immediately before the disposal gave the person disposing of the shares control of the company, any shares not giving control and not quoted on a recognised stock exchange or dealt in on the Unlisted Securities Market.

## C. The Capital Gains Tax Liability of the Deceased

**5.16**  Prior to the date of death, the deceased may have made disposals which gave rise to capital gains tax liability. If this liability has not been discharged prior to the death, the personal representatives must discharge it on the deceased's behalf. The personal representatives calculate tax in accordance with the principles outlined above and will be able to claim, on behalf of the deceased, the benefit of any exemptions or reliefs the deceased could have claimed. Once these exemptions and reliefs have been claimed, the personal representatives will pay tax on behalf of the deceased at the appropriate rate(s).

The deceased may have unrelieved losses in the tax year of death. Section 49(2) provides that such losses can be carried back and set against the gains realised by the deceased in the three tax years preceding the tax year of death, taking later years first. If tax was paid in any of those earlier years, a rebate will be claimed.

If there are still unrelieved losses, these cannot be taken over by the personal representatives to set off against gains they make.

If the deceased made a disposal by way of a *donatio mortis causa*, no chargeable gain arises (section 49(5)).

# D. The Capital Gains Tax Liability of the Personal Representatives

### 1. THE POSITION ON DEATH

There is no disposal of assets on death. Section 49(1)(a) provides that the assets of which a deceased person was competent to dispose shall be deemed to be *acquired* on his death by the personal representatives for a consideration equal to their market value at the date of the death. Since there is a deemed acquisition but no deemed disposal, no capital gains tax liability arises as a result of the death. The same rule applies to a person who held property jointly with the deceased.

Where inheritance tax is payable the *valuation* for capital gains tax purposes will be the same as that used for inheritance tax purposes (section 153) *i.e.* the market value at the date of death. The *value* for inheritance tax purposes may be increased as a result of the related property rules; that increased value will also be used for capital gains tax purposes. The inheritance tax *reliefs* (such as agricultural property or business property reliefs) do not affect the valuation for capital gains tax purposes.

If quoted shares and securities are sold within 12 months from the date of death, at less than market value at the date of death, the personal representatives can elect that, for inheritance tax purposes, the sale price be substituted for the probate value. (See below, Chapter 12). If the reduced value is taken for inheritance tax purposes, it becomes the acquisition price of the personal representatives for capital gains tax purposes as well. The personal representatives cannot keep the original acquisition value for capital gains tax purposes once they have elected for the inheritance tax reduction. If land or an interest in land is sold within three years of death at less than market value at the date of death, the personal representatives can elect that the sale price be substituted for the probate value.

**5.17**

It is not clear whether the reduced value becomes the acquisition value for capital gains tax purposes.

## 2. DISPOSALS BY THE PERSONAL REPRESENTATIVES

**5.18** In the course of administering the estate, the personal representatives may have to sell assets. If they do so, they will be liable to capital gains tax on any gains realised after deduction of any losses they incur on their disposals. The calculation of liability has been outlined in paragraphs 5.2–5.15. Personal representatives will be chargeable to capital gains tax at a rate equivalent to the basic rate of income tax. The indexation allowance is available to personal representatives in exactly the same way that it is available to individuals.

In addition to the normal deductions for incidental selling expenses, personal representatives are entitled to deduct a proportion of the costs of valuing the estate for probate purposes (*I.R.C.* v. *Richards' Executors* (1971)). The Inland Revenue publishes a scale of permitted deductions (SP 7/81). However, the personal representatives are free to claim more than the scale deduction where they can show that the actual cost was higher.

The rights of personal representatives to claim exemptions and relief are limited. In the tax year of death, and the two following tax years, the personal representatives can claim the annual exemption currently £5,000. Thereafter all the gains they realise (other than on assets within paragraph 5.11) are taxable. The only or main residence exemption cannot apply to personal representatives since a continuing body of persons cannot have a residence. However, by concession, if before and after the death, the residence has been used as their only or main residence by individuals who, under the will or intestacy, are entitled to the whole or substantially the whole of the proceeds of sale of the house either absolutely or for life, the exemption can be claimed (see above, paragraph 5.11).

If the personal representatives have made losses on their disposals but have no, or insufficient, gains to set them against, these unabsorbed losses cannot be passed on to the beneficiaries.

Where personal representatives are proposing to sell an asset which has fallen in value since death and have no gains against which the loss can be set, it may be preferable for them to consider vesting the asset in a beneficiary and allowing the beneficiary to sell. Even if the beneficiary has no gains in the current tax year, the loss can be carried forward indefinitely (see paragraph 5.9 above).

## 3. TRANSFERS TO LEGATEES

For capital gains tax purposes, section 47(2) defines the term   **5.19**
"legatee" as including "any person taking under a testamentary disposition or on an intestacy or partial intestacy, whether he takes beneficially or as trustee, and a person taking a *donatio mortis causa* shall be treated . . . as a legatee and his acquisition as made at the time of the donor's death."

Section 49(4) provides that when the personal representatives transfer an asset to a legatee under the terms of a will, or the intestacy rules, no chargeable gain accrues to the personal representatives. The personal representatives' acquisition is treated as the legatee's acquisition. The position is the same if the personal representatives appropriate an asset in or towards satisfaction of a pecuniary legacy or a share in residue. Therefore, such transfers cannot give rise to capital gains tax liability if the asset has risen in value since the date of death and neither can the personal representatives have the benefit of a loss where the asset has fallen in value since the date of death.

If the personal representatives vest assets in trustees (even if they themselves are the trustees) the trustees are treated in the same way as legatees and so acquire the asset at market value at the date of death.

When the personal representatives are deciding which assets to sell and which to vest in beneficiaries, they should take into account their own and the beneficiaries' present and future tax liability.

# E. The Capital Gains Tax Liability of Beneficiaries

As has already been explained, the legatees, whether they are   **5.20**
entitled under a will or the intestacy rules, whether they receive a specific legacy, an asset in satisfaction of a pecuniary legacy or a residuary legacy or whether they are beneficially entitled or are merely entitled as trustees, receive the property at market value at the date of the death.

This means they take the asset with the benefit of any unrealised losses that may have accrued since the death and subject to any unrealised gains that have arisen since that date.

They cannot, however, take over any unrelieved losses which the personal representatives realised.

With regard to the indexation allowance, the beneficiaries acquire the assets at their value at the date of death, together with the benefit of any indexation allowance allowed to the personal representatives.

On subsequent disposals by beneficiaries the gain or the loss must be calculated on the basis of the market value at the date of death, increased by any indexation allowance available.

# 6. Income Tax

In the illustrations given in this chapter, it is assumed except **6.1** where the contrary is stated, that basic rate tax will remain at 25 per cent. for tax year 1991/92 and all subsequent tax years.

## A. Introduction

Many people regard income tax as the bane of their lives and **6.2** would be distressed to discover that the Inland Revenue can pursue them beyond the grave.

When a person dies, income tax must be considered in respect of three different periods:

(1)   the period up to death
(2)   the administration period, and
(3)   the period after the completion of administration.

The purpose of this chapter is to consider the rules that apply to these different periods but before looking at the detailed rules, a brief explanation of the types of receipt on which income tax is levied and the methods of calculating the tax is necessary.

## B. Income Tax Generally

A detailed discussion of the income tax system is beyond the **6.3** scope of this book. Instead we intend merely to make some simple, basic points to put the particular rules relevant on death into context.

It is necessary when considering income tax to ask the following questions:

(1) What is income?
(2) What income is taxable?
(3) In what year of assessment will income be taxed?
(4) How is the tax liability calculated?
(5) What are the rates of tax?
(6) When is the tax payable?

## 1. WHAT IS INCOME?

**6.4** The first problem that arises is to define the kind of receipt which attracts the charge to income tax. Most people would probably not be able to define income but no doubt recognise it when they receive it.

Over the years, lawyers have attempted to define the nebulous concept of "income" that is subject to tax. In the case of *London County Council* v. *Att.-Gen. (1901)* Lord Mac-Naughten said "income tax, if I may be pardoned for saying so, is a tax on income." As a definition this is of little assistance. However, more precise guidelines have developed and it can now be said that the tax is paid on profits of an income nature, as opposed to profits arising on the disposal of a capital asset (although there are cases where capital receipts can be treated as income, such as certain premiums on leases). The distinction between these two types of receipt is, broadly speaking, that to be of an income nature, the receipt should be recurrent. This concept has often been explained by references to apple trees and their fruit—the tree being the capital asset that annually produces fruit (the income). If the tree is sold, a capital gain may arise but if the apples are sold, any profit made is income. The analogy breaks down if the seller *deals* in apple trees. The problems caused by the sale of a branch of the tree are beyond the scope of this book.

## 2. WHAT INCOME IS TAXABLE?

**6.5** If the receipt is of an income nature, it is necessary to determine into which of the five Schedules to the Income and Corporation Taxes Act 1988 ("the Taxes Act") it falls. The Schedules govern the method of calculating the tax on income receipts and the date on which the tax is paid. The Schedules, and the Cases into which they are subdivided, cover all the types of taxable income, *i.e.*

| Schedule A | | −rents |
| Schedule C | | −government securities |
| Schedule D | Cases I & II | −trading and professional income |
| | Case III | −pure income profits (such as annuities, annual payments and interest). |
| | Cases IV & V | −foreign trading income |
| | Case VI | −miscellaneous income |
| Schedule E | | −employment income |
| Schedule F | | −dividends |

**Note**
Schedule B which applied to woodlands was abolished as from April 6, 1988.

A few types of income are exempt (for example, scholarship income) and so are tax-free. Income received from a building society or bank in the tax year 1990/91 and earlier tax years is not liable to basic rate tax in the hands of the recipient but is liable to excess liability (see below, paragraph 6.8).

Each Schedule and Case (apart from those dealing with pure income) lays down rules as to the expenses which can be deducted to determine net income. The tax year in which the income will be taxed is determined by the basis of assessment relevant to the particular Schedule.

3. WHAT IS THE RELEVANT YEAR OF ASSESSMENT?

Tax is calculated by reference to years of assessment (commonly **6.6** called "tax years"). A new tax year commences on April 6 each year.

The Taxes Act lays down two main bases of assessment—the preceding year basis and the actual year basis. The former requires that an individual pays tax on the profits made in the accounting period that ended in the immediately preceding tax year and applies to Schedule D Cases I & II income. The latter requires that tax is assessed in each year on the income of that tax year (this applies for example, to Schedule E).

4. HOW IS THE TAX LIABILITY CALCULATED?

*General*

**6.7** Three steps are necessary:

(a) calculate "statutory income"

(b) deduct "charges on income" to produce "total income"

(c) deduct "personal reliefs" to produce "taxable income."

*What is "statutory income"?*

**6.8** The taxpayer's "statutory income" is found by adding together his receipts (after deducting allowable expenses) from all sources, taking into account the relevant basis of assessment. Statutory income includes sums received gross (such as trading income) and the grossed up amounts of sums which are received net of tax.

It is necessary to gross up sums received net of tax since income tax is calculated on the basis of a person's gross income (credit is given for the basic rate paid). Examples of sums which are received net are salaries paid net of tax under the P.A.Y.E. system, payments made by trustees to beneficiaries and dividend income.

To gross up a net sum where basic rate tax (BRT) has been deducted, simply multiply the sum actually received by

$$\frac{100}{100 - BRT}$$

The reason why this calculation works is that if the basic rate of tax is 25 per cent. and £75 is received net of basic rate tax, then £75 is 75 per cent. of the gross figure (25 per cent. of the gross figure having already been deducted). To calculate 100 per cent. of the receipt simply divide by 75 to find 1 per cent. and then multiply by 100 to find 100 per cent.

*Example*

A shareholder receives a dividend of £3,750 on which basic rate tax of 25 per cent. has already been paid by the company. When calculating the shareholder's statutory income the dividend is grossed up to £5,000.

$$£3,750 \times \frac{100}{100 - 25} = £5,000$$

£5,000 is included in the taxpayer's income tax return as part of gross income. However, it must be remembered that in the above example £1,250 in tax has already been paid. This sum is a "tax credit" so that, when calculating what tax (if any) is due to the Revenue, an allowance must be made for the £1,250 already paid on behalf of the taxpayer by the company. The company is required to supply the shareholder with a certificate of deduction of income tax.

If the taxpayer pays only basic rate tax no additional tax need be sent to the Revenue since the "right" amount of tax has already been paid. If the taxpayer pays higher rate tax, additional tax will have to be sent.

If the taxpayer from whom income tax has been deducted is not liable to even basic rate tax (because of his entitlement to personal reliefs and charges), he can normally reclaim, from the Revenue, the basic rate tax already paid on his behalf. Interest received from a building society or bank in tax year 1990/91 and earlier tax years is, however, subject to the composite rate scheme and is treated rather differently.

(a) The amount received by the taxpayer is not liable to basic rate tax. The bank or building society deduct a composite rate of tax which is rather less than the equivalent to 25 per cent. of the gross interest, before paying interest to their depositor.

(b) No *basic rate* tax is required from the taxpayer.

(c) Where a taxpayer is not required to pay even basic rate tax, nothing can be recovered from the Revenue.

(d) Where a taxpayer is liable to *higher rate* tax, the net receipt must be grossed up at 25 per cent. in order to calculate the taxpayer's "excess" rate liability.

The composite rate will be abolished as from April 6, 1991 and thereafter banks and building societies will deduct the full basic rate of tax. The taxpayer will receive a basic rate tax credit and will be able to reclaim that tax if not liable for even basic rate tax.

*What are "charges on income"?*
Charges on income are "amounts which fall to be deducted in **6.9** computing total income" (Taxes Management Act 1970, s.8(8)). The amounts which are deductible are payments under

charitable covenants satisfying certain conditions, interest payments on qualifying loans (such as loans for the purchase of land and payments made for bona fide commercial reasons in connection with an individual's trade, profession or vocation). They are deducted from "statutory" income when calculating a person's "total" income because the payer is regarded as having alienated a portion of income so that it ceases to be the payer's income and becomes the payee's.

*What is "taxable income"?*

**6.10** From "total income" the taxpayer deducts his "personal reliefs" to leave "taxable income." The reliefs that can be claimed depend on the taxpayer's circumstances, and include the married couple's allowance, the single person's allowance and the age allowance. A husband and wife are each entitled to a personal allowance in the same way as a single person. In addition there is a married couple's allowance available to the husband but transferable to the wife in so far as the husband's income is insufficient to absorb the relief. Personal allowances are only available to individuals and not to personal representatives (see below, paragraph 6.13). In 1990/91 the single person's allowance is £3,005 and the married couple's allowance is £1,720.

5. WHAT ARE THE RATES?

**6.11** Once "taxable income" has been ascertained, the rates of tax are calculated on it. For the tax year 1990/91 these are 25 per cent. on the first £20,700 of taxable income and 40 per cent. thereafter. (The bands and the personal reliefs will in future tax years rise according to the rate of inflation, unless Parliament decides otherwise). These rates are applied to all types of income, both earned income and investment income. Investment income is everything which is not earned income.

An example of a simple calculation of a taxpayer's liability may be helpful.

*Example*
Alec, who is unmarried, has the following income on which he is liable to tax in the year 1990/91.

(1) £26,500 from his solicitor's practice (calculated according to the preceding year basis)

(2) £6,000 gross director's fees from XYZ Ltd., from which the company has deducted £123.75p under the P.A.Y.E. system. This is the correct amount of tax

once the personal relief and the charge on income mentioned below have been set against the fees.
(3) £7,500 from a trust fund paid to him net of basic rate tax.

He has paid £2,500 interest on a £20,000 loan to buy an interest in the firm of solicitors. His tax liability will be calculated as follows:

| | £ |
|---|---:|
| Statutory income | |
| Practice receipts | 26,500 |
| Salary (gross) | 6,000 |
| Income from trust fund (grossed up $7,500 \times \frac{100}{75}$) | 10,000 |
| | 42,500 |
| *Less* | |
| Charge on income | (2,500) |
| Total income | 40,000 |
| *Less* | |
| Personal relief | (3,005) |
| Taxable income | £36,995 |

| | £ |
|---|---:|
| His tax liability is: | |
| On the first £20,700 tax at 25% | 5,175 |
| On the balance of £16,295 tax at 40% | 6,518 |
| | 11,693 |

The total tax bill is therefore £11,693 of which £2,623.75 has already been paid (£2,500 by the trustees of the trust fund and £123.75 by XYZ Ltd.). Therefore, the Revenue will require £9,069.25 direct from Alec.

6. WHEN IS THE TAX PAYABLE?

The basic rule is that tax is paid on January 1, of the tax year **6.12** on the statutory income of that year, or 30 days from the date of the issue of the assessment notice, if later. This is, however, subject to qualifications. For example, tax assessed under Schedule D Cases I & II is payable in two equal instalments on January 1, in the tax year in question and on the following July 1; Schedule E tax is deducted before the employee receives it under the P.A.Y.E. system; any "excess liability" (*i.e.* the difference between the basic and higher rate of tax on income that has already suffered basic rate tax) falls due on the December 1 following the end of the tax year. (All these dates are subject to the 30-day period referred to above).

## C. Income of the Deceased

We will now examine the particular rules which are relevant on death.

### 1.INTRODUCTION

**6.13**   It is the responsibility of personal representatives to deal with the income tax affairs both of the deceased and of the estate during the administration period, to ensure that a full declaration of income, arising before and after the death, is made and that tax, at the appropriate rates, is paid. When performing this duty the personal representatives must make returns both in respect of the income of the deceased up to the date of death and in respect of the administration period.

### 2. INCOME OF THE DECEASED

**6.14**   The personal representatives must ascertain the statutory income of the deceased for the tax year of death. Only income received or receivable before death is included. Income receivable after death is income of the estate (see paragraph 6.15 below). They will calculate his tax liability in the usual way by deducting any charges on income payable before the death together with a *full* year's personal reliefs, regardless of the date of death. This will be the single person's allowance (£3,005) and the married couple's allowance (£1,720) if appropriate. Increased allowances are available when a taxpayer is over 65 provided the taxpayer's income does not exceed certain limits. A further increase is available where a taxpayer is over 75.

There are special rules if the deceased is survived by a spouse, as far as that spouse's right to claim personal reliefs is concerned. If the deceased was a man, his widow will get her own relief on her income from the date of death until the end of the tax year following the tax year in which the death occurred. She can also claim the widow's bereavement allowance given by Taxes Act 1988, s.262 (currently £1,720), provided she was living with him. Unless she remarries before the beginning of the next following tax year she will be entitled to another such allowance.

Once the deceased's taxable income has been calculated, the appropriate rates of tax are applied and any extra tax due is paid or a rebate claimed where relevant.

*Example*

Betty, unmarried, died on May 6, 1990 and her personal representatives find her share of the profits from a solicitor's practice for the tax year 1990/91 is £4,000. They also find she was entitled to a £750 dividend from A Ltd. (declared on May 1, 1990) and that a dividend of £375 on shares which she owned in B Ltd. was declared on June 1, 1990. Only the profits and the dividend from A Ltd. are treated as the deceased's income; the dividend from B Ltd. is treated as income of the estate (see paragraph 6.15 below). The tax calculation will be as follows:

|  |  | £ |
|---|---|---|
| Statutory income | | |
| Profits | | 4,000 |
| Grossed up dividend | | |
| $(£750 \times \dfrac{100}{75})$ | | 1,000 |
| Total income | | 5,000 |
| *Less* | | |
| Personal relief | | (3,005) |
| Taxable income | | 1,995 |

Tax on £1,995 at 25 per cent. is £498.75p but £250 tax has already been paid in respect of the dividend. Therefore the personal representatives will have to pay £248.75.

3. DISTINGUISHING INCOME OF THE DECEASED FROM INCOME OF THE ESTATE

**6.15**   The personal representatives must differentiate between the deceased's income and that of the administration period and this is done by ascertaining when the particular receipt arose. This causes few problems when considering salary or profits from a trade or profession since these sources of income will normally cease with the death. However, other types of income which continue to arise after the death, such as rent, interest or dividends, will cause greater problems since they are often attributable to a period which falls partly before and partly after the death.

Income which is *due* before the death is part of the deceased's income (for example, a dividend on shares due and payable on a date before death) even if paid after death. Income which is *due* after the death is income of the estate (for example a dividend due and payable after death or interest which becomes due and payable on a date after the death). The Apportionment Act 1870 (see below, paragraph 16.48), which provides for the apportionment of income on a day-to-day basis for the purposes of distribution, does not apply for income tax purposes (*I.R.C. v. Henderson's Executors* (1931)). As we saw in paragraph 4.17 a limited income tax relief is available where income received after death has been apportioned for inheritance tax purposes and some of that income has been included as an asset of the estate at death attracting inheritance tax (Taxes Act 1988, s.699, as amended).

4. PRACTICAL PROBLEMS

**6.16**   The income tax liability of the deceased may take a considerable length of time to finalise. This is particularly likely to be the case where the deceased was a sole trader or a partner as there may be delays in preparing the accounts on which the tax liability is to be calculated. There may be additional tax due to the Inland Revenue or there may be repayments of tax due to the deceased as the result, for example, of excessive P.A.Y.E. tax paid by an employer on the taxpayer's behalf.

The personal representatives are normally required to submit an Inland Revenue Account at the latest within 12 months of the death detailing the assets and liabilities of the deceased and showing the amount of inheritance tax due to the Inland Revenue calculated on the basis of the net value of the estate.

At the same time they are required to send a cheque for any inheritance tax due. The value of the estate cannot be accurately determined until all the assets and liabilities are ascertained so any delay in finalising the income tax position of the deceased will prevent the final calculation and payment of inheritance tax due.

Personal representatives are usually anxious to pay inheritance tax promptly, partly because interest starts to run after six months from the end of the month of death but more importantly because they cannot get a grant of representation and therefore cannot start administering the estate until the inheritance tax due has been paid. To prevent delays, personal representatives will frequently estimate the income tax liability of the deceased and pay inheritance tax due on the basis of that estimated figure. When they obtain the final income tax figure, they can if necessary submit a corrective account and make any adjustments to the inheritance tax which prove necessary.

## D. Income Arising after Death

As regards the income received by the estate during the "administration period" different rules apply. This period starts with the day after the date of death and continues until the completion of the administration of the estate (Taxes Act 1988, s.695). It is generally accepted that completion of the administration occurs on the date the residue is ascertained for distribution. Personal representatives cannot claim any personal reliefs since these are only available to individuals. They can deduct interest on a loan to pay inheritance tax when calculating the taxable income of the estate income but only in so far as the loan is to pay tax on personalty vesting in the personal representatives to which the deceased was beneficially entitled, Taxes Act 1988, s.364. Further, this interest is only deductible for one year. **6.17**

The personal representatives pay only basic rate tax on the taxable income regardless of the amount and type of income and, if this taxed income is paid to a beneficiary, they must supply a certificate of deduction of tax.

To the extent that income is paid to beneficiaries, further rules are relevant. These differ depending on the beneficiaries' interests in the estate and firstly we will look at the treatment of payments to residuary beneficiaries.

1. RESIDUARY BENEFICIARIES

**6.18** These rules are themselves sub-divided into those which relate to beneficiaries with limited interests and those which relate to beneficiaries with absolute interests in the residue.

*Limited interest beneficiaries (Taxes Act 1988, s.695)*

**6.19** A beneficiary has a limited interest in the residue where he will be entitled only to the income of the estate or part of it, rather than to capital. For example, where the beneficiary will be the life tenant of a trust fund created from the residue.

Any sums that such a person receives will already have borne basic rate tax in the hands of the personal representatives, accordingly they are net amounts and have to be grossed up when calculating the statutory income of the beneficiary. The beneficiary will include the gross amount in his tax return for the tax year in which the amount is received and will pay any excess liability or reclaim basic rate tax if appropriate (Taxes Act 1988, s.695(2)).

The personal representatives may retain the taxed income for much of the administration period and then hand over, perhaps, several years net income at once. In the absence of special provisions, the unfortunate beneficiary could suffer unnecessarily high rates of tax in such a case. In order to prevent such anomalies section 695(3) and (4) of the Taxes Act 1988 provide that, once the administration is complete, the Revenue aggregate the *net* amounts that have been paid, or are payable, to the beneficiary and spread them evenly over the administration period on a day-to-day basis. The date of death is treated as the last day of the deceased's life and the administration period is treated as beginning on the following day.

It should be noted that these rules require the "spreading" on a daily basis of the *net* amounts. These are grossed-up at the basic rate appropriate for each tax year of the administration period, with the result that there may be differences between the basic rate tax actually paid and the tax credit eventually given to the beneficiary. However, the beneficiary is always treated as having paid his basic rate tax for each year of the administration.

*Example*

Charles dies on March 2, 1991 having by will made Donna the life tenant of a trust of residue. Donna has received the following payments, all net of basic rate tax. Assume that the basic rate of income tax for 1990/91 is 25 per cent. and for 1991/92 it will be 22.5 per cent. and for 1992/93 20 per cent.

|  | Net amounts received £ | Basic rate | Gross amounts included as part of statutory income £ |
|---|---|---|---|
| Tax year 1990/91 | Nil | 25% | Nil |
| Tax year 1991/92 | 2,325 | 22.5% | 3,000 |
| Tax year 1992/93 | 1,600 | 20% | 2,000 |
|  | 3,925 |  | 5,000 |

The administration is completed on July 14, 1992.

(a)  During the administration period the beneficiary includes, as part of her statutory income, the net amounts actually paid to her, grossed up at the appropriate rate for the tax year in question. She has a tax credit for the basic rate tax paid by the personal representatives but if she is a higher rate tax payer, she will have to pay any additional tax due and, if she is not required to pay even basic tax, she can reclaim the tax paid.

(b)  At the end of the administration period the total net amounts received (£3,925) are spread on a day-to-day basis over the administration period. The administration period comprises 500 days (34 days within tax year 1990/91; 366 days within tax year 1991/92; 100 days within tax year 1992/93) and, therefore, £7.85 income is attributable to each day. The amounts treated as received in each tax year are grossed up at the rate appropriate for each tax year.

| Tax Year | Net amount "spread" £ | Basic rate | Gross amount to be substituted as part of statutory income £ |
|---|---|---|---|
| 1990/91 (£7.85 x 34) | 266.90 | 25% | 355.87  (+355.87) |
| 1991/92 (£7.85 x 366) | 2,873.10 | 22.5% | 3,707.23  (+707.23) |
| 1992/93 (£7.85 x 100) | 785.00 | 20% | 981.25  (−1,018.75) |

(c)   The substitution of the new gross income figures in Donna's statutory income *may* mean that income tax is due to or from the Inland Revenue. However, this is not necessarily so. The substituted amounts have already borne basic rate tax and Donna has a basic rate tax credit at the rate appropriate for the year in question. *Extra* tax will only have to be paid by Donna if the additional income now attributed to 1990/91 and 1991/92 takes her into a higher tax band. Tax will only be reclaimed by Donna if the reduction in her income for 1992/93 means that she has unused reliefs.

*Absolute interest beneficiaries (Taxes Act 1988, s.696)*

**6.20**  A beneficiary who is entitled to all or part of the capital of the residue in his own right has an absolute interest.

Such a beneficiary is entitled to both income and capital; income tax is, of course, only payable on income receipts. Therefore, when a beneficiary receives a cash sum from the estate it is necessary to distinguish income from capital receipts.

In order to do this the personal representatives must calculate the "residuary income" of the estate in respect of each tax year. Section 697 of the Taxes Act 1988 defines "residuary income" as (broadly) all income less certain charges (including annuities) and management expenses properly chargeable to income. There is no definition of "management expenses properly chargeable to income." However in *Carver* v. *Duncan* (1985), a case on management expenses "properly" chargeable to income for the purposes of liability to additional rate income tax under the Finance Act 1973, s.16, it was said that "properly means properly under the general law and not properly under the terms of the particular trust instrument." (Examples of expenses properly chargeable to income would be rates or repairs.) Net residuary income is residuary income less basic rate tax.

Payments made to a residuary beneficiary are treated as his income up to the limit of the residuary income. The beneficiary must gross up payments received and include the gross amount in his statutory income. He will be given a tax credit for the basic rate tax paid on his behalf by the personal representatives. Any payments made to the beneficiary in excess of the residuary income are treated as capital and as such are not included in the beneficiary's statutory income.

This procedure could lead to the avoidance of tax. Personal representatives could refrain from paying income to a residuary beneficiary in one year, retain it until a later year and then make a large payment in the later year. The beneficiary would not be assessed to tax on any estate income in the first year, since he would have received no income; in the later year he would only be assessed to tax on that later year's residuary income, the balance being treated as capital.

In order to prevent avoidance of tax, the Revenue reassess the residuary beneficiary at the end of the administration period. In any tax year in which the beneficiary was assessed on less than the residuary income of the estate, the beneficiary is *retrospectively* to be treated as having received the whole of the residuary income for the year in question. In order to achieve this, payments made to the beneficiary in later years are treated as made up of:

(a) the residuary income for the current tax year;

(b) an amount sufficient to cover the difference between the sums actually received by the beneficiary in earlier years and the residuary income for years in which the full amount was not received; this amount is to be treated retrospectively as income for those years; and

(c) capital.

*Example*
Eric died on May 15, 1990, having by his will left his residuary estate to Fiona absolutely. The administration is completed on July 14, 1992. The basic rate of income tax for 1990/91 is 25 per cent. and it is assumed for the purposes of this example that the basic rate of income tax will remain at 25 per cent. Residuary income and payments made to Fiona are as follows:

| Tax year | Residuary income of Estate £ | Net residuary income (i.e. after basic rate tax deducted) £ | Payments to Fiona | £ |
|---|---|---|---|---|
| 1990/91 | 10,000 | 7,500 | October  6, 1990 | 750 |
| 1991/92 | 5,000 | 3,750 | October 12, 1991 | 20,000 |
| 1992/93 | 2,000 | 1,500 | July      14, 1992 | 54,400 |

(a) During the administration period payments made to Fiona are treated as income until the receipts exceed the net residuary income of the estate for the current tax year. Fiona must include the grossed up income receipts as part of her statutory income for the appropriate tax year.

| Tax year | Amount actually received £ | Amount treated as income of Fiona | | Balance treated as capital £ |
|---|---|---|---|---|
| | | Net £ | Gross £ | |
| 1990/91 | 750 | 750 | 1,000 | Nil |
| 1991/92 | 20,000 | 3,750 | 5,000 | 16,250 |
| 1992/93 | 54,400 | 1,500 | 2,000 | 52,900 |

(b) At the end of the administration period (July 14, 1992) Fiona will be reassessed for any tax year in which she received less than the whole of the net residuary income of the estate. The only shortfall occurred in 1990/91 and was a shortfall of £6,750.

Therefore, the payment of £54,400 made at the end of the administration period is finally treated as made up of:

| | |
|---|---|
| Net income for 1992/93 | £1,500 |
| Net income for 1990/91 | £6,750 |
| Capital balance | £46,150 |
| | £54,400 |

(c) The addition of £9,000 gross income (i.e. £6,750 grossed up at 25 per cent.) to Fiona's statutory income for 1990/91 may mean that additional income tax is due to the Inland Revenue. However, this is not necessarily so. The £9,000 has already borne basic rate tax and Fiona has a basic rate tax credit. Extra tax will only have to be paid by Fiona if the additional income now attributed to 1990/91 takes her into a higher rate tax band for that year.

*Inland Revenue Statement of Practice SP 7/80*

**6.21** We saw in paragraph 6.8 above that for tax year 1990/91 and earlier tax years it is normally impossible for a person who is not required to pay even basic rate tax to make a repayment claim to recover tax on building society and bank interest. In the case of beneficiaries with an absolute interest in the residue of an estate the Revenue accepts that a repayment claim can be made in respect of residuary income even though building society or bank interest contributed to that income. The reason for this is that the Revenue was advised that it is not permissible to "look through" the residuary income to identify its component parts.

## 2. NON-RESIDUARY BENEFICIARIES

We must also look at the taxation of specific, pecuniary and **6.22** general beneficiaries.

### Specific beneficiaries

The subject-matter of a specific legacy may earn income from **6.23** the date of death (for example, company shares). A beneficiary only becomes liable to pay tax after the personal representatives have made an assent of the asset to the beneficiary. The liability relates back to the date of death so the assessments for intervening tax years will be reopened and tax will be reassessed for the years in which the income arose.

### Pecuniary and general beneficiaries

Such beneficiaries may be entitled to be paid interest on the **6.24** value of their legacies (see Chapter 16). The question then arises of their liability to income tax on such interest. Often income tax is chargeable on income even if not accepted but in the case of interest, tax is only payable on sums actually received. Thus if a beneficiary disclaims entitlement to interest payable to him on a pecuniary or general legacy or the personal representatives cannot pay it, he is not liable to tax—*Dewar* v. *I.R.C.* (1935) (unless a sum has been specifically set aside to pay the legacy in which case tax must be paid even if the legatee fails to draw the interest—*Spens* v. *I.R.C.* (1970)).

If interest is paid to the beneficiary it is taxed as Schedule D, Case III income in his hands (normally as income of the year of receipt, Taxes Act 1988, s.64, s.66 and s.67).

# 7. Taxation of Trusts and Settlements

## A. Introduction

Where property is held on trust the legal and beneficial interests **7.1** are often held by different people and the Revenue find it convenient and, in some cases necessary, to impose liability on both the trustee and the beneficiary. Where the beneficial interest in property is divided between several people, either at a particular time or successively, special rules are required to ensure that the creation of the settlement cannot be used as a means of saving tax.

Tax definitions of "settlements" for inheritance tax, capital gains tax, and income tax are different and will be considered separately later in this chapter. The definitions for tax purposes are not the same as for other purposes and in particular do not distinguish between trusts for sale and strict settlements.

Settlements may be created *inter vivos*, by the intestacy rules or by will. There are many different types of settlement; we will concentrate mainly on two very common types in this chapter. These are:

(i)   A settlement "to A for life remainder to B" (that is a settlement where property is vested in trustees to pay the income from the property to A until A dies and then to vest the property absolutely in B). For inheritance tax purposes this is a settlement "with an interest in possession."

(ii)  An "accumulation and maintenance settlement." This type of settlement gives the trustees a power to use income for the maintenance of the beneficiaries, and requires them to add any income not so used to capital (*i.e.* to accumulate income). For inheritance tax purposes this is a settlement "without an interest in possession."

We will deal with each tax separately for the sake of clarity but it is important to realise that in deciding whether or not to create a settlement each tax must be taken into account. Furthermore the non-tax consequences of creating a settlement should always be regarded as the first consideration. A gift is unwise, even if it saves tax, if it leaves the settlor or his dependants with insufficient income or capital for their needs.

# B. Settlements and Inheritance Tax

DEFINITIONS

**7.2**  For inheritance tax purposes the term "settlement" is defined, by section 43(2) of the Inheritance Tax Act 1984, as:

" ... any disposition or dispositions of property ... whereby the property is for the time being—
  (a) held in trust for persons in succession or for any person subject to a contingency; or
  (b) held by trustees on trust to accumulate the whole or part of any income of the property or with power to make payments out of that income at the discretion of the trustees or some other person, with or without power to accumulate surplus income; or
  (c) charged or burdened (otherwise than for full consideration. ... ) with the payment of any annuity or other periodical payment payable for a life or any other limited or terminable period. ... "

Section 43(3) adds to the definition a lease for life or lives or for a period ascertainable only by reference to a death which is not granted for full consideration.

It should be noted that a settlement is "any disposition or dispositions of property ... whereby the property is *for the time being*" held in one of the various ways listed in the definition. Whether or not property is settled must, therefore, be considered each time that a potential charge to tax arises. Property ceases to be settled once it ceases to be held in one of the various ways listed in the definition even though it may still be held by trustees (for example where they have not yet vested it in a beneficiary who has become absolutely entitled). A bare trust (that is a trust where the beneficiary is entitled to require the transfer of the legal title to himself) is not a settlement for inheritance tax purposes—the beneficiary of such a trust is treated as an absolute owner. A statutory trust for sale imposed where property is held by co-owners is not a settlement for inheritance tax purposes. The co-owners are treated as absolute owners.

Examples of inheritance tax settlements include:

   (i)   Trustees are holding property for "A for life remainder to B" (successive interest, see section 43(2)(a) above).

  (ii)   Trustees are holding property for "A if he reaches 25" (subject to a contingency, see section 43(2)(*a*), above).

 (iii)   Trustees are holding property "to accumulate the income therefrom for 10 years and then to pay capital to A" (trust to accumulate until the 10 years expires, see section 43(2)(*b*) above).

 (iv)   Trustees are holding property "to pay the income therefrom for 10 years from [date] to such of my children as they shall in their absolute discretion from time to time appoint and thereafter to pay the capital to A" (discretion to pay income until the 10 years expires, see section 43(2)(*b*), above).

  (v)   Property is being held by someone subject to the payment of an annuity to someone else and full consideration was not given for the annuity. For example the will of a testator leaves Blackacre "to my son charged with the payment to X of an annuity of £1,000 per annum for the rest of X's life." In this case there will be a settlement of Blackacre from the death of the testator until the death of X (see section 43(2)(*c*) above).

# C. Inheritance Tax—Settlements with Interest in Possession

## 1. SIGNIFICANCE OF INTEREST IN POSSESSION

It is extremely important to decide whether or not a trust has an **7.3** interest in possession. This is because a trust in which there is an interest in possession is treated quite differently for inheritance tax purposes from a trust in which there is no interest in possession.

Section 49(1) of the Inheritance Tax Act 1984 provides that "A person beneficially entitled to an interest in possession in settled property shall be treated . . . as beneficially entitled to the property in which the interest subsists." This means that a person with an interest in possession is treated for inheritance tax purposes as the owner of the trust assets. Where a person is entitled to part of the income from settled property he is treated as owning a corresponding part of the property. Special rules apply where one or more beneficiary (for example, an annuitant) is entitled to a fixed amount of income rather than a proportion of the whole or where one or more beneficiary is entitled to the use and enjoyment of property rather than the income from it. These rules are not further considered.

As we shall see at paragraphs 7.6–7.15 below, where there is no interest in possession no one person is treated as beneficially entitled to the settled property. Instead inheritance tax is charged on the value of the trust assets periodically over the lifetime of the trust.

The term "interest in possession" is not defined in the legislation. In most cases it is clear whether or not there is an interest in possession. If a beneficiary has an immediate right to receive income or otherwise to use and enjoy trust property then he has such an interest. Thus the life tenant of a settlement usually has an interest in possession. It is also clear that no one has such an interest in the case of an ordinary discretionary trust since no one has a *right* to income. There are, however, some marginal cases where the position is less clear.

For example in *Pearson* v. *I.R.C.* (1980) a trust fund was held for three beneficiaries (all adults) who were entitled to the property subject to powers of appointment and a power to accumulate; they would each receive one-third of the income unless the trustees exercised the power to accumulate or the power of appointment. The House of Lords by a majority of three to two (and overruling the decisions at first instance and in the Court of Appeal) held that there was no interest in possession. The majority held that an interest in possession is one giving "a present right to present enjoyment" and that on these facts there was no such right since the beneficiaries would not receive the income to the extent that the power to accumulate was exercised.

## 2. CREATION OF SETTLEMENT WITH INTEREST IN POSSESSION

A transfer to any type of settlement is a transfer of value by the settlor. Assuming that no exemptions apply, the transfer will be either potentially exempt or chargeable.

A settlor who makes an *inter vivos* transfer to a settlement with an interest in possession on or after March 17, 1987, is treated as making a potentially exempt transfer. Thus, no inheritance tax is payable unless the settlor dies within seven years of the transfer. If death does occur within that period the transfer becomes chargeable at the full rates in force at the date of death (subject to the possibility of tapering relief).

*Example*
On June 5, 1990, S gives £135,000 to trustees to hold on trust for A for life, remainder to B. For the purposes of this example, it is assumed that no exemptions or reliefs apply. S's cumulative total is nil. S dies on December 5, 1990.

No tax is payable on creation. However, on December 5, the transfer becomes chargeable. The first £128,000 will be taxed at the nil rate; the remaining £7,000 will be taxed at 40 per cent.

(A settlor who made an *inter vivos* transfer to a settlement with an interest in possession prior to March 17, 1987, is treated as having made a chargeable transfer. There was an initial charge to tax at half rates. In the event of the settlor dying within seven years of such a transfer tax becomes chargeable at the full rates (subject to the possibility of tapering relief) but credit will be given for any tax already paid.)

As we saw above, a person with an interest in possession in settled property (for example, a life tenant) is deemed to own the trust assets beneficially. Therefore, if a settlor creates a settlement *inter vivos* in which he is the first life tenant there will be no charge to tax. This is because before the creation he *actually* owns the property beneficially; after the creation he is *deemed* to own it beneficially, so for tax purposes the value of his estate has not gone down. Similarly, if the settlor's spouse is the first life tenant, the creation of the settlement (whether *inter vivos* or on death) will not give rise to tax because the spouse exemption will apply.

If the transfer to the settlement is made on the death of the settlor the property to be transferred to the trust will be taxed as part of the settlor's death estate before being transferred to the trustees of the settlement.

A trust with an interest in possession could be used as a preliminary to the creation of a trust without an interest in possession in an attempt to avoid inheritance tax at the settlor's rates were it not for the existence of anti-avoidance provisions contained in the Finance (No. 2) Act 1987. These are dealt with briefly in paragraph 7.12 below.

3. CHARGEABLE EVENTS AFTER CREATION OF SETTLEMENT
WITH INTEREST IN POSSESSION

**7.4**  Since a person with an interest in possession is treated as owning the trust property (or a proportion of it if he is entitled to part only of the income) it follows that a termination of an interest in possession is taxable as a disposition *of the trust property* by that person. Tax may thus become chargeable:

    (i)    On the death of the person entitled to the interest.

    (ii)   On an actual disposal of the interest (for example, the beneficiary gives his interest away, surrenders it or sells it).

    (iii)  On the termination of the interest in any other way (for example, where the interest is determinable at a particular date or on the happening of a particular event, tax will be payable on that day or when that event occurs).

Since the termination of the interest is treated as a transfer of the trust property by the person entitled to the interest, the rate of tax will depend on that person's cumulative total and on whether the termination is on death or during his lifetime.

*Example*

Trustees are holding a fund of £70,000 on trust for A for life remainder to B. A dies having made chargeable lifetime transfers of £40,000, all in the seven years preceding his death, and owning £30,000 worth of unsettled property on his death. The estate on death is £100,000 (*i.e.* the trust fund and the £30,000 owned by A). This is cumulated with the £40,000 chargeable lifetime transfers so the tax on the death estate of £100,000 is calculated at the rates appropriate for a transfer between £40,000 and £140,000. The tax is, therefore, £4,800 (that is £12,000 at 40 per cent). This tax will normally be paid by the trustees of the settlement and the personal representatives in the same proportions that the trust property and the unsettled property bear to the whole estate on death. In this case the trustees will pay seven tenths of the tax and the personal representatives three tenths.

Where a person with an interest in possession sells his interest, tax may be payable even though the sale is for the full value of the interest. This is because the life tenant is treated as owning the trust property absolutely for inheritance tax purposes. However, for the purpose of sale a life interest is valued actuarially taking into account the age and expectation of life of the life tenant. This value will always be less than the value of the settled property itself so that there is bound to be a reduction in the value of the life tenant's estate. The reduction will be the difference between the value of the trust property and the price paid for the life interest.

*Example*
A is the life tenant of a trust fund worth £180,000. The actuarial value of A's life interest is £40,000 and he sells it for that amount. A is treated as making a transfer of value of £140,000. This transfer is a potentially exempt transfer. No tax is payable initially. Tax will be payable if the transferor dies within seven years.

Where an interest in possession comes to an end and at that time the life tenant becomes beneficially entitled to the trust property there is no tax to pay. This is because before the interest ends he is treated as owning the trust property, after it ends he actually owns it so that for tax purposes there is no loss to his (or anyone else's) estate.

*Example*
Trust property is held on trust to pay the income to A until 25 and thereafter to A absolutely. When A reaches 25 no tax will be payable.

The same rule applies where the life tenant becomes entitled to another interest in possession in the same property.

*Example*
Trust property is held on trust for A for 10 years and thereafter to A for life provided he is then married. If at the end of 10 years A is married he will acquire another interest in possession so no tax will be payable.

Where an interest in possession comes to an end and the life tenant then acquires an interest in possession in part only of the trust property tax will be payable on the part in which he does not acquire a new interest in possession.

Despite the above rules there is no tax on the termination of an interest in possession if the property then reverts to the settlor during the settlor's lifetime or to the settlor's spouse during the settlor's lifetime or within two years of his death.

*Example*
A settles property on B for life with a reversion to the settlor. No tax is payable if A is still alive when B dies.

The exemption for reversion to the settlor does not apply where the settlor has purchased the reversion.

*Example*
A settles property on B for life remainder to C. If A purchases C's remainder tax will be payable on B's death even though the property then reverts to A.

Since a person with an interest in possession is deemed to own the trust property absolutely, an advance of capital by the trustees to him does not give rise to tax since he is receiving property which is already treated for the purposes of inheritance tax as his own. An advance of capital to anyone else does give rise to tax since it brings the life tenant's interest in that property to an end.

Various exemptions and reliefs are available on the termination of an interest in possession including the following:

(i) The annual exemption of £3,000 (unless already used to exempt other transfers) is available where the termination occurs *inter vivos*.

(ii) The spouse exemption applies unless the spouse has acquired the reversion for money or money's worth. (For example, settlement to A for life remainder to B—no tax on A's death if he is then married to B. Settlement to A for life remainder to B; C (A's spouse) buys B's reversion and then A dies—tax will be payable).

(iii) Business and agricultural property relief.

## 4. REVERSIONS

**7.5** A reversionary interest (that is a future interest) in settled property is usually excluded property and so no tax is payable on a transfer (*inter vivos* or on death) of such an interest. This rule is really just a consequence of the fact that the person with an interest in possession is deemed to own the trust property absolutely.

*Example*
Property is settled on A for life remainder to B. No tax is payable if B dies or gives away his interest during A's lifetime.

To prevent tax avoidance a reversionary interest is *not* excluded property (so that tax will be payable on the death of its owner or on an *inter vivos* transfer by him) in certain special cases.

# D. Inheritance Tax—Settlements with no Interest in Possession

### 1. INTRODUCTION

There is no interest in possession in a settlement if no individual has "a present right to present enjoyment" of the trust property (*Pearson* v. *I.R.C.* (1980) see paragraph 3 above). The most common examples of such settlements are accumulation trusts and discretionary trusts. In the case of a settlement with an interest in possession, tax is payable on the death of the life tenant and on the termination of the life interest in other ways (see paragraphs 7.4–7.5). In the case of accumulation and discretionary settlements this type of charge cannot arise so that special rules are required to prevent tax avoidance.    **7.6**

Where there is an interest in possession tax is chargeable once for each individual beneficiary's period of enjoyment of the property. The rules for settlements without an interest in possession are designed to achieve the equivalent of one full tax charge every generation thus establishing rough parity of treatment with other settlements and with circumstances where the property is not settled at all.

It is not intended to deal with the rules fully in this book but they are summarised briefly as follows:

### 2. CREATION OF A SETTLEMENT WITH NO INTEREST IN POSSESSION

A transfer to a settlement without an interest in possession is a chargeable transfer by the settlor. If the transfer is *inter vivos*, inheritance tax is charged initially at half rates; tax will be charged at full rates if the settlor dies within seven years of the transfer but credit will be given for any tax already paid. Tapering relief will be available if the settlor dies more than three years after the transfer.    **7.7**

If the transfer is on death, the property is taxed as part of the death estate before being transferred to the trustees of the settlement.

There is no reduction in the amount of tax if the settlor or his spouse is one of the discretionary beneficiaries since a discretionary beneficiary has no interest in the trust property for tax purposes. Furthermore, the fact that the settlor is a beneficiary will amount to a reservation of benefit thus leading to a possible charge on his death (see paragraph 7.10 below).

3. CHARGEABLE EVENTS AFTER CREATION OF SETTLEMENT WITHOUT INTEREST IN POSSESSION

*Periodic charge*

**7.8** Throughout the period when there is no interest in possession tax is charged on each tenth anniversary of the creation of the settlement. The rate of tax is 30 per cent. of the "effective rate" on the value of the settled property. The effective rate means broadly speaking the lifetime rate on the value of the settled property cumulated with the settlor's cumulative total at the date of creation of the settlement and with any capital sums which have left the settlement in the last 10 years.

*Example*

Settlor's lifetime cumulative total was £120,000. He settled £50,000 by will free of inheritance tax on trustees with a discretion as to the payment of income and capital. During the last 10 years the trustees have distributed £20,000 of capital. The settled property on the first tenth anniversary is worth £80,000. This figure will be cumulated with:

|  | £ |
|---|---|
| (lifetime cumulative total) | 120,000 |
| (capital paid out) | 20,000 |
|  | 140,000 |

The tax on £80,000 (treated as the top part of a cumulative total of £220,000) at half the full rates is £16,000. £16,000 is 20 per cent. of £80,000 so that is the effective rate. The tax payable is therefore:

$$\frac{30}{100} \times \frac{20}{100} \times £80,000 = £4,800$$

Special rules apply where the settlor creates two settlements on the same day and where there is an interest in possession in respect of part of the settled property. These rules are not further considered.

### Proportionate periodic charge

There is a charge to tax where property leaves the settlement **7.9** during a 10-year period (whether from creation to the first tenth anniversary or between successive tenth anniversaries). This may happen because the trustees exercise a discretion to distribute capital or because a beneficiary acquires a right to the capital (for example when a contingency is satisfied). There is also a charge where someone acquires an interest in possession in the settled property. When these charges arise the tax is a proportion of the tax which would be payable on a tenth anniversary.

### Reservation of benefit

Where a settlor creates a settlement without an interest in **7.10** possession he may be a beneficiary of the settlement (*e.g.* he is one of the objects of a discretionary trust). In this case he has made a gift "subject to a reservation" and tax may, therefore, be payable *on his death* in respect of that property unless he has been excluded from benefit for seven years before he dies.

### 4. ANTI-AVOIDANCE PROVISIONS

A transfer to a discretionary trust is a chargeable transfer **7.11** attracting inheritance tax at half the full rate. A transfer to a settlement with an interest in possession is a potentially exempt transfer and a transfer from such a settlement will be treated as a transfer by the person with an interest in possession, any tax payable being calculated by reference to his cumulative total and not to the original settlor's cumulative total.

Prima facie, it would seem possible for a person with a high cumulative total who wishes to transfer property to a discretionary trust to make use of a short-term interest in possession trust to save inheritance tax. The settlor would transfer the property to a trust in which a person with a low cumulative total would have an interest in possession for a short time. This would be a potentially exempt transfer. The property would then pass to a trust without an interest in possession. This would be a chargeable transfer, but the inheritance tax would be assessed by reference to the cumulative total of the person with the interest in possession.

To prevent the avoidance of tax by such means the Finance (No. 2) Act 1987 contains provisions designed to ensure that a transfer to a discretionary trust following a transfer to a trust with an interest in possession can be taxed by reference to the cumulative total of the original settlor where certain conditions are fulfilled. A detailed consideration of these provisions is beyond the scope of this book.

### 5. SPECIALLY PRIVILEGED SETTLEMENTS

**7.12** None of the charges to tax outlined above apply where trust property is held for charitable and similar purposes or is held in an accumulation and maintenance settlement.

### 6. ACCUMULATION AND MAINTENANCE SETTLEMENTS

*Introduction*
**7.13** Where settled property is held in an accumulation and maintenance settlement (as defined by section 71 of the Inheritance Tax Act 1984) special tax rules apply which are more favourable than the rules for settlements with or without an interest in possession. The object of the rules is to enable a settlor to give property without any tax penalty to young people with conditions attached which prevent them having access to income and/or capital at too young an age. The charges to tax on 10th anniversaries and on property leaving the settlement do not apply. The creation of an accumulation and maintenance settlement *inter vivos* is a potentially exempt transfer.

*Definition*
**7.14** The accumulation and maintenance settlement rules apply to settled property if four requirements (laid down in section 71 of the Inheritance Tax Act 1984) are satisfied:

(a) one or more persons will, on or before attaining a specified age not exceeding 25, become beneficially entitled to it or to an interest in possession in it; and

(b) no interest in possession subsists in it; and

(c) the income from it is to be accumulated so far as not applied for the maintenance, education or benefit of a beneficiary (*i.e.* one of the persons who will become entitled at 25 or a lower age); and

(d) *either* (i) not more than 25 years have elapsed since the beginning of the settlement (or later time when it satisfied the three requirements above);

*or* (ii) all the beneficiaries had a common grandparent (or are the children, widows or widowers of the original beneficiaries who die before achieving the specified age).

We will now consider each of the requirements in turn.

(a) *Entitlement at 25 or some lower specified age.* A settlement only satisfies this requirement if the beneficiaries *will* be entitled at 25 or some lower specified age. It is not sufficient that a beneficiary *may* be entitled at 25 or some lower specified age. Thus a settlement which gives "capital and income at 25 or on earlier marriage" satisfies the requirement since the beneficiary will get the property at 25 at the latest. A settlement which gives "capital and income on marriage or at 25 whichever is the later" does not satisfy the requirement.

It is not necessary that the beneficiaries obtain a vested interest in *capital* at the specified age. It is sufficient that they acquire an interest in possession in the settlement, that is a right to income as it arises. Thus a settlement which requires income to be accumulated until 25 and then gives the income to the beneficiary is sufficient even if capital is never to vest in that beneficiary.

Section 31 of the Trustee Act 1925 gives the right to receive income to a beneficiary on reaching 18 where the vesting of capital is contingent on reaching a greater age or fulfilling some other contingency. Thus a settlement which gives capital to A at 30 (or any other age) satisfies this condition as long as section 31 has not been excluded since the right to income will then vest at 18.

Section 71 of the Inheritance Tax Act requires that an age of 25 or lower be "specified." It might be argued that where a beneficiary acquires a right to income at 18 under section 31 no age has been *specified*. However, the Revenue has stated that it regards the entitlement to income at 18 under section 31 as satisfying this requirement.

The requirement is that "one or more persons" will be entitled at a specified age. The "persons" can include unborn persons but section 71(7) of the Inheritance Tax Act 1984 provides that the condition is not satisfied "unless there is or has been a living beneficiary." Thus a settlement on "the children of A at 25" is not an accumulation and maintenance settlement if A is childless when the settlement is created (it will become one when A's first child is born). If the settlement were to the children of A and A had a child living at the time the settlement was made the settlement would remain an accumulation and maintenance settlement even if that child were to die since there would then "have been" a living beneficiary.

(b) *No interest in possession.* Once there is an interest in possession in settled property it ceases to be subject to the rules for an accumulation and maintenance settlement. However, where there is more than one beneficiary each part of the settled property must be considered separately.

*Example*
A settlement is made for "such of the children of A asreach 25"; when the settlement is created A has been dead for some time and has two children, B aged 10 and C aged 16. The whole of the settled property will be subject to the rules for an accumulation and maintenance settlement for two years. When C reaches 18 he becomes entitled to half the income under section 31 of the Trustee Act 1925 and, therefore, obtains an interest in possession in half the settled property. The other half of the property remains subject to the rules for accumulation and maintenance settlements. If C dies two years later there will be tax to pay on his half share (since he had an interest in possession); after his death the whole settled property will be subject to the accumulation and maintenance rules for a further four years until B obtains an interest in possession at 18.

(c) *Income to be accumulated so far as not applied for maintenance etc.* The income must be either accumulated or used for the maintenance education or benefit *of the beneficiaries* (*i.e.* the persons who will be entitled at 25 or some lower age). Where the settlement is silent as to how income is to be used and section 31 has not been excluded this requirement will be satisfied because of the terms of section 31.

This requirement will not be satisfied if the trustees are given power to apply the income for other purposes (such as maintenance of persons other than the beneficiaries as defined).

(d) *Common grandparent or less than 25 years since settlement became an accumulation and maintenance settlement.* This requirement is satisfied where all the beneficiaries are children of the same person or grandchildren of the same person. The common grandparent need not be the settlor.

This requirement is also satisfied where the settlement provides for the replacement of beneficiaries who have a common grandparent but die before obtaining a vested right to capital or an interest in possession by their own children, widows or widowers.

*Example*
A settlement "to the children of A equally at 25 or if any of them shall die before that age such deceased child's share shall go to the children of such deceased child at 25" will remain an accumulation and maintenance settlement if a child dies before 18 and is replaced by his own children.

Where the settlement is not on persons with a common grandparent it will only be an accumulation and maintenance settlement for 25 years. Since (as we shall see in paragraph 7.15) adverse tax consequences will then apply it is important in such a case to ensure that all property ceases to be subject to the rules for an accumulation and maintenance settlement within 25 years. If the settlement is on named persons this requirement cannot cause any additional problem (because they must achieve the specified age within 25 years to satisfy requirement (a) above).

*Tax consequences*
As stated above the lifetime creation of an accumulation and **7.15** maintenance settlement is a potentially exempt transfer (see Chapter 4, paragraph 3.1). Thus tax will only be payable where the settlement is created by will or as a result of the intestacy rules or where the settlor dies within seven years of creation. After the creation of the settlement there is no charge to tax on each tenth anniversary, nor on the death of a beneficiary before he acquires an interest in possession, nor on an advance of capital or income to a beneficiary, nor on a beneficiary becoming entitled to an interest in possession or an interest in capital. This usually means that there is no charge to tax other than on the creation of the settlement until after the property ceased to be settled (*i.e.* until the beneficiary gives the property away or dies after acquiring a vested interest in it).

However, tax will become payable at the end of 25 years if the settlement is still an accumulation and maintenance settlement and the beneficiaries did not have a common grandparent. Where tax does become payable the rate is dependent solely on the length of time the property has been in the settlement and is usually much higher than the rate for other settlements with or without an interest in possession.

The main advantages of an accumulation and maintenance settlement are that there is no initial charge if the settlement is created *inter vivos*, no periodic charges during the lifetime of the settlement and usually no charge when property leaves the settlement. In the case of other settlements without an interest in possession there is a charge on creation, on each tenth anniversary and when property leaves the settlement.

# E. Inheritance Tax and Trustee Act 1925, s.31

**7.16**　Section 31 (see Chapter 11 for a full discussion) provides that where there is an income available to an infant (whether he has a vested or a contingent interest) the trustees of the trust may at their sole discretion apply the whole or part of such income for or towards the infant's maintenance, education or benefit and to the extent that they do not they must accumulate the whole or part of such income. If, after reaching the age of 18, the beneficiary has not attained a vested interest in such income the trustees *shall* thereafter pay the income (together with any income produced by investments bought with accumulated income) to the beneficiary until the beneficiary either attains a vested interest or dies or until his interest fails. Section 31 is not part of the inheritance tax legislation. However, as seen above, the effect of the section on dispositions of property has considerable tax consequences.

Where a gift is contingent (for example on the beneficiary reaching a certain age) the contingent beneficiary is entitled to income under section 31 if 18 or over. This means that such a beneficiary has an interest in possession for inheritance tax purposes. The death of such a beneficiary when an adult will, therefore, give rise to a charge to inheritance tax even though the contingency has not been satisfied.

Where a gift is contingent and there is a living beneficiary who is an infant the trustees have a discretion to use income for the maintenance, education and benefit of the beneficiary. There will, therefore, be a settlement without an interest in possession for inheritance tax purposes. The rules for accumulation and maintenance settlements will apply provided the infant will be entitled to capital or income at an age of 25 or less (he will be entitled to income at 18 unless the will has expressly excluded that right).

Where an infant is given a life interest the trustees have a discretion to use income for his maintenance, education and benefit. Any income not so used is accumulated, if the infant dies under 18 accumulated income is added to capital and devolves with capital. The infant does not, therefore, have an interest in possession until he reaches 18 and until that time the settlement will be an accumulation and maintenance settlement.

## F. Settlements and Capital Gains Tax

### 1. INTRODUCTION

The basic structure of capital gains tax was explained in Chapter    **7.17**
5. In this section we will consider the possible liability to capital gains tax, in relation to disposals of trust assets or interests in a trust, of:

    (a)   the settlor,
    (b)   the trustees, and
    (c)   the beneficiaries.

### 2. DEFINITION OF SETTLEMENT FOR CAPITAL GAINS TAX PURPOSES

"Settled property" is defined, by Capital Gains Tax Act 1979,    **7.18**
s.51, as any property held on trust other than property to which Capital Gains Tax Act, s.46, applies.

The property excluded from the definition of settled property by section 46 is assets held by a person:

    (a)   As nominee for another person; *or*
    (b)   As trustee for another person absolutely entitled as against the trustee. Such a bare trust often arises where property has been held on trust for a life tenant who has recently died and the trustees are holding the property while arranging to vest it in the remainderman. Another example of such a bare trust is where the trustees are preparing to transfer the assets to a beneficiary who has satisfied a contingency. The test for deciding whether a person is absolutely entitled as against the trustees is whether he has the exclusive right (subject only to paying the expenses of the trust) to direct how those assets shall be dealt with (section 46(2)). The beneficiary must, therefore, have the right to demand that the assets be handed over to him; *or*
    (c)   As a trustee for any person who would be so entitled but for being an infant or other person under disability. Thus, where land has been left to an infant,

since an infant cannot hold a legal estate in land, trustees will have to hold the property until the child reaches 18. If he must satisfy a contingency (such as reaching 18) before he can become absolutely entitled to the property the exception does not apply (*Tomlinson* v. *Glyn's Executor and Trustee Co.* (1970)).

Where the "trust" falls within one of the section 46(1) exceptions, the Capital Gains Tax Act applies as if the property were vested in the beneficiary and any acts of the nominee or trustee are treated as acts of the beneficiary. Thus, for example, when the trustees transfer assets to the remainderman after the death of the life tenant, no capital gains tax liability can arise.

Property held by two or more persons as joint tenants or tenants in common is not "settled property" provided they are together absolutely entitled to the property.

Trustees of settlements normally pay capital gains tax at a rate equivalent to the basic rate of income tax (in tax year 1990–91 this is 25 per cent.). However, in the case of settlements under which income is to be accumulated or paid at the discretion of any person, the trustees pay capital gains tax at a rate equivalent to the basic and additional rates of income tax (in tax year 1990–91 the additional rate is 10 per cent. so that the capital gains tax rate in such cases is 35 per cent. in all). This 35 per cent rate is payable on all trust gains whenever any part of the trust income for the year of assessment is liable to the additional rate of income tax. Where the settlor or spouse retain an interest in the settlement, gains are charged at the rates appropriate to the settlor (see below).

# G. Capital Gains Tax Liability of the Settlor

## 1. CREATING THE SETTLEMENT INTER VIVOS

**7.19** If the settlor transfers assets to trustees (whatever the terms of the settlement), this is a disposal. The gain or loss will be calculated in the normal way by deducting from the market value of the assets at the time of disposal, the deductions permitted by the Act, and any indexation allowance available (see paragraph 5.6.). The trustees will in turn acquire the assets at market value at the date of the disposal unless the hold-over relief is claimed.

In certain cases hold-over relief may be claimed so that no immediate charge to capital gains tax arises (see paragraph

5.13). Hold-over relief is available where the assets put into settlement are business assets. It is also available, regardless of the nature of the assets which are settled, where the creation of the settlement is a chargeable transfer for inheritance tax purposes but not where it is an exempt or potentially exempt transfer. This means that hold-over relief is available on the creation of a no interest in possession settlement. Where hold-over relief is available because there is a chargeable transfer, the settlor makes the election for relief, the trustees of the settlemet are not required to agree.

Should the disposal give rise to a loss, that loss can only be set against gains made by the settlor on other transfers to trustees of the same settlement since settlors and their trustees are "connected persons" (Capital Gains Tax Act 1979, ss.62(3) and 63(3)).

The potential liability to capital gains tax can arise even if the settlor has an interest as a beneficiary or is a trustee, or the sole trustee, of the settlement (Capital Gains Tax Act, s.53).

The Finance Act 1988 provides that where a settlor or his spouse has any interest in a settlement (for example, as a life tenant or as a beneficiary of a discretionary trust) gains of the settlement will be charged as gains of the settlor personally and not of the trustees. The settlor has a right to recover the tax paid from the trustees.

## 2. CREATING THE SETTLEMENT ON DEATH

**7.20** If the settlement is created on death there will be no disposal and so no capital gains tax liability will arise. The deceased settlor's personal representatives will acquire the assets at their market value at death. This will also be the acquisition price of the trustees (subject to any indexation allowance available to the personal representatives).

# H. Capital Gains Tax—The Liability of the Trustees

## 1. CHANGES IN TRUSTEES

**7.21** During the "life" of the settlement the persons holding office as trustees may change, whether by reason of death, retirement or removal. Whenever a new trustee is appointed the assets will have to be transferred to the newly constituted body of trustees. Section 51(1) of the Capital Gains Tax Act 1979 provides that settlement trustees are a continuing body of persons and disposals to the new trustees do not give rise to capital gains tax liability.

## 2. ACTUAL DISPOSALS

**7.22** The trustees may wish to dispose of items of trust property and replace them with new items. They may wish to sell assets to raise cash, whether to meet expenses or to be able to make a cash advance to a beneficiary. Whatever the reason for the disposal, if the trustees make an actual disposal of trust property they may become liable to capital gains tax.

Whether a gain or loss arises will be determined in the usual way. The indexation allowance is available to trustees.

The trustees can set the exemptions and reliefs they are entitled to claim against any chargeable gains realised. The exemptions and reliefs to which they are entitled include:

(a) the annual exemption which is normally half the exempt amount available to an individual (so that trustees currently get £2,700). However if the settlement is one of a number created by the same settlor the trustees of each settlement can claim one-tenth of the exempt amount available to an individual (so that such trustees will currently get £540) or, the annual exempt amount available to an individual (currently £5,000) divided by the number of trusts in the group, whichever is the greater;

(b) the principal private dwelling-house exemption given in the Capital Gains Tax Act 1979, ss.101–103, provided the house disposed of has been the only or main residence of a person entitled to occupy it under the terms of the settlement (s.104). Therefore, provided the trustees have been given a power to permit the beneficiary to occupy the house the exemption will apply, whether the beneficiary is a life tenant or the beneficiary under a discretionary trust (*Sansom* v. *Peay* (1976)).

(c) "Retirement" relief is available to trustees (under section 70(3) of the Finance Act 1985) on the disposal of shares in a company or assets used in a business which form part of the settled property. However, this relief is only available:

(i) if there is a beneficiary with an interest in possession in the settlement who is at least 60 (or is retiring on the grounds of ill health) and

(ii)   *either* the shares are in a company which has been his family company for at least a year and of which he has been a working director for at least a year but he has now ceased to be a director
*or* the assets have been used for at least a year by the beneficiary in his business.

If a disposal gives rise to a loss the trustees may set that loss against any gains they have made in the year of disposal and may carry forward unabsorbed losses to set against gains made in future years.

## 3. DEEMED DISPOSALS

*Persons becoming absolutely entitled as against the trustees*

Where a person becomes absolutely entitled to trust property as against the trustees, the Capital Gains Tax Act, s.54(1), provides that "all assets forming part of the settled property to which he becomes so entitled shall be deemed to have been disposed of by the trustee, and immediately reacquired by him in his capacity as a trustee within s.46(1) ... , for a consideration equal to their market value." Any capital gains tax payable is assessed at this point and thereafter the trustee holds as a bare trustee.

**7.23**

Section 54(1) applies where:

(a)   the trustees advance assets (other than cash) to a beneficiary (where he is a life tenant or a discretionary beneficiary); *or*

(b)   a beneficiary satisfies a contingency and so becomes entitled to all or part of the trust property; *or*

(c)   the settlement comes to an end as a result of the death of the life tenant and the remainderman becomes absolutely entitled to the property. (However, no tax is payable in this circumstance: see below, paragraph 7.24.).

The deemed disposal and reacquisition takes place as soon as the beneficiary becomes absolutely entitled as against the trustees, even though the assets may not be transferred for some time afterwards. Thus, if a person is entitled to property provided he reaches the age of 25, on his 25th birthday the trustees are deemed to dispose of the assets as settlement trustees and immediately to reacquire them as bare trustees for the beneficiary. Capital gains tax will be payable if a gain has arisen after taking account of exemptions, reliefs and allowances but there is no further liability when the assets are subsequently vested in the beneficiary.

Hold-over relief is available in certain circumstances when a beneficiary becomes absolutely entitled as against the trustees. If the settlement is an accumulation and maintenance settlement at the date the beneficiary becomes absolutely entitled, hold-over relief can be claimed by a joint election of trustees and beneficiary. The relief is also available on a joint election by trustees and beneficiary where there is a transfer by the trustees which is chargeable to inheritance tax; for example, an appointment of assets from a discretionary trust.

When a remainderman becomes absolutely entitled to the settled property following the death of the life tenant there is, again, a deemed disposal and reacquisition but no chargeable gain arises (section 56(1)(a)). This is in accordance with the general principle that death does not give rise to capital gains tax and so the remainderman has the benefit of a tax-free uplift in the base value of the settled property.

If the trustees have accrued losses from earlier transactions that they have been unable to set off against chargeable gains, section 54(2) provides that those losses are to be treated as if they accrued to the person becoming absolutely entitled, and not to the trustees.

*Death of the life tenant where the settlement continues*

**7.24** By section 55(1) of the Capital Gains Tax Act 1979 (as amended by section 84(1) of the Finance Act 1982) when a life interest in settled property (that continues to be settled after the death) comes to an end on the death of the life tenant, there is a deemed disposal and reacquisition at market value of the assets but no chargeable gain accrues on the disposal (subject to tax becoming payable on gains held-over when assets were transferred to the trustees).

Thus, if property is held on trust for persons in succession, for example "to A for life, remainder to B for life, remainder to C absolutely," on A's death there is a deemed disposal and reacquisition. However, no tax is payable on accrued gains unless gains were held-over when the trustees were originally given the assets. The trustees acquire the assets as trustees for B at the market value at the date of A's death. On B's death, the settlement comes to an end and C becomes absolutely entitled to the assets so that the provisions outlined in paragraph 7.23 will apply.

# I. Capital Gains Tax—The Liability of Beneficiaries

If a beneficiary is entitled to an interest in settled property, no **7.25** chargeable gain arises on the disposal of the interest unless it was acquired by the beneficiary (or a predecessor in title) for consideration in money or money's worth, other than consideration consisting of another interest under the settlement (section 58(1)). Thus if a life tenant sells his interest no gain arises but the purchaser may face a tax liability on any subsequent disposal.

If the beneficiary is entitled under one of the types of trusts within section 46 of the Capital Gains Tax Act 1979, (*i.e.* broadly speaking where he is the beneficiary of a bare trust—see above, paragraph 7.18) he is treated as if the assets were vested in him and so any disposals made by the trustees are taxed as if the beneficiary had disposed of the property. This means that the normal rules for calculating capital gains tax liability will apply and exemptions, reliefs and allowances the beneficiary is personally able to claim will be available; losses realised by the trustees can be used by the beneficiary (section 54(2)). Furthermore if the disposal by the trustees is to the beneficiary himself there is no capital gains tax liability.

# J. Settlements and Income Tax—Introduction

In Chapter 6 we considered the general rules for the taxation of **7.26** income and the particular rules that apply when a person dies. We saw that it is the personal representatives' responsibility to pay any outstanding income tax liability of the deceased and to pay tax on income that arises in the course of administering the estate. Once the administration period is complete the personal representatives' liability ceases.

If the beneficiaries have absolute interests in the residue, the capital of the residue will be transferred to them (see paragraph 6.20. for the income tax rules applying in these circumstances). However, if the will creates any type of trust which is to continue after the administration period the property will be vested in trustees and special tax rules will apply.

Will trusts are basically taxed in the same way as other trusts but since the settlor is dead when the trust becomes operative, the special anti-avoidance provisions relating to settlements contained in sections 660–694 of the Taxes Act 1988 (the "income deemed" provisions) cannot apply.

Trust income is taxed in two stages. The trustees are liable for basic rate tax in the first instance (although in certain circumstances they also pay the additional rate of 10 per cent). The position is then adjusted, if necessary, by charging the beneficiaries further tax or refunding tax to them, depending on their particular circumstances.

## K. Income Tax—the Liability of the Trustees

**7.27** The statutory income of trustees is calculated in the same way as for an individual by applying the rules of the various Schedules in the Taxes Act 1988. In calculating this figure, the trustees may deduct the expenses permitted by the appropriate Schedule.

Thus, if the trustees are carrying on a trade, the income derived from the trade is assessed in accordance with the provisions of Schedule D, Case I of the 1970 Act and they can deduct allowable business expenses. However, they cannot deduct the expenses of managing the trust itself (*Aikin* v. *MacDonald's Trustees* (1894)).

Having calculated the income of the trust the trustees are liable to pay income tax at the basic rate on *all* of the income without the deduction of any personal reliefs (which are only available to "individuals" and for these purposes trustees are not "individuals"). Trustees are not liable to higher rate tax regardless of the amount of the income. If trustees make a payment which is income in the hands of the beneficiary the trustee will have to pay basic rate tax on it even though it is paid out of capital (Taxes Act 1988, s.349, and see paragraph 7.28).

If income is paid directly to the beneficiary from its source, it is taxed in the hands of the beneficiary without the trustees paying basic rate tax (such a situation would arise where, for example, trustees ask a tenant of land owned by the trust to pay the rent to the beneficiary). If the trustees receive income net of basic rate tax (for example, as a result of receiving a dividend from a company) their basic rate tax liability has already been met and so need not be paid again.

Section 16 of the Finance Act 1973 requires the trustees of certain trusts to pay the "additional rate" (which is currently 10 per cent.) on so much of the income of the trust *as exceeds the expenses of managing the trust grossed up at basic rate.* The additional rate is payable on income which *inter alia*:—

(a) is income which is to be accumulated or which is payable at the discretion of the trustees or any other person (section 16(2)(*a*)) and

(b) is not the income of any person other than the trustees, nor treated as income of the settlor (section 16(2)(*b*)).

The additional rate will, thus, be payable on income of a settlement which is treated as an accumulation and maintenance settlement for inheritance tax purposes (see above, paragraph 7.7). It will also apply to most settlements which are treated as settlements without an interest in possession for inheritance tax purposes.

It should be noted that for the purposes of calculating liability to the additional rate of 10 per cent. the trustees deduct the trust expenses "properly" chargeable to income grossed up at basic rate from the trust income. The reason for this is that the additional rate is only chargeable on income which can be accumulated (and is not the income of any person other than the trustees). The income which can be accumulated is the trust income *after* the trust expenses have been paid. The expenses are grossed up at basic rate to reflect the fact that they were paid from taxed income. Expenses "properly" chargeable to income are those so chargeable as a matter of general law not those made chargeable to income by the trust instrument (*Carver* v. *Duncan* (1985)).

When the trustees of such a trust make a payment to a beneficiary, they pay it net of both the basic and the additional rate of tax. Therefore, the beneficiary will receive a tax credit of 35 per cent.

The application of these rules can be seen in the following example.

*Example*

The trustees carry on a trade and make a net profit of £20,000 after deduction of allowable expenses. They incur £750 expenses in the course of managing the trust.

(a) *If the additional rate is not payable.* The trustees pay basic rate tax (25 per cent.) on the trust income of £20,000 (this amounts to £5,000). From their net income of £15,000 they will pay the expenses of £750 leaving £14,250 net income available for the beneficiaries.

**Note:**
The beneficiaries will be given a certificate of deduction of income tax and will claim a tax credit for the basic rate tax paid in respect of the sums paid to them. When calculating their statutory income they will gross up the £14,250 to £19,000.

(b) *If the additional rate is payable.* The trustees will be liable to pay the additional rate of 10 per cent. as well as the basic rate tax liability (calculated as in (a) above). The trustees' liability to the additional rate is calculated as follows:

|  | £ | £ |
|---|---|---|
| Trust Income |  | 20,000 |
| *Less:* Trust expenses grossed up |  |  |
| *i.e.* £750 x $\dfrac{100}{75}$ = |  | (1,000) |
| Income liable to additional rate |  | 19,000 |
|  |  |  |
| Additional rate tax (£19,000 x 10%) |  | 1,900 |

| The income available to beneficiaries will be... |  |  |
|---|---|---|
| Trust Income |  | 20,000 |
| *Less:* Income tax (a) basic rate | (5,000) |  |
| (b) additional rate | (1,900) |  |
|  |  | (6,900) |
| Income after tax |  | 13,100 |
| *Less:* expenses paid |  | (750) |
| Net available income |  | 12,350 |

**Note:**
If the trustees pay to or apply any of the net available income for a beneficiary they must supply a certificate of deduction of income tax to that beneficiary. When calculating his statutory income the beneficiary will gross up any amounts received at 35 per cent. In the above example if the whole of the available income of £12,350 was applied to one beneficiary that beneficiary would include in his statutory income £12,350 grossed up to £19,000.

The question of when the trustees must pay the additional rate depends on whether or not a beneficiary has a *right* to trust income; this is discussed in the next paragraph.

## L. Income Tax—the Liability of the Beneficiaries

The position differs depending on whether or not any beneficiary has a right to the trust income.

### 1. BENEFICIARIES WITH A RIGHT TO TRUST INCOME

A beneficiary who has a *right* to trust income is taxed on the income when it arises irrespective of whether or not it is paid over to him. Such a right arises when the beneficiary has a vested interest in the income of the trust. A direction to accumulate income will not destroy a vested interest in it provided the accumulated income *must* be paid to the beneficiary or to the estate of the beneficiary at some time.

**7.28**

Three examples of trusts where beneficiaries have vested interests in the income are where the beneficiary has:

(a) A life interest in a trust fund, for example "to A for life." (However, if A is under 18 and section 31 of the Trustee Act applies there will be no right to income and A will effectively have only an interest contingent on reaching 18).

(b) A vested interest in accumulating income, for example "to A but the income to be accumulated for 10 years and then paid to A or A's estate." A has no right to receive the income immediately but it is certain that A or A's estate will receive it in 10 years' time.

(c) A right to income conferred by section 31 of the Trustee Act (for example, where a beneficiary has an interest in the capital of the fund contingent on reaching an age greater than 18 and has reached 18).

In these circumstances the trustees will have paid the basic rate tax on the trust income and the beneficiary will include in his "statutory income" for the appropriate tax year the income available to him, that is the gross trust income less the trustees' expenses grossed up at basic rate. The grossed up income must be included even if no income is actually paid to (or applied for) the beneficiary. When the tax liability is calculated the beneficiary will claim a basic rate tax credit which satisfies his liability to basic rate tax. If he is not liable to pay even basic rate (*e.g.* because of unused personal reliefs) he can reclaim the tax from the Revenue. If he is a higher rate taxpayer he will have to pay the difference between his higher rate and the basic rate to the Revenue.

When calculating the tax liability the beneficiary is assessed on the income under the Schedule or Case of the Taxes Act 1988 appropriate to the source of the income (*Baker* v. *Archer-Shee* (1927)). Most trust income will be derived from sources which would provide investment income in the hands of an individual. However, some trusts may derive their income from a trade carried on by the trustees. In such a case, the beneficiary would be assessed under Schedule D Case I although the income would be treated as *investment* income, not earned income, since it will not be income immediately derived by the beneficiary from the carrying on by him of the trade.

The following example illustrates the way in which the tax liability of a beneficiary of a trust is calculated.

*Example*
The trustees of a trust for A for life, remainder to B receive £10,000 gross income from the trust property and incur £750 expenses in managing the trust. A has a vested interest in the income of the trust fund and his only other source of income is a share of partnership profits of £18,000. He has no charges on income. The trustees pay to A £6,750 (that is the trust income of £10,000 less basic rate tax of £2,500 and the trust expenses of £750.)

The tax liability of A is calculated as follows:

| | £ |
|---|---|
| *Statutory income* | |
| Profits (DI) | 18,000 |
| Net trust income grossed up at basic rate (*i.e.* £6,750 x $\frac{100}{75}$ ) | 9,000 |
| *Total income* | 27,000 |
| *Less:* Personal relief | (3,005) |
| *Taxable income* | 23,995 |

Tax liability is calculated as follows:

| | | |
|---|---|---|
| £20,700 @ 25% | £5,175 | |
| £3,295 @ 40% | £1,318 | 6,493 |
| *Less* Tax Credit (£9,000 @ 25%) | | (2,250) |
| To pay | | 4,243 |

*Payments from capital.*
If a beneficiary with a vested interest in the trust income receives a payment that is income in his hands, he will pay income tax on it even if the trustees make the payment from capital (*Michelham's Trustees* v. *I.R.C.* (1930)). This situation can arise where the trust fund bears an annuity. If the trust income is insufficient to meet the annuity, the trustees will have to make up the balance by using the capital of the trust. The annuity will be regarded as income in the hands of the beneficiary (*Brodie's Will Trustees* v. *I.R.C.* (1933)).

2. BENEFICIARIES WITH NO RIGHT TO TRUST INCOME

A beneficiary will have no *right* to trust income if his 7.29 entitlement to receive income depends on his satisfying a contingency or depends on the trustees exercising a discretion in his favour. The income is treated as the income of the trustees who will pay the basic and the additional rate of tax (the calculation was illustrated in paragraph 7.27).

The most common examples of trusts falling within this category are discretionary trusts and trusts where the income is being accumulated for a person with no vested right to the income (such as accumulation and maintenance settlements as defined for inheritance tax purposes in Inheritance Tax Act 1984, s.71).

While the income is merely being accumulated, it is not taxed as part of the contingent beneficiary's income. However, if a payment of income is made to a beneficiary the amount paid must be treated as part of the beneficiary's income and he will have to gross it up at the basic and additional rates, that is at 35 per cent. A 35 per cent. tax credit can be claimed and the beneficiary's excess liability or right to claim a rebate will then be calculated in the normal way.

This can best be illustrated by an example.

*Example*

The trustees hold property on trust for the children of A provided they reach the age of 25. The settlement satisfies the requirements of the Inheritance Tax Act 1984, s.71, with regard to the trustees' discretion as to maintenance etc and accumulation. The only child, X, is under 18 and the trustees decide to apply all the income of the trust to X (X has no other income). The trustees receive £20,000 gross income and incur £750 in trust expenses.

(a) The net income available for X's maintenance, education and benefit is £12,350 (the calculation was explained at paragraph 7.27).

(b) X's tax liability:

| | £ |
|---|---|
| *Statutory income* | |
| Trust income grossed up at 35% | |
| $£12,350 \times \dfrac{100}{65} =$ | 19,000 |
| *Less:* Personal relief | (3,005) |
| *Taxable income* | 15,995 |
| Tax liability is: £15,995 @ 25% | 3,998.75 |

From his total tax liability of £3,998.75 X can deduct his 35 per cent. tax credit of £6,650. He has, therefore, a right to claim a rebate of £2,651.25, making his net receipts from the income of the trust £15,001.25.

**Note:**
Since the beneficiary can claim a 35 per cent. tax credit on income applied for his benefit, the trustees should bear this in mind when deciding whether or not to apply income for the beneficiary.

Since the beneficiary only suffers income tax liability on income advanced to him, an accumulation trust may be advantageous from an income tax point of view for individuals suffering the higher rates of tax since the rate of tax on income accumulated is 35 per cent. whereas the highest rate of tax on income received by an individual is 40 per cent. When the accumulations are later paid to a beneficiary they have become capital and so escape further income tax. However, inheritance tax may then be payable if it is not an accumulation and maintenance settlement as defined by the Inheritance Tax Act 1984, s.71 (see above, paragraph 7.7), so that care should be taken with this method of saving tax. Furthermore this course would be most inadvisable if the beneficiaries would be paying less than 35 per cent. tax since they can reclaim tax only in respect of income which has been advanced to them, not in respect of accumulated income. If the settlement gives trustees a discretion to pay income to beneficiaries or to accumulate it, the trustees could maximise tax-saving by exercising the discretion to the extent that the beneficiaries' income would not be liable to more than 35 per cent. tax.

## M. Income Tax, Capital Gains Tax and Trustee Act 1925, s.31

*Income Tax*

Section 31 of the Trustee Act is not a tax provision. However, since it can affect a beneficiary's right to income it can affect the income tax liability of trustees and beneficiaries. **7.30**

Section 31 (see Chapter 11 for a full discussion) provides that where there is income available to an infant (whether he has a vested or a contingent interest) the trustees of the trust may at their sole discretion apply the whole or part of such income for or towards the infant's maintenance, education or benefit and to the extent that they do not they must accumulate the whole or part of such income.

If, after reaching the age of 18, the beneficiary has not attained a vested interest in such income the trustees *shall* thereafter pay the income (together with any income produced by investments bought with accumulated income) to the beneficiary until the beneficiary either attains a vested interest or dies or until his interest fails.

Once the infant reaches the age of 18 the trustees must decide what is to happen to income that has been accumulated (and therefore capitalised).

In all cases, except one, the accumulated income is added to capital and devolves with it. Thus, whoever takes the capital takes the accumulations.

The exceptional case is that of an infant with a life interest. If the infant reaches 18 any income which has been accumulated is paid to him. However, if the infant dies before reaching 18 the accumulated income is added to capital and devolves with it. An infant with a life interest, therefore, has no *right* to receive income until he reaches the age of 18 (since the trustees may decide to accumulate it) and cannot be certain of ever receiving the accumulations (since he may die before reaching 18).

Section 31 can, therefore, *give* certain beneficiaries a right to income where prima facie they had no such right under the terms of the trust. It can also *prevent* beneficiaries having a right to income which under the terms of the trust they would otherwise have enjoyed.

The effect, if any, of section 31 on income tax liability can be illustrated by examples.

(a) *T's will gives 20,000 shares to A for life (A is aged six)*. If section 31 did not apply, A would have *a right* to receive the income from the shares and the trustees would pay basic rate tax only. A would include the grossed up income on his income tax return and might be liable to excess liability or might be entitled to a repayment depending on his circumstances.

However, if section 31 applies the trustees have a discretion whether to apply income for A's benefit and A, therefore, has no *right* to receive current income until he reaches 18. He has no right to receive accumulated income until he reaches 18. A is, therefore, treated as having an interest contingent on reaching 18. The trustees therefore pay basic rate tax *and* the additional rate of tax. A will include income actually applied for his maintenance on his tax return. (Excess liability or a right to a rebate may arise depending on A's circumstances). Once A reaches 18 he will obtain a right to current income. The trustees will pay basic rate tax only.

(b) *T's will gives 20,000 shares to A if he reaches 25 (A is aged six)*. If section 31 did not apply A would have no *right* to the income until reaching 25 and the trustees would pay basic rate tax *and* additional rate tax. Nothing would be included on A's tax return in respect of the trust income.

However, if section 31 applies A will have no right to the trust income *until* 18. The trustees will pay basic rate and additional rate tax. The trustees may choose to apply income for his benefit. Nothing will be included on A's tax return except to the extent that income is applied for his benefit. Amounts actually applied in this way will be included on A's tax return grossed up at 35 per cent. A may have to pay excess liability or may be able to claim a rebate depending on his circumstances.

From 18 to 25 A will have a right to the income and therefore, the trustees will pay basic rate tax only. A will include the grossed up amount in his tax return (grossed up at

25 per cent.) and again may be liable to extra tax or entitled to claim a refund depending on his circumstances.

*Capital gains tax*
Trustees pay capital gains tax on gains realised by them on trust **7.31** assets at the rate of 25 per cent. *except* in the case of accumulation or discretionary trusts when the rate is the sum of the basic and additional rates of income tax (currently 35 per cent). A trust is an accumulation or discretionary trust where all or any part of the income arising to the trustees in a year of assessment is liable to the additional rate of income tax.

Thus, whenever section 31 alters the liability of trustees to pay the additional rate of income tax on any part of the trust income it also alters the rate at which capital gains tax is charged.

# 8. Grants

## A. Types of Grant

A grant of representation is an order of the High Court. The **8.1**
High Court has exclusive jurisdiction to make grants in England
and Wales. Since October 1, 1971 the Family Division of the
High Court has exercised the jurisdiction to make grants
(section 1(4) of the Administration of Justice Act 1970). The
Chancery Division and the county court have certain powers in
probate cases but these do not include a power to make grants;
these powers will be considered in Chapter 9.

There are three basic types of grant of representation:

   (i)   A grant of probate;
  (ii)   A grant of letters of administration with will annexed;
       and
 (iii)   A grant of letters of administration (commonly called
       a grant of simple administration).

A grant once made serves two main purposes. First, it
establishes the authority of the personal representative. Secondly, it establishes either the validity of the deceased's will (in
the case of probate or administration with will annexed) or that
the deceased died intestate (in the case of simple administration).

## B. Capacity to Take a Grant

Any person, including an alien, a minor, a corporation, a **8.2**
bankrupt, a convicted criminal, or a mentally disordered person
may be *appointed* an executor by a will. Similarly any such
person may prima facie be entitled to a grant of letters of
administration.

However, a minor cannot *take* a grant of representation and
therefore the grant is made to an adult for the use and benefit
of the minor. Such a grant will usually be limited to the period

of incapacity so that the minor may take out a grant on attaining majority.

Similar rules apply to mentally disordered persons (that is persons who are incapable of managing their own affairs).

Where an alien resident outside the jurisdiction, a bankrupt or a criminal is entitled to a grant no special rules apply. However, in each case the court may exercise its discretion to pass over the person entitled and make a grant to some other person entitled (Supreme Court Act 1981, s.116).

After the coming into force of the Family Law Reform Act 1987 the fact that a person's parents were not married to each other at the time of his birth is irrelevant for the purposes of succession to property and is therefore irrelevant for the purpose of entitlement to a grant of representation (unless a contrary intention has been expressed in a will left by the deceased). Section 21 of the 1987 Act does provide, however, that a deceased person shall be presumed not to have been survived by any person whose parents were not married to each other at the time of his birth (or who is related through such a person). The presumption can be rebutted by evidence to the contrary. This provision is designed to facilitate the administration by making it unnecessary to carry out investigations.

## C. Grant of Probate

### 1. THE EXECUTOR APPOINTED BY WILL

**8.3** Normally the only person who may obtain a grant of probate is the executor appointed by the deceased in his will (or in a codicil validly supplementing or amending the will). An executor is a person appointed by the will to administer the deceased's property. The will may appoint several executors but not more than four persons may take out a grant in respect of the same part of the estate.

Since most testators want to choose a person to administer the estate, a properly drafted will should expressly provide for the appointment of an executor; for example, by including a clause which says "I appoint X of [address] to be the executor of this will." The person named should be someone suitable to act as executor and who is willing to take a grant. The appointment may describe rather than name the executor; for example, "I appoint the Vicar of St. James's Church in the parish of [....] to be the executor of this will" but such appointments are unwise since they may be ambiguous.

The appointment of an executor may be implied in cases where the will shows an intention that a particular person should perform the functions of an executor even though he is not expressly described as an executor. Such a person is described as "an executor according to the tenor of the will." For example, in *In the Goods of Baylis* (1865) the will directed that named persons should pay the debts of the estate and then hold the estate on trust for sale for the deceased's children. Lord Penzance held that since the "trustees" were to get in the whole estate, pay the debts and distribute the property the clear intention was that they should act as executors; therefore they were entitled to a grant. The appointment of a trustee without a direction that he is to pay the debts of the estate is not sufficient to make him executor according to the tenor (*In The Estate of McKenzie* (1909)).

A firm (for example, of solicitors) may be named as executors. However, since the office is a personal one this is treated as an appointment of all the individual partners in the firm. Great care should be taken with such appointments since, in the absence of clear words to the contrary, the partners in the firm at the date on which the will is made (rather than the partners at the date of death) are the executors and they may be unavailable or unwilling to act at the time of the death. (The drafting problems connected with appointment of a firm will be considered in Chapter 22).

2. APPOINTMENT OTHER THAN BY WILL

**8.4**  A will may validly appoint someone to nominate an executor (in such a case the person appointed may nominate himself). Such a provision in a will would seldom be advantageous but if included a time limit should be imposed on the making of the appointment.

One executor is always sufficient even where there is a minority or life interest. However, the court has a rarely exercised power to appoint an additional personal representative to act with a sole executor in the administration of the estate (Supreme Court Act 1981, s.114(4)). Such a person is not described as an executor but would seem to have the same powers as an executor.

Under the Administration of Estates Act 1925, s.22, trustees of settled land of which the deceased was tenant for life and which remains settled land after his death are deemed appointed executors in respect of the settled land alone.

Under section 50(1)(*a*) of the Administration of Justice Act 1985 the court may appoint a person to be a personal representative in substitution for an existing personal representative. If the substitute is to act with an existing executor he is also an executor, in any other case he is an administrator.

3. CHAIN OF REPRESENTATION (ADMINISTRATION OF ESTATES ACT 1925, S.7)

**8.5**   Where the sole or last surviving executor dies before completing the administration of the estate a grant of letters of administration *de bonis non administratis* may be made to the person entitled under rule 20 of the Non-Contentious Probate Rules 1987 (see below, paragraphs 8.33–8.36). Where one of a number of executors dies there is no need for a further grant; the remaining executor or executors having full power to complete the administration.

However, where a sole or last surviving proving executor (other than an executor substituted under section 50(1)(*a*) of the Administration of Justice Act 1985) dies *having himself appointed an executor*, the latter, on taking a grant of probate in respect of the executor's estate, automatically becomes the executor of the original testator as well so that a grant of administration to the original estate is not needed (Administration of Estates Act 1925, s.7).

*Example*
A appoints B to be his executor and B appoints C. On A's death B will become his executor and may take a grant of probate. If B dies without having completed the administration of A's estate and C takes a grant of probate of B's estate he will automatically become executor of A as well as B.

This is called the chain of representation. There may be more than two links in the chain. To continue the same example, if C appoints D to be his executor and C then dies without completing the administration of the estates and D takes out a grant of probate in respect of C's estate D will automatically become the executor of A and B as well as of C.

The chain of representation only applies where there is a grant of *probate* to the executor of a person who had himself taken out a grant of probate in respect of someone else's estate. Thus, the chain of representation is broken (and a grant of administration *de bonis non* is required) where:

(i) an executor dies intestate or without appointing an executor; or

(ii) an executor dies having appointed an executor but that executor has predeceased; or

(iii) an executor dies having appointed an executor but that executor fails to take out a grant in respect of the original executor's estate.

The chain of representation can be said to pass from *proving executor* to *proving executor*. There is, therefore, no chain of representation where no executor has been appointed. For example, A dies intestate, B takes out a grant of letters of administration and then B dies having appointed C to be his executor. C does not become the executor of A.

The appointment of an administrator will usually break the chain of representation. However, a temporary appointment does not do so.

*Example*

A appoints B to be his executor, B appoints C and dies. C is a minor when B dies. A grant of administration is made in respect of B's estate to D. D does not become A's executor. When, however, C reaches majority he may take out a grant of probate in respect of B's estate. If he does so he will then automatically become A's executor.

Similarly a person who becomes executor through the chain of representation may cease to be executor when someone else takes out a grant of probate in respect of the deceased's estate.

*Example*

A appoints B and C to be his executors: when A dies B is an adult and C a minor. A grant will be made to B alone but C is said to have "power reserved," *i.e.* he can take out a grant when he reaches majority. If B dies without completing the administration of A's estate appointing D his executor while C is still a minor, D will become A's executor on taking out probate of B's estate. However, if on reaching 18 C takes out a grant in respect of A's estate, D will cease to be A's executor.

This is because the chain of representation can only operate on the death of the *last proving* executor.

## 4. LIMITED, CONDITIONAL AND SUBSTITUTIONAL APPOINTMENTS

**8.6** Most wills appoint one or more persons to act as executor for the whole of the deceased's estate and without limit as to time. However, an appointment may be limited, for example a grant may:

(i) be limited in time (the appointment may, for example, appoint one person until another person reaches the age of majority);

(ii) be limited to certain property (for example, one executor may be appointed to deal with the deceased's general estate and another to deal with business property or literary effects).

Limited grants are dealt with in more detail in paragraphs 8.23–8.32 below.

An appointment may also be conditional. For example, "I appoint A to be my executor provided he is a partner in the firm of A B and Co at the date of my death."

A will may also validly provide for a substitutional appointment. For example "I appoint A to be my executor but if he is unable or unwilling to act then I appoint B." B may take out a grant once A has renounced probate or died.

## 5. EFFECT OF GRANT OF PROBATE

*Conclusive proof of content and execution of will*
**8.7** A grant of probate in respect of a particular will is conclusive evidence as to the terms of the will of the deceased and that it was duly executed. If a will is found to be defective (for example, because it is found not to have been properly executed or a later will is discovered) after a grant of probate, the probate must be revoked (see paragraphs 8.38–8.40) if that will is to be made ineffective.

*Confirmation of executors' authority*
**8.8** A grant of probate merely confirms the authority of the executor conferred by the will. The authority derives from the will. An executor may, therefore, deal with the estate of the deceased without first taking out a grant (see Chapter 11). However, a grant is in practice necessary to prove to other people that the executor has authority to deal with the property

of the deceased and to pass a good title to any land in the estate.

## 6. EXECUTOR DE SON TORT

The term executor *de son tort* means literally executor as a result of his own wrong. The expression is unfortunate since the noun is wholly misleading and the adjectival phrase almost as much so. An executor *de son tort* is a person who deals with the estate of a deceased person by intermeddling with it as if he were an executor or administrator. Acts which have been held to amount to intermeddling include selling property, paying debts, collecting debts and carrying on the business of the deceased. However, acts of charity, humanity or necessity are not sufficient. Thus, arranging the deceased's funeral, ordering necessary goods for the deceased's dependents and protecting the deceased's property by moving it to a safe place have been held not to amount to intermeddling.

**8.9**

An executor *de son tort* has no authority to act in the estate of the deceased and can obtain no rights from his intermeddling. However, a person who is in fact the deceased's executor and who intermeddles loses the right to renounce probate and so can be cited to take a grant (see paragraphs 10.61–10.64).

The effect of being an executor *de son tort* is that such a person becomes liable to the creditors and beneficiaries to the extent of the real and personal estate coming to his hands as if he were an executor (Administration of Estates Act 1925, s.28). He is also liable for inheritance tax to the extent of such property.

An executor *de son tort* can bring his liability to creditors and beneficiaries to an end by delivering the assets he has received (or their value) to the lawful executor or administrator before the creditors or beneficiaries bring an action against him.

## 7. POWER RESERVED TO PROVE AT A LATER DATE

A will may appoint several people to act as co-executors. It is unnecessary for them all to join in taking the grant if they do not wish to. Those who do not take the grant may renounce their rights but if they prefer not to renounce they may have power reserved to them to take the grant at a later date if it proves desirable. Where an application for probate is made and power is to be reserved to some executors to prove at a later date, notice of the application must be given to the non-proving executors, and the oath for executors, filed when the application

**8.10**

for the grant is made, must state that this notice has been given (Non-Contentious Probate Rules 1987, rule 27(1)).

# D. Grant of Letters of Administration with Will Annexed

### 1. CIRCUMSTANCES IN WHICH GRANT IS MADE

**8.11** A grant of letters of administration with will annexed (also called a grant *cum testamento annexo*) is made when the deceased has left a valid will and a grant of probate cannot be made to an executor. Such a situation arises where the will makes no appointment of an executor, where the executor predeceases, where the executor has validly renounced probate and where the executor has been cited but has not taken a grant of probate (see paragraphs 10.61–10.64). A grant of administration with will annexed is also made in certain cases where an earlier grant of probate or administration with will annexed has been made but the personal representative appointed by the earlier grant has been unable to complete the administration of the estate (see paragraphs 8.33–8.36).

### 2. PERSONS ENTITLED TO THE GRANT

**8.12** Rule 20 of the Non-Contentious Probate Rules 1987 contains a list of the persons who are entitled to take out a grant of administration with the will annexed. The list follows the order of entitlement to property under the will. Persons who come earlier in the list will take a grant in preference to those who come later. If there is no executor able and willing to act, the following are entitled:

(i) *Any residuary legatee or devisee holding in trust for any other person.* For example, residue is given to X and Y on trust for A and B. X and Y are the residuary legatees holding on trust and so have the first right to a grant. This is logical since the testator by appointing X and Y as trustees has shown that he is willing that they should deal with his property.

(ii) *Any other residuary legatee or devisee (including one for life), or where the residue is not wholly disposed of by the will, any person entitled to share in the undisposed of residue (including the Treasury Solicitor when claiming* bona vacantia *on behalf of the Crown).* For example, residue is given to A, B, C and D in equal shares; each will be entitled to take the grant. If D predeceased the testator and X was entitled to take the quarter of residue undisposed of, X would be equally entitled to the grant.

There are two provisos to this category:

(a)   unless a registrar otherwise directs, a residuary legatee or devisee whose legacy or devise is vested in interest shall be preferred to one entitled on the happening of a contingency, and

(b)   where the residue is not in terms wholly disposed of, the registrar may, if he is satisfied that the testator has nevertheless disposed of the whole or substantially the whole of the known estate, allow a grant to be made to any legatee or devisee entitled to, or to share in, the estate so disposed of, without regard to the persons entitled to share in any residue not disposed of by the will.

(iii) *The personal representative of any residuary legatee or devisee (but not one for life, or one holding in trust for any other person), or of any person entitled to share in any residue not disposed of by the will.* For example, residue is given to A and B in equal shares; A predeceases the testator and X is entitled to take the half share of residue undisposed of. If X and B both die before taking a grant the personal representatives of either will be entitled to the grant.

(iv) *Any other legatee or devisee (including one for life or one holding in trust for any other person) or any creditor of the deceased.* For example, a house is left to A and £1,000 to B. Either is entitled to the grant unless a registrar otherwise directs. A legatee or devisee whose legacy or devise is vested in interest shall be preferred to one entitled on the happening of a contingency.

(v) *The personal representative of any other legatee or devisee (but not one for life or one holding in trust for any other person) or of any creditor of the deceased.* For example, if A and B in the previous example survive the testator but die before taking a grant the personal representatives of either will be entitled to the grant.

Rule 27(4) and (6) of the Non-Contentious Probate Rules 1987 provides that where two or more persons are entitled in the same degree (*i.e.* come into the same paragraph above) a grant may be made to any of them without notice to the others (contrast the position with grants of probate, see paragraph 8.10) and that disputes between persons entitled in the same degree are to be decided by a registrar. (For the procedure see paragraph 10.60).

Living beneficiaries are to be preferred to the personal representative of deceased beneficiaries entitled in the same degree and adults to infants entitled in the same degree unless a registrar directs to the contrary (rule 27(5)). If the whole estate of the deceased is assigned by the beneficiaries, the assignees have the same right to a grant as the assignors (rule 24).

3. THE EFFECT OF A GRANT

*Conclusive proof of content and execution of will*

8.13 A grant of administration with will annexed is like a grant of probate in that it is conclusive evidence as to content and execution of the will.

*Conferral of authority on administrator*

8.14 A grant of probate merely confirms the authority of executors. However, a grant of letters of administration *confers* authority on the administrator and vests the deceased's property in him (until the grant is made the property of a deceased who appoints no executor is technically vested in the President of the Family Division of the High Court). Once made the grant does not relate back to the date of death of the deceased except to the extent that relation back would (at the time of the grant) be beneficial to the estate (see paragraph 11.4).

# E. Grant of Simple Administration

1. CIRCUMSTANCES IN WHICH GRANT IS MADE

8.15 A grant of simple administration is made when there is no will capable of being admitted to probate (or of being annexed to letters of administration).

Simple administration is appropriate in the vast majority of cases where there is a total intestacy. However, if there is an admissible will which does not deal with property (for example, a will merely appointing executors) a grant of probate may be made. Similarly a will is admissible to probate (or may be annexed to letters of administration) where it purports to deal with property but all the gifts fail.

## 2. PERSONS ENTITLED TO TAKE A GRANT

Rule 22 of the Non-Contentious Probate Rules 1987 contains an **8.16** order of the persons who are entitled to take out a grant of simple administration. The order follows the order of entitlement to the estate on intestacy and says that the persons entitled are, in the order listed and provided that they have a beneficial interest in the estate:

   (i)   the surviving husband or wife of the deceased,
   (ii)  children of the deceased (and the issue of a child who has predeceased),
   (iii) the parents of the deceased,
   (iv)  the brothers and sisters of the whole blood of the deceased (and the issue of any brothers or sisters who have predeceased),
   (v)   brothers and sisters of the half blood of the deceased (and the issue of any who have predeceased),
   (vi)  grandparents,
   (vii) uncles and aunts of the whole blood (and the issue of any who have predeceased),
   (viii) uncles and aunts of the half blood (and the issue of any who have predeceased).

Since a beneficial interest is required the entitlement to a grant depends in part on the size of the estate. For example, if the deceased died leaving a spouse but no issue and with an estate of £80,000 (plus personal chattels) the parents (if surviving) or brothers and sisters would not be entitled under this provision since the estate would all go to the spouse. They would, however, be entitled if the deceased's estate was £140,000.

Rule 22(2) provides that if no-one is entitled as being in any of the above categories the Treasury Solicitor may take out a grant if he claims *bona vacantia* on behalf of the crown.

Rule 22(3) provides that a grant may be made to a creditor of the deceased or to a person who would be entitled to a beneficial interest in the estate if there were an accretion to the estate provided that all those entitled according to rule 22(1) and (2) are cleared off. Thus, in the example given above (a deceased with an estate of £80,000 and personal chattels who is survived by spouse but no issue) the parents (if surviving) would have a right to a grant if the spouse had been cleared off. If the parents have predeceased then the brothers and sisters would have a right to a grant.

The personal representative of a person who survives the deceased but dies before taking a grant is entitled in the same degree as the person whom he represents (rule 22(4)). However, unless a registrar otherwise directs where a number of persons are entitled in the same degree, a person of full age is to be preferred to the guardian of a minor and a living person is to be preferred over the personal representative of a dead person (rule 27(5)). Furthermore, relatives in ii–viii above are to be preferred to the personal representative of a spouse unless the spouse is entitled to the *whole* of the estate as ascertained at the time of application for the grant.

*Example*
H dies survived by spouse and children. The spouse dies before obtaining a grant. The spouse's personal representative will be able to take a grant if the estate is not more than £75,000 plus personal chattels but if it is larger then the children will have priority.

3. EFFECT OF A GRANT

**8.17** The effect of a grant of simple administration is the same as that of a grant of administration with will annexed except that it provides conclusive evidence of intestacy rather than as to the contents and terms of the will.

# F. Renunciation

**8.18** A person who is entitled to a grant of probate or administration may renounce his entitlement unless he has lost the right to renounce. Renunciation is made in writing to the registry. The most convenient way to deal with any renunciation is to submit it with the papers submitted by a person who does wish to take a grant.

An executor accepts office and thereby loses his right to renounce if he intermeddles in the estate (the principles are the same as those applying to a person constituting himself an executor *de son tort* so that the performance of acts of charity, humanity or necessity does not deprive the executor of his right to renounce). A potential administrator does not lose his right to renounce if he intermeddles. Both an executor and an administrator lose their rights to renounce if a grant is made in their favour.

A renunciation of probate by an executor does not operate as a renunciation of any right to administration which he may have unless that right is also renounced (Non-Contentious Probate Rules 1987, rule 37(1)). However, a renunciation of administration in one capacity in effect operates to renounce *all* rights to a grant of administration.

Once a renunciation has been made it may only be retracted on the order of a registrar (rule 37(3)). The Court will only allow the retraction of a renunciation if it can be shown to be for the benefit of the estate or of the persons interested in the estate (*Re Gill* (1873)).

## G. Number of Personal Representatives

Section 114(1) of the Supreme Court Act 1981 provides that **8.19** "probate or administration shall not be granted ... to more than four persons in respect of the same part of the estate of a deceased person." This means that if more than four executors are appointed in respect of all or any part of the estate a grant can be made to only four of them. Power may be reserved to the others so that they can take a grant if a vacancy occurs (for example on the death of one of the four who has taken a grant). Similarly if more than four persons are equally entitled to a grant of administration (of either type) the grant cannot be made to more than four. If any dispute arises as to which of more than four persons are to take a grant it is resolved by a hearing before a registrar brought by summons in the principal registry (Non-Contentious Probate Rules 1987, rule 27(6)).

The minimum number of executors is always one although the court has a discretion to appoint one or more additional personal representatives to act with the sole executor while there is a minority of a beneficiary or life interest subsisting in the estate (Supreme Court Act 1981, s.114(4)). An application for such an appointment may be made by any person interested in the estate or the guardian or receiver of any such person.

The minimum number of administrators is generally one unless there is a minor beneficiary or a life interest in the estate where the appointment must normally be made to a trust corporation (with or without an individual) or to not less than two individuals (Supreme Court Act 1981, s.114(2)). However, the court has a discretion to appoint a sole administrator where there is a minority or life interest if it appears to the court "to be expedient in all the circumstances." (Supreme Court Act 1981, s.114(2)).

Where two administrators are necessary they may often be persons who have different entitlements to a grant.

*Example*

T dies intestate survived by a spouse and children and the estate is sufficiently large for the children to have an interest in it. The surviving spouse is entitled to a grant. A second administrator is required and so any adult child may be co-administrator.

There is no requirement in cases of a minority or life interest that the numbers be maintained. Thus, if one of two administrators dies the survivor can continue alone.

# H. Special Rules as to Appointment of Personal Representatives

### 1. AFTER RENUNCIATION

**8.20**   It may appear from what has been said so far that the choice of executor or administrator is automatic. However, this is far from being the case in all circumstances. The person with the best entitlement to a grant may renounce (see paragraph 8.18 above) in which case the rules are applied as if that person had predeceased the testator. Thus:

> (i)   if an executor renounces (unless there is another executor willing to act) a grant of administration with will annexed will be made to the person with the best entitlement to a grant under rule 20;
>
> (ii)  if a person with the best entitlement under rule 20 (or rule 22 if there is an intestacy) renounces the person next in the list will have a right to a grant.

### 2. PASSING-OVER

**8.21**   The High Court has power under the Supreme Court Act 1981, s.116 to pass over the person entitled to a grant if "it appears ... to be necessary or expedient to appoint as administrator some person other than [the person entitled to take a grant]." When this power is exercised the court may appoint any person to be the administrator so that it does not necessarily appoint the person with the next best right to a grant or indeed a person with any right. Under section 115(1)(*b*) the Court also has power to grant administration to a trust corporation either solely or jointly with another person.

The power to pass over the person entitled to a grant is discretionary so that no exact rules can be laid down as to when the power will be exercised. However, two types of case may be recognised.

First, where the persons entitled request the appointment of their nominee. In *Teague and Ashdown* v. *Wharton* (1871) Lord Penzance held that a mere request was insufficient to enable the court to pass over those entitled since " ... persons entitled to grants ... are many of them persons who have no opportunity of knowing their own rights, and are not aware of the dangers that may beset them if they transfer these rights to other persons."

In *Re Potter* (1899) Gorell Barnes J. made a grant at the request of the persons who were entitled to a grant. It should be noted that in that case there were other special circumstances and that in his remarkably short judgment the judge seemed to place reliance on the fact that the appointment was made with the agreement of all the persons *interested* in the estate and not merely with the agreement of the persons entitled to a grant. It would seem, therefore, that the court will not pass over those entitled merely because they request that course.

Secondly, the Court may pass over a personal representative who is himself unsuitable for that office either in general or in the circumstances of the case. For example, in *In the Estate of Crippen* (1911) the deceased had been murdered by her husband; she had died intestate and normally he would have taken her property. He would also have been entitled to take a grant to her estate and, as he was dead, his personal representatives would have taken the grant. However, there is a rule of public policy that a person who slays another loses his entitlement to that person's property (see Chapter 16). The husband had, therefore, lost his beneficial entitlement to her estate and so his personal representative was passed over in favour of the wife's next-of-kin.

In *In the Estate of Hall* (1914) an executor who was in prison was passed over. In *In the Estate of Biggs* (1966) an executor had dealt with property in the estate without taking a grant (and was therefore debarred from renouncing probate—see paragraph 8.9) but was now unwilling to continue acting despite the fact that he had been ordered to take a grant and that proceedings for contempt of court had been started against him. The court passed him over.

Finally, the case of *In the Goods of Edwards-Taylor* (1951) shows that the power to pass over is designed to control the appointment of personal representatives and cannot be used for a collateral purpose. In that case there was an application to pass over a beneficiary who was alleged to be mentally and physically immature. The application was made so that she would not be able to get possession of the deceased's estate immediately. The court refused to pass her over since the reason for the application was not concerned with the administration of the estate.

### 3. ADMINISTRATION OF JUSTICE ACT 1985, S.50

**8.22** Under section 50(1)(*a*) the court has power to remove an existing personal representative and appoint a substitute. Under section 50(1)(*b*) where there are two or more existing personal representatives it can terminate the appointment of one or more, but not all, of those persons.

# I. Limited Grants

### 1. INTRODUCTION

**8.23** Most grants are general in their effect. That is they give the personal representative authority (or, in the case of probate, confirm his authority) to act for all purposes in the administration of the estate and extend to all the property in the estate without time limit.

There are, however, three ways in which grants may be limited in their effect:

(i) they may be limited in time (for example, "until X reaches majority"); or

(ii) they may be limited to part of the estate (for example, "limited to settled land"); or

(iii) they may be limited as to a purpose, that is they may give the personal representative authority to deal with one particular aspect of the administration (for example, "limited to conducting or defending litigation").

## 2. GRANTS LIMITED AS TO TIME

### Grants on behalf of minors

An infant cannot take a grant of probate or of administration.  **8.24**
Where one of several executors appointed by a will is a minor
the adult executors may take a general grant of probate
immediately. Power is reserved to the minor who may take a
grant of double probate when he reaches 18 (see paragraphs
8.26–8.29 below). Where one of several potential administrators
entitled in the same degree is a minor the grant will usually be
made to the adults in preference to the guardians of the minor
(Non-Contentious Probate Rules 1987, rule 27(4)).

Where, however, the executors or the persons with the best
entitlement to be administrators are all minors it is necessary to
make a grant of letters of administration to some other person
until the minors reach 18. This type of grant is commonly called
a grant *durante aetate minore*; it may be a grant of
administration with will annexed or a grant of simple
administration. It confers on the administrator a general power
to deal with the estate but is limited in time until the minor
reaches 18. The grant will usually expire automatically on the
minor reaching 18 although it is possible for some other time
limit to be fixed (for example, the grant may be effective until
the minor himself takes a grant). A grant *durante aetate minore*
is made "for the use and benefit of the minor" and is therefore,
made to the guardian of the minor (subject to the exceptions
mentioned at (i) below) rather than to others entitled to the
estate of the deceased.

The persons entitled to take a grant *durante aetate minore*
under rule 32 of the Non-Contentious Probate Rules 1987 are:

(i)   both parents of the minor jointly or any statutory
      guardian (*i.e.* usually the surviving parent) or tes-
      tamentary guardian or any guardian appointed by a
      court provided that where the minor is sole executor
      and has no interest in the residuary estate of the
      deceased, administration for the use and benefit of the
      minor limited as aforesaid, shall, unless a registrar
      otherwise directs, be granted to the person entitled to
      the residuary estate.

(ii)  an "assigned" guardian; that is someone appointed by
      a registrar under rule 32(2) either because there is no
      one eligible under the rules listed above or because the
      registrar decides to pass over those persons;

(iii) where there is a minority in the estate so that two administrators are required but there is only one person competent and willing to take a grant under the rules listed above that person may nominate a second administrator.

*Mental incapacity*

**8.25** Where the executor or administrator is unable to act because of mental incapacity he *may*, in some cases be passed over in favour of other applicants but, normally a grant will be made to some other person for the use and benefit of the person suffering incapacity (rule 35).

The grant is made in the following order of priority unless the registrar otherwise directs:

(i) to the person authorised by the Court of Protection to apply for a grant;

(ii) where there is no person so authorised, to the lawful attorney of the incapable person acting under a registered enduring power of attorney;

(iii) where there is no such attorney entitled to act, or if the attorney shall renounce administration for the use and benefit of the incapable person, to the person entitled to the residuary estate of the deceased.

Unless a registrar otherwise directs, no grant shall be made under this rule unless all persons entitled in the same degree as the incapable person have been cleared off.

## 3. GRANTS LIMITED AS TO PROPERTY

**8.26** Where a grant is made limited to certain property up to four personal representatives may join in that grant and up to four in the grant made in respect of the rest of the estate.

*Appointment of executors*

**8.27** A will may appoint different executors to deal with different parts of the estate. One example of this is an appointment of a literary executor to deal with literary effects and of a general executor to deal with the rest of the estate. The grant of probate taken by the literary executor will be limited to literary effects only. The grant taken by the general executor, if taken before the grant to the limited part of the estate is described as a grant "save and except" the limited part; if taken after the grant of the limited part it is described as a grant *caeterorum*.

There is no practical difference between these two types of grant.

### The court's discretion
The court can make a grant limited to part of the estate in **8.28** exercise of its discretion under section 116 of the Supreme Court Act 1981. However, the court will not make such a grant unless there are very exceptional circumstances and will usually pass over the person entitled to a grant altogether rather than make a limited grant.

### Settled land
The legal title to settled land is vested in the tenant for life not **8.29** in the trustees of the settlement. When the tenant for life dies and the settlement continues after his death a grant limited to settled land is required in order that the settled land vests in the trustees of the settlement rather than the general personal representatives.

Where the deceased dies testate a grant of probate limited to settled land is made to the trustees of the settlement at the date of death as special executors whether or not they are appointed in the will. (This is because Administration of Estates Act 1925, s.22 deems them to have been appointed if they have not been expressly appointed).

Where the trustees at the date of death fail to take a grant any later trustees of the settlement will take a grant of administration with will annexed limited to settled land.

Where the deceased dies intestate the trustees of the settlement at the date of grant take a grant of simple administration limited to settled land.

Where the property passes to a person absolutely entitled after the death of the tenant for life the settlement comes to an end and the property devolves on the general personal representatives of the deceased tenant for life. There is, therefore, no need for special personal representatives in such a case (*Re Bridgett and Hayes Contract* (1928)). Similarly no special personal representatives are needed where a settlement is *created* by the will of the deceased. The general personal representatives will deal with administration of the property and will vest it in the tenant for life when administration is complete.

The above rules apply only to strict settlements under the Settled Land Act 1925. Where a person is entitled to a life interest under a trust for sale, whether or not of land, the property is vested in the trustees and continues to be vested in them despite the death of the life tenant. The trust property does not, therefore, pass to any personal representative of the life tenant. Where a trust for sale is created by the will or intestacy of the deceased the general personal representatives will deal with the property and will vest it in the trustees of the settlement.

### 4. GRANTS LIMITED AS TO PURPOSE

*Grant ad colligenda bona*

**8.30** The purpose of a grant *ad colligenda bona* is to enable collection and preservation of the assets in the estate before a general grant is made so that any assets in danger may be preserved. Since the grant does not extend to distribution of the estate the will is not annexed to it. There are no particular rules as to who may apply for the grant; application is made to a registrar *ex parte* (Non-Contentious Probate Rules 1987, rule 52(b)).

Although a grant *ad colligenda bona* is usually limited to collecting in the estate the court may grant power to sell or otherwise deal with the assets so as to preserve their value.

*Grant ad litem*

**8.31** A grant *ad litem* is made to enable proceedings in court to be begun or continued on behalf of the estate of the deceased or against it. Any person interested in the litigation may apply *ex parte* to a registrar. Where someone wishes to bring a claim against an estate for family provision under the Inheritance (Provision for Family and Dependants) Act 1975 the Official Solicitor will usually be willing to take out a grant *ad litem*.

*Grant pendente lite*

**8.32** Where there is a probate action in relation to an estate (for example, because the validity of an alleged will is in question), the court may appoint an administrator *pendente lite*, that is until the probate action is concluded. Any person who is a party to the probate action or interested in the estate may apply for the grant to be made but the grant will usually be made to an independent third party. The administrator will not usually be given authority to distribute any of the estate.

## J. Incomplete Administration

**8.33** In most cases the executor or administrator who first takes out a grant will complete the administration of the estate. Sometimes, however, the original personal representative will die or otherwise cease to hold office without completing the administration. In such a case, if there is no chain of representation, a grant to some other person will be required. This will either be a grant *de bonis non administratis* or a cessate grant depending on the circumstances. Sometimes before the administration is completed an executor is added by means of a grant of double probate. A grant of double probate is made where one or some of a number of executors have taken a grant with power reserved to others to take at a later stage and one of those others now obtains a grant.

## 1. GRANT OF ADMINISTRATION DE BONIS NON

A grant *de bonis non administratis* is made to enable the **8.34** administration of the estate to be completed following the death or incapacity of *all* the previous personal representatives or the revocation of the previous grant. (If one of the personal representatives becomes incapable the grant is revoked and a further grant is made to the remaining personal representatives; this is not, however, regarded as a grant *de bonis non*). Although the name "*de bonis non administratis*" means "concerning unadministered goods" it is appropriate in cases where any type of property, including realty, is unadministered.

There are three requirements which must be satisfied before such a grant can be made:

(i) *The administration is incomplete.* Administration is complete once the debts and legacies have been paid, accounts have been prepared and any land or other assets remaining in the estate have been vested in the beneficiaries by means of assents.

(ii) *There is no remaining personal representative.* A grant *de bonis non* cannot be made following the death of one of a number of executors or administrators since the remaining personal representatives have full power to complete the administration. Similarly a grant *de bonis non* cannot be made following the death of the last surviving executor if he has appointed an executor who proves his will and so becomes an executor by representation (see paragraph 8.5 above).

(iii) *There has been a previous grant.* A grant *de bonis non* must always follow a previous grant. An original grant is appropriate where an executor has acted without a grant or someone has partly administered the estate without any authority.

A grant *de bonis non* may be a grant of administration with will annexed or a grant of simple administration. The order of priority for taking the grant is governed by Non-Contentious Probate Rules 1987, rules 20 and 22 which were explained above.

Usually the person (or persons) to whom the grant is made will be the person who was entitled to a grant equally with the previous grantee or who was next entitled after him. Where the previous personal representative was entitled to the whole of the estate the grant will usually be made to his personal representatives (the rule that living persons are to be preferred to the personal representatives of deceased persons only applies as between persons entitled in the same degree).

Where there is a minority or a life interest in the estate at the time when the application for the grant *de bonis non* is made two administrators will be required unless the court orders to the contrary or makes a grant to a trust corporation.

2. CESSATE GRANTS

**8.35** A cessate grant is required where the original grant was limited in time and has ceased to be effective because the time has expired. The most common circumstances in which such a grant is required is where a grant of administration (with will or of simple administration) has been made to a guardian "for the use and benefit" of a minor who would be entitled to a grant but for his infancy. When the minor reaches 18 the limited grant to his guardian automatically ceases to be effective and the minor is entitled to apply for a cessate grant. The cessate grant may be a grant of probate, administration with the will annexed or simple administration depending on the nature of the minor's entitlement.

A cessate grant is also appropriate in other circumstances where a grant is limited in time and the time expires. Thus if a will appoints an executor for life the executor's office ceases altogether with his death and so the chain of representation cannot provide the estate with an executor. A cessate grant is then made to any executor appointed in substitution for the deceased executor by the will (for example, the will may have appointed "A for life and thereafter B"). If no substitutional appointment has been made a cessate grant of administration with will is made to the person entitled under rule 20. If a grant of simple administration is made for the use and benefit of a minor a cessate grant of simple administration is made to the minor when he reaches 18.

A cessate grant is theoretically different from a grant *de bonis non* since it is a general re-grant in respect of the whole estate rather than a limited grant in respect of the unadministered part. However, the practical effect of the two types of grant is the same.

### 3. DOUBLE PROBATE

A grant of double probate is made to an executor when he **8.36** applies for a grant after a grant of *probate* has already been made to another executor. There are three types of case in which a grant of double probate is appropriate:

(i) Where one of a number of executors does not wish to take a grant immediately, does not wish to renounce and has not been cited to take or renounce probate, power will be reserved to him to take a grant later. He may then apply for double probate at any time.

(ii) Where one of a number of executors is a minor at the time of the original grant of probate to the others, power is reserved to him automatically and he can apply for double probate on reaching 18. If the original grant had been a grant of administration he would apply for a cessate grant not a grant of double probate. Thus where a will appoints several executors of whom some are adults and some minors a grant of probate will be made to the adults immediately and a grant of double probate to the minors on reaching majority. Where a will appoints an infant as the only executor a grant of administration with will annexed will be made to the guardians of the executor (or to the person entitled to residue if the infant executor was not so entitled) and a cessate grant of probate to the infant on reaching majority.

(iii) Where an executor is prevented from taking a grant by the rule which restricts a grant to four persons in respect of any part of an estate (Supreme Court Act 1981, s.114(1)) he may apply for a grant of double probate if a vacancy occurs (for example on the death of one of the four proving executors) since power is reserved to him in the original grant.

It should be noted that there is no possibility of double grants of administration. A potential administrator who does not prove in the original grant will only be able to take a grant later if a grant *de bonis non* or a cessate grant is needed or if a second administrator is needed because a life interest or minority arises.

When applying for a grant of double probate the oath must set out, in addition to the usual matters, particulars of the former grant. An office copy of the original grant should accompany the application.

## K. Circumstances in which No Grant is Required

**8.37** Since an executor's authority derives from the will rather than the grant of probate certain steps may be taken without a grant. However, in nearly all circumstances a grant is eventually in fact required so that it can be produced to prove title to the assets of the estate.

There are a number of statutory provisions which enable certain assets to be dealt with without production of a grant but they are all concerned with relatively small amounts of property (see paragraph 12.8).

## L. Revocation of Grants

### 1. JURISDICTION

**8.38** In certain circumstances a grant may be revoked by the Chancery Division (or county court) in contentious cases or by a registrar of the Family Division in non-contentious cases.

Where there is a dispute as to whether a grant should be revoked the case is contentious and every personal representative must be a party to the action. The original grant must be lodged with the court.

If there is no dispute as to the need for revocation the case is non-contentious. However, a grant cannot normally be revoked in non-contentious proceedings except on the application of the person to whom the grant was made.

### 2. GROUNDS FOR REVOCATION

**8.39** A grant will be revoked if it is subsequently found that it ought not to have been made to the person to whom it was in fact made. This may arise in many ways: for example, where a fraudulent application is made by a person with no right to a grant; where a person thought to have predeceased is subsequently found to be alive and better entitled to a grant than the person to whom the original grant was made; where the grant was made despite the entry of a caveat; where a grant was made even though contentious probate proceedings were pending.

A grant will be revoked where a subsequent will is discovered (and in most cases where a subsequent codicil is discovered) or where it is found, after a grant, that the will was invalid or had been revoked before death.

A grant will be revoked where a personal representative becomes mentally or physically incapable, where he disappears or where he wishes to retire.

A grant will be revoked where the "deceased" is not in fact dead.

## 3. CONSEQUENCES OF REVOCATION

Section 27 of the Administration of Estates Act 1925 protects an original personal representative who makes or permits payments or dispositions in good faith. A person who makes a payment to a personal representative in good faith is also protected. Section 39 of the same Act provides that contracts for sale remain binding on and enforceable by the estate despite the revocation of the grant. Section 37 provides that a conveyance of any type of property remains valid despite revocation of the grant provided the conveyance is to a purchaser who gave valuable consideration in good faith (a conveyance is widely defined in this context and includes almost all dealings with property). **8.40**

If property is transferred to the wrong beneficiary under a grant which is later revoked (for example, the property is distributed as on intestacy and then a will is found) the beneficiary is liable to return the asset or to refund its value. The true beneficiary is also entitled to trace the asset or its proceeds and to recover it from the person now in possession so long as it remains identifiable. However, there is no right to trace into the hands of a bona fide purchaser for value without notice.

# 9. Probate Jurisdiction

## A. Jurisdiction—Territorial Limits

**9.1** Grants of representation are made by the English courts where property of the deceased is situated in England and Wales and either an executor is appointed or such property is disposed of in England and Wales. A will which neither appoints an executor nor disposes of English property is not usually admitted to probate although the court has a discretion to issue a grant in such cases.

## B. Nature of Probate Jurisdiction—Contentious and Non-Contentious Business

**9.2** Probate jurisdiction is concerned with three things only. First, the decision as to whether a document may be admitted to probate or annexed to a grant of administration as a testamentary document. Secondly, the decision as to who is entitled to a grant of representation in respect of the estate of a deceased person; thirdly, the decision to amend or revoke a grant.

Since 1970 probate business has been divided between the Family Division (which deals with non-contentious business), and the Chancery Division (which deals with contentious business) and the county court (which has concurrent jurisdiction to deal with contentious business where the value of the estate of the deceased does not exceed a limit laid down by rules of court, the present limit is £30,000).

Non-contentious business (which is also called common form business) is defined by Supreme Court Act 1981, s.128 as:

> "the business of obtaining probate and administration where there is no contention as to the right thereto, including—
> (a) the passing of probates and administrations through the High Court in contentious cases where the contest has been terminated, and

(b) all business of a non-contentious nature in matters of testacy and intestacy not being proceedings in any action, and

(c) the business of lodging caveats against the grant of probate or administration."

The vast majority of probate cases are non-contentious and are dealt with entirely by the Family Division. Non-contentious probate may involve a hearing before a registrar; for example a hearing may be required to decide between persons entitled to a grant in the same degree, or where the court is asked to pass over a person entitled to a grant in favour of some other person (see paragraphs 10.60–10.64).

Where there is a dispute as to what document or documents should be admitted to probate, or as to who is entitled to take out a grant, or as to whether a grant should be revoked, contentious (or solemn form) proceedings may be necessary and will be brought in the Chancery Division or county court. In most cases non-contentious proceedings will begin first and the case will only become contentious when the dispute arises.

A grant of representation in common form does not prevent a probate action for proof in solemn form being brought later. Thus if, after the Family Division has granted probate, someone wishes to challenge the validity of the will he may issue a writ to start contentious proceedings.

Frequently where there is a dispute a caveat or citation will be entered but neither of these steps is, of itself, sufficient to start a contentious probate action. In every case where proof in solemn form is required a writ or summons must be issued.

After a writ or summons has been issued the case remains contentious until the dispute is finally decided by the Chancery Division or the county court. Once the dispute is disposed of the case becomes non-contentious and so is returned to the Family Division which is responsible for the issue of the grant (the Family Division is the only court which actually makes grants).

## C. Financial Limits

**9.3** The jurisdiction of the High Court (Family and Chancery Division) is unlimited as to the amount of the estate. The county court has no jurisdiction in non-contentious cases and its jurisdiction in contentious cases is limited to cases where the estate is less than the county court limit at the time of death.

(In valuing the estate for this purpose debts, funeral expenses and incumbrances are deducted as is property vested in the deceased as trustee and not beneficially). The county court with jurisdiction is the one within whose area the deceased was resident at the date of death. Once proceedings have been commenced in the county court the principal registry should be informed so that no grant is made in common form in the estate. Proceedings in the county court are commenced by summons.

## D. Probate Jurisdiction and Other Jurisdiction Concerning Wills

Probate jurisdiction is concerned only with what documents are admissible as testamentary documents and to whom grants should be made. Litigation concerning wills and administration of estates may, however, arise in at least three other ways; **9.4**

- (i) there may be no dispute as to what should be admitted as a testamentary document but a dispute as to what it means (that is, a question of construction may arise);
- (ii) there may be a dispute as to how the estate should be administered by the personal representatives (so that an administration action becomes necessary); or
- (iii) there may be a claim against a personal representative who is alleged to have acted improperly (and so may be liable for the *devastavit* which he has committed).

Proceedings in each of these three types of case will usually be brought in the Chancery Division. When a question of construction is before the court, it is bound by the decision of the Family Division (or of the Chancery Division in earlier probate proceedings) as to the wording of the testamentary instrument. Questions of construction are not generally decided in probate proceedings except to the extent that it is necessary for the purpose of the probate action. Thus, it is appropriate for the court to decide, in probate proceedings, who the testator intended to appoint as executor and what parts of earlier wills or codicils have been revoked by a later testamentary document.

## E. Solemn Form Procedure

We have already outlined the distinction between common form and solemn form probate. We intend to give no more than an **9.5** outline of the solemn form procedure in the High Court (Chancery Division). (The procedure for obtaining a grant in common form cases is dealt with in Chapter 10).

## 1. ISSUE OF WRIT

**9.6**   Order 76 rule 1(2) of the Rules of the Supreme Court defines a probate action as "an action for the grant of probate of the will, or letters of administration of the estate, of a deceased person or for the revocation of such a grant or for a decree pronouncing for or against the validity of an alleged will (or codicil), not being an action which is non-contentious or common form business." A probate action is begun by writ or summons indorsed with a statement of the nature of the plaintiff's and defendant's interest in the estate of the deceased.

The writ may be issued by the executor or a person interested in the will, a person interested under any other will whose interest would be adversely affected if the will in question were admitted to probate or the persons entitled on intestacy (including the Treasury Solicitor and Solicitors to the Duchies of Lancaster and Cornwall if the Crown or Duchies would be entitled to take the estate as *bona vacantia* on intestacy).

Any person interested who is not a plaintiff in the action must be made a defendant. However, a person whose entitlement will not be affected by the decision need not be a party. It is not, for example, necessary to join a specific legatee who will take a legacy under one will if the only dispute is as to whether that will has been revoked by a later will which repeats the same legacy.

## 2. PLEADINGS

**9.7**   A statement of claim may be indorsed on the writ. If it is not, it must normally be served on each defendant who enters an appearance within six weeks of his entering the appearance.

A defence (and, where appropriate, counterclaim) must be served on the plaintiff within 14 days of the expiry of the time limit for entering an appearance or within 14 days of the service of the statement of claim. The rules make provision for further pleadings where appropriate.

The content of the pleadings will vary with the circumstances but each separate allegation as to the invalidity of the will must normally be separately pleaded (thus if lack of knowledge and approval on the testator's part *and* undue influence are to be relied upon each must be pleaded).

Once pleadings are closed a summons for directions must be taken out. The procedure is the same as in other Chancery Division actions.

### 3. DEFAULT OF APPEARANCE AND PLEADINGS

It is not possible to obtain judgment in default of appearance in a probate action. Where a defendant fails to appear the plaintiff may file an affidavit as to service and then seek an order from the court for trial of the action despite the non-appearance. Similarly the court may order trial of the action where one of the parties has failed to serve pleadings. In such cases the court can order that the trial proceed on affidavit evidence.   **9.8**

### 4. COMPROMISE

A probate action may be compromised where consent is given by or on behalf of all the beneficiaries who are or might be interested in the estate (Administration of Justice Act 1985, s.48).   **9.9**

### 5. COSTS

Costs are in the discretion of the court. The general principle that costs should follow the event (*i.e.* be ordered against the unsuccessful party) usually applies. However, there are a number of circumstances in which the court departs from this principle in the case of probate actions.   **9.10**

An unsuccessful defendant who serves notice with his defence that he is putting those propounding the will to proof in solemn form but that he only intends to cross examine the witnesses who support the will (and not for example to produce his own witnesses in opposition or to try to prove a later will) cannot be made liable for the plaintiff's costs unless it is shown that there is no reasonable ground for opposing the will (R.S.C. Ord. 62, r. 6(1)(*d*)).

### 6. EFFECT OF ORDER

An order in a probate action is binding on the parties to it and also on any person who had notice of the proceedings and knew that he had an interest in the action but nevertheless chose not to intervene.   **9.11**

# 10. Obtaining the Grant (Non-Contentious Cases)

## A. Probate Jurisdiction

Most non-contentious or common form probate business is dealt **10.1** with in the Principal Registry of the Family Division in London or one of the 11 district registries (most of these district registries have sub-registries attached to them). However, in cases of doubt or uncertainty a registrar may refer a matter to a judge of the Family Division (Non-Contentious Probate Rules 1987, rule 61). Registries do not have "catchment areas"; the choice of registry is governed by convenience and personal preference.

It is not necessary for a personal representative to consult a solicitor. The personal representative can make a personal application at the Principal Registry or at a district registry or sub-registry or at certain local probate offices served from the nearest registry. The procedure is simple and will not be considered here. We are concerned only with the procedure where a solicitor is acting for the personal representative.

## B. The Papers Leading to a Grant

The solicitor must send or deliver the following: **10.2**

(a) The Inland Revenue Account, if required, and cheque or money order for any inheritance tax due. The completed account together with a remittance for tax and interest must be sent by post to the Central Accounting Office at Worthing.

   The receipted account is returned to the solicitor who can then deliver it to the Principal or district registry with the other papers.

Cheques should be made payable to "Inland Revenue" and crossed. (In certain circumstances the Inland Revenue may accept assets in satisfaction of the whole or any part of any liability to inheritance tax for example, works of art of "pre-eminent" standard under the Inheritance Tax Act 1984, s.230.)

(b) The appropriate oath sworn or affirmed by the personal representatives before an independent solicitor.

(c) Probate fees. A crossed cheque made payable to H.M. Paymaster General should be used. No fee is payable where the value of the net estate passing under the grant does not exceed £10,000; if the value exceeds £10,000 but does not exceed £25,000 there is a flat fee of £40; if the value exceeds £25,000 but does not exceed £40,000, there is a flat fee of £80; if the value exceeds £40,000 but does not exceed £70,000 there is a flat fee of £150; if the value exceeds £70,000 but does not exceed £100,000 there is a flat fee of £215; if the value exceeds £100,000 but does not exceed £200,000 there is a flat fee of £300 and for every additional £100,000 or part thereof a further fee of £50.

(d) The will (if there is one). A photographic copy of the will is normally annexed to the grant of representation by the registry. However, if the registrar considers that the will is unsuitable for photographic reproduction or if it contains inadmissible alterations or other irrelevant matter the registry will require the applicant's solicitor to supply a typewritten engrossment. In such circumstances, as an alternative to an engrossment the registrar has a discretion to allow a facsimile copy produced by photography in certain circumstances including:

(i) where a complete page is, or complete pages are, to be excluded;

(ii) where the original has been altered but neither re-executed nor republished and there is in existence a photocopy of the original executed document.

If the whole or part of the will has been written in pencil, a copy of the will in which the words which appear in pencil in the original are underlined in red ink must be lodged with the will.

If the original will has been lost or destroyed it may be possible to obtain an order admitting to proof the will as contained in a copy or reconstruction (Non-Contentious Probate Rules 1987, rule 54(1)). If the original will is lodged in a foreign court a duly authenticated copy of the will may be admitted to proof without need for an order (Non-Contentious Probate Rules, rule 54(2)).

(e) Any affidavit evidence that may be required, for example an affidavit of due execution.

(Items (a), (b) and (e) are considered in more detail later in this chapter.)

Once the appropriate papers have been lodged at the registry all testamentary documents are photographed. Searches are made; one to ensure that no caveat has been entered against the estate and one to ensure that no grant of representation has already been issued. Searches are also made to ensure that no application for a grant has been made in a different registry.

The papers are examined and if they are in order the grant of representation is prepared. A photographic copy of the will and codicils (if any) is attached to the grant. Grants are usually signed by a Probate Officer under the authority of the President of the Family Division; they are sealed with the seal of the Division. The grant is sent by post to the extracting solicitor together with any office copies that have been requested.

If there are defects in the papers the registry will contact the extracting solicitor so that the queries can be resolved.

# C. Oaths

## 1. INTRODUCTION

Every application for a grant of representation must be **10.3** supported by an oath. The oath is prepared by the solicitor acting for the personal representatives and it must be sworn (or affirmed) by the personal representatives before an independent solicitor.

The oath performs three functions:

(a)  It sets out the basis of the applicant's claim to be entitled to take the grant (for example, in the case of an executor it recites the fact that the applicant is the person named as executor in the will).

(b)  It requires the applicant to swear that he will duly collect in the assets of the deceased and duly administer the estate.

(c)  In the case of applications for grants of probate and letters of administration with the will annexed, the oath exhibits and identifies the will and any codicils to it.

The three most common oaths are the oaths leading to a first grant of probate, letters of administration with the will annexed or simple letters of administration. The three oaths are similar but differ in points of detail. Points common to all three oaths are considered first and then points relevant to specific types of oath.

## 2. FORMS OF OATHS

**10.4**  The form of the three most common oaths is set out at pages 460–462. The letters printed on the oaths in square brackets refer to points made later in the chapter.

## 3. POINTS COMMON TO ALL OATHS

### Affirmation

**10.5**  Despite the name, an "oath" need not be sworn but can be affirmed. If a person wishes to affirm, the words "make oath and say" which appear twice in the body of the oath can be deleted and replaced by the words "do solemnly and sincerely affirm." The words "sworn by" in the jurat at the end of the form (shown on the blank forms marked F) should then be deleted and replaced by the words "affirmed by."

### Solicitor's name and address

**10.6**  The name and address of the extracting solicitor should appear in the top right hand corner of the oath. Correspondence concerning queries will then be sent to the solicitor and not to the personal representatives themselves. It is desirable to add the solicitor's reference immediately afterwards since the reference will then be included on the grant of representation when it is returned by the registry.

### The deceased's name

The true and proper name of the deceased must always be **10.7** given. The true and proper name of the deceased is normally the name in which the birth was registered or in the case of a married or divorced woman the surname of her husband (if she has adopted her husband's name). The true and proper name may have been changed by:

(a) deed poll; or
(b) habit and repute; however, a name is only regarded as changed by habit and repute if the former name has been completely abandoned over a period of time.

A testator may have been known by a name (or names) other than his true and proper name; such a name is not to be included on the oath unless it is necessary that the name appear on the grant of representation. It is necessary if the will was made in a name other than the testator's true and proper name or if property was owned in a name other than the true and proper name.

An explanation justifying the inclusion of the other name must either be given in a separate affidavit or, if it can be stated sufficiently concisely, added at the end of the oath immediately before the jurat (marked F). Examples of such concise explanations are:

1. "That the true and proper name of the deceased was Jane Brown but she made and duly executed the said will in the name of Jane LeBrun."

2. "That the true and proper name of the deceased was Jane Brown but certain property, to wit ... is vested in her in the name of Jane LeBrun." In such a case at least one property held in the other name must be specified.

### The deceased's address

The address given must have been the usual residential address **10.8** of the deceased at the time of death. In the case of an oath leading to a grant of probate or letters of administration with the will annexed if the latest testamentary document gives an address different from the last address of the testator that former address should be given but all others may be ignored.

### The date of death of the deceased

This must be set out as it appears in the certificate of death. In **10.9** cases where the precise date of death is uncertain the following wording is used:

"who was known to be alive on ... and whose dead body was found on ... "

If a person is believed to be dead but no body has been found (for example, because the deceased was aboard a ship which disappeared) the Family Division can make an order giving leave to swear that the person who is believed to be dead died "on or since" a certain date. The wording of such an order should be repeated in the oath.

*Domicile of the deceased*

**10.10** If the deceased died domiciled in England or Wales this should be recited as "England and Wales" (because England and Wales is one jurisdiction). If there is any doubt as to domicile an affidavit setting out the facts should be filed in support of the oath. The Administration of Estates Act 1971 provides that where a grant of representation is issued in England and Wales, Scotland or Northern Ireland in respect of the estate of a person who died domiciled in one of these countries, the grant will be recognised in the other two countries provided it contains a statement of the deceased's domicile. Thus, if a person dies domiciled in Scotland owning assets in England and Wales, provided the Scottish confirmation contains a reference to the domicile of the deceased it will be recognised as the equivalent of an English grant.

*Age of the deceased at death*

**10.11** If the precise age of the deceased is not known the best estimate possible should be given.

*Settled land*

**10.12** Each oath contains a paragraph (marked B) relating to land settled before the death of the deceased and continuing settled after his death. If there was no such settled land comprised in the deceased's estate the paragraph is left as printed.

If there was settled land the word "no" must be deleted. Normally such settled land devolves not on the general personal representatives but on the trustees of the settlement who take out a special grant of representation limited to the settled land. Therefore normally in such a case the general personal representatives must qualify the later paragraph (marked D) by inserting in the appropriate spaces the words "save and except settled land." If however the settled land is to devolve on the general personal representatives (for example, where they happen to be the trustees of the settlement) the words "including settled land" must be inserted.

*The personal representatives swear to collect and get in the real and personal estate and to duly administer it*

Each oath contains a paragraph (marked D on the specimen blank forms) which sets out the duties of a personal representative. Nothing need be done to this paragraph unless the estate included settled land in which case as stated in paragraph 10.12 above the words "save and except" or "including" settled land must be inserted.

**10.13**

*Gross & net estate*

Each oath contains a paragraph (marked E) dealing with the gross and net value of the estate *which passes under the grant*. The deponent(s) must swear to the gross and net values. The paragraph contains two alternatives one of which must be deleted.

**10.14**

(a) "the gross estate passing under the grant does not exceed £     and the net estate does not exceed £     , and this is not a case in which an Inland Revenue Account is required" or

(b) "the gross estate passing under the grant amounts to £     and the net estate amounts to £     "

The deponent is not concerned with the value of any part of the estate which does not pass under the grant. The following property does not pass under the grant: a life interest, joint property devolving by survivorship, property which is the subject of a *donatio mortis causa* or nomination. The test is whether the grant is necessary to establish a claimant's right to the property. The *gross* value of such property must be stated because the personal representatives swear that they will duly administer the estate, due administration of the estate includes the payment of debts; therefore, they must swear to gross figures not merely to net ones. The net value must be stated since probate fees are calculated on the basis of the value of the net estate passing under the grant.

If the gross estate passing under the grant does not exceed £115,000 and the other circumstances are such that no Inland Revenue Account need be delivered, that is, the deceased died on or after April 1, 1990 and the estate is an "excepted estate" (as defined in paragraph 10.35 below) paragraph (a) should be completed and paragraph (b) deleted. If the recital that this is not a case where an Inland Revenue Account is required is omitted, the oath will be returned for the recital to be inserted and the oath resworn. Paragraph (a) must state that the net estate passing under the grant does not exceed one of the figures on which fixed probate fees are payable.

Where an Inland Revenue account is required to be delivered paragraph (a) must be deleted and paragraph (b) completed with the precise values of the gross and net estate passing under the grant.

In paragraph (b) the figures for gross and net estate passing under the grant are the figures shown on the back of the Inland Revenue Account (IHT 200 or 202).

*The jurat*

10.15    This is marked F on the blank forms. The oath must be sworn by each deponent in the presence of an independent Commissioner for Oaths or solicitor. An independent solicitor is one who is not a member of the extracting solicitor's firm. The place and date of swearing must be given precisely; it is not sufficient to give the name of the town. If there is more than one deponent and each swears at a different time the name of each should be inserted in a separate jurat. Otherwise the name of the deponent(s) need not be inserted at all; it is sufficient for the jurat to refer to "the above named deponents." The wording of the jurat must be altered if there is to be an affirmation.

4. OATH FOR EXECUTORS

10.16    This oath is set out on page 460.

*"[I/we] ... /of ... "*

10.17    The first paragraph of the oath for executors should commence with the words "I" or "we" as appropriate. The names, addresses and occupations or descriptions of each of the deponents should be inserted. The order of names should be the same as that given in the will and the order of names given on the oath will be repeated on the grant of representation. Sometimes the deponents wish to vary the order so that a trust corporation or professional person can be named first and in this case a letter of consent signed by the executors may be filed with the affidavit. However, if no such letter is filed the executors are presumed to have consented to the change.

The true and proper name of each of the executors must be given. Since one of the functions of the oath is to explain the basis of the claimant's right to take a grant by identifying him as the executor named in the will, it is necessary to give an explanation if the true and proper name differs from the name given in the will. The wording used will vary according to the circumstances:

(a)   If the discrepancy is very small it is sufficient to say "in the will called" or if it is a mistake in the spelling "in the will written."

*Example*

"Jennifer Smith in the will called Jenny Smith"

(b)   If a change of name was made by deed poll the date of the deed poll should be recited and the deed itself lodged for inspection.

*Example*

"Charles Coomb, formerly Charles Crumb who changed my name by deed poll dated the 5th day of December 1982."

(c)   If the change of name was made on marriage the previous marital status should be given.

*Example*

"Jennifer Smith, married woman, formerly and in the will called Jennifer Brown, spinster."

(d)   If the change of name was by habit and repute the fact that the former name has been completely abandoned must be recited.

*Example*

"That I was formerly known as David Button but assumed the name of David Betten on or about the 4th of December 1960 since when I have never used the name of David Button but have always been known as David Betten."

*Relationship*

It is quite common for a will to mention a relationship in the appointment of an executor for example, "I appoint my niece Frances Brown."

It is also quite common for testators to make a mistake in such relationships, for example referring to someone as a niece who is in fact a niece of the deceased's spouse. In such a case the oath must state that the deceased had no relative of that name and degree of relationship and recite such facts as will establish that the deponent was the person intended. If the will simply refers to "my wife" or "my husband" the oath must state that the deponent was the lawful spouse *at the time the will was signed.*

*Address*
The full, private and permanent address of the deponent must be given. A solicitor, or other person administering the estate in a professional capacity may give a professional address only. Other persons may give a business address in addition to a private address but only if it can be shown to be for the advantage of the estate.

*Occupations or descriptions*
The occupation of a male or female deponent must be given in precise language (if the person is retired the former occupation should be given qualified by the word retired).

If a woman has no occupation she may be described by reference to her marital status, *i.e.* as "spinster," "married woman," "widow" or in the case of a divorced woman as "single woman" or "single woman, formerly the wife of. ... " The marital status of female grantees does not appear on the grant of representation but if a woman so wishes the word "Mrs" or "Miss" can be included on the oath in which case they will also appear on the grant (Practice Note December 16, 1971—the Practice Note does not mention the possibility of including "Ms").

*"Make oath and say that [I/we] believe the paper writing now produced to and marked by [me/us] to be the true and original last will and testament ... "*

**10.18**  This paragraph (marked A on the oath for executors and on the oath for administrators with will annexed) performs two functions:

  (a)  it makes the oath binding on the deponents. (If the deponent wishes to affirm, the words "make oath and say" must be altered to "do solemnly and sincerely affirm" here, later in the oath (see paragraph 10.19) and in the jurat); and

  (b)  it identifies the documents which it is desired be admitted to probate. The deponent and person before whom the oath is being sworn must sign their names on each document. The signatures should be placed away from the text, if possible, since if the document is made unsuitable for photographic reproduction the

Probate Registry will require an engrossment of the will.

If there are codicils to the will the words "with ... codicils thereto" must be added to "the true and original last will and testament." If a codicil has been revoked by a later codicil, the earlier codicil must still be proved if it altered the terms of the original will or a previous codicil.

If the original will is unavailable the word "original" should be deleted. If the original is lodged in a foreign court an official copy (bearing the seal, if any, of the court) must be marked and the oath must refer to "the true last will and testament as contained in a true and official copy thereof." If the original will is lost or destroyed a court order must be obtained allowing probate to be obtained of a copy, draft or reconstruction. The oath must refer to "the true last will and testament as contained in a copy thereof" or " ... as contained in a completed draft thereof."

*"And [I/we] further make oath and say that [I/we] [am/are] ... the ... [executors/executrices] named in the said will."*
This paragraph is marked C on the oath for executors. If only **10.19** some of the living executors named in the will wish to take probate the number of such executors should be inserted for example, "we are two of the executors named in the said will."

If some of the executors are dead but all the living executors wish to take probate the living ones should be referred to as "the surviving executors." If only one executor was named in the will such a person is referred to as "the sole" executor.

If some of the proving executors are male and some are female, all should be referred to as "executors." If all are female, they should be referred to as "executrices."

If any executors have renounced probate this need not be referred to in the oath but the instrument of renunciation should be filed with the papers. It is not necessary for persons unwilling to take the grant to renounce. Instead power can be reserved to them to prove at a later date.

*"And [I/we] further make oath and say that notice of this application has been given to the executor(s) to whom power is to be reserved"*
Rule 27 of the Non-Contentious Probate Rules 1987 provides **10.20** that notice of an application for a grant of probate must be given to any executor to whom power is reserved. The oath for executors must therefore (in cases where power is reserved to

an executor) include the paragraph set out above stating that such notice has been given. The registrar can dispense with the need to give notice if he is satisfied that to do so is impracticable or will result in unreasonable delay or expense. Application for such dispensation is made by letter.

When an executor wishes power to be reserved to him to prove at a later stage it is not necessary to include a statement to this effect in the oath; but the name of such an executor should be written in the margin.

### 5. THE OATH FOR ADMINISTRATORS WITH WILL ANNEXED

**10.21**  The oath is set out on page 461 of the Appendix.

*Comparison with oath for executors*

**10.22**  This oath is similar to that sworn by executors in that it refers to the will to explain the basis of the deponent's claim to be entitled to administer the estate. It, therefore, has to identify the will in the same way that the oath for executors does. However, the oath must recite that the deponent is the person entitled in priority to take the grant and must explain that persons with prior rights (for example, persons appointed executors in the will) have been cleared off. We will comment only on those parts of the oath which differ from the oath for executors.

*["I/we] ... of ... "*

**10.23**  The same details of name, address and occupations or description that are given in the case of executors must be given for administrators; any discrepancy between will and oath must be explained. The order in which such names appear on the oath is determined by the extent of their interest in the estate.

*"that ... minority ... life interest arises in [his/her] estate"*

**10.24**  If a minority or life interest exists no matter how small it may be (but see paragraph 10.27 for details of certain permitted deductions that may extinguish an apparent minority or life interest) the grant will usually have to be made to at least two individuals or to a trust corporation. Therefore, the oath must state whether or not there is a minority or life interest.

*Clearing off persons with prior rights*

**10.25**  Immediately after the paragraph dealing with settled land (marked B) the deponent must insert a paragraph explaining that any person with a prior right has been cleared off. Priority is governed by rule 20 of the Non-Contentious Probate Rules 1987.

If the will did not appoint executors this must be recited. If the will did appoint executors the reason why they are not seeking a grant must be stated (for example, because an appointed executor died without taking a grant). Similarly the oath must state why any other person with a prior right is not seeking a grant. The reasons are likely to be:

(a)   death, or
(b)   renunciation, or
(c)   failure to appear to citation.

The precise wording of such a recital will vary according to the circumstances, the following is a specimen:

> "That A, the sole surviving executor and trustee appointed in the will, predeceased the deceased [or survived the deceased but has since died without having proved the will] and that B, the residuary legatee and devisee for life named in the will, has renounced letters of administration with the will annexed and that C, the ultimate residuary legatee and devisee, has been duly cited to accept or refuse letters of administration with the will annexed. That in default of appearance of the said C to the said citation it was ordered by Mr. Registrar [...] of this Division on the ... day of ... 199 ... that letters of administration with the will annexed be granted to [me/us]."

It is common practice for an applicant for a grant to file, with the other papers, the renunciation of any executor or any person having an interest prior to his own.

It is not necessary to clear off persons entitled in the *same* degree as the applicant. For example, if there are three specific legatees one of whom wishes to take a grant he must clear off persons with a *prior* right but not the other two specific legatees.

If it is apparent from the will that no trustees of residue were appointed it is not necessary to state this in the oath.

*Recital of deponent's right to grant*

After clearing off any person with a prior right the oath must state (at C) the exact capacity in which the applicant claims the    **10.26** grant. If the applicant is claiming as a person entitled under a partial intestacy the relationship (if any) must be given.

*Examples*

> "one of the residuary legatees and devisees named in the will."
>
> "one of the specific legatees and devisees named in the will."
>
> "a brother of the whole blood of the deceased and one of the persons entitled to share in the undisposed of estate of the said deceased."

If the person entitled to the grant is a minor and the applicants are taking a grant for his use and benefit the oath must recite this and must also show the applicants' authority to take such a grant. Suitable wording would be:

> "That A is the residuary legatee and devisee named in the said will and is a minor, the said A being the age of ... and that there is no testamentary or other lawfully appointed guardian of the said minor and that I, C, am the lawful father and statutory guardian of the said minor and I, D, am the person nominated by an instrument in writing dated the ... day of ... 199 ... under the hand of the said C, for the purpose of joining with him in taking a grant of letters of administration with will annexed of the estate of the said deceased."

Similarly if a grant is to be taken out for the use and benefit of a person who is mentally incapable of managing his own affairs the oath should state this and should show the basis of the applicant's right to take the grant; for example, that the applicant is the person authorised by the Court of Protection.

*Permitted deductions*

**10.27** At the end of any oath immediately before the jurat it is always possible to insert additional necessary information. Sometimes it is desired to show details of "permitted deductions" from the value of the estate which may reduce the value of the estate below £75,000 or £125,000. This is done where the effect of such deductions will be to reduce the value of the estate to such an extent that no life interest or minority interest arise in respect of any undisposed of property so that it may be possible for the grant to issue to a sole administrator.

The permitted deductions are:
- (a) the value of personal chattels,
- (b) debts,
- (c) inheritance tax payable from the estate without a right of recovery from any other person or property,
- (d) fair and reasonable costs incurred and to be incurred,
- (e) probate fees.

## 6. OATH FOR ADMINISTRATORS
The oath is set out on page 462. **10.28**

*Comparison with oath for executors and oath for administrators with the will annexed*
This oath is sworn where the deceased left no valid will. It **10.29** follows that there is no will to identify and no need to refer to a will to establish the basis of the deponent's claim. Instead the oath must recite the relationship of the deponent to the deceased and show that all persons with a prior right have been cleared off. Only those parts of the oath which differ from the previous oaths will be commented on.

*"[I/We] ... of ... "*
The same details of names, addresses and occupations or **10.30** description that are given in the case of executors must be given in the case of administrators although obviously in the case of an intestacy there can be no discrepancy between will and oath to require explanation. The order of names is governed by their priority to take a grant. A change can be made at the request of all applicants.

*Clearing off persons with prior rights*
Immediately after the words "died domiciled in ... intestate" **10.31** (marked A) the applicant must explain in what way persons with prior rights have been cleared off. Priority is governed by the Non-Contentious Probate Rules 1987, rule 22. Clearing off is done either by stating that the deceased left no-one in the prior categories set out in rule 22 or by stating that there were such people at the time of the intestate's death but they have since renounced their rights, failed to appear to a citation or died without taking a grant. A surviving spouse has first claim to a grant so if the intestate left no spouse the oath must first state that the deceased died intestate "a bachelor" or "a spinster" or "a widower" or "a widow" or "a single man" or "a single woman."

Any other persons entitled under rule 22 are cleared off by stating that the deceased died *without* "issue," or "parent," or "brother or sister of the whole [or half] blood" or "their issue," or "grandparent," or "uncle and aunt of the whole [or half] blood" or "their issue." When clearing off any such persons the following words must be added "or any other person entitled in priority to share in his [her] estate by virtue of any enactment." This is to make it clear that there are no adopted or legitimated relatives or relatives whose parents were not married surviving the deceased.

If a person with a prior right has renounced, the wording is as follows:

> "died intestate, a widow, without issue or parent (or any other person entitled in priority to share in her estate by virtue of any enactment) leaving B her brother of the whole blood and the only person entitled to her estate surviving her and that the said B has duly renounced letters of administration."

If a person with a prior right has survived the intestate but died before taking a grant, that person's personal representatives can apply for the grant and the wording is as follows:

> "died intestate leaving W his lawful widow and the only person now entitled to his estate surviving him and that the said W has since died without having taken upon herself letters of administration of the said estate."

It is not necessary to clear off persons entitled in the same degree as the applicant. For example, if there are three children of the deceased one child does not need to clear off the other two.

*"And further make oath and say that [I am/we are] ... of the deceased"*

**10.32**   The applicant must here (marked C) show the precise relationship to the deceased and state whether he or she is "the only person entitled to the estate of the deceased" or "one of the persons entitled to share in the estate of the deceased" or "a person who may have a beneficial interest in the estate of the said deceased in the event of an accretion thereto."

A surviving spouse is described as "the lawful husband" or "the lawful widow." Since the Family Law Reform Act 1987 it is no longer necessary to describe a child as either "lawful" or "natural." An adopted child should be described as "lawful adopted." A child of a deceased uncle or aunt can be described as "a cousin german."

If the application is made by a grandchild, nephew or niece or cousin german the oath must recite that the parent through whom the claim is made died in the lifetime of the deceased.

It is not necessary to swear in the oath that those with an *equal* entitlement to a grant have been informed of this application (contrast the oath for executors where such a statement is required).

*Permitted deductions*
As with the oath for administrators with the will annexed details **10.33** of permitted deductions may be shown.

# D. Inland Revenue Accounts and Payment of Tax

### 1. INTRODUCTION

A grant of representation will not, normally, be issued until the **10.34** personal representatives have lodged an Inland Revenue Account giving full details of the deceased's estate and until they have paid the amount, if any, of inheritance tax for which they are liable (Supreme Court Act 1981, s.109(1)). This account, where it is required, must generally be delivered within 12 months of the end of the month in which the death occurred although it may be delivered later in certain circumstances. However certain estates are excepted from the requirement of delivering an account prior to the issue of the grant. If the estate is not "excepted," the solicitor acting for the personal representatives will complete one of the standard printed forms.

The purpose of the form is to enable the extracting solicitor acting on behalf of the personal representatives to list the deceased's assets and to calculate the inheritance tax liability, if any. The Inland Revenue will then check the extracting solicitor's "self-assessment" to tax to determine whether or not it is correct.

It should be emphasised that, unless the estate is an "excepted estate," the account must be delivered whether or not there is any tax to pay either on delivery of the account or at any time in the future. If tax is to be paid on delivery of the account, a cheque is sent with the form (see paragraph 10.2). If it is discovered at a later date that the Inland Revenue Account does not reflect the true circumstances of the deceased's estate a corrective account must be filed within six months of the discovery.

### 2. "EXCEPTED ESTATES" WHERE NO INLAND REVENUE ACCOUNT NEED BE FILED

The obligation to file an Inland Revenue Account does not **10.35** apply to "excepted estates." These are estates of persons dying on or after April 1, 1990 where, immediately before the death:

(a) the value of the estate is attributable wholly to property passing under that person's will or intestacy or under a nomination of an asset taking effect on death or by survivorship in the case of a beneficial joint tenancy (*i.e.* the estate must not include trust property nor, on a strict interpretation of the conditions, should the deceased have made a *donatio mortis causa*. However if the other conditions are met the Revenue will normally regard the estate as "excepted" even if a *donatio mortis causa* was made);

(b) the total *gross* value of that property did not exceed £115,000;

(c) of that property not more than £15,000 represented value attributable to property then situated outside the United Kingdom;

(d) that person died domiciled in the United Kingdom and without having made any chargeable transfers (or potentially exempt transfers which have become chargeable as a result of the transferor's death within seven years) during his lifetime.

**Note**
Where death occurred prior to April 1, 1990 the rules are slightly different and will not be dealt with here.

Thus if the deceased died with a relatively small estate and a nil cumulative total, no account need be filed. For the purposes of determining the size of the estate, if the deceased was a joint tenant, only the value of his beneficial interest is taken into account when considering the £115,000 limit. If the estate later proves not to be an "excepted estate" because, for example, further property is discovered which increases the value of the estate to a figure over £115,000 an Inland Revenue Account must be delivered within six months of the discovery.

An estate cannot be excepted if the deceased gave away property *inter vivos* subject to a reservation and at his death the reservation is still subsisting or if the reservation was released within seven years before the donor's death.

The Inland Revenue has power to require, by notice in writing within the "prescribed period," the delivery of an Inland Revenue account even where the estate is excepted. The "prescribed period" begins with the death and ends 35 days after the date of the first general grant of representation.

### 3. IHT FORM 202

If the estate is not "excepted" from the need to file an Inland **10.36** Revenue Account, the personal representatives will have to complete and deliver the appropriate IHT Form. The first one we shall consider is the four-page IHT Form 202. A completed example of this form is set out in the Appendix at pages 472–475.

It is obviously important to use the correct form appropriate to the circumstances of the deceased. The IHT Form 202 can be used in the case of relatively small and straightforward estates complying with the conditions set out below. The Probate Registry have requested that solicitors should always use this form when possible to avoid unnecessary time and trouble spent completing and reading the longer IHT Form 200.

The headnote to the printed IHT Form 202 states that it is to be used for an original full grant where:

- (a) the deceased died on or after March 18, 1986 domiciled in the United Kingdom;
- (b) the estate comprises *only* property which has passed under the deceased's will or intestacy, or by nomination, or beneficially by survivorship and all that property was situated in the United Kingdom. (Therefore, the form cannot be used where the deceased was entitled to an interest in settled property, nor interpreting the wording of the form strictly, where a *donatio mortis causa* was made. However, as with an "excepted estate," if the other conditions are satisfied the existence of a *donatio mortis causa* will not normally lead the Revenue to refuse to allow the use of this form);
- (c) the total *net* value of the estate, after deducting any exemptions and reliefs claimed does not exceed the threshold above which inheritance tax is payable at the date of death.

**Note**
(In cases where death occurred prior to March 27, 1981, the rules are rather different and will not be considered here. In cases where the above conditions are met save only that the deceased died on a date between March 27, 1981 and March 17, 1986 inclusive, the appropriate form is CAP 202.)

The Form goes on to state that in all other cases (unless the estate is excepted) Form 200 or 201, as appropriate, must be used. On the second side of the Form are eight statements in seven paragraphs none of which can be altered. Three of the paragraphs in effect impose four further conditions which must be satisfied if this Form is to be used. These four further conditions are that:

(a) The deceased made no transfers of value or potentially exempt transfers chargeable with inheritance tax (*i.e.* no transfers of value that were not covered by inheritance tax exemptions) within seven years of the death (paragraph 3); and

(b) The deceased made no gifts subject to a reservation to the donor, on or after March 18, 1986 and within seven years of the death (paragraph 4); and

(c) The deceased did not have an interest in settled property at his death (paragraph 8); and

(d) The deceased did not have an interest in settled property nor did he settle any property within seven years of his death (paragraph 8).

If these conditions are not satisfied the appropriate form in cases where the deceased was domiciled in England and Wales will be IHT Form 200.

Since IHT Form 202 cannot be used where the value of the deceased's estate at death exceeded the nil rate band, nor where he had made chargeable transfers, it follows that inheritance tax will never be payable when IHT Form 202 is used.

**10.37** The first page of the Form contains the following:

(1) The extracting solicitor's name, address and reference.

(2) The name of the registry to which the application for a grant is to be made.

(3) The details of the deceased, that is his full name and title, date of birth and death, occupation, last usual address (this will not be the hospital in which the deceased died unless he was a permanent resident), surviving relatives and place of domicile.

(4) The names and addresses of the persons applying for the grant. It is sufficient simply to state the names and addresses of the personal representatives. Their entitlement to the grant will be explained in the oath for executors or administrators.

Page 2 commences with eight paragraphs. There is a note which forbids paragraphs 2 to 8 being altered. Paragraph 1 must be completed to identify the kind of grant desired, that is, a grant of probate, letters of administration or letters of administration with the will annexed as appropriate. Paragraphs 3, 4, 7 and 8 recite various conditions for the use of the Form. If these statements cannot be made, the Form cannot be used. Paragraphs 2, 5 and 6 state that various parts of the IHT Form are true and accurate.

The IHT Form 202 must be signed and dated by the personal **10.38** representatives but there is no need for the form to be sworn. However, even though not sworn, the personal representatives are liable to prosecution and penalties if they fail to make full enquiries or to verify personally that the statements in the account are true.

On the rest of the form, the personal representatives must set out full details of the estate and its liabilities.

The account is divided into two parts, Account A and Account B.

In Account A, the personal representatives set out, to quote the head note, "a full description of the property, real and personal, *in respect of which the grant is to be made.*" (The important words are those which we have put in italics). Therefore, in Account A the personal representatives list the values of the deceased's assets which will vest in them and in respect of which the personal representatives need a grant of representation to prove title. This means assets other than nominated property and property as to which the deceased was a joint tenant (which will appear in Account B). The total of these assets is the gross estate for probate purposes which appears in the oath sworn by the personal representatives. From this figure the liabilities of the estate are deducted to give the net estate. The figure for the net estate is also entered in the oath and it determines the amount of the probate fees (see paragraph 10.2 above.)

Account A is divided into two parts, the first lists assets which do not attract the instalment option; debts, other than those charged on property attracting the instalment option, are listed and deducted to give a net figure. The second part lists instalment option property; debts charged on such property are listed and deducted to give a net figure.

Page 4 commences with a questionnaire which asks for full particulars of any joint property (*i.e.* property passing by survivorship) held by the deceased at death. Particulars requested include the date when the joint ownership began, the names of the other owners and the extent of contributions made to the purchase price. The form then continues with Account B in which the personal representatives set out property in respect of which the grant is not made, *i.e.*:

(1) a full description and value of property nominated by the deceased in his lifetime,
(2) a description of any property (real or personal) held jointly by the deceased with any other person or persons, the beneficial interest in which passed by survivorship, and the value of the deceased's interest in such property.

When valuing a joint tenancy the deceased's interest is valued at the moment before death.

When valuing a joint tenancy in land the property as a whole must be valued and that value is then divided amongst the co-owners. Thus, if there were three co-owners the value of each share would prima facie be 1/3rd of value of whole. However, it is usual to apply a discount of about 15 per cent. (*Wight & Moss* v. *I.R.C.* (1982)) to reflect the fact that a co-owner has no right to exclusive possession and, despite the Law of Property Act 1925, s.30, may not be able to compel co-owner(s) to sell. In the case of husband and wife the related property rules (see paragraph 4.16) apply and no discount is available.

(The rules on valuation apply equally to tenancies in common. The value of the deceased's interest as tenant-in-common is included in Account A since the interest will vest in his personal representatives.)

After Account B the personal representatives must show the gross and net value for *probate* purposes. This is the value of property which vests in the personal representatives. The gross figures are brought forward from Account A together with the debts from Account A. The debts are deducted from the value of the gross estate to give the net figure.

Both gross and net figures will be repeated on the oath sworn by the personal representatives.

The final portion of the Form shows the value of the estate for *tax* purposes. The net value of Account B property is added to the net value of Account A property to give the total estate potentially chargeable to inheritance tax. Exemptions and reliefs are then deducted to give the final value of the estate for inheritance tax purposes.

4. IHT FORMS 200 AND 201

*Introduction*

If the estate is not "excepted" and IHT Form 202 cannot be **10.39** used, the personal representatives must deliver either IHT Form 200 or IHT Form 201. A completed example of the former appears in the Appendix at pages 480–491 and will be considered in this section, the latter is used for the estate of persons who died domiciled otherwise than in the United Kingdom. Foreign domicile must be proved by a statement attached to the Form. IHT Form 201 will not be considered further. Inheritance tax is charged (subject to double tax relief) on all property in the United Kingdom regardless of the owner's domicile and on foreign property where the owner is deemed domiciled here for tax purposes (see paragraph 10.40) although actually domiciled elsewhere.

IHT Form 200 like Form 202 sets out the assets and liabilities of the estate of the deceased and in addition is used to claim inheritance tax exemptions and reliefs and to calculate the amount of tax, if any, payable on the estate. The Form is a self-assessment form so that the solicitor acting for the personal representatives' will send with it a cheque for any inheritance tax payable on delivery of the account. (Usually all the tax for which the personal representatives are liable is payable on delivery of the account but in some circumstances the instalment option may be claimed—see above, paragraph 4.42). The procedure for delivery of the account and payment of the inheritance tax has been considered in paragraph 10.2 above.

It will be seen from the print of IHT Form 200 in the Appendix that it is a 12-page form of some complexity. Supplied with it are Forms 37 and 40. The Capital Taxes Office have published an explanatory booklet, Form 210, which contains detailed guidance for the completion of the Form.

The Form is divided into four main Sections, the division of the first three being based on liability to pay inheritance tax. This was considered fully in paragraphs 4.33–4.35; it should be remembered that the following are concurrently liable for the payment of inheritance tax on the deceased's estate:

(a)   the personal representatives for inheritance tax on the deceased's free estate ("free estate" includes property held as joint tenant and tenant in common) and on United Kingdom settled land which devolves on the personal representatives (as a result of the death of the life tenant bringing the strict settlement to an end);

(b)   the trustees for inheritance tax in respect of property which was settled immediately before the death;

(c)   any person in whom property is vested after death, or who is beneficially entitled to an interest in possession or for whose benefit property or income is applied out of property settled before death.

The fourth section is designed to discover whether any debts are non-deductible under section 103 of the Finance Act 1986 (see paragraph 4.18 above.)

We will consider the Form page by page and it will therefore be useful to refer to the Appendix where the Form is printed in full. The present print of the Form is used for deaths on or after March 18, 1986.

*Pages 1 and 2*

**10.40**   Page 1 of IHT Form 200 is very similar to the first page of IHT Form 202 in that the extracting solicitor's name, address and reference should be set out as well as details of where the application for the grant is to be made and details of the deceased. The deceased's full name, dates of birth and death, last usual address, marital status, surviving relatives, occupation and domicile are set out. The information given will be the same as that which appears in the oath. Thus, the extracting solicitor will set down the last permanent address of the deceased (as with IHT Form 202, the address of a hospital where the deceased died should not be given unless he was a *permanent* resident). The domicile is determined according to general law save that the Inheritance Tax Act 1984, s.267 provides that a person not domiciled in the United Kingdom shall be treated as so domiciled if he was domiciled in the United Kingdom within the three years preceding death or if he was resident in the United Kingdom in not less than seventeen of the twenty years of assessment ending with the year of assessment in which death occurs. It should be remembered that normally if the deceased was domiciled outside the United Kingdom IHT Form 201 is used.

The tax district at which the deceased's tax affairs were handled must be stated together with the tax district reference.

At the bottom of page 1, the names and addresses of all *proving* personal representatives are set out. If appointed by will, the names are set out in the order they appear in the will. If administrators are taking out a grant, they appear in order of entitlement.

On page 2 of the Form, the personal representatives have to sign, but not swear, a declaration that to the best of their knowledge and belief all the details that appear in the Form are true. Should the details prove to be false, the personal representatives may be liable to prosecution and penalties.

In statement 1 on page 2, the personal representatives state the nature of the grant of representation for which they are applying for example a grant of probate, letters of administration or a grant *de bonis non*.

Statement 3 is completed only if the personal representatives are, for some reason, unable to value some of the deceased's property.

Where the estate includes property which attracts the instalment option, statement 4 will have to be amended as appropriate. Whether the personal representatives will exercise the option to pay the tax by instalments will depend on the facts and the wishes of the recipients but the mere fact that property attracts the option does not necessarily mean it should be exercised. For example, if the amount of the outstanding tax is small, the personal representatives and the recipient may agree to discharge the liability immediately. However, where the liability is large the option will, in most cases, be exercised, since exercising it may remove the necessity of borrowing money to discharge the inheritance tax liability.

*The Questionnaire (page 3)*
The function of the questionnaire is to ascertain information **10.41** relevant to the liability to tax of the deceased's estate. Questions are asked to ascertain the size of the deceased's cumulative total (hence the reference to "Gifts, etc." in the first part of question 1). The questions also relate to the value of the estate at death and therefore ask whether the deceased disposed of any property by way of gift which was subject to a reservation (the second part of question 1); they also ask for details of the deceased's entitlement to interests in settled property (question 2), nominations made by him (question 3) and joint property in which he was interested (question 4). The value of the property referred to in the second part of question 1 and in questions 2, 3 and 4 will appear in the Form as it affects the value of the death estate and so the amount of inheritance tax that may be payable.

When answering the questions on *inter vivos* gifts full answers must be given, even though a full declaration of *inter vivos* gifts (and payment of tax, if appropriate) has been made in the past.

The questions are designed to ascertain the total chargeable transfers made by the deceased, the questionnaire is not intended merely to reveal transfers as yet undeclared.

Prima facie all transfers of value must be reported. However, certain transfers are exempt from reporting. These are set out at the bottom of page 2 opposite the questionnaire and include, *inter alia*, certain gifts falling within the annual exemption of £3,000 and the small gift exemption of £250.

*Section 1 (pages 4–7)*

**10.42** From page 4 to page 9, the personal representatives set out the details of the deceased's property. The value of the various items must be set out but there is no need, in this or any of the other sections of the form, to include pence. (Pence must appear in any Schedules to the Form). Pence are, however, included in the calculation of the tax on page 11.

The headings to each section give clear instructions as to which items are to be included.

Section 1 is a "**schedule of all the property of the deceased** within the U.K. to which the deceased was beneficially entitled and **in respect of which the grant is made,** ... " All property of the deceased situated in the United Kingdom which *vests in the personal representatives* appears in this section. If it does not vest in the personal representatives, for example because it is trust property the legal title to which is vested in trustees or is property subject to a nomination, *donatio mortis causa,* or a general power of appointment exercised by the deceased by his will or joint property passing by survivorship or is property gifted by the deceased *inter vivos* subject to a reservation, it appears in either Section two or in Section three.

*Section 1A (pages 4 to 6)*

**10.43** Section 1 is subdivided into two parts. Section 1A contains all the United Kingdom property of the deceased which vests in the personal representatives and which does *not* attract the instalment option.

On pages 4 and 5 are lists of the type of property falling within this heading. The value of property owned by the deceased falling within each category appears in the appropriate place on the Form. Page 4 requires little explanation but it should be noted that the reference to stocks, shares, etc., only includes items for which the instalment option is not available. To save space, if necessary, only the total value of such securities need appear on page 4, the full details will then appear on Form 40.

Certain items on page 4 relating to income merit attention.

(a) *"Income accrued due but not received prior to the death arising from real and personal property in which the deceased had a life or other limited interest."*

Income accrued *due* is income which was actually owed to the life tenant of a trust but not yet paid over to him by the trustees (or other payer). (The capital value of the trust assets will be included in section 3 not here).

(b) *"Apportionment of income from that source to date of death."*

It is necessary to examine the trust instrument to ascertain whether income payable after the death of a life tenant is to be apportioned between his estate and the beneficiary next entitled or whether the whole of such income is to be paid to the beneficiary next entitled. If as a result of the Apportionment Act the income is to be apportioned the pre-death portion is an asset of the deceased life tenant's estate and will be included for inheritance tax purposes. If the trust instrument states that there is to be no apportionment of income after the death of a life tenant, the deceased life tenant will have had no entitlement at death to such income and it will not be included here as an asset of the estate.

(c) *"Any other income apportioned where necessary to which the deceased was entitled at his death (e.g. pensions, annuities, director's fees, etc.)"* The treatment of income due from these sources differs from the treatment of income due to a deceased life tenant from a trust.

It is necessary to include the pre-death portion of all such payments as assets of the estate for inheritance tax purposes.

The will may exclude the need for apportionments for the purpose of *distribution* amongst beneficiaries of the estate but this does not alter the inheritance tax position on the death of the deceased. Amounts due to the deceased at death are assets of the estate and must be included for inheritance tax purposes.

(d) *Policies of insurance and bonuses (if any) thereon, on the life of the deceased.* These are included only if they were in the beneficial ownership of the deceased immediately before his death, (*i.e.* if the proceeds are payable as of right to the estate). If the policies were in the beneficial ownership of another, (*e.g.* having been assigned by the deceased *inter vivos*) they are not assets of the estate and are not included on the Form.

Section 1A continues on page 5 on which there are three points worthy of note:

(1) The details of any reversionary interest held by the deceased must be included in Section 1A even if it is "excluded property" (see paragraph 4.3). If the reversionary property *is* excluded property, relief is claimed on page 10 of the Form.

(2) The reference to "income tax payable" means refunds of income tax due to the estate.

(3) At the end of page 5, personal representatives include "other personal property not comprised under the foregoing heads." The items that can appear here include superannuation benefits where the personal representatives have a legally enforceable claim to those benefits, that is, if they are payable to the deceased's estate. If the trustees are given a *discretion* as to whom the benefits are paid, the benefits are not part of the death estate and so escape tax.

The total value of items shown on pages 4 and 5 of the Form are carried forward to page 6, on which appears the "Schedule of Liabilities and Funeral Expenses" and also to the Probate Summary on page 12.

On page 6, the personal representatives list the outstanding liabilities of the deceased except those charged on property attracting the instalment option. Examples of outstanding liabilities are domestic debts, such as insurance premiums, rates, electricity and gas bills as well as income tax outstanding at the date of death. These, together with "reasonable funeral expenses", are deducted from the gross value of Section 1A property and the net figure is carried to the Assessment of Tax on page 11 and to the Probate Summary on page 12. Further information relating to liabilities is required on page 9 to ascertain whether the debts are non-deductible under section 103 of the Finance Act 1986 (for example where the deceased directly or indirectly provided consideration, see paragraph 4.18 above).

*Section 1B (page 7)*

**10.44** In Section 1B, details are given of all United Kingdom property *which vests in the personal representatives* and which can attract the instalment option. This covers land, business interests and certain shares and securities which were in the absolute ownership of the deceased. (The detailed requirements which must be satisfied for the option to be available were discussed in paragraph 4.42.) The value and details of the property is shown on this page whether or not the option is to be exercised. The personal representatives state whether tax on this property is to be paid on delivery of the account or is to be paid by instalments. If the tax is to be paid by instalments each instalment is paid yearly.

The following property appears in this section:

(a) Land (freehold or leasehold) owned by the deceased in the United Kingdom (not being land subject to a Settled Land Act settlement which continues after the death of the deceased) whether or not subject to a statutory trust for sale. If, however, the deceased was a *joint tenant*, no reference to the land must appear here because the interest will not vest in the personal representatives but will pass by right of survivorship to the surviving joint tenant. If the deceased was a tenant in common the deceased's interest will vest in the personal representatives and will appear here. Details of land coming within this heading are set out in Form 37. Included in this section is land that *was* the subject-matter of a strict Settled Land Act settlement where the settlement has been brought to an end by the death of the life tenant (the deceased). In this circumstance the land vests in the personal representatives and they are liable for the inheritance tax. The grant is required to prove their title, so details of the land have to appear in Section 1.

(b) Business interests. Here the personal representatives insert the net value of the deceased's interests in unincorporated businesses, whether run by him as a sole proprietor or in which he was a partner. A statement or balance sheet showing the net value of the interests must be annexed to the Account.

(c) Shares, provided they either give control or are unquoted minority shareholdings satisfying the requirements of the Inheritance Tax Act 1984. The details of these shares are contained in Form 40.

Any liabilities charged at the date of death on the property (such as mortgages of land, amounts outstanding on business loans) are deducted from the total value of the section 1B property. The net "instalment option" property in the United Kingdom is carried to the Assessment of Tax on page 11. (The gross value is carried to the Probate Summary on page 12, as is the total of debts and liabilities). In the event of such liabilities exceeding Section 1B assets, the balance can be set against

Section 1A assets. Again, further information on liabilities is required on page 9 in order to establish whether any are non-deductible under Inheritance Tax Act, s.103.

*Section 2 (page 8)*

**10.45** The head-note to Section 2 requires the personal representatives to include on this page "**all other property on which the personal representatives are liable to pay tax** (or would be liable if any tax were payable) including all nominated property and property passing by survivorship and all property situated outside the United Kingdom."

In Section 2 appears all the deceased's United Kingdom "free estate" which does not vest in the personal representatives together with all free estate situated outside the United Kingdom.

Therefore the personal representatives list here details of all property subject to a nomination or *donatio mortis causa* and property held under a joint tenancy. Property on which the instalment option is not available appears in Section 2A, property on which the instalment option is available appears in Section 2B. Thus while the deceased's share in a joint building society account will appear in Section 2A, his interest in a joint tenancy in land will appear in Section 2B. (It should be noted that it is only the value of the *deceased's* interest in joint property which is shown, not the value of the *whole* property). In relation to the valuation of a deceased person's interest in property held jointly, whether as beneficiary joint tenants or as tenants in common, see the comments made above in respect of IHT Form 202.

As the head-note states, foreign property appears in Section 2A or 2B as appropriate.

Liabilities attaching to the Section 2A or 2B property (if any) are deducted from the respective gross totals. The net amounts are carried to the "Assessment of Tax" on page 11. Further information on liabilities is required on page 9 in order to establish whether any are non-deductible under Inheritance Tax Act, s.103.

*Section 3 (page 9)*

**10.46** In Section 3 appears "**any other property in the UK and elsewhere** in which the deceased had or is treated as having had a beneficial interest in possession immediately before his death including property over which the deceased had and exercised by will a general power of appointment, and property outside the UK comprised in a settlement made by a UK domiciled person and property gifted by the deceased subject to a reservation retained by the deceased."

The only trust property included in Section 3 is trust property in respect of which the liability to pay inheritance tax falls on the trustees of the settlement. The tax on property subject to a reservation is primarily the liability of the donee (although the personal representatives will *become* liable if the tax remains unpaid 12 months after death).

The Section is to be subdivided into Parts 1 and 2, the former including "property on which tax is **elected to be paid** on delivery of this Account," the latter containing "Property on which tax is **not to be paid on delivery of this account**." At first sight it may be difficult to visualise what property would appear in Part I since the section contains property in respect of which the trustees or donees are liable to pay tax.

Part 1 of Section 3 will include details of, *inter alia*:

(a)   any trust property (other than settled land where the strict settlement comes to an end by virtue of the death of the life tenant, when it appears in Section 1B) where the trustees are also the personal representatives of the deceased, in which case it may be administratively more convenient for the personal representatives to pay tax on both parts of the estate at the same time;

(b)   any property where the personal representatives of the deceased have been given money by the separate trustees or by the donees to discharge the tax liability on behalf of the trustees or donees.

Under the heading "Part 1" the personal representatives must show separately the property that does, and does not attract the instalment option since these figures, after deduction of any liabilities, appear in different places in the "Assessment of Tax" on page 11. If the instalment option is to be taken up the personal representatives must state this.

Under the heading "Part 2," the personal representatives list the property in respect of which tax is *not* to be paid when they deliver the Account. Even though the tax may be paid separately, the value of the property still has to appear in the Form since it will affect the size of the death estate and, therefore, the amount of the inheritance tax liability, if any.

The personal representatives include in Part 2 details of, *inter alia*:

(a)  Settlements of personalty;
(b)  Land held on express trusts for sale (but *not* land held on a statutory trust for sale which will appear in section 1B if it is a tenancy in common or section 2B if it is a joint tenancy;
(c)  Settled Land Act settlements where the settlement continues after the death of the life tenant;
(d)  Property gifted *inter vivos* subject to a reservation.

Form 210 gives illustrations of how the information required to be set out in Section 3 should appear. Broadly speaking in Part 1, the personal representatives identify and value the settlement and its property or the property subject to a reservation and deduct any liabilities from the property to which they are attached. In Part 2, the personal representatives in addition identify the settlement and its trustees or the *inter vivos* donees (to enable the Revenue to collect the tax from them). Any liabilities attached to the property are deducted from the value of the property. The net totals of Parts 1 and 2 are then transferred to separate places in the "Assessment of Tax" on page 11. No reference to reliefs or exemptions are made on page 9; they appear on page 10.

*Section 4 (page 9)*

**10.47**  Section 4 requires the personal representatives to state whether in the case of any of the debts and liabilities incurred on or after March 18, 1986, and deducted in the three earlier sections of the Form, the consideration consisted of property derived from the deceased or was consideration given by a person at any time entitled to or amongst whose resources there was at any time included any property derived from the deceased.

If the answer is yes, it is likely that such a debt will prove to be non-deductible under section 103 of the Finance Act 1986. The Capital Taxes Office will decide this at a later stage; the initial amount of inheritance tax assessed in IHT Form 200 will include all liabilities listed. This has the advantage of reducing the amount of the tax payable initially. If the tax is later increased as a result of certain debts being disallowed, it is likely that the personal representatives will find it easier to obtain funds from the deceased's estate as they will have obtained the grant of representation.

*Exemptions and reliefs (page 10)*

**10.48**  On page 10, all the exemptions and reliefs the personal representatives wish to claim are set out, except quick succession relief and double taxation relief which are claimed on page 11.

The personal representatives identify the property attracting the relief or exemption by reference to the Section in which it appears and then identify the relief, whether it is the spouse exemption or business property relief, etc. Having done so, the net value of the property is stated and the amount of the exemption or relief claimed.

Thus if property within Section 1A has been left to the deceased's spouse, the property is identified, valued and its entire value claimed as an exemption. If a reversionary interest that is excluded property was included in Section 1A it must be identified and deducted on page 10 to ensure it is left out of account when calculating the value of the death estate.

Where the property set out in Section 1B attracts business or agricultural property relief, the appropriate percentage reduction will be claimed as a relief.

When completing page 10, the reliefs available in respect of the various sections and sub-sections are claimed separately and the separate totals of deductions for each Section are carried to page 11.

*Assessment of tax (page 11)*
The purpose of page 11 is:                                        **10.49**

(a) to calculate the total amount of inheritance tax payable on the death estate, taking into account the deceased's lifetime cumulative total and the reliefs and exemptions available on death including quick succession relief; and

(b) to calculate the proportion of that tax which must be paid by the personal representatives on delivery of the IHT Form. This is done by apportioning the total tax payable between firstly, the property in Sections 1A, 2A and 3, Part 1 (*i.e.* the property for which the personal representatives are liable—or in the case of Section 3, Part 1 have agreed to be liable—and on which the instalment option is not available) in respect of which inheritance tax is payable on delivery of the account and secondly, the property in Sections 1B, 2B and Section 3, Part 1, (*i.e.* the property for which the personal representatives are liable—or in the case of Section 3, Part 1 have agreed to be liable—and on which the instalment option is available) in respect of which inheritance tax is not payable on delivery of the account if the option is exercised. The proportion of the tax which relates to the Section 3, Part 2 property is not dealt with further on this form. It is a matter for the Capital Taxes Office and the person(s) liable.

In the first part of page 11, the summary for determining taxable rates, the net totals from the various parts of the first three sections of the Form are entered and the appropriate exemptions and reliefs deducted. The values of each category of property after the deduction of reliefs are added together to give a total net value after reliefs. This is labelled "A" on the form and represents the taxable value of the death estate. To this is added the cumulative total of chargeable transfers made *inter vivos*. This is labelled "B." The result described as "Aggregate chargeable transfers" is labelled "C."

In the right-hand top corner of page 11, tax is calculated on total "C" at the full rates. Since this total includes the *inter vivos* chargeable transfers of the deceased, inheritance tax at the full rates on this figure is later deducted, leaving the amount of inheritance tax payable in respect of the death estate. From this is deducted any quick succession relief in accordance with the Inheritance Tax Act 1984, s.141 to leave the total tax payable in respect of the death estate (Total D).

Not all this tax will be paid on the delivery of the account since some of the property may be property in respect of which others, such as the trustees of the settlement are liable to pay the tax. Furthermore some of the property may attract the instalment option so that only part of the tax will be paid now, *i.e.* to the extent that the instalments are due.

In the bottom portion of page 11 (labelled "the amount payable on this account") the tax payable by the personal representatives is apportioned between the non-instalment property and the instalment option property. The calculations shown on the Form ensure that each part of the estate bears the appropriate proportion of the total tax liability.

The reference to deducting "Reliefs against tax other than relief for successive charges" is to any double taxation relief that may be available (exemptions and reliefs against capital such as spouse, business property etc., will already have been claimed on page 10).

Although the account need only be delivered within 12 months of the end of the month of death, interest (currently 11 per cent.) is payable on tax outstanding from six months after the end of the month of death. (For the position as regards outstanding instalments where the instalment option is claimed, see paragraph 4.42).

At the foot of page 11 on the left-hand side the personal representatives have to insert the amount of any tax due on any potentially exempt transfers made within seven years of the death and any additional tax due on chargeable transfers made before death (and interest if appropriate) if relevant even if they are not liable to pay it. The donee of a gift made within seven years of the death is primarily responsible for the inheritance tax due but recourse can be made to the estate if it proves necessary either because the tax due exceeds the value of the asset that the recipient has or because the tax has not been paid by the recipient (see paragraph 4.35).

*Probate summary (page 12)*
The purpose of the Probate Summary is two-fold.

**10.50**

First it sets out the gross and net value of the assets vesting in the personal representatives, which figures appear on the oaths sworn by the personal representatives and determine the probate fees.

Secondly it sets out the amount of tax and interest payable on the Account, the receipt of which is acknowledged by the Inland Revenue.

*Payment of tax*
The IHT Form and the cheque for any tax the solicitor has assessed as being payable are submitted together with the other probate papers.

**10.51**

It is not normally necessary to submit the Inland Revenue account for examination and assessment of tax before applying for the grant, however this has to be done in certain cases, *i.e.* where, *inter alia*:

(a) the deceased was domiciled outside the United Kingdom and died on or after March 13, 1975;

(b) a tax exemption is claimed in relation to property said to be of national, scientific, historic or artistic importance, or land or buildings of outstanding interest;

(c) tax is to be paid in the form of delivery of national savings certificates or premium bonds;

(d) the personal representatives wish to pay tax on unquoted shares or securities by instalments;

(e) the grant is to relate only to settled land or is one for which IHT Form 200 or 202 is inappropriate.

5. FURTHER FORMS

In addition to the forms already described, other forms may have to be completed.

**10.52**

*Corrective accounts*

**10.53** If the information originally provided by the personal representatives proves to be incorrect, whether as a result of a mistake or because they discover additional property or liabilities, a corrective account, Form D-3, will have to be sent to the Capital Taxes Office. If the alteration is trivial, they may agree to dispense with the requirement.

*Second or Subsequent Grants*

**10.54** If the applicant is applying for a grant of double probate or a cessate grant or a grant *de bonis non administratis,* Form A-5c is normally used.

Otherwise (for example, when a new grant is applied for after the previous grant has been revoked) IHT Form 200 (or 201 if appropriate) is used. Where the grant follows a revocation, any inheritance tax payable has to be paid again and the original grantee applies for a refund. However, the tax originally paid can be treated as paid by the new grantee provided it can be shown that it was paid from the deceased's estate or that the original grantee agrees.

# E. Affidavit Evidence

## 1. AFFIDAVIT OF DUE EXECUTION

**10.55** Before a will or codicil can be admitted to probate the registrar must be satisfied that it was duly executed.

If a will or codicil contains an attestation clause, which recites that the proper formalities were complied with, a presumption that the will was duly executed arises. Under the Non-Contentious Probate Rules 1987, rule 12(1) if the will contains no attestation clause or the attestation clause is insufficient or where it appears to the registrar that there is some doubt about the due execution of the will he must require an affidavit as to due execution before admitting the will to probate in common form. The affidavit should be from one of the attesting witnesses or, if no attesting witness is conveniently available, from any other person who was present at the time the will was executed. If no such affidavit evidence is obtainable, the registrar may (under rule 12(2)) accept affidavit evidence from any person he may think fit to show that the signature on the will is in the deceased's handwriting or on any other matter which may raise a presumption in favour of due execution. The registrar may require notice of the application to be given to any person who may be prejudiced by the will. If the registrar after considering the evidence is satisfied that the will was not duly executed he must refuse probate and mark the will accordingly.

The maxim *omnia praesumuntur rite ac solemniter esse acta* may assist when actual evidence of due execution cannot be obtained. In certain circumstances it allows the inference to be drawn that the necessary formalities have been complied with.

> "The maxim expresses an inference which may reasonably be drawn when an intention to do some formal act is established; when the evidence is consistent with that intention having been carried into effect in a proper way; but where the actual observance of all due formalities can only be inferred as a matter of probability." *Per* Lord Lindley L.J. in *Harris* v. *Knight* (1890).

The presumption can only be of use where the appearance of the document in question is consistent with the formalities having been complied with. The presumption applies very strongly where there is a formal attestation clause and less strongly where there is an informal clause or no clause at all. *In the estate of Denning* (1958) is an example of the application of the presumption in the absence of an attestation clause. The dispositive part of a will, together with the testator's signature, was contained on one side of a piece of paper. On the reverse side two signatures were written in different handwriting, one below the other. Sachs J. applied the presumption and declared that the will was duly executed. He said:

> "that there is no other practical reason why the names should be on the back of the document unless it was for the purpose of attesting the will."

However, the presumption will not be applied where the evidence available suggests that the will was not duly executed.

## 2. AFFIDAVIT AS TO KNOWLEDGE AND APPROVAL

**10.56**   Under rule 13 of the Non-Contentious Probate Rules 1987, before admitting to proof a will which appears to have been signed by a blind or illiterate testator or by another person by the testator's direction or which for any other reason gives rise to doubt as to the testator having had knowledge of the contents of the will at the time of its execution, the registrar must satisfy himself that the testator had such knowledge. The registrar may require affidavit evidence for this purpose under the Non-Contentious Probate Rules 1987, rule 16.

A solicitor who is present when a will is signed by such persons ought to ensure that the attestation clause states that the will was read over to the testator and that the testator appeared to understand and approve the contents.

### 3. AFFIDAVITS OF ALTERATION, CONDITION AND DATE OF EXECUTION

**10.57** The following matters are dealt with in Non-Contentious Probate Rules 1987, rule 14.

*Alteration*

If a will appears to contain an unexecuted alteration (other than the completion of a blank space) the registrar must require evidence to show whether the alteration was present at the time the will was executed (rule 14(1)) and may require affidavit evidence for this purpose (rule 16). In the absence of evidence to the contrary the alteration is presumed to have been made after execution. The registrar may, however, disregard an alteration which is of no practical importance (for example, an alteration to a legacy which has lapsed).

*Incorporation*

**10.58** If a will contains a reference to another document in such terms as to suggest that it ought to be incorporated in the will the registrar may require the document to be produced and may call for such evidence in regard to the attaching or incorporation of the document as he may think fit (rule 14(3)). The registrar may require affidavit evidence for this purpose (rule 16).

*Date of execution*

**10.59** If there is doubt as to the date on which a will was executed the registrar may require such evidence as he thinks necessary to establish the date (rule 14(4)) and may require affidavit evidence for this purpose (rule 16).

### 4. AFFIDAVIT OF ATTEMPTED REVOCATION

**10.60** Any appearance of attempted revocation by burning, tearing or otherwise destroying must be accounted for to the registrar's satisfaction (rule 15) and the registrar may require affidavit evidence for this purpose (rule 16). It is not desirable to attach anything to an original will since the existence of marked pin holes, staple holes or clip impressions may suggest that there has been an attempted revocation in which case the registrar will call for affidavit evidence.

# F. Caveats

A caveat is a notice entered at any probate registry by post or **10.61** in person the effect of which is to prevent a grant of probate or administration being made without notice first being given to the person who enters the caveat, called the caveator, (Non-Contentious Probate Rules 1987, rule 44).

Once a caveat is entered it is effective for a period starting with the day after the day on which it is entered and ending six months after the day on which it was entered. A caveat may be renewed for an additional six months during the last month of the six-month period and again in the last month of each successive six-month period. The probate registry's own internal procedures ensure that no grant can be made in any registry while the caveat is effective. The caveat must contain the name and address of the deceased, the date and place of death and the name and address for service of the caveator.

Any person interested may issue a "warning" to the caveat under rule 44(5). The index to caveats has been kept since August 1, 1988 at the Leeds District Probate Registry and not at the Principal Registry. As a consequence, warnings must be issued either personally, through the post or through the document exchange at Leeds District Probate Registry. The "person warning" must state the nature of his interest and the date of the will (if any) in the warning which must then be served on the caveator. The warning must also require the caveator to state the nature of his interest. A person whose application for a grant was blocked by a caveat may issue a warning since he is a "person interested."

Once the warning has been served on the caveator one of four things will happen depending on what right the caveator is alleging and what steps he chooses to take:

(a) *The caveator may withdraw his caveat* (rule 44(11)). A caveator is free to withdraw his caveat at any time whether a warning has been issued or not. A caveator who withdraws after receiving a warning must give notice to the person warning. Once the caveat is withdrawn it becomes ineffective and the person warning is free to proceed with his application for a grant (unless, of course, there is another caveat in force).

(b) *The caveator may enter an appearance* (rule 44(10)). An appearance should be entered within eight days of the service of the warning on the caveator. If it is not the person warning may thereafter take steps to "warn off" the caveator (see paragraph

(d) below). An appearance can only be entered by the caveator if he has an interest contrary to that of the person warning. For example, entry of an appearance would be the appropriate step to take where the caveator claims to be an executor under a valid will and the person warning claims to be entitled to letters of administration on the grounds that the will is invalid. The appearance must be entered personally at the Leeds District Probate Registry.

Once an appearance has been entered the caveat remains in force until a registrar of the Family Division otherwise directs (rule 44(13)). Often the entry of the appearance will be followed by the commencement of a probate action (although neither the warning nor the entry of the appearance itself amounts to the commencement of such an action). Where this happens the caveat is no longer necessary since the fact that a probate action has been started has the effect of preventing a grant being made (rule 45(3)).

(c) *The caveator may issue and serve a summons for directions* (rule 44(6)). This step must be taken within eight days of service of the warning, otherwise the caveator risks being warned off. A summons for directions may only be issued by a caveator who has no interest contrary to that of the person warning. It is, therefore, the appropriate step to take where the caveator is entitled to a grant in the same degree as or a lower degree than the person warning but wishes to show cause why that person should not take a grant (for example because he is unsuitable and the caveator wishes the court to pass him over).

After a summons for directions has been issued there will be a hearing before a registrar (or in case of difficulty a judge) at which he will decide to whom a grant should be made.

(d) *The caveator may do nothing*. In this case the person warning may file an affidavit after the time limit for entering an appearance (eight days) has expired (rule 44(12)). The affidavit must show that the warning was served on the caveator. The caveat is then said to be "warned off" and is no longer effective so that the person warning is now free to proceed with his application.

## G. Citations

**10.62** Citations are documents issued by the principal or district registry which call upon the party cited to show cause why a certain step should not be taken. They are used for a variety of purposes but all are designed to give a remedy where a person actually or possibly entitled to a grant is refusing to take steps to take the grant or to renounce so that others may do so. Although citations were formerly issued in contentious cases they are now only used in non-contentious cases.

There are three types of citation:

(a)   A citation to take probate;
(b)   A citation to accept or refuse a grant (of probate or letters of administration);
(c)   A citation to propound a will.

### 1. CITATION TO TAKE PROBATE

An executor may normally renounce his right to take a grant. **10.63** However, once he has "intermeddled" (so as to constitute himself an executor *de son tort*) in the estate he is no longer free to renounce and so may be cited to take probate. The citation may be issued at the instance of any person interested in the estate but cannot be issued until at least six months after the testator's death nor at any time while proceedings as to the validity of the will are pending (Non-Contentious Probate Rules 1987 rule 47(3)). An administrator does not, by intermeddling, lose his right to renounce and so he cannot be cited to *take* administration; (an administrator who intermeddles will, however, make himself liable up to the limit of assets coming into his hands as an executor *de son tort.*)

### 2. CITATION TO ACCEPT OR REFUSE A GRANT

A citation to accept or refuse a grant may be issued at the **10.64** instance of any person who would be entitled to a grant if the person cited were to renounce (Non-Contentious Probate Rules 1987, rule 47(1)). This type of citation is, therefore, used where a person with an inferior right to a grant wishes to force the person or persons better entitled to make up their minds whether to apply or not. Where there are several persons with a superior right they must all be cited before the person with the inferior right can take a grant. Where power has been reserved to a person to take a grant of probate, the proving executor may cite him to take or refuse probate (rule 47(2)). In other cases it is not necessary or possible to cite a person with an equal right to take a grant since the court can issue a grant to any of the persons equally entitled.

A citation to accept or refuse a grant may be issued to a person with a right to either a grant of probate (unless he has lost the right to renounce) or letters of administration. A citation of this type may be made at any time after the death of the testator or intestate.

### 3. CITATION TO PROPOUND A WILL

**10.65** The object of this type of citation is to force the persons interested in the alleged will to seek probate of it if they can. The application may be made by any person with a contrary interest (which in effect means a person who is entitled on intestacy or under an earlier will). The citation must be directed to all the persons interested under the alleged will and not only to the executors of it (Non-Contentious Probate Rules 1987, rule 48(1)).

An executor of a will who doubts the validity of a later codicil is not entitled to cite the beneficiaries of the alleged codicil to propound it. His proper course is to bring a probate action in which he will seek to establish the validity of the will and the invalidity of the codicil.

### 4. PROCEDURE ON CITATION

A person (called a citor) who wishes to obtain a citation must first issue a caveat (Non-Contentious Probate Rules 1987, rule 46(3)). The citor must then swear an affidavit confirming every averment in the citation (rule 46(2)) and the registrar must settle the form of citation before it is issued (rule 46(1)). Any will referred to in the citation must be lodged in a registry before the citation is issued unless it is not in the citor's possession and it is impractical to lodge it (rule 46(5)). The citation will set out the steps which the court will take if the person cited does not show cause to the contrary.

A citation must normally be personally served on the person cited but other modes of service, including advertisement, may be ordered by the registrar (this will be done, for example, where the difficulty in obtaining the grant has been caused by the disappearance of the person entitled).

A person cited must enter an appearance within eight days of service (rule 46(6)). If he does not the citor may apply for an order for a grant to himself if the citation was a citation to accept or refuse a grant (rule 47(5)(a)). Where the person cited was cited to take probate he can be ordered to do so within a stated time if he fails to enter an appearance (rule 47(5)(c)) although the court may exercise its discretion to pass him over (see, for example, *In the Estate of Biggs* (1966), paragraph 8.21). If the person cited was cited to propound a will and has failed to enter an appearance the citor may apply for a grant in common form as if the will were invalid.

Where the person cited does enter an appearance he may show cause why the steps contemplated by the citation should not be taken. Alternatively if he is now willing to take a grant he may apply *ex parte* to a registrar for an order for a grant (rule 47(4)) to himself.

Where power to take a grant has been reserved to an executor a citation to accept or refuse a grant may be made at the instance of the proving executors (or the person who is executor by representation) against that person.

## H. Standing Searches

An entry of a caveat has the effect of ensuring that notice of an application for a grant is given to the caveator. However, it is an abuse of the process of the court for a person to enter a caveat where there is no dispute as to an issue concerned with a probate matter (such as the validity of a will or a right to a grant of probate or administration). A person who merely wishes to know when a grant is made so that he can make a claim against the estate should not therefore enter a caveat. Such a person could, in most cases, enter a citation since a creditor is entitled to a grant of administration on clearing off the beneficiaries. However, it will usually be more appropriate for him to make a "standing search."   **10.66**

A standing search is made by lodging the appropriate form together with the prescribed fee at the principal registry. An office copy of any grant made within 12 months before or six months after the search will then be given to the applicant. The period of search can be extended by further periods of six months on payment of a fee for each extension.

## I. Guarantees

Before 1972 almost all administrators were required to enter into bonds for the due administration of the estate of the deceased. This requirement was repealed by the Administration of Estates Act 1971 and replaced by a much less stringent   **10.67** provision requiring a guarantee in certain limited circumstances and no guarantee or bond at all in most circumstances.

The present law is contained in section 120(1) of the Supreme Court Act 1981 which provides that:

" ... the High Court may ... require one or more sureties to guarantee that they will make good, within any limit imposed by the court on the total liability of the surety or sureties, any loss which any person interested in the administration of the estate of the deceased may suffer in consequence of a breach by the administrator of his duties as such."

The Non-Contentious Probate Rules 1987 (unlike the rules which they replace) do not require guarantees in any particular type of case.

# 11. Powers and Duties of Personal Representatives

## A. Duties of Personal Representatives

### 1. DUTY TO COLLECT ASSETS

The first duty of a personal representative is "to collect and get **11.1** in the deceased's real and personal estate" (Administration of Estates Act 1925, s.25 as amended by Administration of Estates Act 1971, s.9). Once the assets are collected the personal representative must administer the estate by paying debts and legacies and by disposing of the residue (these duties are dealt with in Chapters 15, 16 and 18). All duties of personal representatives must be performed with "due diligence." The personal representative must, therefore:

(a) take reasonable steps to collect money due to the deceased (by bringing proceedings if necessary);

(b) collect the assets as quickly as is practical. (Money which is due to the deceased and which is secured by mortgage or other charge need not be collected immediately unless the security is in danger.)

No absolute rule can be laid down as to what is a reasonable time for collection of assets nor as to what steps must be taken in order to collect assets. In each case the personal representative will only be liable for loss resulting from his failure to act if he has acted unreasonably.

### 2. PROOF OF TITLE TO ASSETS

The personal and real property of the deceased devolves on the **11.2** personal representatives at death, in the case of an executor or on the making of the grant, in the case of an administrator. This

only applies to interests in property which continue notwithstanding the death so that a life interest does not devolve
on the personal representatives nor does an interest in joint
property (which passes to the remaining joint tenant(s) by right
of survivorship). The legal title to property held by the deceased
as a trustee devolves on the personal representative if the
deceased was a sole trustee but on the remaining trustees if
there are any at the time of death. If the deceased owned an
interest as a tenant in common in equity, it will devolve on the
personal representatives, unless it was a life interest in which
case it will cease to exist on death.

An interest held as beneficial joint tenant will not devolve on
the personal representatives but will pass by right of survivorship to the surviving joint tenant(s). Property subject to a
nomination or *donatio mortis causa* will not devolve on the
personal representatives but can be claimed by the nominee or
donee immediately after death. Such property is an asset of the
estate but the grant of representation is not required to make
title.

Insurance policies on the deceased's life written in trust for
third parties or taken out under the Married Women's Property
Act 1882 will not be assets of the estate. Such policies are
payable to the trustees on proof of death; the grant of
representation is not required. The personal representatives will
not be concerned in the collection of the proceeds of such
policies (unless there is no trustee named in which case the
proceeds will be paid to them—even so the proceeds will still
not be assets of the estate for tax purposes). A lump sum
payable under a discretionary pension scheme will not be an
asset of the estate and the personal representatives will not be
concerned in its collection. The trustees of the pension scheme
will pay direct to the person(s) they have selected.

In order to collect the assets which devolve on them personal
representatives will have to prove their entitlement to the
people who are in possession of the assets at the time of death.
This can be done by production of the original grant of probate
or administration or of an office copy of the grant. Office copies
can be obtained from the registry on payment of a small fee.
Personal representatives should apply for sufficient office copies
to enable them to deal with the estate of the deceased
promptly—the more items of property included in the estate the
greater the number of copies which should be obtained. It is
not, however, necessary to have a copy for each item of
property. A person in possession of estate assets must hand over

the assets on production of the original or office copy grant which he must then return to the personal representative.

## 3. ENFORCEMENT OF PERSONAL REPRESENTATIVES' DUTIES

A personal representative who accepts office (by taking a grant **11.3** or by acting as executor) is liable for loss resulting from any breach of duty which he commits. A breach of duty by a personal representative may consist of misappropriating the property of the deceased for his own benefit, maladministration (such as distributing to the wrong people even though in good faith) or negligence (such as an unreasonable delay in dealing with the collection or distribution of the estate). Any breach of duty by a personal representative is called a *devastavit*.

An action may be brought against the personal representative by a beneficiary or creditor who is not paid in full as a result of a *devastavit* by a personal representative. A personal representative can protect himself against certain types of breach of duty in a number of ways (see Chapter 14). In particular a personal representative cannot be held liable to an adult who has consented to the way in which he has performed his duties with full knowledge of the circumstances.

Where several personal representatives are appointed each is liable for his own breach of duty but not for breaches by his co-executor or co-administrator. However, a personal representative who permits a breach of trust by another personal representative will be liable since he has then failed to perform his own duty of safeguarding the estate. He may also be liable in negligence if he fails to attend to his duties and thus allows a breach by another personal representative to go unnoticed.

# B. Powers of Personal Representatives before Grant

The authority of an administrator derives from *the grant*. The **11.4** powers of an administrator before the grant is made are, therefore, very limited.

An administrator may not bring any action before grant and if he purports to do so a later grant does not cure the defect in the original proceedings (*Ingall* v. *Moran* (1944)). A new action must be brought once the grant has been made. In order to protect an estate from wrongful injury in the period between death and the obtaining of the grant the authority of an administrator will relate back for the limited purpose of giving validity to acts done before letters of administration were obtained. However, such relation back occurs only in those cases where the acts done are for the benefit of the estate. The test of whether or not an act is for the benefit of the estate is entirely objective. Thus in *Mills* v. *Anderson* (1984) an "administrator" agreed before the grant to accept on behalf of the estate a sum in full and final settlement of a claim for damages. It later became apparent that the settlement was too low. It was held that there could be no question of the administrator's authority relating back to validate the agreement as it would not be to the benefit of the estate.

An administrator has no power to vest property in any person before obtaining a grant.

The power of an executor derives from *the will* of the deceased and not from the grant which merely confirms his authority. An executor can therefore, in principle, exercise all his powers without obtaining a grant. An executor can sue or be sued before obtaining a grant. If he brings an action (for example, against a creditor) the action is valid even though no grant has been issued. However, before judgment is entered in his favour a grant must be obtained since the court will, at that stage, require proof of his authority to act as executor if the action depends on his title to act in that capacity.

An executor is also entitled to deal with the collection and distribution of the estate without first obtaining a grant. In practice, collection of assets without a grant may prove impossible since the persons in possession may refuse to hand them over without proof of the executor's title. Similarly, as far as distribution is concerned, a purchaser will require proof of title before paying for assets. A beneficiary in whose favour an assent or conveyance of a legal estate in land is made is entitled to have a notice of the assent or conveyance endorsed on the original grant of representation; thus, the grant will have to be obtained before the assent is made.

# C. Implied Administrative Powers

### 1. INTRODUCTION

**11.5** The Administration of Estates Act 1925 gives personal representatives various powers in connection with the administration. The Trustee Act 1925 and Trustee Investments Act 1961 give various powers to trustees and since the definition of "trustee" contained in that Act includes a personal representative, personal representatives have these powers also. The most important of these implied powers are outlined briefly in this section. Many of these powers are, however, subject to awkward limitations with the result that it is common for professionally drawn wills to extend them and to confer additional powers. In this section we have pointed out the limitations where appropriate and in Chapter 22 we have dealt more fully with the express clauses commonly included to extend the powers.

It is always possible for a testator to exclude an implied power by stating in the will that it is not available to the personal representatives or trustees.

## 2. POWERS OF PERSONAL REPRESENTATIVES TO SELL, MORTGAGE AND LEASE

Section 39 of the Administration of Estates Act 1925 gives the **11.6** personal representatives very extensive powers; they are given "the same powers and discretions" in dealing with the deceased's real and personal estate as are enjoyed by trustees for sale of land (*i.e.* all the powers of a tenant for life and of the trustees of a settlement under the Settled Land Act 1925). Thus, personal representatives can sell or exchange any property or part thereof, can raise money by mortgage or charge and can grant leases and accept surrenders of leases. These powers exist "until the period of distribution arrives," that is until the end of the administration period.

A receipt given by a personal representative for money, securities or other personal property is a sufficient discharge to the person paying or transferring (Trustee Act 1925, s.14) unless that person acts in bad faith (for example, by purchasing property at a fraudulent undervalue) in which case the transaction is vitiated and a beneficiary or creditor of the estate may have the transaction set aside. If trustees sell land, it is necessary for a receipt to be given by at least two trustees or a trust corporation. However, a sole personal representative may give a good receipt for capital money (Trustee Act 1925, s.27(2)).

The personal representatives obviously have very wide powers to sell assets and raise money. These powers are necessary since cash is required for a number of purposes in connection with the administration; for example, the payment of funeral, testamentary and administration expenses, inheritance tax, debts and pecuniary legacies. Deciding *which* assets to sell is a complex decision and the personal representatives have to consider a number of matters; for example, which assets have been specifically given to beneficiaries, which assets occur first in the statutory order for property available for payment of debts (see Chapter 15), which assets will fetch the best price and which assets will attract the least liability to tax for the estate and for the beneficiaries. These matters are discussed more fully in Chapter 12.

### 3. POWER TO APPROPRIATE

**11.7** Section 41 of the Administration of Estates Act 1925 gives the personal representatives power to appropriate any part of the estate in or towards satisfaction of any legacy or interest or share in the estate of the deceased, provided that such an appropriation does not prejudice any specific beneficiary.

*Example*
T leaves X a pecuniary legacy of £1,000 and the residue of the estate to Y. The residue includes a clock valued at £750. The personal representatives may let X take the clock in partial satisfaction of the legacy.

An appropriation can only be made by the personal representatives if the appropriate consents are obtained. There are two situations to consider.

(a) *If the beneficiary is absolutely and beneficially entitled to the legacy* the consent required is that of the beneficiary or, if the beneficiary is an infant or mentally incapable of managing his own affairs, the consent must be that of the beneficiary's parent or guardian or receiver.

(b) *If the legacy is settled* the consent must be that of the trustees (provided they are not also the personal representatives) or of the person for the time being entitled to the income provided such a person is of full age and capacity. If the personal representatives are the only trustees and there is no person of full age or capacity for the time being entitled to the income no consents are required. However, in this case the appropriation must be of an investment authorised by law or by the will. This limitation as to the type of property appropriated does not exist in other cases.

The asset is valued at the date of the appropriation, not at the date of death (*Re Collins* (1975)); in times of rising property values, therefore, a pecuniary legatee will be anxious that the appropriation be made as quickly as possible. The personal representatives will have to ascertain and fix the value of assets for this purpose as they see fit but must strive to be fair to all beneficiaries. A duly qualified valuer should be employed where necessary. Thus, in *Re Bythway* (1911) it was held that an executrix was not entitled to appropriate to herself shares in an unquoted company at her own valuation.

If the asset is worth more than the legacy to which the beneficiary is entitled it would appear that the power granted by section 41 cannot be exercised since in such a case the asset cannot be said to be appropriated "*in or towards satisfaction*" of the legacy (*Re Phelps* (1980)). The personal representatives can, however, exercise their power of sale under section 39 of the Administration of Estates Act 1925 to sell the asset to a beneficiary in consideration of a part payment of cash and the satisfaction of the legacy.

Because section 41 requires consent, the Inland Revenue regard appropriation as a "conveyance or transfer on sale" so that any instrument giving effect to the appropriation attracted ad valorem stamp duty (*Jopling* v. *I.R.C.* (1940)). For that reason it was common for wills to provide that the personal representatives need not obtain the consent of a legatee to an appropriation. The Stamp Duty (Exempt Instruments) Regulations 1987 exempt from duty all instruments giving effect to an appropriation in or towards satisfaction of a general legacy executed on or after May 1, 1987. Such instruments must be certified as falling within the appropriate category of the Schedule to the Regulations. (See paragraph 22.37).

Where a personal representative sells an asset to a beneficiary partly in consideration or satisfaction of a legacy and partly in consideration of an additional cash payment it would appear that ad valorem stamp duty may have to be charged on any instrument effecting the transaction. This is because it cannot be said in such a case there has been an appropriation *in or towards* satisfaction of a legacy.

The Intestates' Estates Act 1952 provides that the surviving spouse of a person who dies intestate has a *right* to require the personal representatives to appropriate any dwelling house comprised in the residuary estate in which the spouse was resident at the time of the intestate's death in or towards satisfaction of the spouse's entitlement (see Chapter 3). Since the spouse can compel the personal representatives to make the appropriation there is no contractual element and ad valorem stamp duty has never been payable. (Schedule 2, paragraph 5(2) of the Act gives the spouse the right to *require* appropriation even where the house is worth more than the spouse's entitlement, provided equality money is paid.)

### 4. POWER TO APPOINT TRUSTEES OF A MINOR'S PROPERTY

**11.8** When a personal representative vests property in a beneficiary absolutely entitled (or person otherwise entitled to assets, for example, a trustee) the personal representative obtains a discharge from liability by means of a receipt signed by the person entitled. In the absence of an express direction to the contrary in the will a minor cannot give a good receipt for money or securities nor can his parents, guardian or adult spouse give one on his behalf (a married minor may give a good receipt for income). Personal representatives who, without authority, pay a child's legacy to a parent, guardian or adult spouse are in danger of personal liability to account to the minor when the minor attains majority. To overcome this difficulty the Administration of Estates Act, s.42 gives personal representatives power, where a minor is absolutely entitled to property, to appoint a trust corporation or two or more individuals, not exceeding four (whether or not including one or more of the personal representatives) to be trustees of the property for the minor. The personal representatives may transfer property to the trustees and a receipt signed by those trustees will be a good discharge to the personal representatives. However, the power is not available where the minor merely has a contingent interest. In the absence of express authority the personal representatives will either have to continue holding the property until the minor reaches majority or use one of the alternatives set out in Chapter 18 (appropriation, payment into court).

### 5. POWER TO POSTPONE DISTRIBUTION

**11.9** Section 44 of the Administration of Estates Act 1925 provides that the personal representatives are not bound to distribute the estate of the deceased before the expiration of one year from death. This does not affect their duty to pay debts with due diligence and simply means that a beneficiary cannot insist on earlier payment of a legacy, even if a testator directed payment within a short period after the death. In a case where such a direction for payment is included in the will a pecuniary or general legatee is merely entitled to interest at 6 per cent. per annum from the date fixed for payment. (There are cases where there is a right to interest from the date of death—see Chapter 16). The personal representatives cannot necessarily be compelled to pay a legacy even after the 12-month period has expired although they may thereafter be required to explain the delay and all pecuniary and general legatees (other than contingent ones) will thereafter be entitled to interest at 6 per cent. per annum.

6. POWER TO INSURE

Section 19 of the Trustee Act 1925 provides that a trustee or personal representative may insure against loss or damage *by fire* (no other risks are mentioned) for up to three-quarters of the value of the property, the premiums to be payable out of income. It is perhaps strange that this power is so limited and it is clearly desirable that personal representatives should have power to insure against all risks and up to not only the full market value of the property but also up to the cost of reinstatement; it may also be desirable that they should have a discretion as to whether premiums are paid from income or capital. It is common, therefore, for a will to extend the statutory power.

**11.10**

The power to insure under section 19 does not extend to any property which the personal representatives or trustees are bound forthwith to convey absolutely to any beneficiary upon being requested to do so (section 19 (2)). It is up to such a beneficiary to insure if he wishes to do so. However, since a personal representative cannot normally be *required* to transfer assets until the personal representative has indicated, by means of an assent, that the asset is not required for payment of debts, this limitation is not relevant to personal representatives until they have assented. (Assents are discussed more fully in Chapter 18).

Insurance money received under a policy is held as capital money. It may be applied in reinstatement of the property lost or damaged provided the personal representatives or trustees obtain the consent of any person whose consent is required to investment (Trustee Act 1925, s.20). Nothing in the section prejudices the rights of any persons (such as a tenant) interested in the premises to require, under the Fire Prevention

(Metropolis) Act 1774 or any other statute or otherwise, that the money be applied in reinstatement.

### 7. POWER TO RUN A BUSINESS

**11.11** A deceased person may have run a business either as a sole trader, a partner or through the medium of a limited company. The personal representatives of such a person must consider their position in relation to the business and determine what powers and duties, if any, they have.

*Sole traders*

**11.12** Where the will is silent the personal representatives have implied power to continue the business *for the purpose of realisation only*, that is to enable it to be sold as a going concern. Such a period will not usually exceed one year (*Re Crowther* (1985)). It is preferable to give them express power to continue the business so long as they see fit (thus avoiding the possibility of a forced sale in a poor market).

Unless the will makes express provision the personal representatives will only have authority to use those assets used in the business at the date of the deceased's death. It may be desirable to give them power to use other assets of the estate if they see fit.

When the personal representatives have authority to carry on a business they are personally liable for any debts they incur. However, they are entitled to an indemnity from the estate. If the business is being carried on for the purpose of *realisation only* the right of indemnity may be exercised in priority to all creditors of the deceased and beneficiaries. If the business is being carried on under authority given by the will the right of indemnity may be exercised in priority to beneficiaries but not in priority to creditors of the deceased. The reason for this is that the beneficiaries are bound by the terms of the will but the creditors of the deceased are not (unless a creditor has expressly assented to the carrying on of the business). In this case the indemnity extends only to assets which the will authorised them to use.

*Partnerships and limited companies*

**11.13** Where a partner or shareholder in a limited company dies the personal representatives of the deceased normally have no power to intervene in the management of the business. Death dissolves a partnership unless, as is usually the case, the partnership agreement provides otherwise.

A company is a legal person which continues to exist despite the death of shareholders or directors. In the case of a "one man" company there may, however, be difficulties in directing its activities once the major shareholder/director dies.

In either case the personal representatives will be mainly concerned with ascertaining the beneficial entitlement to the deceased's interest in the business and, if appropriate, arranging a sale of the interest. It is important that personal representatives should be aware that a partnership agreement frequently contains provisions relating to death of partners. For example, many agreements provide for automatic accruer of a deceased's share of goodwill and/or for the exercise by surviving partners of an option to purchase the deceased's share in the capital assets. Similarly the Articles of Association of a company or an agreement between the shareholders may give other shareholders pre-emption rights or options to purchase a deceased shareholder's shares. Personal representatives should discover whether or not such rights exist and should not look only at the deceased's will.

### 8. POWER TO MAINTAIN INFANTS

Section 31 of the Trustee Act gives trustees (and personal representatives) a power to apply available income for the maintenance, education or benefit of infant beneficiaries. **11.14**

*What happens to income—the general rule*
Where a testator directs that property is to be held on trust for beneficiaries (for example "to A if A becomes a solicitor"), the question arises of what happens to any income produced by the property after death. If the testator has left express directions, they must be carried out. If not, there are general rules (see Chapter 16). We can summarise these rules by saying that most testamentary gifts carry with them the right to intermediate income. This means that income produced by the property is added to capital and devolves with it, so that whoever becomes entitled to the capital also becomes entitled to the intermediate income. Certain gifts do not carry with them the right to intermediate income; the most common example of such a gift is a contingent pecuniary legacy (apart from certain exceptional contingent pecuniary legacies dealt with in Chapter 16). A contingent pecuniary legatee is entitled to nothing but the capital (unless there is a delay in payment after the contingency has been fulfilled in which case the legatee becomes entitled to interest at 6 per cent. per annum). In such a case if the legacy **11.15**

fund is invested any interest produced is paid to the residuary beneficiary or if there is none to the person entitled on intestacy.

*The effect of section 31 of the Trustee Act*

**11.16** Section 31 of the Trustee Act provides that where property is held for a minor beneficiary and the gift carries with it the right to intermediate income the trustees have a discretion as to what they do with that income, whether the minor's interest is vested or contingent. The trustees are entitled under section 31 to choose to apply the income for the maintenance, education and benefit of the minor but to the extent that they do not, they must accumulate it. In exercising this discretion they are directed to consider the age and requirements of the minor, the circumstances of the case generally and in particular what other income, if any, is applicable for the same purposes. If they have notice that more than one trust fund is available for those purposes the trustees must so far as is practicable, unless the entire income of the funds is applied or the court otherwise directs, apply only a proportionate part of each trust fund. Accumulated income may be applied during the minority of the beneficiary as if it were income of the current year.

*Example*
T makes two settlements. T gives his shareholding in X Co. to trustees to hold for A if A reaches 25 and his shareholding in Y Co. to trustees to hold for B for life, remainder to C. At T's death both A and B are minors. A has a contingent interest, B has a vested interest. The trustees may choose to apply the income from the respective shares for the benefit of A and B but in so far as they do not apply it, they must accumulate it.

Section 31(1) provides that if the minor reaches 18 and still has an interest which is contingent the discretion of the trustees ceases and from that date they *must* pay the income to the beneficiary until the contingency is fulfilled or the gift fails. In the above example, therefore, as soon as A reaches 18 the trustees must pay current income to A until A reaches 25 or dies without fulfilling the contingency. B will be entitled to income at 18 and until his death.

Once the minor reaches 18 (or marries earlier) the trustees must consider what is to happen to income which has been accumulated. Section 31(2) provides that with one exception (dealt with below) such accumulations are to be added to capital and will devolve with it. Thus, if a gift is contingent on reaching

21 the beneficiary will be entitled to both capital and accumulations if he reaches 21 but if he does not they will both pass to the person entitled in default.

The exceptional case where accumulations do not devolve with capital is that of a minor with a life interest. Section 31(2) provides that *if* such a minor reaches 18 he is entitled to any income that has been accumulated. If he fails to reach 18 (or marry earlier), the accumulations will devolve with the capital. The effect is that a minor with a life interest has no right to receive income until he reaches 18 (or marries earlier); he can neither insist on receiving income as it arises nor can he be certain of receiving the accumulations.

*Example*
T gives his shareholding in Y Co to trustees to hold for A for life remainder to B. A is aged 6 at the time the settlement comes into effect. Until A reaches 18 the trustees must accumulate the income to the extent that they do not choose to apply it for the benefit of A. If A dies before reaching 18 the accumulated income (together with the shares in Y Co) will pass to B. If A reaches 18 the trustees must pay the accumulated income to A.

*Express clause varying section 31*
A professionally drawn will may extend the statutory power of **11.17** maintenance to give the trustees an unfettered discretion (so that, for example, they need not consider other sources of income available to the minor).

Where a gift is contingent on reaching an age greater than 18 (for example, 25) the person drafting the will should consider removing the right to receive income at 18. One reason for removing the right is that its existence gives the beneficiary an interest in possession at 18 for inheritance tax purposes. If such a beneficiary dies aged between 18 and 25 the value of the trust property will be included in his estate when calculating inheritance tax payable even though the beneficiary had no right to capital (see Chapter 7). Another reason for considering the removal of the right to income at 18 is that if the right remains and the settlement is converted into an interest in possession settlement at 18, holdover relief for capital gains tax will not be available when the beneficiary becomes absolutely entitled to capital at 25. If the settlement were to continue as an accumulation and maintenance settlement until 25, holdover relief would be available. However, draftsmen should be aware of the capital gains tax *disadvantage* of removing the right to income; any gains realised by the trustees will be liable to capital gains tax at the rate of 35 per cent., instead of 25 per cent. (See Chapter 7.)

### 9. POWER TO ADVANCE CAPITAL

**11.18**    Section 32 of the Trustee Act provides that trustees (and personal representatives) have an absolute discretion to apply capital for the advancement or benefit of any person who has either a vested or contingent interest in capital. Property may be advanced under this section to new trustees to be held upon new trusts containing powers and discretions not contemplated by the original instrument (although the perpetuity period will run from the time that the original settlement was created).

If a beneficiary with a contingent interest dies after receiving an advance and without fulfilling the contingency the trustees have no right to recover property from the estate of the deceased beneficiary. The section does not apply to land or capital money under a Settled Land Act settlement (it does, however, apply to the proceeds of sale of land held upon trust for sale).

There are three limitations on the statutory power:

(a)    The trustees may only advance up to one-half of the beneficiary's vested or presumptive share. (For example, if a settlor gives a trust fund of £30,000 to be divided amongst X, Y and Z provided they reach 25, each has a presumptive share of £10,000. The trustees may advance up to half of £10,000 to each or any of them.) If an advance is made to a person who dies without fulfilling the contingency the trustees have no right to recover the advance from that person's estate.

(b)    Any advance made must be brought into account when the beneficiary becomes absolutely entitled.

(c)    Any person with a prior interest (*e.g.* the right to receive income from the trust property) must consent to the advance.

It is common for a will to include an express clause removing the three limitations and to leave the trustees to exercise an unfettered discretion.

### 10. POWER TO DELEGATE

**11.19**    Under the Trustee Act 1925, s.23(1) trustees and personal representatives may, instead of acting personally, employ and pay an agent to do any *act* (but not to exercise any discretion) in connection with the trust or administration. They will not be vicariously liable for the default of any such agent if employed in good faith. Although not vicariously liable, trustees or personal representatives may be liable for their *own* breaches of duty if they do not take care in their choice of agent or fail to exercise proper supervision over the trust or administration.

Under section 30 of the Trustee Act 1925 they are liable only for money and securities actually received by them and are answerable only for their own defaults and not for those of any co-trustees or banker, broker or other person with whom trust property may be deposited unless a loss happens through their own wilful default. The section specifically provides that this is so even if the trustee signed a receipt for the sake of conformity. "Wilful default" was defined in *Re City Equitable Fire Insurance Company Limited* (1925) as "a consciousness of negligence or breach of duty or a recklessness in the performance of a duty."

Under section 9 of the Powers of Attorney Act 1971 trustees or personal representatives may delegate by power of attorney for a period not exceeding 12 months the exercise of any of the trusts, powers and discretions vested in them. However, if this power is exercised the trustees remain liable for the acts of the delegate as if they were their own.

### 11. IMPLIED INDEMNITY

Section 30(2) of the Trustee Act 1925 authorises trustees and personal representatives to reimburse themselves for all expenses incurred in the execution of their powers and duties. **11.20**

### 12. POWERS OF INVESTMENT

The Trustee Investments Act 1961 gives trustees power to invest money in those investments listed in the First Schedule. There are three lists of investments. **11.21**

*Narrow range not requiring advice*
This includes such items as National Savings Certificates and deposits in the National Savings Bank all of which could be described as "small savers" investments and which a trustee may select without taking expert advice. **11.22**

*Narrow range requiring advice*
This includes such items as debentures in United Kingdom companies complying with certain conditions (set out below in **11.23**

connection with company shares), mortgages of freeholds or of leaseholds with not less than 60 years to run and Government Stock. They are basically "safe" investments and correspond approximately to the old "Statutory List" of approved investments for trustees.

*Wide range investments*

**11.24** These were introduced as possible investments by the 1961 Act and the list includes such items as authorised unit trusts, shares in designated building societies and most importantly shares in United Kingdom companies complying with the following conditions:

    (a)  the company is quoted on a recognised stock exchange;

    (b)  the shares or debentures are fully paid up or required to be paid up within nine months of issue;

    (c)  the company has a total issued and paid up share capital of at least one million pounds;

    (d)  the company has paid a dividend on all shares ranking for dividend in each of the immediately preceding five years;

    (e)  the company is incorporated in the United Kingdom.

A trustee who wishes to invest in wide range investments must first divide the fund into two equal parts (a written valuation made by a person reasonably believed by the trustees to be qualified to make it shall be conclusive for this purpose). One part *must* be invested in narrow range investments; the other part can be invested in either narrow range or wide range investments (section 2(1)). If property is transferred from one part of the fund to another a compensating transfer must be made in the opposite direction (section 2(1)).

If property subsequently accrues to the trust fund the trustees must ensure that the value of each part of the fund is increased by the same amount (which may require compensating transfers) (section 2(3)). However, if property accrues in right of ownership of property in one part of the fund (for example bonus shares) it is treated as accruing only to that part of the fund and no apportionment or compensating transfer is required (section 2(3)). A trustee is free to *withdraw* property for trust purposes (for example, advances to beneficiaries under section 32 of the Trustee Act 1925) from *either* part of the fund. There is no need to make any compensating transfer even if the withdrawal exhausts that part of the fund.

Before making an investment in wide range or narrow range investments requiring advice the trustees must obtain and consider written advice on the suitability of the investment from a person reasonably believed to be qualified by his ability in and practical experience of financial matters; such advice must be obtained and considered periodically while retaining such investments (section 6 (2)–(7)). The advice must relate to:

(i)   the need for diversification of investments;
(ii)  the suitability of investments of the type proposed and of the particular investment as an example of the type (section 6(1)).

(Section 6(1) provides that trustees must have regard to these matters in the exercise of any powers of investment; the provision is not limited to the exercise of their powers under the Act.)

The will or trust instrument may extend the statutory power in which case investments purchased under the express power are set aside as "special range" property and the provisions of the Act apply only to the remainder of the fund. Because the Act provides for only a limited range of investments and because the rules on division make administration of the trust rather complicated it is usual for wills to confer on trustees an unfettered discretion in their choice of investment giving them the power to invest as though they were absolute beneficial owners.

### 13. POWER TO PURCHASE LAND

**11.25**  Land is not an authorised investment under the Trustee Investments Act 1961. Indeed, the purchase of non-income producing land is not regarded as an investment at all and would not be authorised by even the widest express *investment* clause. In *Re Wragg* (1919) "to invest" was defined as "to apply money in the purchase of some property from which interest or profit is expected and which property is purchased in order to be held for the sake of the income which it will yield." Trustees of *personalty* have no statutory power to purchase land.

However, trustees of a strict settlement under the Settled Land Act 1925 have power to apply capital money in the purchase of freehold land or of leasehold land with 60 years or more unexpired at the time of purchase (although they must normally exercise such power according to the direction of the tenant for life). Section 28 of the Law of Property Act 1925 confers on trustees for sale of land the powers of a tenant for life and of the trustees of a settlement under the Settled Land 1925 and, therefore, such trustees can purchase land. One problem is that, according to *Re Wakeman* (1945), if the trustees sell all the land subject to the trust they cease to be trustees for sale of land and lose the power to purchase land even if their intention was to use the proceeds of sale to purchase more land immediately. However, *Re Wellsted's Will Trusts* (1949) casts doubt on this and suggests that the power might not be lost if the proceeds of sale of the original land are kept together in an identifiable investment pending the purchase of replacement land.

It is common for professionally drawn wills to confer on trustees an express power to purchase land for purposes other than investment so that, for example, a house may be purchased as a residence for a beneficiary.

## D. Administrative Powers Granted by Will

**11.26** As indicated in the previous section it is common to extend many of the statutory powers of trustees and personal representatives. It is also common to confer on them certain additional powers such as the power to make loans to beneficiaries or to advance capital to a surviving spouse to whom a life interest has been given. These matters are dealt with more fully in Chapter 22.

## E. Rights of Beneficiaries During the Administration

**11.27** As we have seen it is the function of the personal representatives to administer the deceased's estate by collecting the assets, paying off the debts and liabilities and distributing the estate to the beneficiaries under the will or the intestacy rules. The beneficiaries may wish to know what rights they have against the personal representatives during the administration period.

### 1. THE RIGHT TO COMPEL DUE ADMINISTRATION

*Beneficiaries have no equitable interest in assets*

**11.28** The assets of the deceased vest in the personal representatives and those assets come to the personal representatives "in full ownership without distinction between legal and equitable interests" (*Commissioner of Stamp Duties (Queensland)* v.

*Livingston* (1965)). In view of this, until the administration of the estate is complete, the beneficiary, whether under a will or intestacy, can have neither a legal nor an equitable interest in the deceased's assets (*Dr Barnardo's Homes National Incorporated Association* v. *Commissioners for Special Purposes of the Income Tax Acts* (1921)). A personal representative cannot be regarded as holding the assets of the estate on trust for the beneficiaries since, until the administration has been completed, it is impossible to say which assets will be available to the beneficiaries and which will have to be used to pay debts and administration expenses. A trust can only exist where there are "specific subjects identifiable as the trust fund" (*Commissioner of Stamp Duties (Queensland)* v. *Livingston*, above). The effect of this is that the beneficiaries cannot claim the assets until the administration has been completed because until then the beneficiaries cannot be certain of entitlement to any assets. They cannot object simply because the personal representatives sell, or intend to sell, an asset given to them in the will. They can only object if the asset should not be sold because, for example, there is no need to sell the asset in the circumstances.

### The beneficiaries' chose in action

Although the beneficiaries have no legal or equitable interest in the deceased's assets, they do have a chose in action; that is a right to ensure that the deceased's estate is properly administered. **11.29**

The chose in action can be transmitted to another person, as is illustrated by the case of *Re Leigh's Will Trusts* (1970). In this case the testatrix left "all shares which I hold and any other interest ... which I may have" in a named company. She did not hold any shares in that company but at the date of her death she was the sole beneficiary of her husband's estate which included shares in that company. It was held that the gift took effect as a gift of her chose in action in her husband's estate.

### The position of specific legatees

While the general rule is that beneficiaries acquire merely a chose in action, in *I.R.C.* v. *Hawley* (1928) it was suggested that a specific legatee takes an equitable interest in the property given under the terms of the will from the date of death, even though the property may be used to discharge the debts and liabilities of the estate by the personal representatives in whom the legal estate will vest. **11.30**

However, this decision is inconsistent with the personal representatives receiving both the legal and equitable interests, as suggested in *Commissioner of Stamp Duties (Queensland)* v. *Livingston* above. In *Re Hayes' Will Trusts* (1971) Ungoed-Thomas J. said "no legatee, devisee or next of kin has any beneficial interest in the assets being administered." In view of this conflict it seems likely that even a specific legatee will have only a chose in action to ensure due administration.

### 2. GENERAL ADMINISTRATION ACTIONS

**11.31** Where difficulties arise while the estate is being administered, whether because of a problem which the personal representatives have encountered or a dispute arising over the conduct of the administration (for example, where the beneficiaries allege that the personal representatives have committed a *devastavit*) an application can be made to the court to have the difficulty resolved. These proceedings which are intended to ensure that the administration is conducted properly are called "administration proceedings." There are two types of administration proceedings:

(a) actions for general administration of the whole or part of the estate by the court. If the court makes such an order the personal representatives cannot exercise their powers to sell or distribute the assets without the consent of the court. The order stops time running under the Limitation Act for creditors' claims; or

(b) actions for specific relief, such as the determination of one specific problem.

Administration proceedings are not necessarily the result of any wrong-doing. The court's help may be sought by the personal representatives themselves if they are anxious about a particular point; this is particularly likely in the case of an action for specific relief and this is, therefore, dealt within Chapter 14 which is concerned with protection of personal representatives. Alternatively, the beneficiaries may seek the help of the court; this is more likely in the case of a general administration action and, therefore, the rest of this section deals with such actions.

*Jurisdiction*

**11.32** The Chancery Division of the High Court has jurisdiction in these matters but the following also have jurisdiction:

(a) the county court if the estate does not exceed in amount or value the county court limit (at present £30,000), and

(b)   the bankruptcy court if the estate is insolvent.

In some cases administration proceedings can be avoided under sections 2(4) and 3(1) of the Public Trustee Act 1906 which provides that where an administration action could be brought the Public Trustee can be required to administer the estate provided that:

(a)   the gross capital value of the estate is less than £1,000,
(b)   the estate is solvent, and
(c)   the beneficiaries are of "small means."

An action is commenced by originating summons or writ. A writ should be used where there are likely to be substantial disputes of fact and a writ *must* be used if there is an allegation of fraud or a claim for damages for breach of duty (for example, where the personal representatives have committed a breach of trust or a *devastavit*).

*The parties*
The action can be commenced by any personal representative, **11.33** any beneficiary under the will or intestacy or any creditor. All the personal representatives must be made parties to any action; those who consent are made plaintiffs and those who do not are made defendants (R.S.C. Ord. 85, r. 3(1)).

*The order for administration*
If the whole estate is to be administered under the court's **11.34** direction the court can order that an account be taken of:

(a)   property that forms part of the residue of the estate which has come into the possession, either of the personal representatives or of some other person by the order or for the use of the personal representatives;
(b)   the deceased's debts and funeral and testamentary expenses. If the deceased died more than six years before the date of the order the court can order that an enquiry be made as to whether any such liability of the deceased remains outstanding;
(c)   legacies and annuities;
(d)   any parts of the deceased's estate that have not yet been collected or distributed after enquiries have been made and any charges attaching to such property have been ascertained.

If an instance of wilful default is established against the personal representative the account may be ordered on the footing of wilful default, that is that the personal representative accounts for property which would have come into his possession but for his wilful default.

Once accounts and enquiries have been taken and made, the court will order distribution to the beneficiaries.

As an alternative to making a general order the court can order that:

(a)   specific accounts and inquiries be taken and made to deal with particular problems that have arisen; or
(b)   the personal representative should produce particular accounts within a stated period of time.

*Costs*

**11.35**   The personal representatives are entitled to have their costs paid from the assets of the estate, unless they have acted unreasonably or unless the result of such an order would be to diminish the estate to such an extent that claimants to it would be unfairly prejudiced (*Evans* v. *Evans*). The costs of other parties are in the court's discretion.

*Appointing a judicial trustee*

**11.36**   Where the personal representatives cannot administer the estate and are unwilling to incur the expense of an administration action they (or a beneficiary) can apply for a judicial trustee to be appointed. He will be appointed to act either alone or with others and can be appointed to replace the existing personal representatives. Since he is an officer of the court, once appointed, he does not need the court's consent to exercise his powers.

*Substitution or removal of personal representative*

**11.37**   The High Court has a discretionary power under section 50 of the Administration of Justice Act 1985 on an application made by a beneficiary of an estate (or by or on behalf of a personal representative):

(a)   to appoint a substitute to act in place of an existing personal representative; or
(b)   where there are two or more existing personal representatives to terminate the appointment of one or more, but not all, of these persons.

# F. Other Remedies of Beneficiaries

## 1. PERSONAL ACTION AGAINST PERSONAL REPRESENTATIVES

When a personal representative accepts office he accepts the **11.38**
duties of the office. A failure to carry out those duties properly
is a *devastavit* for which the personal representative will be
personally liable to the disappointed beneficiaries (or next of
kin). The court may, however, grant relief either wholly or
partly from personal liability to a personal representative for a
breach of trust where it appears that a personal representative
acted honestly and reasonably and ought fairly to be excused
(Trustee Act 1925, s.61).

## 2. THE RIGHT TO TRACE

A beneficiary (or next-of-kin or creditor) has the right to trace   **11.39**
and recover *property* of the estate (or property representing
property of the estate) from the personal representative or from
any recipient of it other than a bona fide purchaser for value (or
person deriving title from such a purchaser). The right to trace
is lost where the property of the estate has been dissipated or
where tracing would produce an inequitable result.

*Example*
X, a personal representative, takes £1,000 belonging to an estate
he is administering and spends it on a car which he gives to Y.
The beneficiaries can recover the car from Y. If Y sells the car
for £900 to Z, a bona fide purchaser for value, the beneficiaries
have no right to trace the car into the hands of Z. They can,
however, recover the £900 from Y. If Y dissipates the £900 by
spending it on a holiday the right to trace is lost.

In some cases a beneficiary may prefer to rely on tracing
rather than on bringing a personal action against the personal
representatives (for example, where he is anxious to recover a
particular asset rather than its value). In some cases the
personal remedy may be valueless (for example, where the
personal representative is bankrupt) so that tracing may be the
only effective remedy.

A full discussion of the law on tracing is beyond the scope of
this book and the reader is referred to any standard equity
textbook.

3. A PERSONAL ACTION AGAINST RECIPIENTS OF ASSETS OF THE ESTATE

**11.40** Where all the other remedies of a beneficiary, next-of-kin or creditor have been exhausted a personal action may be brought against a person who has wrongly received assets of the estate. This was established by the judgment of the House of Lords in *Ministry of Health* v. *Simpson* (1951). In this case, personal representatives had paid large sums of money to various charities in the mistaken belief that they were entitled to do so under the terms of the will. The next-of-kin of the deceased had established that the personal representatives were not so entitled and had exhausted their personal remedies against the personal representatives. They had been able to trace some of the payments into the hands of the charities and to recover them. However, some of the charities had dissipated the money with the result that the right to trace was lost. It was held that the next-of-kin were able to bring an action against the recipients personally to recover an amount equal to that which had been wrongly paid to them.

# 12. Practical Considerations During Administration

## A. Introduction

In previous chapters we have studied the legal rules that are **12.1** relevant to the administration of an estate. When applying the legal rules the circumstances of the estate and of the beneficiaries must be borne in mind. In this chapter we will consider some of the problems which can arise.

## B. Raising Money to Pay Debts and Inheritance Tax

### 1. INTRODUCTION

Before the personal representatives can obtain a grant of **12.2** representation they will need to pay any inheritance tax that is due. However the problem which faces them is that in order to get access to money in the deceased's bank or building society or to raise money by selling assets they will normally need the grant. They will therefore need to find a way of raising money to pay the tax which does not require a grant of representation.

### 2. BORROW MONEY FROM A BANK

One of the most common methods of raising money is to **12.3** borrow it from a bank. The bank may be the deceased's bank or the personal representatives may prefer to approach their own bank.

Banks normally insist on an undertaking being given by the personal representatives to the effect that they will account to the bank from the first obtained assets of the estate. If the personal representatives have appointed solicitors to act for them, the bank may require a further undertaking to be given by the solicitors. In this case the solicitor should obtain the personal representatives' irrevocable authority to give such an undertaking.

The disadvantage of borrowing from a bank is that the loan will carry interest. Therefore, (irrespective of any undertaking that has been given) the loan should be outstanding for as short a time as possible. It is advisable to arrange the loan immediately before the application for the grant is to be made and, once the grant has been obtained, to use it to realise sufficient assets to repay the debt as quickly as possible.

The Income and Corporation Taxes Act 1987, s.364(1) provides that the personal representatives may for the purposes of calculating income tax liability deduct interest paid as a charge on their income to the extent that it is paid on a loan to meet an inheritance tax liability on the delivery of the Inland Revenue Account, in respect of personal property to which the deceased was beneficially entitled immediately before his death and which vests in the personal representatives (or would do so if the property were situated in the United Kingdom). Even if the loan satisfies this requirement, the interest is only deductible to the extent that it is paid in respect of a period ending within one year from the making of the loan. Furthermore, the personal representatives must open a separate loan account, and not merely allow the deceased's bank account to become overdrawn.

The liability to pay interest may make this method unattractive to personal representatives and to beneficiaries.

### 3. BANK AND BUILDING SOCIETY ACCOUNT BALANCES AND PROCEEDS OF INSURANCE POLICIES PAID DIRECT TO THE INLAND REVENUE

**12.4** Where the deceased had invested money in a building society or had an insurance policy the proceeds of which are payable to the estate, the building society or the insurance company will not normally release money to the personal representatives until the grant can be presented as proof of the personal representatives' entitlement. The building society or insurance company may, however, agree to send the balance, or an appropriate part of it, direct to the Inland Revenue's Capital Taxes Office.

### 4. BORROW FROM A BENEFICIARY

**12.5** Beneficiaries may object to the personal representatives borrowing money from banks to meet the inheritance tax liability since the interest paid will reduce the income from the estate available to them. In many cases, the beneficiaries have to accept the payment as unavoidable but it may be possible to borrow money from a beneficiary interest-free.

Since the loan will facilitate the administration, beneficiaries will often be amenable to such a suggestion, provided they have the money available. This may come from their own resources or from the proceeds of an insurance policy taken out by the deceased and payable direct to the beneficiary. Such a policy may be a Married Women's Property Act 1882, s.11 policy or one written in trust for a particular person. In such cases the insurance company will simply require proof of death, in the form of a death certificate and will not require production of a grant.

If the deceased contributed to a superannuation scheme and a lump sum is paid by the trustees to a beneficiary on the death, the beneficiary may be willing to use such a sum to make an interest-free loan.

Where easily realisable property (such as money in a building society account) was held jointly with the deceased, the survivor may be willing to lend to the personal representatives out of such property.

The beneficiary will be reimbursed from the assets of the estate once the grant has been obtained.

## 5. SALE OF ASSETS

An executor's authority derives from the will, whereas an administrator's authority derives from the grant. An executor, therefore, has power to sell assets before a grant of representation is made whereas an administrator has no such power. However, an executor may find that it is, in fact, difficult to sell some types of assets since a prospective purchaser may insist on seeing the grant in order to confirm that the person claiming to be the executor is, in fact, the person entitled to the grant. Moreover, while the executors may be able to sell items of moveable personal property such as clothes, paintings and furniture such items may not raise sufficient funds. Land cannot be sold without the grant because the purchaser will want to examine the original grant and endorse a memorandum of the sale on the original grant. It is, however, possible to sell quoted shares before the grant is issued as a result of Stock Exchange rules.

**12.6**

## 6. ASSETS HANDED DIRECT TO INLAND REVENUE

Generally, inheritance tax is required to be paid by cheque. However the Revenue has a discretion to accept assets in total,

**12.7**

or partial, satisfaction of the tax liability on an estate (Inheritance Tax Act 1984, s.230).

To be acceptable, land must have some kind of amenity value and the public must be able to enjoy reasonable access. Other items which the Secretary of State is satisfied are pre-eminent for their national, scientific, historic or artistic interest are also acceptable.

## 7. SUMS PAYABLE WITHOUT A GRANT

*Small payments*

**12.8** Various provisions permit small sums to be paid or transferred on death without the need to produce a grant of representation. In all cases this power is discretionary, not obligatory and orders made under the Administration of Estates (Small Payments) Act 1965 place an upper limit on these payments of £5,000. If the sum due to the deceased is in excess of £5,000 the grant is needed for the *whole amount*, not just the excess over £5,000.

Subject to the £5,000 limit the payment can be made to the person appearing to be entitled to the grant or to be beneficially entitled to the sums in respect of *inter alia*:

(a) Money held in the National Savings Bank, Trustee Savings Bank, Savings Certificates or Premium Bonds. It should, however, be noted that despite these rules, the Director of Savings will, in practice, require sight of a grant if the deceased held more than £5,000 *in total* in the National Savings Bank, Savings Certificates and Premium Bonds. In certain circumstances, the Director of Savings must obtain a statement from the Inland Revenue to the effect that either no inheritance tax is payable or that it has been paid, before he will make the payment without the production of the grant;

(b) Moneys payable on the death of a member of a trade union, an industrial or provident society or a friendly society;

(c) Arrears of salary, wages or superannuation on benefits due to employees of government departments;

(d) Police and firemens' pensions, Army and Air Force pensions.

Schedule 7 para. 1 Building Societies Act 1986 contains corresponding provisions in respect of moneys invested in a building society.

These small payments may be a useful source of funds to pay inheritance tax for personal representatives and may be preferable to seeking loans from beneficiaries.

## C. Sale of Assets—Which to Sell?

### 1. INTRODUCTION

When the personal representatives have to sell assets whether to raise money to pay inheritance tax or in the course of administering the estate after the grant has been obtained, they must bear in mind a number of considerations:

    (a)   the terms of the will,
    (b)   the wishes of the beneficiaries,
    (c)   the tax consequences of selling individual items.

**12.9**

### 2. THE TERMS OF THE WILL AND THE WISHES OF THE BENEFICIARIES

When deciding which assets to sell first, the personal representatives must have due regard to the statutory order for payment of debts (see Chapter 16). Should the personal representatives use the wrong items to satisfy the debts then "marshalling" may be necessary so that the appropriate beneficiary bears the burden of the debt. Therefore, if the will gives specific items of property to beneficiaries these items should not be considered for sale until the other assets in the estate have been exhausted.

When the personal representatives are choosing which assets to sell, the wishes and needs of the beneficiaries should be considered. For example, if the residuary beneficiary wants a valuable antique which has not been specifically dealt with in the will, his wishes should be respected if at all possible.

**12.10**

### 3. FUTURE DESTINATION OF PROPERTY

If the terms of the will or the intestacy rules create a trust, the personal representatives should ensure that any property retained is suitable in view of the nature of the trust. Thus only investments authorised by the terms of the will or the Trustee Investments Act 1961 should be retained. Within these limits the personal representatives should consider the needs of the

**12.11**

beneficiaries when deciding whether to retain high income as opposed to high capital growth investments.

## 4. THE SALE OF SHARES

**12.12** The sale of shares in a quoted company should cause few problems but if the shares are in an unquoted company it may be less easy to find a market for the shares. In this circumstance, the personal representatives could seek a buyer among the other members of the company. The company itself may be willing to buy the shares under the provisions of section 162 of the Companies Act 1985. When a payment is made by the company in these circumstances to the deceased member's personal representatives any profit made on the sale will attract income tax liability unless the requirements of sections 219–229 of the Income and Corporation Taxes Act 1988 are satisfied. (The details of these rules are beyond the scope of this book).

Clearly, where unquoted shares are concerned, the personal representatives must take professional advice as to the price they should obtain for the shares. They should also be aware of the fact that the company's Articles of Association may contain pre-emption rights.

## 5. TAX CONSIDERATIONS—INHERITANCE TAX

**12.13** The sale of assets does not normally affect the amount of inheritance tax payable. However, Inheritance Tax Act 1984, ss.178–198 contains provisions giving relief where certain assets are sold for less than their market value at the date of death.

*Relief for sales of shares at a loss*

**12.14** If "qualifying investments" are sold by the "appropriate person" within 12 months of the death at less than their market value at the date of death, the sale price can be substituted for the market value at the date of death. Depending on the size of the death estate and the deceased's cumulative total, this may lead to a repayment of tax.

"Qualifying investments" are shares and securities which are quoted at the date of death, on a recognised stock exchange or the unlisted securities market and units in authorised unit trusts (Inheritance Tax Act 1984, s.178(1) and Finance Act 1987, s.272). The relief also applies to any such investments held in a settlement of which the deceased was a life tenant.

The "appropriate person" is defined in section 178(1) as "the person liable for tax attributable to the value of those investments or, if there is more than one such person, and one of them is in fact paying the tax, that person." In view of the wording of the definition, it is important that the sale be made by the person who has paid the tax (usually the personal representatives or trustees) if the relief is to be available. For example, if the personal representatives had paid the inheritance tax on quoted shares, they must be the ones to sell those shares. The relief would not be available if the shares were vested in a specific legatee even if the legatee sold the shares at a loss within 12 months.

The loss is calculated by deducting from the market value of the shares at death, the sale price. However, the Revenue have the power to substitute the best consideration which could reasonably have been obtained (section 179(1)(b)). Expenses incurred as a result of the sale, such as stockbrokers commission and stamp duty, cannot be used to increase the loss.

*Example*
On X's death he had a nil cumulative total and an estate worth £133,000, including shares in a public quoted company worth £3,000. Inheritance tax of £2,000 was paid on the estate. If X's personal representatives sell the holding for £2,500 within 12 months of the death, they can claim the relief and so receive a rebate of £200 (40 per cent. of £500).

If a number of sales of qualifying investments are made within the 12 month period the sale proceeds of all transactions must be aggregated to discover the overall gain or loss. If, overall, a loss has arisen the claim for the relief may be made. If, overall, a gain has been made the Revenue cannot demand extra inheritance tax but no loss relief can be claimed on the particular shares sold at a loss.

*Example*
The figures for X's estate are the same as for the previous example save that X held shares in three separate public companies, each holding being worth £1,000 at his death. If X's personal representatives sell the three holdings for £500, £750 and £1,250 respectively within 12 months of the death, they must aggregate the three sale prices to calculate the overall loss of £500. It is *not* possible to take account only of the first two sales.

The relief is available whenever a sale is made within the specified period but, if the sale proceeds are reinvested in other qualifying investments within two months of the last such sale, the loss relief available will be reduced or extinguished (section 180(1)). This is because the purpose of the relief is to give assistance where shares are sold to raise money to pay inheritance tax or other debts. If the sale is to improve the estate's portfolio of investments, the relief will not be available to the personal representatives.

If the sale is to be eligible for the relief, it must occur within 12 months of the death. The operative date is the sale date unless there was a contract to sell in which case, the contract date determines whether the sale qualifies for relief.

*The inter-relation of inheritance tax loss relief on shares and capital gains tax*

**12.15** When sales which can potentially give rise to claims within paragraph 12.14 take place, the personal representatives will realise an allowable loss for capital gains tax purposes. If the election for the inheritance tax relief is claimed, however, the sale price becomes the personal representatives' acquisition value for capital gains tax (Inheritance Tax Act 1984, s.187 and Capital Gains Tax Act 1979 s.153). The personal representatives will then be treated for capital gains tax purposes as selling for the same amount as the acquisition value and will not be able to claim a capital gains tax loss.

Inheritance tax is chargeable at 40 per cent. on the value of the portion of an *estate* exceeding the nil rate band (after cumulation). Since capital gains tax is payable by personal representatives at 25 per cent. of the chargeable *gain*, it will always be preferable to claim inheritance tax loss relief unless the amount of the capital gains tax loss is more than the amount by which the nil rate band is exceeded and there are (or are likely to be) future gains against which the loss can be set in excess of any exemption or relief the personal representatives can claim.

*Relief for sales of land at a loss*

**12.16** If the deceased was entitled to an interest in land at the time of death and that interest is sold for less than the market value at death, the personal representatives can claim to have the sale price substituted for the market value at death, provided the sale takes place within three years of death, the operative date being the date of the contract for sale (sections 190–198 Inheritance Tax Act 1984). This can lead to a rebate in the way illustrated in paragraph 12.14.

As with sales of quoted shares the sale must be by "the appropriate person" which has the same meaning as in paragraph 12.14 above. Furthermore section 196 prevents the claim being made where the sale is to one of the beneficiaries (or to certain persons closely connected to a beneficiary). Section 191 provides that small decreases in value are ignored. Thus, the relief is not available if the reduction in the value of the interest is less than either £1,000 or 5 per cent. of its value on death, whichever is the lesser.

The Revenue are given the power to substitute the best consideration that could reasonably have been obtained on the sale if this is higher than the sale price, thereby preventing the personal representatives artificially creating or increasing the loss.

Where several interests in land are sold within the three year period, if one is revalued in order to claim loss relief, all the interests sold must be revalued. If any interest has increased in value, there may be more inheritance tax to pay as a result. Care must, therefore, be taken when deciding whether to make the claim in these circumstances since if the personal representatives make an overall *gain*, additional inheritance tax *can* be levied. (This is an important distinction as compared with the position on shares).

Sections 192 to 195 require certain adjustments to be made which may reduce the amount of loss relief that can be claimed. For example, when the sale proceeds are reinvested in any other interest in land within four months of the last qualifying sale, the relief may be reduced or extinguished.

The sale must take place within three years from death, the operative date being the date of the contract.

*The inter-relation of inheritance tax loss relief and capital gains tax*
Unlike the provisions which deal with loss relief on the sale of shares, the provisions which deal with loss relief on the sales of interests in land contain no section which states expressly that the capital gains tax acquisition value is to be reduced in the event of a claim for inheritance tax loss relief. It is therefore arguable that in the case of sales of land no such reduction is to be made for capital gains tax purposes, with the result that a loss could be claimed for capital gains tax at the same time that a claim for inheritance tax loss relief is made.    **12.17**

6. TAX CONSIDERATIONS—CAPITAL GAINS TAX

Personal representatives will, prima facie, be liable to pay capital gains tax at 25 per cent. on gains made on sales of    **12.18** assets. However, as personal representatives are chargeable only on gains arising since death and as relief may be available to exempt gains, in many cases, no capital gains tax will be payable.

If the personal representatives vest assets in the beneficiaries, the beneficiaries will acquire the assets at their market value at the date of death (increased by any indexation allowance available). When the beneficiaries dispose of the assets they will be chargeable at their own rates on any gains realised by them and entitled to the benefit of any allowable losses realised by them. The personal representatives will not have any capital gains tax liability on such disposals.

If the personal representatives wish to sell assets, they should, when deciding which assets to sell, consider the possibility of a capital gains tax liability arising. They should consider the following factors:

(a) *Will a chargeable gain arise?* The assets may have risen in value since the date of death. However, the personal representatives will be able to claim an annual exemption of £5,000 in the tax year of death and the two following tax years. They may also claim the indexation allowance. Where possible sales of assets which have risen in value during the administration should be spread over two or more tax years so that more than one annual exemption may be claimed.

(b) *Will a loss arise?* A loss must be set off against any gains which the personal representatives realise in the same tax year. To the extent that the loss cannot be set off against gains of the same tax year, it is carried forward and set off against gains made by the personal representatives in future tax years. If the personal representatives are unlikely to make future gains they may wish to consider vesting the loss-making asset in a beneficiary, thus allowing the beneficiary to sell the asset. The beneficiary can then set the loss off against any gain that he may make in the future. If the assets sold are shares or land, the inheritance tax loss relief discussed above should be considered.

(c) *Is it better to sell an appreciating asset or a depreciating one?* Selling an asset that is increasing in value may avoid the payment of tax but equally will deprive the estate of a valuable asset. Selling a depreciating one will give rise to a loss which may lead to a tax saving but the personal representatives must not delay too long before selling since the value of the estate may be unnecessarily reduced. However, it would be foolish to sell if there is any possibility of the asset recovering its value in the near future.

(d) *What are the wishes of the beneficiaries?* When choosing which assets to sell and which to retain, the personal representatives should consult with the beneficiaries to obtain their views. Most beneficiaries will want to ensure that the value of their entitlement is maintained so will advocate selling depreciating assets and retaining appreciating ones. However, a beneficiary with a substantial capital gains tax liability from other disposals may be anxious to receive a depreciating asset so that he can sell it, thus realising a loss that can be set against his gains. Similarly a beneficiary with unrelieved losses can have an appreciating asset vested in him. The asset can be sold by the beneficiary, the gain being reduced by his allowable losses.

(e) *Higher rate beneficiaries* A beneficiary may want an asset which has been left to him to be sold. A beneficiary who is a higher rate taxpayer will prefer the *personal representatives* to sell assets which show capital gains rather than having the asset vested in himself. This is because personal representatives pay capital gains tax at a rate equivalent to the basic rate of income tax and are not liable to pay at the higher rate. Therefore, unless such a beneficiary has an unused annual exemption tax will be saved if the personal representatives sell and make the *proceeds* available to the beneficiary.

## D. General Duties

In addition to the detailed points set out above, the personal **12.19** representatives must bear in mind more general considerations when administering the estate. The personal representatives must ascertain the deceased's debts and liabilities, obtain the grant, pay debts and distribute the assets to the beneficiaries.

While administering the estate they must ensure that the value of the assets are maintained.

This obligation will be discharged in a number of ways. The personal representatives must ensure that when any asset is damaged or falls into disrepair it is repaired. This can be expensive and so they should take out insurance cover. If the deceased had taken out property insurance the personal representatives should as soon as possible after the death notify the insurance company and either have their interest noted on the policy or a fresh policy issued.

For estates which include shares, personal representatives must constantly review their portfolio, taking expert advice as appropriate, and ensuring as far as possible that the portfolio maintains its value. Therefore the personal representatives must consider selling shares that are dropping in value with a view to replacing them with a better investment. Equally the personal representatives should avoid speculative investments even though they might realise substantial profits. Any investments other than stocks and shares of the deceased should also be looked at critically.

Finally the personal representatives should ensure that they complete their task quickly and efficiently by anticipating difficulties before they arise (so far as possible) and not delaying the performance of their duties.

# 13. Duties of Solicitors

## A. Drafting and Execution of a Will

A person who wishes to make a will often asks a solicitor to **13.1** prepare the will on his behalf. The solicitor's principal duty is to ensure that the will is drafted so as to comply with the client's instructions. Taking instructions and will drafting are considered in Chapter 22. A failure by the solicitor to draft a will so as to comply with the client's wishes is an especially serious matter since the mistake which has been made is not likely to become apparent until the client is dead or may never be discovered at all. It is too late to correct certain types of mistake once the client is dead. The will (or part of it) may be refused probate on the grounds that the client did not have knowledge and approval of the contents but this will not necessarily ensure that the testator's true wishes are put into effect. Section 20 of the Administration of Justice Act 1982 allows rectification of a will to correct clerical errors or failure to understand the client's instructions but as we saw in Chapter 2 this does not enable every type of mistake to be corrected. Even if rectification is possible the mistake will cause considerable delay and expense.

The solicitor is also under a duty to ensure that the will is properly executed in accordance with the formalities required by the Wills Act 1837 (as amended). If the will is not properly executed it will be refused probate and nothing can be done to correct the error once the testator is dead.

If a solicitor makes a mistake in advising on the execution of a will, liability to his client for breach of contract will arise but since the client has suffered no financial loss his estate can claim only nominal damages in respect of the breach. The case of *Ross* v. *Caunters* (1980) shows that the solicitor *also* owes a duty of care (in tort) to the beneficiaries whom the testator intended to benefit. In that case the testator made a will leaving a part of the residue of his estate to the plaintiff. Two years later he sent instructions to his solicitor proposing changes to the will. The solicitor entered into correspondence with the testator during

287

which the testator asked if he was right in thinking that "beneficiaries may not be witnesses." The solicitor did not reply to this question. The client wrote to the solicitor asking that the draft will be sent to an address in Ealing, West London, which was the plaintiff's address (as the solicitor could have seen from the will) and said "I will have the will signed and witnessed there." The solicitor sent the will to the specified address with instructions as to the method of execution which told the testator that attestation was required "by two independent witnesses" (*i.e.* not somebody benefiting under the will)." The will was executed and returned to the solicitor. One of the witnesses was the husband of the plaintiff. The plaintiff therefore lost her legacy. Sir Robert Megarry V.-C. held that the solicitor had been negligent because:

"1. he had failed to warn the testator that a spouse of a beneficiary should not witness;
2. he had failed to check whether the will was properly attested when it was returned to him;
3. he had failed to observe that the attesting witness was the spouse of a beneficiary;
4. he had failed to draw this to the testator's attention."

The Vice-Chancellor went on to decide that the solicitor owed a duty of care to the beneficiary. The solicitor's duty of care to his client extends to third parties whom the client intended to benefit and so the plaintiff was entitled to damages to compensate for the loss of the legacy to which she would have been entitled had the will been properly executed.

*Ross* v. *Caunters* was concerned with negligent failure to ensure the proper execution of the will but the judgment makes it clear that a solicitor who *drafts* a will negligently could also be in breach of his duty of care to the beneficiary.

When drafting a will a solicitor should ensure that he understands the client's instructions fully. In most cases a personal interview is desirable. Special care should be taken when initial instructions come from a third party such as a relative or bank. The solicitor must always confirm the instructions with the client in such a case.

The solicitor's role in taking instructions should not be entirely passive; he should ensure that the client is not under some misapprehension as to the effect of his instructions which if corrected might lead to different instructions. It is not possible to give an exhaustive list of all the points which should be drawn to a client's attention but the following are among the most important:

1.  Jointly held property will pass to the surviving joint tenant even if the will says otherwise.
2.  If dependants and certain relatives are not provided for family provision claims may be made.
3.  Gifts of specific items will be adeemed if the items are sold or changed in substance unless specific provision is made.
4.  Unless contrary provision is made most types of gift will lapse (and fall into residue or pass on intestacy) if the donee predeceases. A gift will, however, take effect if the beneficiary survives for a very short time or is deemed to survive under section 184 of the Law of Property Act 1925. This may not correspond with the client's wishes so that a survivorship clause should be considered.
5.  Payments from pension funds and insurance policies may be payable to beneficiaries independently of the terms of the will. In the case of pension schemes where lump sums are payable at the discretion of the trustees of the scheme, it is usually possible for an employee to leave a statement of his wishes for the destination of the sum payable. Such a statement is not binding on the trustees but will be considered by them. A client who has the benefit of such a scheme should be advised to make a statement.

## B. Records

A solicitor who prepares a will for a client should keep an **13.2** attendance note with details of the time and place of execution and of the names and addresses of the witnesses in case any doubts as to due execution later arise. The solicitor or a member of his staff should attend at the execution of the will if possible. If execution is to take place at the solicitor's offices the partners must not witness the will if there is a charging clause in their favour but employed solicitors, articled clerks or long-standing employees may do so. Temporary staff should not witness since they are likely to be hard to contact later.

A solicitor who is present at the execution of a will by a testator who is frail (whether mentally or physically) should always make a full and careful attendance note. (See paragraph 13.4 below).

After execution the solicitor should "make up" a copy of the will (*i.e.* write in particulars of the date, signature and witnesses) or take a photocopy for his file. Made-up copies and photocopies are admissible as proof of the terms of the will if the will is lost (see paragraph 2.31). It is especially important to keep a copy if the will itself is to be kept by the client or deposited elsewhere such as at a bank. The solicitor's filing system must be so arranged that the original will (if kept by the solicitor) and copy can be found many years after execution. Nothing should be attached to an original will since the presence of pin holes or clip impressions may lead the registrar to suspect attempted revocation in which case affidavit evidence will be required. (See paragraph 10.59).

## C. General Advice

**13.3**  A solicitor taking instructions for a will should also take the opportunity to explain to the client any tax rules which may be relevant and should point out any disadvantages of the dispositions proposed by the client. It may also be appropriate to advise on other methods of disposal such as lifetime gifts and on the possible advantages of taking out insurance policies expressed to be for the benefit of third parties. If the solicitor thinks it necessary he may also advise the client to obtain expert investment advice. If the solicitor himself gives investment advice he must be authorised under the Financial Services Act 1986.

It is also very important to warn clients that a will should never be regarded as permanent. Changed circumstances should lead to a review of the will (particularly changes in family circumstances such as marriage, separation, divorce and the birth of children and changes in financial circumstances such as inheritance of property or retirement). A solicitor who is acting for a client in relation to other matters (such as a divorce) should always suggest the making of a new will if he suspects it may be desirable. When advising a married client who intends to make a will it is desirable to suggest that the spouse also considers making a will so that the dispositions of the spouses can be considered together.

Although it is a breach of the rules of professional conduct for a solicitor to tout for business there can be no objection to a solicitor informing his existing clients of changes in the law which make it desirable for them to make new wills. This may be especially necessary when tax rules change.

## D. Capacity of Testator

A solicitor who has prepared a will should ensure, as far as **13.4** possible, that the testator has testamentary capacity at the time of execution. If there is any doubt about this the solicitor should make inquiries of the testator's medical advisers. Such inquiries should be made in any case where, because of age or infirmity, the solicitor has any cause to suspect possible impairment of the client's judgment. It is obvious that such inquiries must be conducted with great tact and so as to ensure complete confidentiality.

Where there is any possibility of doubt as to the testator's capacity "the will ... ought to be witnessed and approved by a medical practitioner who satisfies himself as to the capacity and understanding of the testator and makes a record of his examination and findings. I hope the Law Society will consider whether sufficient guidance is given to students and practitioners" (*per* Templeman J. in *Re Simpson (Deceased)* (1977)).

Where a solicitor is satisfied that a testator has capacity but fears that the will may be challenged on the basis that the testator lacked capacity, precautions should be taken. Medical advisers should be asked to make a written statement as to the testator's state of mind. The solicitor should try to be present when the will is executed and should make a full and careful file note.

## E. Solicitor as Beneficiary

Where a person is a beneficiary of a will which he has himself **13.5** prepared positive evidence will be required of the testator's knowledge and approval of the contents of the will (*Wintle* v. *Nye* (1959)). Furthermore, the Law Society has directed that a solicitor receiving a benefit from a client must *insist* that the client goes to another solicitor for independent advice and for the drafting of the will. It is not sufficient that the client is merely *advised* to take such advice (see paragraph 2.27).

Neither of these rules prevents a solicitor from preparing a will which appoints the solicitor or his partner as an executor even though the will contains a charging clause.

## F. Solicitor Acting for Personal Representatives

**13.6**   Personal representatives will frequently retain a solicitor to act for them in the administration of an estate. The personal representatives are then the solicitor's clients. The beneficiaries or family of the deceased are not. If there is any dispute arising out of the administration the solicitor must be careful not to allow an actual or potential conflict of interest to arise by advising the beneficiaries or family of the deceased while he continues to act for the personal representatives.

The duties of a solicitor in acting for personal representatives include giving advice and taking action in the administration on the clients' behalf. Immediately after the death the solicitor will be called upon to obtain any will of the deceased, advise on its validity and take steps to obtain a grant including the preparation of the appropriate oath and the Inland Revenue Account (if required). In some cases it will also be necessary to obtain affidavits in support of the application (such as affidavits of due execution).

Once the grant has been obtained the solicitor's duty is to advise the personal representatives on their duties. In particular the solicitor will be required to advise on the collection and realisation of the estate, the payment of debts and the distribution of the estate to the beneficiaries.

Once the administration is complete the solicitor will prepare (or will supervise the preparation of) the estate accounts prior to the distribution of residue. Solicitors have frequently been criticised (for example, by the Lay Observer of the Solicitors Disciplinary Tribunal) for failure to prepare such accounts promptly.

# 14. Protection of Personal Representatives

## A. Introduction

Personal representatives are personally liable for any loss arising **14.1** from a failure to carry out their duties. If they have incurred personal liability they may be able to obtain relief in one of three ways.

(a) *The will may contain a relieving provision.* Many wills include a clause limiting the liability of personal representatives to liability for wilful fraud or wrongdoing and giving protection from liability for mistakes made in good faith.

(b) *The court may grant relief under Trustee Act 1925, s.61.* The court has a discretion to grant relief where a trustee "has acted honestly and reasonably and ought fairly to be excused." For example, this discretion was exercised in *Re Kay* (1897) where a personal representative paid a legacy which appeared small in comparison to the estate at a time when he was unaware of liabilities which exceeded the total value of the estate.

(c) *The beneficiaries may grant a release.* The personal representatives can obtain a release from personal liability from all the beneficiaries affected by the breach. Such a release is only effective where the beneficiaries induced the personal representatives to perform the wrongful act (*Trafford* v. *Boehm* (1746)) or if the beneficiaries are *sui juris* and fully aware of the breach.

(d) *Limitation.* Where personal representatives have incurred personal liability, they may be able to plead the defence of limitation. Creditors cannot bring an action against personal representatives for non-payment of debts after a period of six years has elapsed from date of distribution of the estate (Limitation Act 1980, s.2). Beneficiaries cannot bring an action

293

against the personal representatives to recover land or personalty after the expiration of 12 years from the date on which the right of action accrued (Limitation Act 1980, ss.23 and 15(1)). No limitation period applies where a personal representative is fraudulent or where the personal representative is in possession of trust property or the proceeds thereof. The limitation period will not start to run against a beneficiary who is under a disability or where there has been fraud, concealment or mistake (Limitation Act 1980, ss.28, 38 and 32).

Personal representatives will obviously be anxious to avoid incurring personal liability. It is possible for them to prevent personal liability ever arising by complying with certain statutory provisions which offer protection. Where a solicitor acts on behalf of personal representatives, the solicitor should endeavour to ensure that they obtain protection. These methods of obtaining protection are considered below.

## B. Statutory Advertisements (Trustee Act 1925, s.27)

14.2 Personal representatives who have distributed the assets of the deceased are personally liable to any beneficiaries or creditors for any unpaid debts and liabilities even though they were unaware of them at the time for distribution (*Knatchbull* v. *Fearnhead* (1837)). However they can protect themselves from such liability if they advertise for claimants under Trustee Act 1925, s.27.

### 1. THE ADVERTISEMENTS

14.3 Under section 27, the personal representatives may give notice of their intention to distribute the assets of the estate, requiring any person interested to send in particulars of his claim (whether as a creditor or as a beneficiary *Re Aldous* (1955)) to the personal representatives within a stated time, not being less than two months from the date of the notice. This notice must be brought to the attention of the general public by:

(a) placing an advertisement in the *London Gazette*; and
(b) placing an advertisement in a newspaper circulating in the district in which land to be distributed (if any) is situated; and
(c) giving "such other like notices, including notices elsewhere than in England and Wales, as would, in any special case, have been directed by a court of

competent jurisdiction in an action for administration." (In an action for administration the court would order the advertisement to be placed in such local or national newspapers as might be appropriate having regard to the circumstances of the case. In cases of doubt, personal representatives should apply to the court for directions as to where to place the advertisements since failure to comply with all the requirements denies them the protection of the section.)

## 2. SEARCHES

Section 27(2) provides that personal representatives are not **14.4** freed "from any obligation to make searches or obtain official certificates of search similar to those which an intending purchaser would be advised to make or obtain." Although this subsection does not list the searches that have to be made the prudent personal representative will make the same searches as a purchaser of land would make in the Land Registry or Land Charges Register, as appropriate, and the local land charges register, as well as searching in bankruptcy against the deceased and any beneficiary receiving assets.

## 3. DISTRIBUTING THE ESTATE

Once the time limit on the notices has expired the personal **14.5** representatives can distribute the estate having regard only to the claims of which they have notice. If a claim is made after distribution by someone of whom they had no notice, the personal representatives are not personally liable. In these circumstances the disappointed claimant must recover the assets from the persons who received them from the personal representatives. So as to avoid delay in the distribution of the estate, these searches and advertisements should be made as early in the administration as possible. The section does not relieve personal representatives from liability if they have actual knowledge of a claim. For example, if they know of a debt they are under an obligation to pay it even though the creditor does not respond to the advertisement.

A problem with section 27 is that having decided what are the appropriate newspapers, it may prove difficult actually to place the advertisement. For example in *Re Gess* (1942), the deceased was Polish and died in England in 1939. Due to the war, no advertisements could be placed in Polish newspapers. Section 27 was of no assistance to the personal representatives who had to seek a different form of protection (they obtained a Benjamin Order—see paragraph 14.7 below).

## 4. CONTINGENT LIABILITIES

**14.6** Although section 27 gives protection against claims of which the personal representatives have no notice, it gives no protection where personal representatives have distributed the estate with knowledge of a future or contingent liability.

If the personal representatives know that a debt will fall due at some time in the future, they will simply set aside a fund to meet that future liability when the time comes. Contingent liabilities are less easy to deal with. For example the deceased may have guaranteed a debt from a third party; the personal representatives cannot know whether or not the estate will be called upon to honour the guarantee. Similarly, there may be a threat of legal proceedings against the estate; while the personal representatives may suspect that the plaintiff will not take the matter further they cannot be certain of this. The personal representatives must decide what to do in such a case and there are four courses of action open to them.

First, they can set aside assets from the estate sufficient to meet the contingent liability should it actually arise. This course of action will be unpopular with the beneficiaries since they will only receive the assets once the personal representatives decide the contingent liability can no longer arise (for example when the loan guaranteed by the deceased is paid off or the plaintiff in the proposed action abandons his claim). It does, however, give the personal representatives total protection provided they have set aside sufficient assets.

Secondly, they can distribute all the assets to the beneficiaries but obtain the beneficiaries' agreement to indemnify the personal representatives if the liability ever crystallises. This will be more popular with the beneficiaries but the personal representatives should be wary since an indemnity is only as financially sound as the beneficiary who gives it. Thus, if the personal representatives distribute assets to a beneficiary who spends the money received on a holiday an indemnity from him will be worthless if he has no other assets. Furthermore, it may not be possible to obtain an indemnity; for example, where a beneficiary is a minor, mentally incapacitated or simply refuses to give one. Even where an indemnity has been obtained from a beneficiary who is financially sound, the inheritance may have been invested in assets which are not easily realisable, for example, a house. In this case calling in the indemnity could cause severe financial hardship, since the beneficiary would have to sell his house to meet his obligation.

Thirdly, the personal representatives could insure against the liability arising. If cover can be obtained (and it depends very much on the risk involved) the only expense will be the premium on the policy; the assets will pass to the beneficiaries free of any liability as far as they are concerned. Provided the premium is not too high, the beneficiaries are likely to find this the most attractive solution.

Finally, as a last resort the personal representatives can apply to the court for directions. This course of action is not one to be undertaken lightly. However, the personal representatives should apply where the potential liability is large and insurance cover is not available. Provided the personal representatives act in accordance with the directions of the court, they are completely protected from liability and need take no further steps to protect themselves.

The Inheritance Tax Act 1984 has created several problems for personal representatives. Where a person dies within seven years of making a potentially exempt transfer such a transfer becomes chargeable. The *inter vivos* transferee is primarily liable for the tax but the personal representatives of the transferor become liable if the tax remains unpaid for 12 months. There is no obligation to report potentially exempt transfers *inter vivos* and such transfers may remain undiscovered until after the personal representatives have distributed the assets. Moreover, the discovery of hitherto unknown *inter vivos* transfers will increase the cumulative total of the transferor at the date of death; this may result in the withdrawal of the nil rate band from all or part of the death estate with a consequent increase in the amount of inheritance tax due.

Personal representatives who are solicitors are to some extent protected by the Solicitors' Indemnity Fund. In an announcement contained in the Law Society's Gazette of November 22, 1989, it was stated that:

"Personal representatives are liable for the inheritance tax paid on potentially exempt transfers where the transferor dies within seven years of the transfer if the tax has remained unpaid by the transferee for 12 months after the end of the month in which the death of the transferor occurred (s.199(2) of the Inheritance Tax Act 1984) and any additional tax on *inter vivos* chargeable transfers payable as a result of the death. A similar problem for personal representatives exists where property is treated as part of the death estate by virtue of the reservation of benefit rules. Such property will be treated as part of the donor's estate on death (s.102(3) of the Finance Act 1986).

The Solicitors' Indemnity Fund Ltd. confirm that where a solicitor incurs a civil liability in the course of his private practice then, subject to the provisions of the indemnity rules currently in force, this liability will be indemnified by the indemnity fund but only to the extent that otherwise funds are unavailable."

Non-solicitor personal representatives and solicitors who are not acting in the course of their practice have no such protection and must therefore consider insurance if they have any suspicion that there may be undiscovered potentially exempt transfers.

## C. Benjamin Orders

**14.7** The personal representatives will not be protected by the provisions of section 27 if they are aware of the rights of a claimant but simply cannot find him. In these circumstances the personal representatives can apply to the court for a *Benjamin Order* permitting them to distribute the estate on the basis of a particular assumption.

For example, in the case from which the order took its name (*Re Benjamin* (1902)), the deceased by his will left a beneficiary a residuary gift. The beneficiary disappeared some nine months before the testator died and despite advertisements the beneficiary did not claim his share of the estate. In the circumstances the court permitted the assets to be distributed as if the beneficiary had predeceased the testator. The order may allow the estate to be distributed on some other footing. Thus in an unreported case the estate was distributed on the basis that a child who predeceased the testatrix left no child surviving the testatrix.

In *Re Gess, Gess* v. *Royal Exchange Assurance* (1942), the administrators of a Polish national, who died domiciled in England, were unable to advertise for Polish claimants against the estate because of the outbreak of war. They knew of some debts and applied for permission to distribute the estate. The court held that they could distribute the estate, after setting aside a fund to meet the known Polish liabilities, without making further inquiries or advertisements on the basis that all the debts and liabilities of the estate had been ascertained.

Naturally there must be some factual basis for the assumption set out in the order so that full inquiries must be made by the personal representatives before the court will grant the order. The court will obviously require evidence. An order may be made without the court inquiring further into the circumstances if it is satisfied that the statutory advertisements have proved unsuccessful in tracing the missing person. The making of the order is not conditional on the personal representatives having complied with the requirements of section 27 as to advertisement and searches; the court will decide what, if any, advertisements ought to be made.

If the assumption on which the order was made proves to be wrong, because the supposedly dead beneficiary is shown to be alive, he can claim his share of the assets from the other beneficiaries. However, the personal representatives are relieved of personal liability in these circumstances. Once an order is obtained, the personal representatives need take no further steps to protect themselves.

## D. Illegitimate and Adopted Beneficiaries

The Family Law Reform Act 1987 abolished the concept of illegitimacy. This means that a person may take on the intestacy of a relative even though he, the relative or some person through whom they are related was born of parents who were not married to each other at any time. Similarly, references to relationships in wills made after April 4, 1988 are, unless a contrary intention appears, construed as including persons whose parents never married or who are related through such persons. The statutory protection previously given to personal representatives who distribute an estate in ignorance of such potential beneficiaries has been withdrawn. However, with respect to intestacy only, a person whose father and mother were not married to each other at the time of his birth is presumed not to have been survived by his father or by any person related to him only through his father unless the contrary is shown.

**14.8**

These rules leave personal representatives in a difficult position. Inquiries should be made of relatives or others to discover any beneficiaries who may exist, and naturally these inquiries should be conducted with the maximum delicacy and tact. Presumably, if personal representatives advertise under the Trustee Act 1925, s.27 and wait the appropriate period they will obtain the protection of that section. However, they may wish to consider the possibility of insuring against liability and of taking indemnities from the known beneficiaries.

A personal representative is protected if he distributes an estate in ignorance of an adoption of which he does not have notice. Disappointed beneficiaries can claim their share of the estate from the other beneficiaries but not from the personal representatives. The personal representatives, therefore, need take no special steps to protect themselves.

# E. The Personal Representatives' Liability in Respect of the Deceased's Leaseholds

## 1. GENERAL

**14.9** On death, a leasehold interest held by the deceased devolves on his personal representatives by operation of law, whether or not they enter into possession of the premises. The nature of their liability for rent or breach of covenants depends on whether their liability is:

(a) representative, that is deriving from their office; or
(b) personal, that is arising when they enter into possession of the premises as assignees of the deceased's interest.

## 2. REPRESENTATIVE LIABILITY

**14.10** The personal representatives are liable as the deceased's personal representatives for rent due, and any breach committed prior to the death as well as for rent due and breaches committed from death to the expiry, or assignment, of the lease (unless the deceased was the original lessee in which case the personal representatives are liable until the expiry of the lease irrespective of any assignment).

In their representative capacity the personal representatives are liable to discharge any liability on a lease to the extent of the assets of the deceased which they have received. If the deceased was an assignee of the lease, the personal representatives can end their liability by surrendering or assigning the lease. If the deceased was the original lessee, assignment will not end their liability. The Trustee Act 1925, s.26, however, protects the personal representatives from further liability once they have assigned (this protection cannot be excluded by the terms of the will). Section 26 as amended provides that the personal representatives will not be liable for a future claim if they do three things:

(a)  satisfy all existing liabilities under the lease which may have accrued and been claimed up to the date of the conveyance to a purchaser or beneficiary; and

(b)  where necessary, set apart a fund to meet any future claims that may be made in respect of any fixed and ascertained sum which the lessee agreed to lay out on the demised premises, although the period for so doing may not have arrived; and

(c)  assign the lease to a purchaser, legatee, devisee, or other person entitled to call for a conveyance.

Thereafter the personal representatives may distribute the deceased's residuary real and personal estate to or amongst the persons entitled thereto without setting aside a fund to meet any future liability under the lease and the personal representatives will not be personally liable in respect of any subsequent claim under the lease.

The lessor can follow the assets of the estate into the hands of the beneficiaries and claim payment from the assets or their proceeds (section 26(2)).

### 3. PERSONAL LIABILITY

Personal liability arises where the personal representatives enter **14.11** into possession, whether physically or constructively (for example, by receiving rent from a sub-tenant). The personal representatives are then personally liable for the rent and for any breaches of covenant arising while the lease is vested in them as assignees of the deceased's interest. As the personal representatives are not the original lessees, liability ceases once the personal representatives assign their interest.

Oddly, there are different limits on the extent of the personal representatives' personal liability. For rent, the liability is limited to the amount actually received (or that which with reasonable diligence might have been received) during their period as assignees (*Rendall* v. *Andreae* (1892)). For breaches of other covenants the personal representatives are liable without limit.

The personal representatives have no protection under section 26 against *personal* liability; they should either obtain an indemnity from the beneficiaries or create an indemnity fund from the estate. This fund will be distributed to the beneficiaries once the personal representatives cease to be personally liable, for example, as a result of assigning the lease or termination. Such a fund may be unpopular with the beneficiaries who are likely to prefer an immediate distribution of property. It is, therefore, modern practice to insure against this liability, thus reducing the drain on the estate's assets.

## F. Liability for Acts of Agents

**14.12**   We saw in Chapter 11 above, that the Trustee Act 1925, s.23 gives wide power to personal representatives to appoint agents but the section gives rise to uncertainty as to the circumstances in which the personal representatives are liable for loss caused by their agents.

Section 23(1) provides that the personal representatives "shall not be responsible for the default of any such agent if employed in good faith."

It would appear, therefore, that the personal representatives are not liable for the acts of the agent provided the agent is appointed in "good faith." They may, however, be liable for their own wrongdoing if they fail to supervise the conduct of the administration sufficiently. It would appear that the personal representatives are liable for loss caused by an agent who was not appointed in good faith.

Section 30 of the Trustee Act states the extent of a single personal representative's liability for the acts of his co-personal representatives. The section provides that "a [personal representative] shall be chargeable only for money and securities actually received by him notwithstanding his signing any receipt for the sake of conformity, and shall be answerable and accountable only for his own acts, receipts, neglects, or defaults, and not for those of any other [personal representative] ... , nor for the insufficiency or deficiency of any securities, nor for any other loss, unless the same happens through his own wilful default." Thus each individual personal representative is protected from the wrongful acts of his fellow personal representatives provided he is not in "wilful default" and this protection is not denied him simply because he innocently signed a receipt or similar document at the instigation of a personal representative who is acting wrongly.

## G. The Six-Month Time Limit

The Inheritance (Provision for Family and Dependants) Act **14.13** 1975 (see Chapter 20) gives personal representatives protection provided they wait until the expiry of six months from the grant of representation before distributing the estate, if the court then permits an out-of-time application to be made. Similarly, if the personal representatives wait for the same period before distributing the estate, they suffer no personal liability if the court then makes an order permitting an out-of-time application to have the deceased's will rectified under section 20 of the Administration of Justice Act 1982. However in neither case are the successful applicants denied the right to recover assets from the beneficiaries who received them from the personal representatives.

Personal representatives are wise to wait six months from the grant before distributing the estate.

## H. Administration Proceedings for Specific Relief

As we have seen if the personal representatives distribute the **14.14** estate to the wrong person or become liable for some expense that was not properly incurred for the benefit of the estate, they are (unless specifically protected) personally liable to make good any loss.

In cases of doubt, prudent personal representatives will apply to the court (Chancery Division or county court where the net estate does not exceed in amount or value the county court limit, at present £30,000). They can apply to have the estate administered in whole or in part by the court but as this is an expensive and time-consuming procedure, they are more likely to apply to the court for specific relief.

Some instances where specific relief can be obtained are contained in R.S.C., Ord. 85, r. 2(2) and (3):

(a) Settling a problem arising out of the administration; for example, the construction of a gift or whether a gift has been adeemed;

(b) Determining who are the beneficiaries; for example, where a query arises on an intestacy as to the identity of the deceased's relatives;

(c) Requiring the personal representatives to supply accounts of particular transactions if there is a dispute as to whether they have exercised their powers for the benefit of the estate;

(d) Ordering the personal representatives to perform, or refrain from performing, a particular act. This order is most commonly made when there is uncertainty as to the personal representatives' authority to carry on the deceased's business or as to which assets they can use in the course of trading. However, it is also used to authorise a legal action to be taken (or defended) by the personal representatives. It is desirable to obtain such consent since the costs will be the personal responsibility of the personal representatives if they cannot prove the action was taken for the benefit of the estate.

Such an action is commenced in the Chancery Division by filing an originating summons. All the personal representatives must be parties to the action. Since these proceedings are normally brought to deal with a particular problem the personal representatives are normally the plaintiffs. Any personal representative who does not consent to being joined as plaintiff must be joined as defendant.

The costs incurred by *all* the parties involved in the action for specific relief are usually paid from the estate provided it can be shown that there was a problem which justified the application being made.

# 15. The Payment of Debts

Personal representatives have a duty to pay the debts of the **15.1**
deceased and must do so with due diligence (*Re Tankard*
(1942)). Different rules as to the payment of debts apply
depending on whether an estate is solvent or insolvent.

## A. The Solvent Estate

An estate is solvent when the assets are sufficient to pay **15.2**
funeral, testamentary and administration expenses and debts
and other liabilities in full. Provided these can be paid, it is
irrelevant that legacies cannot be paid in full. The beneficiaries
of the estate will be concerned to know which assets of the
estate will be used in payment of the debts and which will be
available for distribution.

Section 34(3) of the Administration of Estates Act 1925
provides that assets shall be taken in the order set out in Part II
of the First Schedule to the Act. However, special rules apply
where property of the deceased was charged during the
deceased's lifetime with payment of a debt. This situation will
be considered first.

### 1. DEBTS CHARGED ON PROPERTY

Where a debt has been charged on property of the deceased **15.3**
*during the lifetime of the deceased* (for example, a mortgage debt
charged on the deceased's house) section 35 of the Administration of Estates Act provides that such property will be primarily
liable for payment of that debt. Thus, a beneficiary who accepts
the property must accept it subject to the mortgage. The
deceased may exclude section 35 by showing a contrary
intention in the will, a deed or other document. A charge is
usually expressly created by the deceased but may also arise by
operation of law; for example an Inland Revenue charge for
unpaid tax or a charge imposed by the court on land belonging
to a judgment debtor.

The case of *Re Birmingham* (1959) illustrates the difference between a simple debt and a debt charged on property. T agreed to buy Blackacre from V for £3,500; contracts were exchanged and T paid a deposit of £350. T died before completion. In her will T left Blackacre to her daughter, D, and the residue to R. T's solicitors completed the purchase of Blackacre. The court held that D took Blackacre subject to an unpaid vendor's lien for the balance of the purchase price. However, the solicitor's costs were to be paid from the general estate since at the time of T's death they were not charged on Blackacre.

### Several properties charged with one debt

15.4 If several properties are charged as security for one debt, each property bears a proportionate part of the debt (section 35(1)) and thus, if each property is given to a different beneficiary, each beneficiary will take his property subject to a charge for a proportionate part of the debt. This is so even if some of the properties are specifically given by the will while some merely pass as part of the residue. In *Re Neeld* (1962) the Court of Appeal said that in such a case the testator is not to be presumed to have thrown the whole debt on to the properties comprised in the residue.

### Separate debts

15.5 Where separate properties are charged with separate debts and the debt charged on one property exceeds the value of that property the amount of the deficit will be made up from the deceased's general estate and not from the other charged properties. This will be so even if all the charged properties are given to one beneficiary (*Re Holt, Holt* v. *Holt* (1916)). The only exception is where the testator makes it clear that a gift of several different properties is *one* gift the whole of which is to be treated as charged with several different debts. In that case the deficit will be made up from the other charged properties (*Re Kensington* (1902)).

### The rights of creditors

15.6 Section 35 is only concerned with competition amongst beneficiaries as to the property to be used to pay debts. It does not affect the rights of creditors. A secured creditor may be paid by the personal representatives from the general estate instead of from the charged property; if this happens the doctrine of marshalling will apply as between the beneficiaries so that ultimately the debt falls on the charged property (see below, paragraph 15.23).

*Options to purchase*
A testator may give an option to purchase a property in the **15.7** will. The option may be at an undervalue but even so the person exercising it will be treated as taking the property as a purchaser not as a beneficiary. A purchaser is entitled to have any debt charged on the property paid off from the general estate (*Re Fison's Will Trusts* (1950)) so that he will take the property free from any debt charged on the property.

## 2. CONTRARY INTENTION

*Methods of showing contrary intention*
Section 35 may be varied if the testator shows a contrary **15.8** intention. Contrary intention is not shown by a simple direction in the will (or any other document) that debts be paid from *residue*; such a direction is to be construed as relating only to debts other than those charged on particular items (section 35(2)(*a*) and (*b*)). An additional indication of intention is required. Thus a gift of specific property *free from the debt* charged on it will suffice; as will an express direction that a mortgage or other charge be paid from residue. Less obviously, if a testator directs that debts be paid from a special fund (*other than residue*) the direction will be construed as extending to all debts including those charged on specific items of property.

For example, if a testator has a mortgage debt charged on Blackacre and in his will directs that "my debts be paid from the proceeds of sale of my shares in X company and the residue of my estate be held for A," all the testator's debts including the mortgage debt will be paid from the proceeds of sale. If the special fund is insufficient to pay off all debts, any unsatisfied balance of a charged debt will remain charged on the property and will not be paid from the general estate (*Re Fegan* (1928)).

*Taking instructions*
A solicitor drafting a will for a client should always inquire **15.9** whether there are any debts charged on property. If there are, the solicitor should ask whether or not the client wishes such debts to be paid from the general residue and draft the will accordingly.

*Mortgage protection policies*
The most common example of a debt charged on property **15.10** during the deceased's lifetime is a mortgage. A client who

wishes to make a will should be asked about his mortgage arrangements so that he can consider from what source the mortgage debt is to be paid. It is, however, becoming increasingly common for mortgagors to take out a mortgage protection policy. This is a life assurance policy which, on the mortgagor's death, pays either a fixed amount (equal to the original loan) or an amount sufficient to pay off the amount of the loan outstanding at the date of death (*i.e.* a reducing amount). If the proceeds are to be paid to the estate of the mortgagor they will increase the size of the estate for inheritance tax purposes. The policy may, however, be written in trust for a named beneficiary, in which case the proceeds will be paid to that person and will not increase the size of the deceased's estate for inheritance tax purposes.

If two people are buying property jointly they normally each take out such a policy. The terms of the policy may state that the proceeds are to be paid to the surviving joint tenant to the exclusion of the estate of the deceased; if no such statement is included the parties may write each policy in trust for the other. A solicitor, drafting a will, should inquire whether such a policy exists and, if one does, should make sure that the client takes it into account when deciding what directions to leave as to the payment of the mortgage debt.

If the client has bought a house in his or her sole name and has taken out such a policy the solicitor should point out the desirability of leaving the proceeds of the policy to the person who is taking the property subject to the mortgage, so that there will be funds available to that beneficiary for the discharge of the mortgage debt.

### 3. THE STATUTORY ORDER FOR UNSECURED DEBTS

**15.11** The deceased may make express provision for the payment of debts. In the absence of such provision the statutory order of application of assets applies and is set out in Part II of the First Schedule to the Administration of Estates Act. It is as follows:

(1) Property of the deceased undisposed of by will, subject to the retention thereout of a fund sufficient to meet any pecuniary legacies.

(2) Property of the deceased not specifically devised or bequeathed but included (either by a specific or general description) in a residuary gift, subject to the retention thereout of a fund sufficient to meet any pecuniary legacies, so far as not already provided for.

(3) Property of the deceased given for the payment of debts.

(4) Property of the deceased charged with the payment of debts.

(5) The fund, if any, retained to meet pecuniary legacies.

(6) Property specifically devised or bequeathed, rateably according to value.

(7) Property appointed by will under a general power (including the statutory power to dispose of entailed interests) rateably according to value.

### Undisposed of property

Such property may arise where a will does not deal with all the assets of the deceased (*i.e.* where there is no residuary gift); it may also arise where a residuary gift fails wholly (*i.e.* where the residuary beneficiary predeceases the testator) or partly (*i.e.* where residue is given to two or more beneficiaries in *equal shares or equally* and one or more of the beneficiaries predeceases the testator, the share of the predeceased beneficiary lapses and passes to the testator's next-of-kin). Before debts are paid from the undisposed of property a fund is set on one side for payment of any pecuniary legacies.    **15.12**

### Residue

Any general gift of property, that is one which is not comprised in a specific bequest or devise, will be a residuary gift. Thus in *Re Wilson* (1967) T made some specific and pecuniary legacies and then gave "all my real estate and the residue of my personal estate." Pennycuick J. held that T's devise of realty fell within paragraph (2) despite the fact that there was no prior specific devise.    **15.13**

Before any debts are paid from residue, a fund is set on one side for payment of pecuniary legacies to the extent that sufficient property was not set aside from any undisposed of property.

### Property specifically given for or charged with payment of debts

Property is specifically *given* for payment of debts where a testator *directs in the will* that it be used for this purpose and leaves no directions as to what is to happen to any balance left over after the debts are paid, for example, "my debts are to be paid from the proceeds of my premium bonds."    **15.14**

Property is *charged* with payment of debts when a testator *directs in the will* that it be used for this purpose and directs that any balance left over after the debts are paid be given to a particular beneficiary; for example "my debts are to be paid from the proceeds of sale of my shares in A Co and any balance is to go to X" or "I give X the proceeds of sale of my shares in A Co subject to payment of debts." This is quite different from the "charge" referred to in section 35 which deals with debts charged *during the deceased's lifetime* on particular assets. In the case of section 34 the assets were unincumbered during the deceased's lifetime and the charge is imposed by the will.

*The retained pecuniary legacy fund*
**15.15** A fund will have been set on one side from the undisposed of property and/or residue to meet pecuniary legacies; if necessary that fund (or part of it) is taken to pay debts. Pecuniary legacies abate proportionally unless the deceased directed that certain legacies be paid in priority to the others.

"Pecuniary legacy" is defined widely in section 55 (1)(ix) of the Administration of Estates Act to include an annuity, a general legacy and a demonstrative legacy in so far as not discharged out of designated property (for definitions see paragraphs 16.4 and 16.5).

*Property specifically devised or bequeathed rateably according to value*
**15.16** The order makes no distinction between devises and bequests; both are equally available.

(a) *Value* means value to the testator. Thus a mortgage charged on the property would be deducted when calculating the value of the property but a legacy charged on the property by the testator in the will would not (*Re John* (1933)).

*Example*
T owns Blackacre value £10,000 but subject to a mortgage of £4,000. T owns Whiteacre value £10,000. T's will gives Blackacre to B and Whiteacre to W but charges Whiteacre with payment to L of a legacy of £6,000. There are debts to pay of £2,000 (apart from the mortgage) and no other assets. Blackacre had a value to the testator of £6,000 (£10,000 − £4,000). Whiteacre had a value to the testator of £10,000.

Therefore

$$\text{Blackacre bears } \frac{6,000}{16,000} \times 2,000 = \text{£750 of the debts}$$

Whiteacre bears $\dfrac{10,000}{16,000} \times 2,000 = £1,250$ of the debts

In addition Blackacre is charged with payment of the mortgage (unless the will directed otherwise) and Whiteacre with payment of the legacy.

(b) *Option to purchase.* T's will may give a person an option to purchase property at a stated price. This price may well be at an undervalue in which case the will gives the "purchaser" a benefit. The personal representatives may wonder whether such property is available for payment of debts as if it were a specific gift.

In *Re Eve* (1956) Roxburgh J. directed that when personal representatives were calculating what property to use for payment of debts they should not regard property subject to an option to purchase as equivalent to a specific gift of that property. They should first calculate whether once the purchase price for the property was paid there would be sufficient assets to meet all the debts of the testator. If there would, the purchaser is free to exercise the option and will purchase the property subject to the option. If there would not, the option cannot be exercised and the personal representatives must take the property and use it for payment of debts. Roxburgh J. concluded that "the property subject to an option is the last to be available for the payment of debts. For, indeed, in so far as the property subject to the option is required for the payment of debts, the option over the property cannot be exercised at all and the benefit of it is totally destroyed by the operation of law."

*Property appointed under a general power of appointment*
Where the testator has a general power of appointment (that is, **15.17** a power to appoint property to anyone he pleases) and exercises the power *expressly* in the will, such property is taken last for payment of debts.

Section 27 of the Wills Act 1837 provides that where a testator has a general power of appointment which is not exercised expressly in the will it is deemed (subject to a contrary intention in the will) to have been exercised by any general gift contained in the will. Thus, for example, if X has a general power of appointment over Blackacre but makes no mention of the power or of Blackacre in the will a general gift of "all the rest of my property" or "all my realty" would be sufficient to dispose of Blackacre. However, if (as a result of section 27) property is included in a general gift it will be treated as available for payment of debts as part of residue not as property subject to a general power.

*Property outside the statutory order*

**15.18** Property subject to a *donatio mortis causa* or to a statutory nomination is available for payment of debts but is not mentioned in the statutory order. It would, therefore, be taken after all the other assets were exhausted. According to *Re Eve*, if a testator gives a person an option to purchase property at an undervalue the property subject to the option is taken to pay debts when it is necessary to do so because all other assets are exhausted, and not otherwise. It is, however, impossible to say in what order assets subject to an option to purchase, *donatio mortis causa* or nomination would be taken as between themselves.

### 4. VARIATION OF THE STATUTORY ORDER

**15.19** A testator has a right to vary the statutory order. There are two ways in which this is commonly done.

*A gift of residue "subject to" or "after" payment of debts*

**15.20** If residue is given to several beneficiaries in equal shares and one of those beneficiaries predeceases the testator that share of residue lapses and becomes undisposed of property. Undisposed of property is normally taken first for payment of debts and any balance will then be available to the testator's next-of-kin. If, however, the testator directs that residue be taken *after* payment of debts (or gives the residue *subject* to payment of debts) that is construed as an express direction that debts be paid from the whole residue before it is divided into shares. Thus, the living beneficiaries and the testator's next-of-kin will bear a proportionate part of the debt and will, therefore, receive a proportionate share in the balance.

*Example*

(a) *No contrary intention.* T gives certain specific bequests and leaves the residue to A and B in equal shares. B predeceases T. The estate, after setting aside the specific bequests but before paying debts and other liabilities, amounts to £20,000. Debts amount to £8,000. B's lapsed share amounts to £10,000. The debts will be paid from that lapsed share leaving a balance of £2,000 available to T's next-of-kin. A will take £10,000.

(b) *Contrary intention.* The same situation but T leaves the residue *after payment of debts* to A and B in equal shares. The debts must be paid from the £20,000 before it is divided into shares. £12,000 will be left after payment of debts and A and T's next-of-kin will divide this equally. A will, therefore, take £6,000 and T's next-of-kin will take £6,000.

*Property "given for" or "charged with" payment of debts— intention to exonerate residue*
If a testator merely gives property for or charges property with payment of debts this will not in itself be sufficient to vary the statutory order. Such property will merely fall within paragraphs (3) or (4) of the statutory order (*i.e.* property specifically given or charged with payment of debts) and will, prima facie, be taken after property within paragraphs (1) and (2) of the statutory order (*i.e.* undisposed of property and residue) is exhausted. However, if the will shows an intention to exonerate the property which would otherwise be taken first, this will vary the statutory order. It has been held that where a will contains a gift of residue to a beneficiary together with a direction that debts be paid from a specified fund this shows an intention to exonerate the residue and the statutory order will be varied.

15.21

In *Re James* (1947), for example, the testator charged certain specific property with payment of debts and gave the residue to his wife. Roxburgh J. held that the will showed a clear intention to exonerate the residue and therefore the debts would be paid from the charged property.

Conversely in *Re Gordon* (1940) a testatrix directed that her debts be paid from a sum of £50 and any balance therefrom be paid to a named charity. There was no gift of residue. It was held that the statutory order was not varied as there was no indication of an intention to exonerate other property; therefore, the debts were to be paid from the undisposed of property and the £50 was to be paid in full to the charity.

Presumably any form of words could be used in a will to show an intention to exonerate other property. Thus in *Re Gordon* had T expressly declared that debts were to be paid from the £50 "in exoneration of any undisposed of property" the result would have been different.

*Desirability of making express provision for payment of debts*
When drafting a will it is desirable to discuss with the testator the possibility of making express provision for the payment of debts since this will allow a testator to consider the question of

15.22

debts and to make his own decision as to the property to be used.

### 5. THE DOCTRINE OF MARSHALLING

**15.23**  If a personal representative takes assets falling within one of the later paragraphs in the statutory order to pay debts before assets falling within the earlier paragraphs are exhausted, the creditors will be entirely unconcerned. Creditors merely want payment; the source of the payment is irrelevant to them. A beneficiary, on the other hand, will be very concerned if property which that beneficiary hopes to take is wrongly used to pay debts. Marshalling is a way of adjusting the assets so as to compensate a disappointed beneficiary where a payment has been made from the wrong assets.

*Example*
X is administering the estate of T. T's will left shares in ABC Ltd. (value £2,000) to S and the residue of the estate to R (the residue consists of land worth £20,000). There is a debt of £2,000 to pay. The debt *should* be paid from residue. If X uses the shares to pay the creditor, S will be disappointed. However, S can be compensated from property falling within any of the earlier paragraphs. S is therefore entitled to £2,000 from the residuary assets.

## B. Insolvent Estates

### 1. INTRODUCTION

**15.24**  An estate is insolvent if the assets are insufficient to pay all the funeral, testamentary and administration expenses, debts and liabilities. The beneficiaries of the deceased's will or the deceased's next-of-kin under the intestacy rules will receive nothing and the creditors of the estate will not all be paid in full. It is important to know in what order creditors are entitled to be paid. The order in which the debts of the deceased are to be paid is:

    (i)   funeral, testamentary and administration expenses, and then

    (ii)  the bankruptcy order.

This order cannot be varied by the testator. If the personal representatives do not follow the statutory order they will incur personal liability for "superior" debts which have been left unpaid. Therefore, if there is any possibility that an estate may be insolvent the personal representatives should observe the statutory order when paying debts.

## 2. ASSETS AND LIABILITIES

When a living person is declared bankrupt there are special rules of bankruptcy which swell the bankrupt's assets. These rules also apply to an insolvent estate by virtue of the Administration of Insolvent Estates of Deceased Persons Order 1986 (S.I. 1986 No. 1999). The same Order provides that where a bankruptcy petition is presented and then the debtor dies, the bankruptcy proceedings may continue despite the death of the debtor.

**15.25**

All debts and liabilities, present or future, certain and contingent, liquidated or unliquidated are provable against an insolvent estate. If the value of a liability is uncertain (because it is contingent or for any other reason) its value must be estimated (Insolvency Act 1986). A debt which is statute-barred is not provable where the estate is insolvent.

## 3. SECURED CREDITORS

A creditor may have security for a debt; for example a bank may have given a loan to the deceased and taken a charge over the deceased's house or other assets as security. Such a creditor has a choice.

**15.26**

(a) He may rely on his security and not prove for his debt at all. This is a safe course provided the security is sufficient to cover the debt.

(b) He may realise the security and if the security is inadequate prove for any balance as an unsecured creditor.

(c) He may value the security and prove for any balance as an unsecured creditor. Care must be taken in such a valuation. If the creditor puts too low a value on the security the personal representatives can insist on redeeming it at that value leaving him to prove as an unsecured creditor for the balance. If he puts too high a value on it and proves as an unsecured creditor for the balance, he will prove for an insufficient amount.

(d) He may surrender his security and prove for the whole debt as an unsecured creditor.

In so far as the secured creditor obtains payment by realising the security, he has priority over all unsecured creditors of the estate and receives payment in priority to the funeral, testamentary and administration expenses.

## 4. FUNERAL, TESTAMENTARY AND ADMINISTRATION EXPENSES

**15.27** These are paid in priority to all unsecured debts and liabilities of the deceased and are paid in priority to preferred creditors. Where an estate is insolvent "reasonable" funeral expenses are likely to be on a lower scale than would be the case with a solvent estate.

## 5. OTHER DEBTS AND LIABILITIES

**15.28** The Administration of Insolvent Estates of Deceased Persons Order 1986 provides that the bankruptcy order is to apply to the payment of all other debts and liabilities.

*The bankruptcy order*
**15.29** The bankruptcy order is as follows:

(a) Preferred debts.
(b) Ordinary debts.
(c) Deferred debts.

Within each category the debts rank equally and if the assets are insufficient to meet the debts of one category in full all debts in that category abate proportionally.

*Preferred debts include*:

**15.30**     (i) Wages or salary or accrued holiday remuneration owed by the deceased to an employee in respect of the whole or any part of the period of four months before death, such amount not to exceed the limit prescribed by the Secretary of State (currently £800).

(ii) Sums due from the deceased in the 12-month period before death in respect of Class 1 or Class 2 contributions under the Social Security Act 1975 (or the Social Security (Northern Ireland) Act 1975).

(iii) Sums due from the deceased under Schedule 3 to the Social Security Pensions Act 1975 in respect of contributions to occupational pension schemes and State scheme premiums.

(iv) Sums due from the deceased to the Inland Revenue on account of deductions of P.A.Y.E. income tax which the deceased was liable to make from wages or salary paid during the period of 12 months before death (less repayments due to the deceased from the Inland Revenue).

(v) Value added tax referable to the six-month period before death and which became due during that period.

If a landlord carries out a distraint on the deceased's goods within three months of death the preferred creditors have a first claim on the goods (or the proceeds of sale). This is to prevent a landlord making use of the special remedy of distraint to obtain payment from the assets of the estate before the preferential creditors. However the landlord is entitled to replace in the order of priority any creditor who is paid as a result of such a claim (Insolvency Act 1986). So to this extent a landlord will get priority over other ordinary creditors.

If the landlord recovers an amount in excess of six months' rent accrued due before death any excess must be held for the estate.

*Ordinary debts*
These are all other debts which are not deferred. **15.31**

*Interest*
Any surplus remaining after the payment of preferred and **15.32** ordinary debts shall be used to pay interest on preferential and ordinary debts from death till payment (ordinary debts ranking equally with preferential debts for this purpose). The rate of interest payable is whichever is the greater of:

(a) the rate specified in section 17 of the Judgments Act 1838 at death; and

(b) the rate otherwise applicable to that debt.

*Deferred debts*
Deferred debts are debts owed in respect of credit provided by **15.33** a person who (whether or not the deceased's spouse at the time the credit was provided) was the deceased's spouse at the date of death. Such debts are payable after the payment of preferred and ordinary debts and the interest thereon.

6. LIABILITY FOR UNPAID DEBTS

*Personal liability of personal representatives*
If a personal representative pays an inferior debt knowing of the **15.34** existence of a superior debt, the payment is taken as an admission by him that he has sufficient assets to pay all debts of

which he has notice which rank in priority to the inferior debt. He will, therefore, be personally liable to pay all such debts.

However, he is not personally liable if, without undue haste, he pays an inferior debt without notice of a superior one. (This is unlike the position of a personal representative who pays a *beneficiary* without notice of the existence of a debt of the deceased).

*Limited protection*

**15.35** A personal representative is under a duty to pay all debts in the same category *pari passu* (*i.e.* proportionately) and has no right to prefer one creditor above others in the same class.

However, under section 10(2) of the Administration of Estates Act 1925 there is limited protection for a personal representative who pays a debt in full at a time when he has no reason to believe the estate is insolvent. A personal representative who makes a payment in such circumstances to a creditor (including himself, unless he took a grant of representation in the capacity of creditor) is not liable to account to other creditors of the *same* class as the creditor who has been paid, if it subsequently apears that the estate is insolvent.

The section does not protect a personal representative against creditors in a *superior* category nor does it protect a personal representative who had any reason to believe that the estate was insolvent.

# 16. Legacies and Devises

## A. Legacies and Devises

A legacy is a gift in a will of personalty; a devise is a gift in a **16.1** will of realty.

## B. Classification of Legacies

Legacies may be classified as specific, general, demonstrative, **16.2** pecuniary or residuary. The classification is important because different types of legacy have different characteristics.

### 1. SPECIFIC LEGACIES

A specific legacy is a gift of a particular item of property owned **16.3** by the deceased at the time of death and distinguished from all other property owned by the deceased of a similar type.

Examples of specific legacies are:

"I give the gold ring I bought in Manchester to X."
"I give my shares in ABC Ltd. to Y."

Specific legacies suffer from the disadvantage that they may fail as a result of the doctrine of ademption. Ademption means that a specific legacy fails if the subject-matter has ceased to form part of the deceased's estate at death. This may be because the property has been sold or has been destroyed or has completely changed its substance. The disappointed beneficiary will receive no compensation from the rest of the estate. Only specific legacies suffer ademption; therefore when construing a will the court tends to construe a legacy as general rather than specific where possible (*Re Rose* (1949)). (For a fuller discussion of ademption, see paragraphs 16.14–16.19).

As we saw in Chapter 15 specific legacies (and devises) are available for payment of debts, but only after such items as undisposed of property, residue and any retained pecuniary legacy fund have been exhausted.

## 2. GENERAL LEGACIES

**16.4** A general legacy is a gift in a will of an item of property which is not distinguished from property of a similar type. If the deceased does not own property at the date of death corresponding to the description in the will, the personal representatives must purchase suitable property using funds from the estate (in determining from which part of the estate such funds are to be provided a general legacy is treated as a pecuniary legacy so that the same rules which apply to the incidence of pecuniary legacies—see paragraphs 16.37–16.41— apply to the incidence of general legacies).

An example of a general legacy is:

"I give 100 shares in ABC Ltd. to Y."

This is a gift of *any* 100 shares in ABC Ltd. The mere fact that at the time of making the will the testator owned exactly 100 shares in the company is not sufficient to turn the legacy into a specific legacy (*Re Willcocks* (1921)). If a legacy is to be construed as specific there must be a clear indication in the will itself that the testator is referring to particular property owned at the time of the will. A general legacy is not liable to ademption but will be taken for payment of debts before specific legacies. (See paragraph 16.8.)

## 3. DEMONSTRATIVE LEGACIES

**16.5** A demonstrative legacy is "in its nature a general legacy but there is a particular fund pointed out to satisfy it" (*Per* Lord Thurlow, *Ashburner* v. *MacGuire* (1786)).

Examples of a demonstrative legacy are:

"I give £100 to X to be paid from my current bank account."
"I give £100 to Y to be paid out of my National Savings Certificates."

A demonstrative legacy combines the attributes of general and specific legacies. It is treated as a specific legacy to the extent that the particular fund is in existence at the date of death and is therefore taken for payment of debts after general legacies. If, however, the particular fund is not in existence at the date of death the legacy is not adeemed (as a specific legacy would be) instead it is treated as a general legacy and paid from any other property available in the estate.

## 4. PECUNIARY LEGACIES

### Description

A pecuniary legacy is a gift in a will of money. Most commonly **16.6** a pecuniary legacy is general (for example, "I give £100 to X") but it may be specific (for example, "I give the £100 I keep in a box under the bed to Y") or demonstrative (for example, "I give £100 to Y to be paid from my current bank account)."

### Annuities

An annuity is a pecuniary legacy payable by instalments. **16.7**

### *The Administration of Estates Act 1925, s.55(1)(x)*

*Special definition.* Section 55(1)(x) defines a "pecuniary **16.8** legacy" for the purposes of the Act. The expression

"includes an annuity, a general legacy, a demonstrative legacy so far as it is not discharged out of the designated property, and any other general direction by a testator for the payment of money, including all death duties free from which any devise, bequest or payment is made to take effect."

Thus, a gift of "the £100 I keep in a box under my bed" being a specific legacy is not treated as a pecuniary legacy for the purposes of the Administration of Estates Act; the £100 would, therefore, rank with the other specific legacies for payment of debts.

*Availability for payment of debts.* In the order of availability of property for payment of debts set out in the Administration of Estates Act, the fund set on one side for payment of pecuniary legacies is taken fifth, whereas specific legacies (and devises) are taken sixth after the retained fund has been exhausted. If only part of the retained fund is required for payment of debts the various pecuniary legacies will abate proportionally (unless the testator indicated that one legacy was to be paid in priority to the others in which case the indication is binding on the personal representatives).

## 5. RESIDUARY LEGACIES

**16.9** A residuary gift in a will passes the property of the deceased not otherwise disposed of. It may be a gift of the entire net estate if no other dispositions have been made or it may be a gift of what is left after payment of specific and general gifts. It may be limited to personalty not otherwise disposed of but more usually it will not be so limited and will pass all property whether realty or personalty.

## C. Devises

**16.10** A devise is a gift of realty and can be either specific or residuary. If specific it is subject to the rules on ademption.

## D. Failure of Legacies and Devises

### 1. INTRODUCTION

**16.11** A gift made in a valid will can fail for a number of reasons. Some of the more important are listed below:

- (a) disclaimer
- (b) ademption
- (c) the beneficiary predeceases the testator
- (d) divorce
- (e) uncertainty
- (f) the beneficiary witnesses the will
- (g) the gift is contrary to public policy or for an illegal or immoral purpose
- (h) the gift is induced by force, fear, fraud or undue influence (this has already been considered in Chapter 2)

(j) the gift infringes the rules against perpetuity and accumulations (a consideration of these rules and their consequences is beyond the scope of this book).

## 2. EFFECT OF FAILURE

Any legacy or specific devise which fails, falls into residue unless the testator has included a substitutional gift. If a residuary gift fails the property is undisposed of and passes under the intestacy rules to the testator's next-of-kin.   **16.12**

## 3. DISCLAIMER

No one can force another to accept a benefit under the will. Beneficiaries are free to disclaim any property given by will. However, it is not normally possible to pick and choose—unless the will provides to the contrary, the whole of a gift must be disclaimed or the whole must be accepted; if, however, two entirely separate gifts are made one may be accepted and the other disclaimed. Once a person has accepted any benefit from a gifted property (for example, income from or interest on it) it is too late to disclaim. (It may, however, be possible to vary the terms of the deceased's disposition by a variation agreement). A fuller discussion of the practical considerations involved in disclaimers and variations will be found in Chapter 19 below.   **16.13**

## 4. ADEMPTION

*Introduction*
As we saw in paragraph 16.3 and in paragraph 16.10, a specific legacy or devise will fail if the subject-matter does not form part of the testator's estate at death. Ademption may occur as a result of sale or destruction of the asset or a change in substance. A disappointed beneficiary has no rights to receive the proceeds of sale where property has been sold nor any rights to the proceeds of any insurance policy where property has been destroyed. There are a number of aspects of the doctrine of ademption which warrant fuller consideration.   **16.14**

*A change in substance*
A change in substance will cause ademption to take place but a mere change in form will not. It is sometimes difficult to decide whether a change is one of substance or of form. In *Re Clifford* (1912), T gave 23 "of the shares belonging to me" in a named company. After the date of the will the company changed its   **16.15**

name and subdivided each share into 4. Swinfen Eady J. held that the legacy was not adeemed since the subject-matter remained exactly the same although changed in name and form. The beneficiary, therefore, took 92 of the new shares. In *Re Slater* (1907), a testator made a gift of shares in Lambeth Waterworks Company. After the date of the will the company was taken over and amalgamated with other waterworks companies into the Metropolitan Water Board which issued stock to replace shares held in the old companies. The Court of Appeal held that the legacy was adeemed since the new stock was in an entirely different organisation.

### Effect of republication

**16.16**  If a legacy has been adeemed and the testator afterwards makes a codicil which republishes the will, it normally has no effect on the ademption. For example, if T left Blackacre to B, sold Blackacre, then made a codicil republishing the will B would still have no rights to the traceable proceeds of sale even if they were identifiable.

However, as a result of the republication the will may be construed in such a way that a gift which would otherwise have been adeemed will be saved. For example, T gives "the house in which I now reside to X." Such a gift is a specific devise and if T sells the house after the date of the will it will be adeemed; if T buys another house X is not entitled to the replacement. However, if T makes a codicil to the will after the purchase of the replacement house the will is republished as at the date of the codicil and, since the wording used in the gift is wide enough to cover *any* house in which T is residing at the appropriate time, X will be entitled to the replacement house.

A codicil republishing a will can only have the effect of passing a replacement asset if the wording used in the original will is sufficiently wide. If, for example, T gave "the 3 stone diamond ring I bought in London in 1971 to X" and the ring was stolen the gift would be adeemed; if the ring was insured T might use the insurance money to buy an identical three stone ring but even if T made a codicil republishing the will the wording would be too specific to cover the replacement and X would get nothing.

### The effect of the doctrine of conversion

**16.17**  When a vendor enters into a binding contract to sell realty the equitable doctrine of conversion applies so that the vendor is treated from the date of the contract as having an interest in the proceeds of sale rather than in the realty. If T makes a will leaving freehold property, Blackacre, to B and then enters into a binding contract to sell Blackacre, the devise is adeemed from the date of the contract. If T dies between contract and completion B is entitled to any rent or other income Blackacre may produce until completion but B is not entitled to the proceeds of sale, which will fall into residue.

The anomalous rule in *Lawes* v. *Bennett* (1785) can in certain circumstances convert property retrospectively; this may lead to ademption. If T makes a will leaving Blackacre to B and residue to R, later grants an option to purchase Blackacre to O and dies before the option has been exercised, Blackacre passes to B. However, if O subsequently decides to exercise the option this effects a retrospective conversion so that Blackacre is deemed to have been converted into proceeds of sale from the date of T's death. The sale proceeds are therefore paid to R and not to B— B is not, however, required to repay any rents or income received since the date of death.

The rule in *Lawes* v. *Bennett* was extended to a gift of shares subject to an option to purchase in *Re Carrington* (1932). The result was that, when the option to purchase the shares was exercised, the shares were deemed to have been sold as at the date of the testator's death. The gift of shares was treated as adeemed and the proceeds of sale fell into residue.

If the will is made or republished after the date of the grant of the option the testator is deemed to have intended to pass to the beneficiary the property *or* the proceeds of sale so that no ademption will take place even if the option is exercised. The beneficiary will be entitled to the proceeds of sale (*Drant* v. *Vause* (1842)).

*Property to be ascertained at date of death*
A testator may make a gift of assets to be ascertained at the **16.18** date of death, for example a gift of "all the shares in ABC Co. which I own at my death." Such a gift is not subject to the doctrine of ademption as such, although it will fail if the testator owns no assets corresponding to the description at the date of death.

*Problems when drafting a will*
The effect of the doctrine of ademption should always be **16.19** explained to a client who wishes to make a bequest or devise of a specific item.

It is possible to include words of substitution so that a testator might give "my shares in ABC Co. or any shares representing that investment at the time of my death." However, such a gift may well create problems for the personal representatives in identifying such shares, particularly if the death occurs some time after the will is made. It may, therefore, be preferable simply to point out to the client the importance of reviewing the will periodically so that it can be changed if an asset specifically given is sold, destroyed or substantially changed.

Alternatively, it may be possible to word the gift so that the precise property is to be ascertained at the date of death (as suggested in paragraph 16.18 above) or to give a pecuniary legacy in substitution for a legacy failing by reason of ademption.

## 5. BENEFICIARY PREDECEASES TESTATOR

*Introduction*

**16.20** In order to take a gift under a will a beneficiary must survive the testator. If the beneficiary predeceases the testator a legacy will lapse and fall into residue or if it is a residuary gift will pass under the intestacy rules. A beneficiary need only survive for a very short period—a minute or a second will suffice.

If a gift is to joint tenants or is a class gift, it will not lapse unless all the joint tenants or members of the class predecease the testator; if one joint tenant or class member survives the testator, that one person takes the whole gift. If a gift is to tenants in common, the share of any tenant who predeceases the testator will lapse.

A testator cannot exclude the doctrine of lapse by declaring that it is not to apply. A testator can, however, include a substitutional gift providing that if the beneficiary predeceases, the property is to pass to another person.

A solicitor should always point out to a client the possibility that a beneficiary may predecease so that the client can consider including a substitutional clause. It is also common to include a survivorship clause in a will. A survivorship clause states that a beneficiary is only to take a benefit under the will if the beneficiary survives the testator for a stated period (usually 28 days). The effect is to prevent a beneficiary who only survives the testator by a very short period from benefiting under the will. The importance of such a clause is obvious when it is remembered that a beneficiary may be *deemed* to survive under the Law of Property Act 1925, s.184 (see paragraph 16.21 below). Without a survivorship clause, the testator's property would pass under the terms of the beneficiary's will or to the beneficiary's next of kin under the intestacy rules. Such a devolution of property might be contrary to the testator's wishes.

Substitutional and survivorship clauses, as well as giving the testator control over the ultimate destination of his property, may have the effect of saving inheritance tax overall. For a fuller discussion of this topic see Chapter 22.

*Where the order of deaths is uncertain*
*The statutory presumption.* It can sometimes happen that **16.21** there is no evidence as to the order in which people have died, for example where two people die in a car accident. In such a case, section 184 of the Law of Property Act 1925 provides that for the purposes of succession to property the deaths are presumed to have occurred in order of seniority so that the elder is presumed to die first. The section applies equally on intestacy (with one exception which will be considered later).

*Example*

```
    Mother              Mother
      |                   |
    Harold     =       Winifred

     30                  29
```

Harold and Winifred both die in a car accident; the order of their deaths is uncertain. They have each made wills leaving all their property to the other. They have no children. Each has a mother who survives.

Harold, being the elder, is presumed to die first. His property therefore passes under the terms of his will to Winifred who is presumed to have survived him. It forms part of her estate. The gift to Harold in Winifred's will lapses and her estate (which now includes Harold's property) passes to her mother under the intestacy rules. It is unlikely that Harold would have wished his property to pass to Winifred's mother in preference to his own, had he included a survivorship clause in his will his property would not have passed to Winifred and so would not have gone to her mother.

*Special rule where the elder of two spouses dies intestate.* Section 1(4) of the Intestates Estates Act 1952 amends section 184 where the elder of two spouses dies intestate. When administering the estate *of the elder spouse only* the younger spouse is presumed to have predeceased; when administering the estate of the younger spouse section 184 applies in the ordinary way.

*Example*

|        |   |          |
|--------|---|----------|
| Mother |   | Mother   |
| \|     |   | \|       |
| Harold | = | Winifred |
| 30     |   | 29       |

As in the previous example Harold and Winifred die in a car accident; the order of their deaths is uncertain. They have no children. This time Harold has died intestate. When dealing with Harold's estate section 1(4) of the Intestates Estates Act provides that Winifred is presumed to have predeceased Harold. His property therefore passes under the intestacy rules to his mother. When dealing with Winifred's estate, whether she dies intestate or leaves a will, section 184 of the Law of Property Act applies so that she is presumed to have survived Harold. If, as in the previous example, her will left everything to Harold the gift will lapse and the property will pass under the intestacy rules to her mother. If she died intestate her property would also pass to her mother as next-of-kin.

*Exceptions to the doctrine of lapse*
**16.22**  There are three situations where, despite the fact that a beneficiary has predeceased a testator, a gift will not fail.

> (a)  Gifts in discharge of a moral obligation.
> (b)  Section 32 of the Wills Act 1837.
> (c)  Section 33 of the Wills Act 1837.

Both (a) and (b) are of comparatively minor importance and can be dealt with briefly; (c), however, warrants a more detailed examination.

*Gifts in discharge of a moral obligation*
If a testator makes a gift to a beneficiary in order to discharge a moral obligation and the beneficiary predeceases the testator the gift will not lapse but will form part of the beneficiary's estate. Examples of gifts which have been held to be in discharge of a moral obligation are a direction to pay a statute-barred debt (*Williamson* v. *Naylor* (1838)) and a mother's direction that the creditors of her deceased son be paid (*Re Leach's Will Trusts* (1948)).

The precise limits of the rule are uncertain and it may be that it applies only to directions to pay debts and not to ordinary gifts (*Stevens* v. *King* (1904)).

## Section 32 of the Wills Act 1837

Section 32 provides that a gift of entailed property will not lapse if at the death of the testator there are any issue living who are capable of taking under the entail. The testator can exclude the section by showing a contrary intention in the will.

## Section 33 of the Wills Act 1837

*The section.* Section 33(1) (as substituted by the Administra-   **16.23** tion of Justice Act 1982) applies where a testator dies after December 31, 1982. (The rules contained in the original section 33 which applied before 1983 are not dealt with in this book.) The substituted section 33 provides that where:

(a) a will contains a devise or bequest to a child or remoter descendant of the testator; *and*
(b) the intended beneficiary dies before the testator, leaving issue; *and*
(c) issue of the intended beneficiary are living at the testator's death;

then, unless a contrary intention appears by the will, the devise or bequest shall take effect as a devise or bequest *to the issue* living at the testator's death.

Section 33(3) provides that such issue take "according to their stock, in equal shares if more than one, any gift or share which their parent would have taken."

*Example*

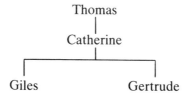

Thomas leaves Catherine a legacy of £20,000 in his will but Catherine predeceases Thomas. Normally the gift to Catherine would fail; however, as a result of section 33 the gift does not fail but passes equally to Giles and Gertrude who take £10,000 each.

Section 33(3) goes on to provide that no issue shall take whose parent is living at the testator's death and so capable of taking.

*Example*

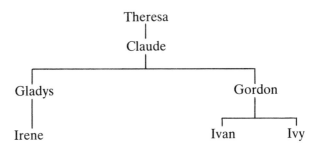

Theresa leaves Claude a legacy of £20,000. Claude and Gordon predecease Theresa. The gift does not lapse but passes to Theresa's issue. Gladys receives one-half (her issue are entitled to nothing as she is still alive); Gordon has predeceased Theresa and therefore his share of £10,000 is divided equally between his issue, Ivan and Ivy, who take £5,000 each.

If the gift to the primary beneficiary is contingent it is not clear from the wording of the section whether a substituted beneficiary would have to satisfy the same contingency. It is, therefore, desirable when drafting a will containing a contingent gift to a child (or remoter descendant) of the testator to make express provision for the possibility that the child (or remoter descendant) might predecease leaving issue and to state expressly whether or not the substitutional gift is subject to the same contingency.

*Class gifts*. Section 33(2) provides that where:

(a) a will contains a devise or bequest to a class of persons consisting of children or remoter descendants of the testator, and

(b) a member of the class dies before the testator, leaving issue, and

(c) issue of that member are living at the testator's death

then, unless a contrary intention appears in the will, the devise or bequest shall take effect as if the class included the issue of its deceased member living at the testator's death. Under section 33(3) the issue take *per stirpes* according to their stocks, in equal shares if more than one, the share which their parent would have taken and no issue whose parent is living at the time of the testator's death shall take.

*Example*

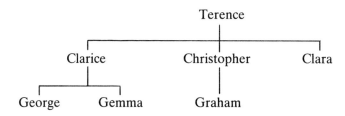

Terence leaves £30,000 to be divided "amongst all my children." Clarice predeceases Terence. Her one-third share (£10,000) will be divided *per stirpes* amongst such of her issue as survive Terence. Section 33(3) will apply so that no issue shall take whose parent is living at the testator's death. Therefore Graham will take nothing.

*Contrary intention.* Both section 33(1) and section 33(2) are expressed to be subject to contrary intention. There is, however, some uncertainty as to precisely what constitutes "contrary intention" for this purpose. The original section 33 of Wills Act 1837 stated that it was not to apply when an interest was determinable at or before death. Thus, that section did not save a life interest to a child of the testator who predeceased, nor a gift to a child of the testator as a joint tenant or as a member of a class who predeceased leaving surviving joint tenants or class members; nor did it apply to a gift contingent on an event which had not occurred when the child predeceased. The substituted section 33 does not contain such exclusions and it is not clear whether or not a testator making gifts on such terms thereby demonstrates a contrary intention. If a testator does not wish the issue of a deceased child (or remoter descendant) to take a benefit the safest course is to include a provision stating what is to happen in the event of such predecease. (See the discussion of the new section 33 and will drafting below).

*Children whose parents were not married and children en ventre sa mere.* Section 33(4) provides that for the purposes of section 33 the illegitimacy of any person is to be disregarded. Thus, a child whose parents were not married can take in the same way as a child whose parents were married. The subsection also provides that a child *en ventre sa mere* is living for the purposes of the section.

*The effect of the substituted section 33 on will drafting.* As explained above if a testator does *not* want section 33 to apply it is desirable for the avoidance of doubt to state in the will what is to happen where a child predeceases. However, even in those cases where a gift to a testator's deceased child (or remoter descendant) *is* to pass to the child's issue, it is desirable to include an express provision to this effect rather than to rely on the section for the following reasons:

(a) If the substitution is set out in the will, a solicitor can be certain that the effect of the statutory provision is brought to the attention of the client; this gives the client the opportunity to request an alternative if the statutory provision does not correspond with his wishes.

(b) If the gift to the testator's child (or remoter descendant) is contingent it is desirable to provide expressly for the possibility that the child might survive the testator but die without fulfilling the contingency leaving issue.

(c) If the gift to the testator's child (or remoter descendant) is contingent it is desirable to state expressly whether or not a substituted beneficiary is to take subject to the same contingency.

In cases where a gift is made to anyone other than a child (or remoter descendant) of the testator (for example "to the children of my brother") an express substitutional gift to issue *must* be included if the testator wants the gift to pass to issue in substitution for a beneficiary who predeceases. Section 33 applies only to gifts to the testator's children (or remoter descendants).

## 6. DIVORCE

*Section 18A of the Wills Act 1837*

**16.24** As we saw in Chapter 2, the Administration of Justice Act 1982 introduced a new section 18A into the Wills Act 1837. It applies in the case of deaths occurring after December 31, 1982. The provision (which is expressed to be without prejudice to the right of the former spouse to apply for financial provision under the Inheritance (Provision for Family and Dependants) Act 1975) provides:

"18A—(1) Where, after a testator has made a will, a decree of a court dissolves or annuls his marriage or declares it void,—

   (a)   the will shall take effect as if any appointment of the former spouse as an executor or as the executor and trustee of the will were omitted; and

   (b)   any devise or bequest to the former spouse shall lapse, except in so far as a contrary intention appears by the will."

The effect of subsection 1 is that a gift to a former spouse lapses as soon as a marriage is dissolved. In *Re Sinclair (decd.)* (1985) the Court of Appeal had to consider the meaning of the word "lapse." It found that the word "lapse" as used in the section has no special or technical meaning. Thus, the word is to be construed as meaning simply "fail," no more and no less, and a former spouse is not to be treated as having *predeceased* the testator.

The decision has important implications on will drafting. In *Re Sinclair* itself a gift of residue had been made to a testator's wife but in the event of her predeceasing or failing to survive the testator by a period of one month the property was to pass to a named charity. The testator's wife was alive at the time of his death and did survive him for one month but the marriage had been terminated by divorce so that, as a result of section 18A, the gift to her lapsed. The Court of Appeal held that the gift over to the charity was expressed to take effect only if the wife *predeceased* or *failed to survive* and as neither of these events had occurred the gift over could not take effect and there was an intestacy, the property passing to the testator's next of kin. The Court rejected counsel's argument that the word "lapse" could be regarded as meaning "deemed to fail as if the spouse had predeceased the testator."

*The effect of section 18A on will drafting*

It is important when drafting a will for a married person to bear **16.25** in mind the possibility of divorce and not to draft a substitutional clause too narrowly. A gift over could be expressed to take effect if a spouse "predeceases, does not survive for [a specified period] or if *the gift fails for any reason*"; alternatively, a clause could be included in the will stating that after termination of the marriage a spouse is to be treated as having predeceased.

In any event it is always desirable to suggest that clients who are contemplating divorce should review their wills and that they should do so as early as possible since the mere fact of separation (or even a decree of Judicial Separation) will not revoke testamentary dispositions.

## 7. UNCERTAINTY

*Introduction*

**16.26** If it is impossible to identify either the subject-matter or the objects of a gift, it will fail for uncertainty.

*Uncertainty of subject-matter*

**16.27** Gifts of "some of my best table linen" (*Peck* v. *Halsey* (1726)) or of "a handsome gratuity" (*Jubber* v. *Jubber* (1839)) have been held to be void for uncertainty. (In some cases such gifts may now be saved by the Administration of Justice Act 1982, s.21).

A gift may prima facie be of an uncertain amount and yet be capable of assessment in which case it will not fail. For example, a clause giving a beneficiary a power to select such items as he wishes is valid; so also is a direction that a beneficiary enjoy "a reasonable income" from the testator's properties (*Re Golay* (1965)) since the court can, if necessary, determine what is a reasonable income.

*Uncertainty of objects*

**16.28** If the beneficiaries are not clearly identified the gift will fail. Thus, a gift to "the son of A" where A had several sons fails for uncertainty (*Dowset* v. *Sweet* (1753)). It is, therefore, important when drafting a will to take care to check the names of individuals and institutions intended to benefit. The only case where a gift will not fail for uncertainty of objects is where a testator wishes to make a charitable gift and does not sufficiently identify the charity which is to benefit. The gift will not fail so long as it is clear that the gift is for exclusively charitable purposes. The court will direct a scheme to give effect to the gift.

## 8. THE BENEFICIARY WITNESSES THE WILL

*The general rule*

**16.29** Section 15 of the Wills Act provides that a gift made to a beneficiary fails if:

(a)   the beneficiary witnesses the will; or
(b)   the spouse of the beneficiary witnesses the will.

The validity of the will itself is not affected. The rule exists to ensure that wills are reliably witnessed by independent persons.

### Beneficial gifts only

Section 15 applies only to beneficial gifts. Thus, if a gift is made **16.30** "to X as trustee to hold for Y" and X or X's spouse witnesses the will the gift does not fail. The gift would fail if Y or Y's spouse witnessed the will.

### Subsequent events irrelevant

It is the time of execution which is important. Subsequent **16.31** events are irrelevant. Thus, if a witness marries a beneficiary *after* the date of execution of the will the gift remains effective (*Thorpe* v. *Bestwick* (1881)). Similarly, if a gift is to the holder of an office or to a person fulfilling a description the gift will remain effective even though a witness later takes up the office or comes to fulfil the description (*Re Ray's Will Trusts, Public Trustee* v. *Barry* (1936)).

### Gift made or confirmed by independently witnessed will or codicil

A gift will not fail if there is a codicil or will which can be said **16.32** to confirm the will and which is not witnessed by the beneficiary (or the beneficiary's spouse). It is not necessary to find any express reference to the gift in the independently witnessed will or codicil. In *Re Trotter* (1899) T made a gift by will to B, a witness; there were two later codicils to the will; B did not witness the first but did witness the second. The court held that as there was one independently witnessed codicil the gift to B did not fail.

### Secret trusts

If T creates a secret (or half secret) trust in favour of X and X **16.33** or X's spouse witnesses the will, X does not lose his entitlement. This is because X takes under the trust and not under the will (*Re Young* (1951)).

### Superfluous attesting witnesses

In the case of a testator dying after May 29, 1968, the Wills Act **16.34** 1968 provides that the attestation of a will by any beneficiaries or their spouses is to be disregarded if without them the will is duly executed.

Thus, if a will is witnessed by three people, one of whom is a beneficiary (or spouse of a beneficiary) that person may take a gift in the will; however if two of the three witnesses (or their spouses) are beneficiaries their signatures cannot be disregarded and neither can take.

If a person (other than the testator) has signed a will it is presumed that the signature is as a witness. The presumption can be rebutted—for example, by evidence that the signature was to indicate approval of the testator's disposition. If a beneficiary (or spouse of a beneficiary) is able to show that a signature was in such a capacity there is no question of loss of entitlement.

*Charging clauses*

**16.35** A trustee or personal representative is unable to charge for services without express authority in the trust instrument or will. It is, therefore, usual for a solicitor (or other professional person) who is appointed a personal representative or trustee to request that a charging clause be included authorising him to charge for his services.

Such a clause is treated as a legacy so that entitlement is lost if the solicitor witnesses the will.

Where there is no express charging clause or where the benefit has been lost a solicitor/personal representative who is a partner in a firm of solicitors cannot pay his own *firm* to act because he is then in effect acting as his own solicitor. This is so even if there is express agreement that he will not share in the profits (*Re Gates* (1933)). However, it is possible for such a solicitor-trustee to employ and pay individual *partners* in the firm provided there is express agreement that the solicitor/personal representative shall not participate in the profits nor derive any benefit from the charges (*Re Gates*). If the firm is being appointed rather than an individual solicitor (this takes effect as an appointment of the partners in the firm; see Chapter 2) none of the partners or their spouses at the date of execution should witness the will; if an articled clerk or assistant solicitor witnesses the will and later becomes a partner the benefit is not lost (see paragraph 16.31 above). Even so most firms of solicitors prefer not to let prospective partners witness wills in order to avoid any possible suggestion of impropriety; in an emergency, however, it can be done.

Banks have their own approved forms of charging clauses (available from any branch) and will not accept appointment unless these clauses are used.

A charging clause is always strictly construed against the trustee and, therefore, such a clause must be carefully drafted. In particular it should authorise charging for *any* work done in connection with the administration or trust whether or not it could have been done by a lay person; otherwise charges can only be made for strictly professional services.

Since a charging clause is treated as a legacy, it will, in the absence of express direction to the contrary, abate with any other pecuniary legacies if there are insufficient funds to pay the legacies in full. In order to avoid this, it is common to provide that charges are to be paid in full in priority to other legacies.

### 9. THE GIFT IS FOR AN ILLEGAL OR IMMORAL PURPOSE OR CONTRARY TO PUBLIC POLICY

Such a gift cannot take effect. The principles to be applied in deciding whether a gift is illegal, immoral or contrary to public policy are the same as in the law of trusts. The law relating to public policy is not fixed but changes with the passage of time. It is, however, a well established rule of public policy that a person shall not profit from a crime. Thus, if one person, (B) is found guilty of murder or, subject to what is said below, manslaughter of another (T), B cannot take any benefit under the will of T or under the intestacy rules if T dies intestate. Any person claiming through B's estate (for example, B's issue) are also excluded. B will not, however, lose entitlement if the killing was carried out while B was insane within the McNaghten rules.    **16.36**

This rule of public policy has been modified by the Forfeiture Act 1982. The Act does not apply where a person has been convicted of murder but applies in any other case where one person has unlawfully killed another (for example, manslaughter). An offender may apply to the court within three months of the date of conviction (section 2) for an order modifying the forfeiture rule in respect of any beneficial interest which the offender would have acquired from the deceased (but for the forfeiture rule) *inter alia*:

    (a)   under the deceased's will or on intestacy;
    (b)   on a nomination by the deceased;
    (c)   as a *donatio mortis causa* (section 2(4)(*a*)).

An application may also be made where property had been held on trust for any person and as a result of the deceased's death but for the forfeiture rule the offender *would have* acquired an interest in the trust property (section 2(4)(*b*)).

Section 4(5) of the Act *appears* to provide that where there is more than one interest in property to which the forfeiture rule applies the Court may exclude the rule in respect of any *but not all* and where there is one such interest the Court may exclude the rule in respect of *part only* of that interest. However, in one of the first applications to come before the Court (*Re K.* (1985)) Vinelott J. stated that the Act was a private members bill and is not couched in technical language but is intended to be understood by persons other than lawyers specialising in property and trust matters. He said that in his view section 4(5) was intended to enlarge the powers of the court by making it abundantly clear that the court is not bound to relieve against the forfeiture rule entirely or not at all but that the court is free if it chooses to modify the effect of the rule to a limited extent. His first instance judgment was approved by the Court of Appeal.

The court must not make an order unless satisfied that the justice of the case requires the forfeiture rule to be modified having regard to the conduct of the offender and of the deceased and to such other circumstances as appear to the court to be material (section 2(2)).

No application may be made after the expiry of the three month period (section 2(3)).

A personal representative, who is administering an estate where the deceased was unlawfully killed by another person who would but for the forfeiture rule have received any of the interests in the property set out above, should wait for the expiry of the three months from conviction before distributing such property to others.

Section 3 of the Act provides that the forfeiture rule is not to be taken to preclude any person from making an application under the Inheritance (Provision for Family and Dependants) Act 1975. Such an application can be made if the requirements of *that* Act are complied with. Thus, an applicant must be able to show that the disposition of the deceased's estate affected by the will or by the intestacy rules did not make reasonable financial provision for the applicant (*Re Royse* (1984)).

# E. Incidence of Pecuniary Legacies

## 1. INTRODUCTION

**16.37** Throughout this section the term "pecuniary legacy" is used in the Administration of Estates Act sense to cover a general legacy, an annuity or a demonstrative legacy so far as it is not discharged from the designated property.

If a will gives a pecuniary legacy to a beneficiary, the personal representatives will need to know from which part of the estate they are entitled to take assets to pay the legacy. We saw in Chapter 15 that personal representatives have exactly the same problem when deciding which assets are to be used for payment of debts and that there are statutory rules which govern availability of assets for payment of debts. The position with regard to pecuniary legacies is, however, much less certain. This area of the law has been described as "tortuous" and "notoriously obscure" (*per* Salt, Q.C., Ch., in *Re Taylor's Estate* (1969)). It is most desirable that anyone drafting a will should avoid any problems of statutory interpretation by stating expressly what property is to be taken for payment of pecuniary legacies.

## 2. PRE 1926 RULES

**16.38**

These rules have been partly replaced by section 33 of the Administration of Estates Act 1925 but they remain important in those circumstances where section 33 does not apply. We will, therefore, look at the pre-1926 rules first.

Prior to 1926 in the absence of contrary intention pecuniary legacies could only be paid from general personalty. In so far as general personalty was insufficient to cover them, the legacies abated. General personalty was any personalty not specifically disposed of. No distinction was drawn between undisposed of personalty and personalty comprised in a gift of residue; every part of the general personal estate was liable for a proportionate share of the pecuniary legacies. The result was that if residue was left in equal shares to A and B and A predeceased the testator so that A's share lapsed, any pecuniary legacies would be paid equally from A's lapsed share and from the share going to B. There was no possibility of arguing that the undisposed of property should be taken first leaving the share of the surviving residuary beneficiary intact.

Realty was not available at all unless there was an indication of contrary intention in the will. Contrary intention could be shown in two ways:

(a) *The rule in Greville v. Brown.* If a testator gave residue (both real and personal) in one mass to a beneficiary the realty was available to pay pecuniary legacies *but only* in so far as the personalty was exhausted. The precise wording of the gift was irrelevant so long as the testator made it clear that there was one single gift consisting of both realty and personality. An example of such wording would be "I give all my residue, both real and personal, to X."

(b) *The rule in Roberts* v. *Walker*. If a testator directed that pecuniary legacies be paid from a mixed fund of realty and personality, the legacies were payable *proportionately* from both realty and personality. An example of such wording would be "I give my residue, real and personal, on trust for sale to my trustees to use the proceeds to pay my legacies and hold any balance for X."

The question of whether or not realty was available was important in three cases:

(i) If residuary realty was given to one person, R, and residuary personality to another person, P, R would obviously want to insist that legacies be paid exclusively from personality (P would be equally anxious that realty be made available).

(ii) If realty was not available pecuniary legacies would have to abate when the personality was exhausted.

(iii) If a pecuniary legacy was paid from realty the legatee bore any estate duty whereas if it was paid from personality the duty was paid from residue. This is no longer an important consideration; as, in the absence of contrary intention inheritance tax on pecuniary legacies is a testamentary expense irrespective of whether the legacy is paid from personality or realty.

## 3.   POST 1925 RULES: THE EFFECT OF SECTION 33 OF THE ADMINISTRATION OF ESTATES ACT 1925

**16.39** Where a person dies partially intestate, section 33(1) provides that a statutory trust for sale is imposed on the undisposed of property. Section 33(2) provides that the personal representatives shall pay from the money arising from the sale such "funeral, testamentary and administration expenses, debts and other liabilities as are properly payable ... and out of the residue of the said money ... set aside a fund sufficient to provide for any pecuniary legacies bequeathed by the will (if any) of the deceased." The effect of section 33(2) is, therefore, to make undisposed of property primarily liable for payment of pecuniary legacies. It is irrelevant whether the undisposed of property is realty or personality.

*Example*
T's will leaves a pecuniary legacy of £6,000 to L and the residue
to A and B in equal shares. A predeceases T and the gift to him
lapses. The estate amounts to £20,000. There are no debts. The
pecuniary legacy will be paid from the lapsed share of residue
irrespective of whether it is realty or personalty. Therefore B
gets £10,000 and A's lapsed share of £10,000 is used to pay L's
legacy of £6,000. The balance of £4,000 left after payment of the
pecuniary legacy will pass under the intestacy rules to T's next
of kin. (Since section 33(2) expressly directs that pecuniary
legacies be paid from the proceeds of sale, realty and personalty
will be available proportionately for the payment of legacies.)

4. THE POSITION IF SECTION 33(2) DOES NOT APPLY

Section 33(2) provides for what is to happen to the proceeds of     **16.40**
sale arising from the statutory trust for sale imposed by section
33(1). However, as we saw in Chapter 3, the statutory trust for
sale is expressly made subject to any express trust for sale
imposed by the will; there cannot be two trusts for sale one
statutory and one express, applying to the same property (*Re
McKee* (1931)). The express trust takes precedence over that
imposed by section 33(1). If section 33(1) does not apply then
neither does section 33(2) which deals only with the proceeds of
sale arising under the statutory trust.

*Example*
A testator leaves a pecuniary legacy of £6,000 to L and directs
that the residue is to be held *on trust for sale* for A and B in
equal shares. A predeceases T and the gift to him lapses. The
estate amounts to £20,000. Since the testator has imposed an
express trust for sale on the residue there is no room for a
statutory trust for sale to apply to the residue. Thus, section
33(1) does not apply to the undisposed of property and
therefore section 33(2) (which deals only with the proceeds of
sale arising from the statutory trust) cannot apply. The question
then arises of what property is to be used to provide for the
payment of the legacy to L. Unfortunately the answer is by no
means certain.

The better view appears to be that if section 33(2) does not
apply the position is governed by the pre-1925 rules; therefore,
the legacy in the above example would be paid from the *general*
estate not primarily from the undisposed of property (realty
would be available under the rule in *Greville* v. *Brown*). The

effect is that the legacy would be paid before the residue is divided into shares; this would leave £14,000 to be divided into two shares, B would take £7,000 and £7,000 would pass under the intestacy rules to T's next of kin.

However, there have been attempts to argue that even where section 33(2) does not apply the burden of pecuniary legacies still falls primarily on undisposed of property. Such arguments are based on a construction of section 34(2) of the Administration of Estates Act 1925 together with Part II of the First Schedule thereto which provide for the order in which assets are to be taken for payment of debts. We saw in Chapter 15 that the property which is to be taken first for payment of debts is "undisposed of property subject to the retention out of such property of a fund sufficient to meet any pecuniary legacies." It has been claimed that the result of section 34(2) is that the personal representatives are under an obligation to set aside a fund from undisposed of property which must be used to pay pecuniary legacies. This argument was accepted in *Re Midgely* (1955), but rejected in *Re Beaumont's Will Trusts* (1950) and in *Re Taylor's Estate* (1969). In the latter two cases the court took the view that when section 33(2) does not apply the payment of legacies is still governed by the pre-1925 rules. Personal representatives should, therefore, only set aside a legacy fund from undisposed of property if and in so far as such property would have been available for payment of legacies under the old rules.

## 5. WILL DRAFTING

**16.41** In order to avoid arguments as to the construction of the Administration of Estates Act, it is desirable when drafting wills to state expressly what property is to be used for payment of pecuniary legacies. For example, a testator may leave residue "subject to payment of legacies." An express direction is particularly desirable, in view of the problem with section 33(2), where residue is left on express trust for sale. It is common for such trusts for sale to direct that legacies be paid from residue before division into shares; this is certainly a solution to the problem of uncertainty but it does not necessarily reflect the wishes of testators. Many testators might prefer a direction that, where residue is left on trust for sale, in the event of any residuary beneficiary predeceasing the testator, pecuniary legacies should be paid from the lapsed share of residue, thus reducing the amount passing under the intestacy rules.

# F. Income from and Interest on Legacies and Devises

## 1. INTRODUCTION

A personal representative cannot be compelled to pay legacies **16.42** and distribute the estates before the expiry of one year from the death (Administration of Estates Act 1925, s.44). Even in a very simple administration there will inevitably be delay between the death and the distribution. Beneficiaries will want to know what rights they have to income or interest in that period.

This section is concerned with the rights of a beneficiary:

(a) to receive *income* which has been produced by assets in the period between the death of the testator and the vesting of the assets in the beneficiary; and

(b) to receive *interest* paid from the estate on the value of a pecuniary (or general) legacy in the period between the death of the testator and the payment of the legacy to the beneficiary.

## 2. INCOME

Some assets by their very nature are incapable of producing **16.43** income (for example, a painting, a ring, a piece of furniture) in which case the question of a beneficiary's right to income is irrelevant. Other assets do, however, produce income (for example, a house which is rented to a tenant, company shares, government stock). We are concerned with the rights of beneficiaries to receive this income. It is necessary to distinguish the following types of gift:

(a) immediate specific gifts
(b) contingent and deferred specific gifts
(c) immediate residuary gifts
(d) contingent and deferred residuary gifts.

*Immediate specific gifts*

A specific legacy or devise which is to take effect immediately **16.44** carries with it the right to any income accruing to the property in the period between the death of the testator and vesting. The beneficiary is not, however, entitled to receive the income *as it arises*; instead, the beneficiary must wait until the personal representatives vest the property in the beneficiary by means of an assent. The assent operates retrospectively to give the beneficiary the right to receive the income which has accrued since the date of death.

An assent can be oral in the case of all assets other than land, for which a written assent is required. An assent indicates that the asset is not required for payment of debts and is available to the beneficiary. (See Chapter 18.) A specific beneficiary must bear all liabilities relating to the asset after the assent and thus, must bear any costs of transporting, insuring or transferring the asset unless there is a direction to the contrary in the will. It is common for a clause to be included in a professionally drawn will directing that such expenses be paid from residue.

*Contingent and deferred specific gifts*

**16.45**  An example of a contingent specific gift is "to X if X becomes a solicitor" and an example of a deferred specific gift is "to X after the death of A." Prior to 1925 neither type of gift carried with it the right to receive income. However, section 175 of the Law of Property Act 1925 provides that such gifts do carry with them the right to income (unless the testator has indicated otherwise). Such income will, therefore, be added to the capital and will devolve with it. Income can, however, only be accumulated and added to capital for so long as the statutory rule against accumulations permits (Law of Property Act 1925, ss.164–166 as amended by the Perpetuities and Accumulations Act 1964, s.13). Thereafter the income will either fall into residue or pass under the intestacy rules.

*Immediate residuary gifts*

**16.46**  An immediate residuary gift whether of realty or personalty carries with it the right to income accruing after the testator's death.

*Contingent and deferred residuary gifts*

**16.47**  Contingent residuary bequests have always carried the right to income, contingent residuary devises carry the right to such income as a result of the Law of Property Act, s.175. In the absence of contrary direction such income will be added to capital (subject to the rule against accumulations) and will devolve with it.

Section 175 does not mention *deferred* (or deferred, contingent) bequests which are, therefore, subject to the pre-1926 rules and do not carry the right to income. In the absence of a direction to the contrary income will pass to the person entitled to undisposed of property.

There is some uncertainty as to whether a *deferred* residuary *devise* carries the right to income. The better view appears to be that it does with the result that income will be added to capital (subject to the rule against accumulations).

The effect is that probably all residuary gifts carry the right to income apart from deferred (or deferred, contingent) residuary bequests. Examples of such gifts would be "my personalty to X after the death of A" or "my personalty to X after the death of A if X becomes a solicitor."

*Apportioning Income*

It is necessary to consider how the income accruing after death **16.48** is to be ascertained and we will, therefore, look at the effect of the Apportionment Act 1870.

In the absence of any direction to the contrary in the will section 2 of the Apportionment Act 1870 provides that: "All rents, annuities, dividends and other periodical payments in the nature of income ... shall, like interest on money lent, be considered as accruing from day to day and shall be apportionable in respect of time accordingly." Interest is required at common law to be apportioned on a daily basis.

An asset which has been specifically devised or bequeathed may produce income which is paid to the personal representatives after the death of the deceased but which covers a period partly before and partly after the death. The personal representatives will have to decide whether the whole of the income passes to the specific beneficiary or whether it must be apportioned; if it is apportioned that part of the income attributable to the period before death will fall into residue and only that part which is attributable to the period after death will pass to the specific beneficiary.

*Example*

T leaves shares in ABC Ltd to X and residue to R. A dividend of £365 is declared for a period 100 days of which precede the death and 265 days of which follow the death. The dividend must be apportioned between X and R. R will get the pre-death income attributable to the 100-day period and X will get the post-death income attributable to the 265 day period.

$$R \text{ will get } \frac{100}{365} \times £365 = £100$$

$$X \text{ will get } \frac{265}{365} \times £365 = £265$$

If the dividend is declared for a period which wholly precedes the death but is not actually paid until after the date of death it will not pass to the specific beneficiary; it will be treated as belonging to the deceased and will, therefore, form part of the residue. If a payment is made *before* death for a period falling partly before and partly after (or even wholly after) the death no apportionment is required and the specific beneficiary is not entitled to claim any portion of the advance payment from the estate. (Apportionments will also be dealt with in Chapter 18).

Apportionments may involve personal representatives in complicated calculations and they are often regarded as more trouble than they are worth. The result is that most professionally drawn wills exclude the need to apportion so that if rents, dividends or other income are paid after death such income will pass entirely to a specific beneficiary even if it did partly relate to a period preceding the death.

Whether the need to apportion has been excluded or whether it applies is of no relevance when it comes to determining the liability of beneficiaries to income tax. Such liability is determined by reference to the income tax rules explained in Chapter 6. Similarly the exclusion of the need to apportion has no relevance to the valuation of the estate for inheritance tax purpose. Such valuation is determined by reference to the inheritance tax rules explained in paragraph 4.17. The exclusion is only effective for distribution purposes and does not affect the Revenue.

### 3. INTEREST

*Introduction*

**16.49**  Interest at 6 per cent. per annum is paid to a pecuniary legatee (or general legatee or demonstrative legatee if the designated fund has been exhausted) from the time at which the legacy is payable. The interest is to compensate the legatee where payment of the legacy is delayed. The interest is paid from residue and is treated as an administration expense. The testator may make express provision and order that more or less interest be paid.

*Time for payment*

**16.50**  In the absence of any direction to the contrary from the testator, the general rule is that a legacy is payable one year from the testator's death (this period is sometimes referred to as the executor's year). It may well be impossible to pay a legacy at the end of the year because of problems with the administration. If the legacy is not paid by the end of that period the legatee becomes entitled to interest from that date.

A testator may specify that a legacy is to be paid at a particular date; for example "£2,000 to X to be paid immediately after my death" in which case interest will be payable from the date specified. Similarly, if a testator directs that a legacy is contingent on the happening of an event or is deferred until a future date interest will be payable not from the end of the executor's year but from the date of the specified event or the future date. However, if a testator directs that a contingent or deferred legacy be severed from the rest of the estate and set aside for the benefit of the legatee it will carry interest from the end of the executor's year.

*Four special cases when interest is paid from death*
There are four exceptional cases when a pecuniary legacy (or general legacy or demonstrative legacy if the designated fund has been exhausted) carries interest from the date of death.

**16.51**

(a) *Satisfaction of a debt.* A legacy to a creditor which is to satisfy a debt carries interest from the date of the death unless the will fixes a later date for payment.

(b) *Legacy charged on realty.* For historical reasons a vested legacy charged on realty carries interest from the date of death, unless the testator fixed a later date for payment.

(c) *Legacy to a testator's infant child.* If a testator gives a legacy to his infant child or to an infant to whom he is *in loco parentis* the legacy carries interest from the date of death. The rule is an old one designed to provide maintenance for the child; if, therefore, any other fund is designated for its maintenance the legacy will not carry interest.

Moreover, the rule only applies where the legacy is given to the child directly; interest is not payable from death if the legacy is given to trustees to hold for the child (*Re Pollock* (1943)).

Interest is payable from death if the legacy is contingent on the child reaching full age or marrying earlier but it is probably not so payable if the contingency has no reference to the child's infancy (for example reaching an age greater than majority).

(d) *Legacy to an infant with intention to provide maintenance.* If a testator gives a legacy to any infant (not necessarily the testator's own child or a person to whom the testator is *in loco parentis*) and shows an intention to provide for the child's maintenance it carries interest from death unless the will designates some other fund for maintenance. Unlike the previous rule interest will be carried from death by a legacy contingent on reaching an age greater than majority.

*Will drafting*

**16.52** A person who is drafting a will may prefer to make express provision for the payment of interest rather than leaving personal representatives and beneficiaries to rely on these rather technical rules.

# 17. Construction of Wills

Entire books have been written on the principles governing the **17.1** construction of wills. One chapter can do no more than give a very brief introduction to some of the more important principles involved.

Questions of construction are dealt with by the Chancery Division on a construction summons.

## A. The Object of the Court is to Ascertain the Testator's Expressed Intention

### 1. THE BASIC RULE

The object of the court is to ascertain the testator's intention *as* **17.2** *expressed in the will*. In other words the court is simply concerned to determine the meaning of the words written; it will not speculate or conjecture as to what the testator's "real" intention may have been. Thus, in *Re Rowland* (1963) a testator made a will leaving all his property to his wife but in the event of her death "preceding or coinciding" with his own everything was to go to his brother. The testator and his wife were declared dead after a boat on which they were sailing disappeared. The wife was the younger and was, therefore, presumed to have survived her husband. The court declared that the substitutional gift to the brother could not take effect as there was no evidence that the wife's death had preceded or coincided with her husband's; she might have survived him. The husband might well have "really" intended his brother to take in such circumstances but the court was not at liberty to speculate. "The will must be in writing and that writing only must be considered." (*Per* Harman L.J.)

### 2. ORDINARY WORDS GIVEN THEIR ORDINARY MEANING

If the words used in the will are clear and unambiguous, it is **17.3** not possible for the court to attribute to them meanings they do not normally bear in order to produce a result which is thought to be more in accordance with the testator's intentions. If, however, such an interpretation gives rise to some obvious absurdity or is manifestly inconsistent with the will read as a whole, the sense of such words may be modified or extended so far as is necessary to avoid the consequences but no further. The mere fact that a disposition seems rather strange is not sufficient to justify departing from the ordinary meaning of words.

Some words have several meanings in which case the court must try and determine in what sense the testator used the word. "Money" is a good example of such a word since it can mean merely notes or coins, can include money "in the bank" or can be used loosely to cover assets in general. The House of Lords in *Perrin* v. *Morgan* (1943) took the view that the word was capable of having a very wide meaning indeed and that courts should carefully consider the context before attributing a narrow meaning to the word (particularly if the result of such an interpretation would be to leave a large part of the estate undisposed).

### 3. TECHNICAL WORDS MUST BE GIVEN THEIR TECHNICAL MEANING

**17.4** If a testator uses a technical word or expression, for example "my realty" or "my personalty", such an expression must be given its technical meaning unless the will shows a *very* clear intention to use it in a different sense. Thus, in *Re Cook* (1948) a testatrix in a home-made will left "all my personal estate" to X; there were no other gifts in the will and the greater part of her estate consisted of realty. Harman J. held that the expression "personal estate" was a technical one and must be given its technical meaning despite the fact that doing so meant that the bulk of the testatrix's property passed on intestacy.

### 4. THE DICTIONARY PRINCIPLE

**17.5** A testator is free to show that words used in the will are used in an unusual way. This may be done expressly, by including a definition clause; for example, a testator may say that wherever he refers to "my monkey" he means "my son." It is more likely, however, that the will as a whole may suggest that an unusual meaning is attached to one word. Thus, in *Re Lowe* (1890) a testator made a gift "to all my children, apart from X." (X was illegitimate.) At that time the word "children" did not include illegitimate children unless the testator indicated that he wanted it to do so. It was held that the specific exclusion of X indicated that the testator regarded the word "children" as including legitimate and illegitimate ones, so that all the testator's illegitimate children, apart from X, could take.

## 5. RECTIFICATION OF A WILL

**17.6** Section 20 of the Administration of Justice Act 1982 provides that "if a court is satisfied that a will is so expressed that it fails to carry out the testator's intentions, in consequence:

(a) of a clerical error; *or*
(b) of a failure to understand his instructions,

it may order that the will shall be rectified so as to carry out his intentions."

A fuller discussion of this provision is contained in paragraph 2.26.

# B. Extrinsic Evidence

## 1. THE GENERAL RULE

**17.7** The general rule is that the court construes the words written in the will and will not admit extrinsic evidence of the testator's intention. However there are certain circumstances where extrinsic evidence is admissible. The first three are long established; the others were introduced by the Administration of Justice Act 1982.

## 2. WHERE THE WORDS USED ARE NOT APT TO FIT THE SURROUNDING CIRCUMSTANCES

**17.8** This is sometimes referred to as "the armchair principle." "You may place yourself, so to speak, in [the testator's] armchair, and consider the circumstances by which he was surrounded when he made his will to assist you in arriving at his intention," *per* James L.J. *Boyes* v. *Cook* (1880). An illustration of this rule is *Thorn* v. *Dickens* (1906) where the testator left "all to mother" but did not have a mother living at the time he made his will; extrinsic evidence of the testator's circumstances was admitted to show that he was in the habit of calling his wife "mother" with the result that she was able to take. Similarly, in *Re Fish* (1893) the testator left property to "my niece, Eliza Water-house" but did not have a niece of that name; extrinsic evidence was admitted to show that his wife had a great-niece of that name and it was found that the testator had used the word "niece" in a wide sense so that the great-niece was able to take the gift. In both these cases there was no-one who fitted the description used in the will. If there had been (for example, if in *Thorn* v. *Dickens* the testator's mother had been alive at the time the will was made) no extrinsic evidence could have been admitted and the apparent beneficiary would have taken. Declarations made by the testator as to his intention are not admissible; only evidence *of the surrounding circumstances* is admissible.

### 3. WHERE THERE IS A LATENT AMBIGUITY

**17.9**   A latent ambiguity is one which does not become apparent until an attempt is made to give effect to the dispositions in the will. Thus, if a testator makes a gift of "my motor car" and it turns out that at the time of the will, he owned six cars or, if a testator makes a gift to "my nephew, John Jones" and it turns out that he had several so named, extrinsic evidence *including evidence of declarations made by the testator* as to his intention will be admitted to show which car was intended to be the subject-matter of the gift or which nephew was intended to benefit. If there is no evidence available the whole gift will fail for uncertainty.

An example of a latent ambiguity is *Re Jackson* (1933). The testator made a gift "to my nephew, Arthur Murphy"; he had one illegitimate nephew and two legitimate nephews of that name. At that time illegitimate relationships were ignored unless the will showed a contrary intention. Therefore, had there been only one legitimate nephew that nephew would have fitted the description and would have taken the gift (even if there had been evidence that the testator's *intention* was that that person should not take). However, as there were two such nephews there was a latent ambiguity and extrinsic evidence, including evidence of the testator's intention, was admitted. This evidence showed that, in fact, the testator had intended to refer to the illegitimate nephew and he, therefore, took the gift.

### 4. TO REBUT A PRESUMPTION OF EQUITY

**17.10**   In certain circumstances equity raises presumptions; for example, that a legacy from a father (or person *in loco parentis*) to his child will be adeemed if the father (or person *in loco parentis*) after the date of the will gives the child an *inter vivos* portion. These presumptions may be rebutted by extrinsic evidence (including evidence of declarations made by the testator as to his intention).

5. THE ADMINISTRATION OF JUSTICE ACT 1982

**17.11** In the case of deaths occurring after December 31, 1982, section 21 provides that extrinsic evidence *including evidence of declarations as to the testator's intention* may be admitted to assist in the interpretation of a will in so far as:

(a)  any part of it is meaningless,
(b)  the language used in any part of it is ambiguous on the face of it,
(c)  evidence other than evidence of the testator's intention shows that the language used in any part of it is ambiguous in the light of the surrounding circumstances.

An example of subsection (b) is a gift of "my money" or "my effects."

Paragraph (c) appears to have extended the existing rules on extrinsic evidence in two ways. First, evidence of surrounding circumstances (though not direct evidence of the testator's intention) can now be admitted to *raise the possibility* that an ambiguity exists, whereas, prior to the 1982 Act, evidence could only be admitted where the words did not fit the surrounding circumstances. Thus, where a testator makes a gift to "my niece, Ann" it would now be possible to admit evidence to show that, although the testator had only one niece called Ann, there was a niece of his spouse also called Ann. Secondly, it is now possible to admit direct evidence of the testator's intention in cases other than latent ambiguity.

In a helpful judgment (*Re Williams, deceased* (1985)), Nicholls J. stated the principles to be applied when considering the admissibility of extrinsic evidence. He reminded practitioners that the section is merely *an aid* to construction. Thus, evidence may be admitted to show which of several possible meanings a testator was applying to a particular word or phrase (for example "my money," "my effects"). The meaning may be one which without the evidence would not have been at all apparent but so long as the word or phrase is *capable* of bearing that meaning in its context this does not matter. However, it may be that the extrinsic evidence reveals a meaning attached by the testator to a word or phrase which no matter how liberal the approach of the court, the word or phrase cannot bear. The court will not allow extrinsic evidence to vary or contradict the language used in the will since this would amount to rewriting the will for the testator and this can only be done, if at all, under the rectification provisions.

## C. The Will Speaks from Death

### 1. SECTION 24 OF THE WILLS ACT 1837

**17.12** Section 24 provides that as regards property every will shall be construed "to speak and take effect as if it had been executed immediately before the death of the testator, unless a contrary intention shall appear by the will." Thus, a gift of "the contents of my house" will pass the contents owned at the date of death, not merely those owned at the date of the will.

### 2. CONTRARY INTENTION

**17.13** A will may expressly state that the testator is giving an asset owned at the date of the will. In the absence of an express statement, certain words and expressions are commonly found to show contrary intention.

*"My"*

**17.14** If the testator couples the word "my" with a gift of a specific item (for example, "my piano") it is possible that the court will construe the gift as a gift of the particular piano owned at the date of the will. Therefore, if the piano is sold or destroyed after the date of the will the gift is adeemed and cannot pass a piano purchased later and owned at the date of the death. However, if the word "my" is coupled with a description of property capable of increase or decrease (for example "all my shares") there is no contrary intention and the gift will pass any shares owned at the time of the death.

*"Now" or "at present"*

**17.15** The use of such words will be taken as showing a contrary intention (that is, as referring to the date the will is made) if they are an essential part of the description. Thus, in *Re Edwards* (1890) the testator made a gift of "my house and premises where I now reside." After the date of the will he let a part of the property. The court held that the word "now" indicated a contrary intention so that the whole of the property occupied at the time the will was made (including the part subsequently let) passed to the beneficiary, not merely the part occupied at the date of the death.

If, however, the words are regarded as mere additional or superfluous description which has simply become inaccurate by the date of the will the court is unlikely to find that they show a contrary intention. In *Re Willis* (1911) a testator gave "all my freehold house and premises situated at X and known as Y and in which I now reside." After the date of the will he acquired two further plots of land which he enjoyed with the original house. The court held that there was no contrary intention so that the gift was to be construed at the date of death; thus the additional plots were included.

3. SECTION 24 HAS NO APPLICATION TO PEOPLE

Section 24 only applies to property; as regards people a will is **17.16** construed at the date it is made (unless there is a contrary intention).

A gift made "to the eldest son of A" is contrued as a gift to the person fulfilling that description at the date the will is made. If that person predeceases the testator the gift fails and does not pass to the eldest *surviving* son.

It is important to remember that where a will is republished it is construed as if made at the date of the republication.

If a testator makes a gift to a beneficiary who fulfils a particular description (for example "the wife of X") and to the testator's knowledge no-one fulfils that description at the date of the will the court will construe the gift as one made to the first person to fulfil the description. Once a person has fulfilled the description the gift is construed as a gift to that person even if the description later becomes inaccurate; thus, if in the previous example X and his wife were divorced after the date of the will she would still be entitled to the gift on Y's death, even if X had remarried.

# D. Property Subject to a General Power of Appointment

1. GENERAL AND SPECIAL POWERS OF APPOINTMENT

Instead of making an outright gift of property to a named **17.17** beneficiary, a testator may give one person a power to appoint property to others. The power may be entirely unlimited, so that the appointer can appoint to anyone, in which case it is referred to as a "general" power, or the power may be limited, so that the appointer can appoint only amongst certain specific people (for example the children of X), in which case it is referred to as a "special" power of appointment.

A person with a general power of appointment is free to deal with the property exactly as he pleases and is therefore for many purposes treated as the owner of the property subject to the general power of appointment. For example, if a person exercises such a power by will, the property subject to the power is available for payment of the deceased's debts. (See Chapter 15.)

### 2. METHOD OF EXERCISING A GENERAL POWER OF APPOINTMENT

**17.18** A testator may make an express appointment by will but this is not essential. Section 27 of the Wills Act provides that, where a testator has a general power of appointment exercisable by will, it can be exercised by any general devise or bequest without the necessity for an express reference to the power. A general devise or bequest is one where the subject-matter is described in a general manner, for example "all my leasehold land," "all my land in Hampshire" or "all my shares." If property subject to a general power is to pass under the terms of such a gift, it must correspond to the general description.

Section 27 is subject to contrary intention. However, the court will not readily find such an intention. Thus, in *Re Jarrett* (1919) the fact that the testator had made an express appointment in the will which failed was found not to show a contrary intention and the subject-matter of the power passed as part of the residue.

The section does not apply if the terms of a general power of appointment require an express reference to the power or the property. Special powers of appointment are not covered by the section and therefore need to be expressly exercised (unless the terms of the power provide otherwise).

## E. Special Rules Relating to Children

### 1. ADOPTED CHILDREN

**17.19** The Adoption Act 1976 applies to any adoption order made by a court in the United Kingdom, the Isle of Man or the Channel

Islands and to certain foreign adoptions. It provides that when construing the will of a testator who dies after December 31, 1975:

(a)   an adopted child is to be treated as the legitimate child of the married couple who adopt it or, if the adoption is by one person, as the legitimate child of that one person (but not as a child of any actual marriage of that person); and

(b)   an adopted child is to be treated as if it were not the child of any person other than the adopting parent(s).

It is immaterial whether the adoption order is made before or after the testator's death. For example, if T gives property "to A for life, remainder to the children of A" any child adopted by A, whether before or after T's death, will be entitled to share in the gift, unless there is any contrary intention shown. (In the case of deaths occurring prior to January 1, 1976 an adopted child can only benefit if the order was made before the death of the testator).

Where a disposition by will depends on the date of birth of a child or children the disposition is to be construed, in the absence of contrary intention, as if:

(a)   the adopted child had been born on the date of the adoption; and

(b)   two or more children adopted on the same date had been born on that date in the order of their actual births.

*Example*
T makes one gift "to the children of A living at my death" and one gift "to the children of A born after my death." T dies in 1976 and after T's death A adopts a child who was born in 1974. This child is treated as born on the date of the adoption and is therefore not a child living at T's death and cannot take under the first gift. However, it is a child born after T's death and can take under the second gift.

It is expressly provided that these rules do not affect any reference to the *age* of a child. Thus, if T gives property "to the first child of A to reach age 25" and A has a natural child born in 1978 and an adopted child adopted in 1980 at age 12, it is the adopted child who will reach age 25 first and be entitled to the gift. A gift to "the eldest child of A" would probably not be construed as containing a reference to an age so that the general rule would be applied; thus, the adopted child would be treated as born on the date of the adoption and therefore as being younger than the natural child.

### 2. CHILDREN WHOSE PARENTS WERE NOT MARRIED

**17.20**   In any will or codicil made after April 4, 1988 references to relationships are construed without regard to "whether or not the father and mother of either [person], or the father and mother of any person through whom the relationship is deduced, have or had been married to each other at any time" (Family Law Reform Act 1987, s.1(1)). Thus a gift "to my children" includes both legitimate and illegitimate children. A gift "to my grandchildren" includes all the testator's children's children regardless of whether the testator was married at any time and regardless of whether his children were married at any time. The will may show a contrary intention should the testator so wish.

In the case of wills and codicils made after December 31, 1969 and before April 4, 1988, the Family Law Reform Act 1969, s.15 applies. This makes provision the effect of which is similar, in most respects, to the 1987 Act.

## F. Class Gifts

### 1. THE CLASS CLOSING RULES

*Necessity for such rules*

**17.21**   A class gift is a gift of property to be divided amongst persons fulfilling a general description (for example "the children of A," "the children of A who reach 18"). The size of any individual's share will depend upon the number of persons who fulfil the description. This makes distributing the property difficult since until A dies it is always possible that the number of persons fulfilling the description will increase. Personal representatives would, therefore, have to wait till A's death before giving any child a share in the property.

To avoid this inconvenient result, certain rules of construction known as "the class closing rules" have been developed; the effect of the rules is to close a class at an artificially early date in order to allow earlier distribution. Beneficiaries who are born after the class has closed lose their entitlement; the unfairness that this may cause is thought to be outweighed by the convenience of allowing early distribution. However, if a testator does not want the class to close early the rules can always be expressly excluded (subject to the rules against perpetuity). Clear words should be used to exclude the rules. An example of sufficiently clear wording is "to the children of A *whenever born.*"

The precise details of the rules vary according to the type of gift (immediate, deferred or contingent) but the principle is that the class closes as soon as there is one beneficiary entitled to immediate distribution.

Throughout this section the word "living" includes a child *en ventre sa mere.*

*Immediate class gifts*

An example of such a gift is "to the children of A." If there is any child of A living at the date of the testator's death the class closes and the personal representatives distribute to the class members then in existence (*Viner* v. *Francis* (1789)). No child born after the class has closed can take any interest. If there are no children living at that date, there is no class closing rule applicable and the class will remain open until A dies.

**17.22**

*Deferred class gift*

An example of such a gift is "to X for life remainder to the children of A." In this case the property cannot be distributed while X is alive and the class, therefore, remains open until X dies. It will include any children living at the testator's death and any children born thereafter and before the death of X. If any such child dies before the property is actually distributed, his share will be paid to his estate. No child born after the class has closed can take any interest. If there were no children living at the testator's death and none born before X's death, there is no class closing rule applicable and the class will remain open until the death of A.

**17.23**

*Contingent class gift*

An example of such a gift is "to the children of A who reach 18." If any child has reached 18 when the testator dies, the class closes at that date and will include any child living at that date who reaches the age of 18. If a child dies without fulfilling the contingency his "share" is divided amongst the other members of the class who fulfil the contingency. If no child has reached 18 at the date of the testator's death, the class remains open until a child reaches 18 and will include any child living at that date who reaches 18. Again if any child dies without fulfilling the contingency his "share" is divided amongst any others who

**17.24**

do fulfil the contingency. No child born after the class has closed can take any interest.

*Deferred and contingent class gifts*

**17.25** An example of such a gift would be "to X for life, remainder to the children of A who reach 18." In this case the property cannot be distributed whilst X is alive and the class, therefore, remains open until X's death. It will close at X's death if any child living at the testator's death has reached 18 and will include any children living at the testator's death or born since who reach 18. If any child, living at the testator's death, reaches 18 but dies before distribution the class closes on X's death and the share of the deceased child is paid to his estate. If no member of the class has reached 18 at the time of X's death the class remains open until the first child reaches 18. No child born after the class has closed can take any interest.

### 2. ACCELERATION OF THE DATE FOR CLOSING A CLASS

**17.26** If there is a postponed class gift (for example "to X for life, remainder to the children of Y") it may happen that the prior interest fails, perhaps because the life tenant predeceases the testator or because the gift to the life tenant is void. In such a case the gift to the class is accelerated so that it is treated as an immediate class gift. The class will, therefore, close at the testator's death (if there are any members then living) and any later born children will be excluded (*Re Johnson* (1893)).

A life tenant may wish to disclaim or surrender the life tenancy and the question then arises of whether one person can by voluntarily dealing with his own interest affect the membership of the class. In *Re Davies* (1957) Vaisey J. held that where a life tenant disclaimed, the gift to the class would be accelerated and would close immediately thereby excluding any later born members. However, the decision has been criticised as not reflecting the probable wishes of a testator; Goff J. refused to follow it in *Re Harker's Will Trusts* (1969) and held that where a life tenant surrendered her life interest the class would remain open until her death.

### 3. GIFTS OF A SPECIFIED AMOUNT TO PERSONS FULFILLING A DESCRIPTION

**17.27** If a testator gives "£1,000 to each of the children of A," it is not a class gift since the amount each child is to receive does not vary according to the number of persons fulfilling the description. However, problems arise in distributing such a gift and these problems are similar to the problems which arise in connection with class gifts. The number of persons fulfilling the description may increase at any time before A's death and so the personal representatives cannot know how much money they should retain to cover the possibility of future children being born. In order that the personal representatives should be able to complete the distribution without difficulty, there is a rule of construction which provides, in the absence of contrary intention, that only persons who are alive at the testator's death can take; if there is no-one alive at that date fulfilling the description, the entire gift fails. This is a drastic rule but it enables the personal representatives to distribute the estate without having to worry about retaining assets to cover a possible future liability.

### 4. CLASS GIFTS TO CHILDREN OF THE TESTATOR WHO PREDECEASE

Normally a person who predeceases the testator can take no benefit under a class gift. Section 33 of the Wills Act 1837 as substituted by Administration of Justice Act 1982, s.19 provides that, in the absence of contrary intention, where a class gift is made to children or remoter issue *of the testator* and a member of the class predeceases the testator leaving issue who survive the testator, the issue take *per stirpes* the share which their parent would have taken (see paragraph 16.23).

**17.28**

## G. Deciding Whether a Gift is Absolute or Limited

### 1. SECTION 22 OF THE ADMINISTRATION OF JUSTICE ACT 1982

Testators who draft wills without professional advice sometimes give property to X and then direct that on X's death what remains should pass to Y. This is because non-lawyers often think that it is possible to give the rights of an absolute owner to persons in succession. The effect of such an attempt depends on the precise words used in the will but may be construed in any of the following ways:

**17.29**

    (a)    an absolute gift to X, the gift over to Y failing, either as a trust which is void for uncertainty, or because it is repugnant to X's absolute interest;

   (b)   a life interest to X, with remainder to Y absolutely;
   (c)   a life interest to X, with remainder to Y absolutely but subject to X's power to dispose of the capital *inter vivos*.

Section 22 of the Administration of Justice Act 1982 introduces a presumption where a testator gives property to his *spouse* in terms which would in themselves give an absolute interest but by the same instrument purports to give *his issue* an interest in the same property, the gift to the spouse is presumed to be absolute despite the purported gift to issue. The presumption applies in the case of deaths occurring after December 31, 1982.

   This section solves the problem of unintended life interests in the case of gifts to spouses but problems still remain where such a gift is made to persons other than spouses.

### 2. THE RULE IN LASSENCE V. TIERNEY

**17.30**   This rule attempts to reconcile inconsistent provisions in a will. "If you find an absolute gift to a legatee in the first instance and trusts are engrafted or imposed on the absolute interest *which fail* either from lapse or invalidity or any other reason, then the absolute gift takes effect so far as the trusts have failed, to the exclusion of the residuary legatee or next of kin, as the case may be." (*Hancock* v. *Watson* (1902)). The rule imputes to T an intention that the absolute gift be modified only so far as is necessary to give effect to the trusts.

*Example*
T gives property to A absolutely and later in the will directs that the property given to A absolutely is to pass, after A's death, to the children of B. If B dies without children, A (or A's estate) will be entitled to the capital.

   The difficulty in such cases is deciding whether or not there was an absolute initial gift. It is comparatively simple to find such a gift where the testator makes the absolute gift in the will and engrafts the trust in a later codicil or where, as in the previous example, there is an absolute gift followed by a later clause engrafting the trust but difficult questions of construction will arise where a series of gifts is made in one continuous sentence.

# 18. Completing the Administration

Once the personal representatives have paid all the debts and **18.1** liabilities of the estate they must vest the available assets in the beneficiaries who are entitled to them and must prepare an account to show the amount of residue available to the residuary beneficiaries.

## A. Assents

### 1. POSITION OF BENEFICIARIES BEFORE ASSENT

As we saw in paragraphs 11.26–11.29 a beneficiary (with the **18.2** possible exception of a specific beneficiary) under a will or a person entitled under the intestacy rules has no legal or equitable proprietary interest in any asset comprised in the estate. He has merely a chose in action in the estate (*i.e.* the right to have the deceased's estate properly administered) and he only obtains rights to assets when the personal representatives indicate by means of an assent that these assets are not required for the purposes of the administration.

### 2. ASSENTS IN RESPECT OF PURE PERSONALTY

*Where there is a will*

An executor (and probably an administrator with the will **18.3** annexed) passes title to pure personalty by means of an assent. An assent is an indication from the personal representative that a particular asset is not required for the purposes of the administration. It is not required to be in a particular form; it can be oral (for example where a personal representative tells a beneficiary that his legacy is ready for collection) or implied from conduct (for example where a personal representative allows a beneficiary to take possession of an asset). The beneficiary actually derives title from the will not from the assent; the effect of the assent is merely to activate the gift in the will.

If particular formalities are required to transfer the legal title to an asset, the assent cannot itself pass the legal title. In such a case once the assent has been made the personal representative holds the asset as trustee for the beneficiary until the appropriate formal requirements have been complied with. Most choses in action require special formalities; money in a Post Office Savings Bank, Trustee Savings Bank or National Savings Certificates require withdrawal or transfer forms; company shares require a share transfer. Although the personal representatives may have themselves registered as members of a company, section 183 of the Companies Act 1985 provides that unless the articles of the company state otherwise a personal representative may transfer stocks and shares without first being registered. There are no formalities required by law to transfer money from a bank account; a letter of instruction should be sent to the bank manager together with an office copy of the grant of representation.

In the case of a specific legacy (but not a residuary or general legacy) the assent is retrospective to the date of death so that the legatee becomes entitled to income produced by the subject-matter of the gift since the testator's death. Thus, in *I.R.C.* v. *Hawley* (1928) the personal representatives did not make an assent of company shares in favour of a specific legatee for nearly three years after the testator's death. It was held that, because an assent to a specific legacy is retrospective, once the assent had been made the Inland Revenue were entitled to assess the beneficiary to income tax on dividends which had been declared in the intervening years. Similarly, after assent a specific legatee is responsible for the costs of transferring the property. This includes costs of packing, delivering and insuring bulky or delicate chattels and the costs of obtaining a share transfer for company shares. Many testators would prefer such costs to be paid from residue and it is, therefore, common for an express direction to this effect to be included in a will.

*Where there is an intestacy*

**18.4**   At common law an administrator had no power to assent in the case of an intestacy (Williams, *Law Relating to Assents*, p. 96).

Section 36(1) of the Administration of Estates Act 1925 gives administrators as well as executors the power to make title to land (freehold or leasehold) by means of a written assent but it does not mention other property. Administrators must therefore pass title to other property by the method appropriate to the nature of the subject-matter. Chattels, money and bearer securities pass by delivery, shares, stock and debentures by transfer and most other choses in action by assignment.

### 3. ASSENTS IN RESPECT OF LAND

*Administration of Estates Act 1925, s.36*

In general a document which is to convey or create a legal **18.5** estate in land must be a *deed* (Law of Property Act 1925, s.52(1)). However, as an exception to this rule, section 36(1) of the Administration of Estates Act gives personal representatives (both executors and administrators) power to *assent* to the vesting of any estate or interest in land (whether freehold or leasehold) in any person entitled (whether beneficially, as trustee or as personal representative of a deceased beneficiary who is entitled to property) *whether by devise, bequest, devolution, appropriation or otherwise*. An assent is a form of conveyance and becomes an essential link in the title of the assentee.

"*Devolution*" covers a person taking under the intestacy rules. The meaning of "*or otherwise*" presents some problems. The other words in the section all refer to transactions which a personal representative would be called upon to effect in the course of the administration of the estate. Probably therefore the words "or otherwise" should be construed *ejusdem generis* and should not be taken to cover any transaction which is not part of the administration; thus, if a personal representative is selling property or is asked by a beneficiary to transfer the property to a purchaser from the beneficiary the personal representative should not risk using an assent but should use a conveyance. There is in any event little advantage to using an assent in such a case for while it may be a rather shorter document, ad valorem stamp duty is payable on a sale whether an assent is used or whether a conveyance to the purchaser is used.

*Form of assent*

Section 36(4) of the Administration of Estates Act provides that **18.6** "an assent shall be in writing, signed by the personal representative and shall name the person in whose favour it is given and shall operate to vest in that person the legal title to which it relates; and an assent which is not in writing or not in favour of a named person shall not be effectual to pass the legal estate."

It is clear that an assent of land by a personal representative in favour of another person must comply with the requirements of section 36(4) if it is to pass the legal estate. According to Pennycuick J. in *Re King's Will Trusts* (1964) the same requirements must be complied with where a personal representative wishes to vest land in himself (whether beneficially or as trustee or as personal representative of another deceased). The reasoning of Pennycuick J. has been criticised by various writers (see R. R. A. Walker (1964) 80 L.Q.R. 328) but even if the criticisms are justified the provision of a signed, written assent by a personal representative in his own favour is hardly an onerous task and has the merit of avoiding any possible doubt or uncertainty.

It is important to remember that a personal representative is always free to convey land by means of a deed and will often choose to do so (for example, where indemnity covenants are required from the beneficiary).

### The effect of an assent

**18.7** Section 36(2) of the Administration of Estates Act provides that an assent relates back to the date of death of the deceased unless a contrary intention appears. This is unlike the position in respect of assents of personalty where only an assent to a specific legacy relates back. Thus, a specific or residuary devisee would appear to be entitled to any rents or profits produced by land from the date of death of the deceased.

### Protection of purchasers and beneficiaries

**18.8** A person in whose favour an assent or conveyance is made may require that notice of the assent is endorsed on the grant of representation at the cost of the estate under section 36(5).

A purchaser will insist that a conveyance from personal representatives contains a statement that the personal representatives have not previously given or made any conveyance or assent in respect of the legal estate. If this statement is incorrect it cannot prejudice the title of any previous *purchaser*; but if there was a previous assent in favour of a *beneficiary* the purchaser will take the legal title in preference to that beneficiary if, and only if, there was no notice of the previous assent endorsed on the grant of representation *and* the purchaser accepted the conveyance on the faith of the statement in the conveyance (section 36(6)).

There is no point in such a statement being included in an assent in favour of a beneficiary since section 36(6) only protects *purchasers*.

A purchaser has no right to examine a will to ascertain that land was assented to the person actually entitled. However, section 36(7) protects such a person by providing that in favour of a purchaser, unless notice of a previous assent or conveyance has been endorsed on the grant of representation, an assent or conveyance made by a personal representative is "sufficient evidence that the person in whose favour [it] is given is the person entitled to have the legal estate conveyed to him." The section only says that an assent is "sufficient" evidence not "conclusive" evidence; thus, if facts have come to the purchaser's knowledge before completion which indicate that the assent was in fact made in favour of the wrong person, the purchaser cannot rely on the assent (*Re Duce and Boots Cash Chemists (Southern) Ltd's Contract* (1937)).

*Protection of personal representatives*

A personal representative will not want to distribute assets until **18.9** satisfied that all liabilities have been dealt with. Section 36(10) provides that personal representatives may, as a condition of giving an assent or making a conveyance, require security for the discharge of any duties, debts or liabilities to which the property is subject (for example, a mortgage debt or charge for capital transfer tax or inheritance tax). If reasonable arrangements have been made for discharging such liabilities, however, the personal representative cannot refuse to make the assent to a beneficiary entitled to the property.

If the personal representative is uncertain whether or not land will be required for the payment of liabilities he may under section 43 of the Administration of Estates Act allow a beneficiary to take possession of the land prior to the making of a formal assent. The personal representative can subsequently retake possession of the property and dispose of it if it becomes necessary in the course of the administration.

If the deceased owned land which was subject to covenants for breach of which the personal representatives will remain liable (for example where the deceased was an original lessee or where there have been indemnity covenants) the personal representatives will wish to protect themselves by obtaining an indemnity covenant from the beneficiary. They will therefore have to use a deed when transferring the property to the beneficiary instead of merely an assent.

# B. Personal Representative or Trustee

## 1. PERSONAL REPRESENTATIVE FOR LIFE

**18.10** A personal representative retains office for life and is not discharged from office even when all the debts and liabilities have been paid and all the assets distributed. If there are any subsequent accretions to the estate (for example if a debt which had been regarded as irrecoverable is paid to the estate or if someone dies leaving a legacy to the deceased which is saved from lapse by one of the exceptions to the doctrine of lapse) the personal representative must distribute such accretions and conversely if legal proceedings are brought or claims made against the estate the personal representatives must deal with them on behalf of the estate.

## 2. COMPARISON WITH TRUSTEES

**18.11** A personal representative may be a trustee of property left by will or passing under the intestacy rules. This may be because:

(i) the testator expressly appointed the personal representative as trustee; or

(ii) the testator left property on trust but did not expressly appoint trustees; or

(iii) a trust arises under the intestacy rules (although there is some doubt as to whether administrators become trustees in such a case).

Even where a personal representative is not also a trustee there are certain similarities between personal representatives and trustees:

(a) Personal representatives, like trustees, are in a fiduciary position. They must act with the utmost good faith and must not profit from their position.

(b) The provisions of the Trustee Act 1925 apply equally to personal representatives where the context admits.

However, there are also important differences:

(a) The function of a personal representative is to wind up the estate and distribute the assets, whereas the function of a trustee is to hold assets for the beneficiaries.

(b) Executors (and probably administrators) have joint and several authority to deal with *personalty* (they must act jointly if they are to convey *land* although one personal representative can enter into a contract for sale binding on any other personal representatives *Fountain Forestry Ltd.* v. *Edwards* (1975)). Trustees must always act jointly.

(c) A sole personal representative may give a good receipt for money for the sale of land whereas at least two trustees (or a trust corporation) are required.

(d) The period of limitation is 12 years against a personal representative but only six years against a trustee.

(e) If a sole personal representative dies without having completed the administration there will either be transmission of office under the chain of executorship or a grant *de bonis non administratis* must be taken out by the person entitled under the Non-Contentious Probate Rules 1987. If, however, a sole or last surviving trustee dies the trust property devolves on the trustee's personal representatives.

(f) A trustee has power to appoint additional or substitutional trustees. A personal representative has normally no power to appoint additional or substitutional personal representatives (although a person entitled to administration may nominate another administrator in certain cases where two administrators are needed because of a minority or life interest).

(g) Personal representatives owe their duty to the estate as a whole, trustees to the individual beneficiaries (*Re Hayes Will Trusts* (1971)).

In view of such differences it is obviously important where a personal representative is also a trustee to ascertain at what point the personal representative ceases to hold assets as personal representative and starts to hold them as trustee.

### 3. TRANSITION FROM PERSONAL REPRESENTATIVE TO TRUSTEE

*Intestacy*

**18.12** Under the Administration of Estates Act 1925 undisposed of property may have to be held on trust either for a spouse for life or on the statutory trusts until a beneficiary achieves a vested interest. There is some doubt as to whether administrators on intestacy ever become trustees in the true sense or whether they continue to hold property as administrators. The better view would seem to be that they do not become trustees. However, Romer J. in the case of *Re Yerburgh* (1928) stated that administrators become trustees as soon as all liabilities have been discharged and the amount of residue to be held on trust has been ascertained. Romer J. went on to state that the administrators ought to mark the moment when residue was ascertained by making an assent to the property vesting in themselves as trustees. It is unclear whether the judge meant that the assent was essential in order to vest the property in the administrators in their capacity as trustees or whether he meant that the assent was merely desirable in practice in order to indicate that the change in capacity had occurred, the change occurring automatically once the residue was ascertained.

*Where the will does not appoint the personal representative as trustee*

**18.13** In the case of a specific legacy, once personal representatives have indicated by means of an assent that an asset is not required for payment of debts the asset is held on trust for the specific beneficiary (*Re Grosvenor* (1916)).

In the case of residue the position is rather unclear. In *Harvell* v. *Foster* (1954) the Court of Appeal stated that the personal representatives remain liable in their capacity as such for the residue of the estate until it is vested in the beneficiary entitled. If the vesting is delayed (as it may be for example where the beneficiary is an infant and cannot give a good receipt) liability as a personal representative will continue and the personal representatives will not become trustees.

It is difficult to see why, if *Re Yerburgh* is correct, there should be a conversion to trustees in the case of intestacy but not in a case where there is a will.

*Where the will appoints the personal representative as trustee*
If personal representatives are directed to hold residue on trust **18.14** there is some authority for saying that as soon as liabilities are discharged and the residue ascertained the personal representatives automatically start to hold the property in their capacity as trustees (*Re Cockburn's Will Trusts* (1957)). However, the position is far from clear and there are dicta in *Attenborough* v. *Solomon* (1913) which suggest that the change does not take place automatically but only when the personal representatives assent the property to themselves in their capacity as trustees.

An assent is certainly desirable since it will avoid any doubt as to whether or not a change in capacity has occurred.

# C. Receipts and Discharges

## 1. INTRODUCTION

A beneficiary discharges a personal representative from liability **18.15** by means of a receipt signed by the beneficiary. A residuary beneficiary normally signs the estate accounts.

## 2. MINORS CANNOT GIVE A GOOD RECEIPT FOR MONEY

Unless the will provides otherwise, a minor cannot give a good **18.16** receipt for money (*Re Somech* (1957)) nor can a parent, guardian or spouse of a married minor give a good receipt on the minor's behalf (unless the will provides otherwise). A married minor can give a good receipt for income but not for capital (Law of Property Act 1925, s.21). Personal representatives must, therefore, either hold the legacy until the minor reaches 18 or use one of the following methods of divesting themselves of the legacy:

(a) *Appointment of trustees to hold the legacy.* Under the Administration of Estates Act 1925, s.42 personal representatives have power where a minor is absolutely entitled to a legacy to appoint a trust corporation or at least two individuals (and not more than four) to hold the property on trust until the minor reaches 18. The trustees can give the personal representatives a good receipt. However, section 42 does not apply where the infant's interest is contingent (for example on reaching 18).

(b) *Appropriation of assets.* Under section 41 of the Administration of Estates Act a personal representative has power to appropriate any asset (not specifically bequeathed or devised) in or towards satisfaction of any pecuniary legacy or interest under the intestacy rules. The personal representative must obtain the consent of a beneficiary who is absolutely entitled or, if that person is not of full age or capacity, the consent of that person's parent or guardian (or if there is no such parent or guardian, the court). If a beneficiary is not absolutely entitled the consent of the trustee (not being also the personal representatives) must be obtained. If, independently of the personal representatives, there is no trustee no consent is required but in this case the personal representatives can only appropriate an investment authorised by law or by the will.

It is common for a will to exclude the need for personal representatives to obtain consents to an appropriation. This used to be done to avoid stamp duty. It is no longer necessary for this purpose. However it is convenient for the personal representatives to be relieved of the need to seek consent.

(c) *Payment into court.* Personal representatives can pay money into court and the receipt of the proper officer of the court will be a sufficient discharge for the money paid in (Trustee Act 1925, s.63). However, because of the personal representatives' wide powers under sections 41 and 42 this power is rarely used.

(d) *Maintenance and advancement.* Personal representatives may apply income or capital for the benefit of infant beneficiaries under sections 31 and 32 of the Trustees Act 1925, or under any express power in the will or any court order.

These matters have been dealt with in Chapter 11.

# D. The Equitable Rules of Apportionment

**18.17** These rules exist to try to achieve fairness between tenants for life and remaindermen. If residuary personalty is left to persons in succession there is an obligation under the rule in *Howe* v. *Lord Dartmouth* (1802) to sell wasting, hazardous, and unauthorised assets. Pending sale the tenant for life is not entitled to the income from such assets since otherwise he might obtain a benefit from the personal representatives' delay. Instead he is entitled to interest at 4 per cent. per annum on the value of the assets (the assets are valued at one of three possible dates depending on the circumstances). Any surplus income is treated as capital and invested in authorised investments. This rule exists to protect remaindermen.

The rule in *Re Earl of Chesterfield's Trusts* (1883) exists to protect the life tenant. There is an obligation to sell reversionary interests and other non-income producing assets. There will inevitably be some delay before such a sale can be effected and no income is earned during the period. Therefore the proceeds of sale of such assets are not treated as exclusively capital but are apportioned between capital and income under the rule in the *Earl of Chesterfield's Trusts*.

Although these rules were originally developed to achieve fairness between the life tenant and the remainderman they do lead to extremely complicated calculations and most professionally drawn wills exclude them as a matter of course. If the rules have not been excluded they will affect the items treated as capital and income on the accounts presented to the residuary beneficiaries. The calculations will not, however, affect liability to income tax of the estate or of the life tenant since the Inland Revenue ignores equitable apportionments.

There is another type of equitable apportionment known as the rule in *Allhusen* v. *Whittell* (1867). This rule provides that where residue is left to persons in succession debts and other outgoings (such as legacies) are to be treated as paid partly from capital and partly from income accruing to that portion of capital during the period between the testator's death and the payment of the outgoings. The principle is that the life tenant is entitled to income from the net residue after payment of debts and other liabilities but not to income from those assets which are needed for the payment of debts and which, therefore, do not form part of the net residue.

*Example*

A will leaves residue to L for life, remainder to R. The personal representatives wish to pay legacies of £11,000 one year after

T's death. The estate has produced income at the rate of 10 per cent. per annum. The legacies will be treated as paid with £10,000 of capital and £1,000 of income. Thus the net residuary estate will be reduced by £10,000 and the income of the estate will be reduced by £1,000.

Like the other equitable apportionments the rule exists to achieve fairness between life tenant and remainderman. It is, however, usually excluded in professionally drawn wills. If it is not excluded it will affect the capital and income accounts presented to the residuary beneficiaries. The Inland Revenue will ignore any apportionments effected under this rule and will assess the liability of the estate to income tax on all the trust income before apportionments.

# E. The Legal Rules of Apportionment

As explained in paragraph 16.48, income is treated as accruing on a daily basis under the common law rules of apportionment of interest and the Apportionment Act 1870. Thus, income received after death must be apportioned if it relates to a period part of which falls before and part of which falls after death.

Most professionally drawn wills exclude the need for such apportionments. If the will creates a trust in favour of a life tenant the need for apportionments should be expressly excluded on the life tenant's death as well as on the testator's death.

Even if the will does exclude the need for apportionments, the exclusion is only effective for *distribution* purposes. Apportionments will still have to be made to calculate the value of the estate at death for *inheritance tax purposes* (see paragraph 4.17). Moreover, when calculating the liability of the estate to *income tax* no apportionments are made no matter what the will says; any income which is payable after death is treated as income of the estate and not of the deceased even though part or all of the income may be attributable to a period falling before death (however, as we saw in Chapter 6 there is an income tax relief available where income has been apportioned and charged to inheritance tax). The position is rather different on the death of a life tenant of a trust. For income tax purposes the Inland Revenue will follow the terms of the trust instrument. If that does not exclude the need for apportionment of income on the death of a life tenant the income tax liability will be apportioned between the life tenant's estate and the person next entitled but if it does exclude the need for apportionment tax on all income payable after death will be treated as the liability of the person next entitled.

# F. Accounts

## 1. THE PURPOSE OF ACCOUNTS

The personal representatives will prepare a variety of accounts **18.18** for different purposes. At an early stage of the administration they must complete an Inland Revenue Account (unless the estate is an "excepted estate" in which case no Account is required). They will also keep records of any income of the estate so that any income tax liability of the estate can be calculated.

In addition, before the personal representatives can complete the administration they must produce estate accounts for the residuary beneficiaries. The purpose of such accounts is to list all the assets of the estate, all the debts, liabilities and expenses that have been paid, all the legacies that have been paid and then to show the balance which is available for distribution to the residuary beneficiaries. The personal representatives will also show how the entitlement of each residuary beneficiary is to be paid. Thus, if the personal representatives propose to pay part of the entitlement in cash and to transfer assets *in specie* to make up the balance this must be explained. The residuary beneficiaries signify their approval of the accounts by signing them and acknowledging receipt of any amount due. This discharges the personal representatives from liability (see paragraph 18.20).

## 2. THE FORM OF THE ACCOUNTS

There are no rules as to the form of estate accounts. However, **18.19** they *must* be clear and easy to understand since their purpose is to convey information to the residuary beneficiaries. An account may be prepared vertically showing assets less liabilities or as a double sided account showing receipts on one side and payments on the other.

An account normally commences with a narrative which sets out such matters as the date of death of the deceased, the date of the grant of representation, a summary of the dispositions made in the will (or of the effect of the intestacy rules), the value of the gross and net estate and any other information relevant to the administration (for example, whether any interim payments have already been made to the residuary beneficiaries, whether it is proposed to transfer assets *in specie* to the residuary beneficiaries). The purpose of such a narrative is to make the account more intelligible to the beneficiaries. In order to cut down the amount included on the account details of investments may be relegated to separate Schedules.

It is usual, except in the case of very small estates, to divide the account into a capital account and an income account. Such a division is essential if a life interest has been created in the residue since one person will be entitled to capital and another to income.

If separate capital and income accounts are prepared it will be necessary, unless the need to apportion has been excluded, to make apportionments of any income received after death which is attributable partly to the period before and partly to the period after death. The former will be shown on the capital account as part of the residuary cash. The latter will be shown on the income account; if the income-producing asset was specifically bequeathed the income will pass to the specific beneficiary, if it was not it will pass as part of the residuary income.

If residuary personalty has been left to one person for life, remainder to another, equitable apportionments of certain types of income and of the proceeds of sale of certain types of asset may have to be made for *distribution* purposes. These were discussed in paragraph 18.17 above. If such apportionments of income and capital are made they will obviously affect the entries made in the Estate Accounts. However, it is usual for professionally drawn wills to exclude the need for equitable apportionments.

A simple estate account is set out below.

## MRS. AMY TESTOR DECEASED

Mrs. Amy Testor of the Restwell Nursing Home, Bognor Regis, died on January 4, 1990 at the age of 96.

Probate of her will was granted by the Principal Probate Registry on April 6, 1990 to her daughter, Miss Catherine Testor.

By her will Mrs. Testor left £2,500 to each of her two grandchildren, Mr. David Kay and Mrs. Elizabeth Forbes. The residue was given after payment of debts, funeral, testamentary and other expenses and legacies to Mrs. Briony Kay and Miss Catherine Testor. The will excluded the need to apportion income. The personal effects have been taken by Miss Catherine Testor in partial satisfaction of her entitlement at an agreed valuation of £410.

## Capital Account

|  | £ | £ |
|---|---|---|
| Investwell Building Society Deposit A/C |  | 31,500 |
| Northern Crest Unit Trust |  | 38,700 |
| Current A/C |  | 950 |
| Cash in Hand |  | 70 |
| Personal effects—estimated value |  | 410 |
| GROSS ESTATE |  | 71,630 |
| *Less debts and other expenses* |  |  |
| Funeral Expenses | 450 |  |
| Solicitors' fees | 520 |  |
| Arrears at Nursing Home | 760 |  |
| Inheritance tax | 900 |  |
|  |  | (2,630) |
| NET ESTATE |  | 69,000 |
| *Less Legacies* |  |  |
| Mr. D. Kay | 2,500 |  |
| Mrs. E Forbes | 2,500 | (5,000) |
| *Residue available to beneficiaries* |  | 64,000 |
| ½ Mrs. B. Kay | 32,000 |  |
| ½ Miss C. Testor | 32,000 | 64,000 |

## Income Account

|  | £ | £ |
|---|---|---|
| *Income received since death* |  |  |
| Investwell Building Society | 1,100 |  |
| Northern Crest Unit Trust | 1,400 |  |
|  |  | 2,500 |
| *Less:* Interest on bank loan taken out to pay I.H.T. |  | (10) |
| *Income available to beneficiaries* |  | 2,490 |
| ½ Mrs. B. Kay | 1,245 |  |
| ½ Miss C. Testor | 1,245 |  |
|  |  | 2,490 |

**Note**

Having calculated the entitlement of the two residuary beneficiaries to capital and income it would then, strictly speaking, be necessary to produce an account for each showing how their entitlement is to be made up. However on these facts each will receive her entitlement in cash (apart from the personal effects valued at £410 which are to go to Catherine Testor) so that the preparation of additional accounts is not essential.

### 3. SIGNATURE OF THE ACCOUNTS

**18.20** A receipt of a residuary beneficiary is normally given by signing the accounts. Such a receipt normally includes an indemnity, for example "I agree to accept the assets shown in full satisfaction of my entitlement and hereby discharge X as executor and indemnify him against all claims and demands." However, such a release and indemnity is only effective if the beneficiary had full knowledge of all the assets, accounts and dealings.

If a beneficiary persists in a refusal to approve accounts he may commence an administration action for examination of the accounts. If he does not the personal representatives may pay the outstanding funds into court under the Trustee Act 1925, s.63 as amended by section 36(4), Schedule III of the Administration of Justice Act 1965. However, this involves the estate in extra expense and should not be done unless there is no satisfactory alternative. It will rarely be necessary since a recalcitrant beneficiary will not wish to be deprived of the estate assets indefinitely and will usually either approve the accounts or commence proceedings relatively quickly. If the reason that approval is not forthcoming is that a beneficiary is missing, the personal representatives may have taken steps earlier in the administration to obtain a "Benjamin order"; if they have not they should consider either obtaining an indemnity from the other beneficiaries or obtaining insurance cover or retaining assets.

A residuary beneficiary may be unable to approve the accounts as a result of disability (minority or lack of mental capacity). In the case of a minor the personal representatives may be able to appoint trustees under section 42 of the Administration of Estates Act; if they are not able to do so they will have to retain the assets until the minor's majority.

In the case of a beneficiary suffering from a mental disorder it may be that a receiver has been appointed by the Court of Protection to deal with that person's affairs. In this case the personal representatives should inform the court of the entitlement and act in accordance with the court's directions. Provided the personal representatives act in accordance with the court's directions they will obtain a good discharge. If no receiver has been appointed an application should be made to the Court of Protection for the appointment of a receiver. Such an application is normally made by a close relative of the disabled beneficiary. The personal representatives will retain the assets pending the application. However, if the relatives are reluctant to make such an application, the personal representatives will have to consider alternative arrangements such as payment into court under the Trustee Act 1925, s.63.

# 19. Post-Mortem Alterations

## A. Introduction

The persons entitled to a deceased person's property under the **19.1** terms of the will or under the intestacy rules may not need or want the property left to them. It is sometimes possible for the disposition of a deceased person's estate to be altered after the death. An alteration may achieve a more satisfactory disposition of the property of the deceased and in certain cases may result in a saving of tax. There are a number of ways in which alterations after death to the dispositions of a deceased person's property can be achieved. In this chapter we will consider the following methods:—

   (a)   A "disclaimer"
   (b)   A "variation"
   (c)   An order made under the Inheritance (Provision for Family and Dependants) Act 1975
   (d)   A "two-year discretionary trust"
   (e)   A "precatory trust."

In each case we will consider the effect on succession to property and on taxation. We will also look at the right of a surviving spouse under the intestacy rules to elect to capitalise his or her life interest. This is not, strictly speaking, an *alteration* of the intestacy rules merely an application of them; however the exercise of the right can alter the inheritance tax liability of the estate and it is, therefore, convenient to consider it in this chapter.

## B. Disclaimer

1. THE SUCCESSION EFFECT OF DISCLAIMER

It was said as long ago as 1819 that "the law certainly is not so **19.2** absurd as to force a man to take an estate against his will" (*per*

Abbot C.J. in *Townson* v. *Tickell* (1819)); the right of disclaimer is long established. The beneficiary is free to disclaim any property. A person entitled on intestacy is also apparently free to disclaim entitlement under the intestacy rules (*Re Scott* (1975)). A disclaimer is simply a refusal to accept property.

*Limitations on the right to disclaim*

**19.3** The right to disclaim a gift is lost altogether once any benefit from it has been accepted by the beneficiary. This will be the case where, for example, the beneficiary has had the property vested in him or where he has received income from a specific legacy or interest on a pecuniary legacy.

Unless the will provides to the contrary, it is not possible to disclaim part only of a single gift, the entire gift must be given up. If a beneficiary is entitled to two separate gifts, he can disclaim one while accepting the other. Thus a beneficiary given two legacies, one of £1,000, the other of a clock, can disclaim the clock and still accept the money (or *vice versa*).

*The effect of disclaiming*

**19.4** If a beneficiary disclaims a gift in the will or an entitlement under the intestacy rules, the property passes as if the gift to him had failed. The destination of the disclaimed property thereafter depends on the nature of the gift or entitlement that has been given up.

If a non-residuary gift in a will is disclaimed the property will fall into residue. If a residuary gift is disclaimed, the property passes under the intestacy rules, unless the gift is a class gift in which case it passes to the other members of the class. If it is a gift to joint tenants, it passes to the other joint tenant.

If a gift in a will is disclaimed, this does not prevent the beneficiary receiving the property (in whole or in part) under the intestacy rules. Thus, if a deceased died leaving a spouse and children having by will given his entire substantial estate to his wife, she could disclaim her interest under the will and still share in the property with her children under the intestacy rules, if this distribution is acceptable. If it is not, a "variation" might be more appropriate (see below, paragraph 19.11).

Disclaiming an interest on intestacy will either result in the property passing to the other members of the same class of beneficiaries or, if there are none, to the next category of relatives. Thus, if one of a number of children disclaims, the result is that the others enjoy a larger share of the deceased's estate. If an only child disclaims, the result is that the deceased's parents or brothers and sisters benefit.

It can be seen that a disadvantage of disclaimer is that the original beneficiary has no control over the ultimate destination of the property, which must pass under the terms of the deceased's will or the intestacy rules. This may be acceptable to the beneficiary who merely wants to give up his rights to certain property (perhaps because it carries with it onerous covenants or unacceptable conditions), but it will not be acceptable if he wants to ensure that someone, other than the residuary beneficiary or next of kin, takes in his place. In the latter case a "variation" would ensure he achieves his wishes.

*Method of disclaiming*
There are no statutory provisions governing the method of  **19.5**
disclaiming a gift in a will or an entitlement under the intestacy rules. It is sufficient for the beneficiary to indicate his intention to the deceased's personal representatives either orally or in writing. Written notice is advisable. A letter stating that the beneficiary does not want the property is sufficient.

2. THE TAXATION EFFECT OF DISCLAIMER

*The inheritance tax rules*
Under general principles a beneficiary who refuses to accept an  **19.6**
entitlement is treated as making a transfer of value for the purposes of inheritance tax. Thus, if the beneficiary were to die within seven years of disclaiming, tax would (subject to any exemptions and reliefs available) be payable. If certain conditions are complied with, a disclaimer will not be treated as a transfer of value. Inheritance tax will, instead, be payable as if the deceased had left his property to the person entitled once the disclaimer takes effect. The conditions are set out in Inheritance Tax Act 1984, s.142:

(a) the disclaimer must not be made for consideration in money or moneys worth (other than the making of a disclaimer or variation in respect of another disposition),
(b) the disclaimer must be in writing,
(c) the disclaimer must be made within two years of the death.

Provided these conditions are complied with, no further formalities are required. The property disclaimed will pass to the person next entitled under the terms of the deceased's will (or on his intestacy). The original beneficiary will not be treated as making a transfer of value. If the change of entitlement results in a change in the amount of inheritance tax payable on the deceased's estate (for example, where the spouse exemption becomes available on more or on less of the estate) the personal representatives will recalculate the tax and submit a corrective account to the Inland Revenue.

A disclaimer is unilateral. The consent of the personal representatives is not required to a disclaimer even if its effect is to increase the tax due.

Section 142(1) refers to the disclaimer of property comprised in the deceased's estate immediately before death "whether passing by will, intestacy *or otherwise.*" As a result of the reference to property passing "otherwise" than by will or intestacy, it is possible to disclaim an interest in joint property passing by survivorship. (Property in which the deceased had merely an interest in possession is not treated as a part of the deceased's estate for the purposes of disclaimer (section 142(5)).

*The capital gains tax rules*

**19.7**   Under general capital gains tax principles a disclaimer will amount to a disposal by the original beneficiary for capital gains tax purposes.

However, the Capital Gains Tax Act 1979, s.49(6) provides that if certain conditions are complied with a disclaimer will not be treated as a disposal. Instead the property will be treated as if left by the deceased to the person entitled once the disclaimer has taken effect. As death is not a disposal, no capital gains tax will be payable. The conditions are identical with those required for inheritance tax relief. No further formalities are required.

*The income tax rules*

**19.8**   *General principles.*

There is no statutory provision which makes a disclaimer retrospective for income tax purposes. Therefore, the position with respect to income from the property disclaimed is governed by the general law.

A disclaimer can only be made where no income or interest has been accepted. Where the gift disclaimed is a pecuniary legacy it carries with it, in certain circumstances, the right to receive interest (see Chapter 16, paragraph 16.49). If such interest is disclaimed, the beneficiary will not be liable to tax on it (*Dewar* v. *I.R.C.* (1935)) unless a fund to meet the legacy has been set aside (*Spens* v. *I.R.C.* (1970)).

The position with regard to disclaimers made by specific and residuary beneficiaries is less clear but is probably the same as in the case of variations (see paragraph 19.14). Where a beneficiary who is absolutely entitled disclaims, he will be assessed to income tax on income of the estate up to the date of disclaimer (despite having received no income); the new beneficiary will be assessed to income tax on income of the estate thereafter. Where a residuary beneficiary with a life interest in residue disclaims the effect is that the absolute interest is accelerated. It is the practice of the Inland Revenue to assess the new absolute beneficiary to tax on income of the estate after the date of the disclaimer; prior to the date of the disclaimer the Revenue will require basic rate tax from the personal representatives but will not seek to recover higher rate tax from either of the residuary beneficiaries.

*Disclaimer by parents.*                                                   **19.9**

A disclaimer is a refusal to accept an entitlement rather than a gift of the entitlement to a new beneficiary. This can have an important and beneficial income tax consequence for parents.

Under the Income and Corporation Taxes Act 1988, s.663, a parent who during his lifetime settles income or income producing assets on an infant, unmarried child will have the income assessed to income tax as part of his own income (unless the settlor makes an irrevocable capital settlement and the income is lawfully accumulated s.664). "Settlement" is widely defined and includes any disposition, arrangement or transfer of assets.

If a parent *disclaims* an entitlement it may happen that the person next entitled to the disclaimed property under the deceased's will (or under the intestacy rules) is the parent's infant, unmarried child. The Revenue appear to accept that in such a case the parent is not making a settlement on the child but is simply refusing to accept a benefit. The parent will not, therefore, be assessed to income tax on income produced by the disclaimed property. The position is otherwise where a parent makes an *inter vivos* gift to or a variation in favour of an infant, unmarried child.

*The stamp duty rules*

A disclaimer does not attract any form of stamp duty and the       **19.10**
instrument giving effect to it does not need to be presented to the Stamp Office.

## C. Variations

### 1. THE SUCCESSION EFFECT OF VARIATION

**19.11** A variation is a direction from a beneficiary to the personal representatives to transfer property to someone other than the original beneficiary. There are no special rules on the form of a variation for succession purposes since it is, in effect, an ordinary *inter vivos* gift.

For succession purposes, a variation is similar to a disclaimer in that the original beneficiary gives up his rights to receive property under the terms of the will or the intestacy rules but a variation differs from a disclaimer in three material respects:

    (a)  A variation is possible even though the original beneficiary has accepted the property, whether by receiving income or by having the property vested in him. It is even possible to vary the deceased's dispositions once the administration of the estate is complete.

    (b)  The original beneficiary can make a partial variation of a gift by, for example, giving up part of a gift. (This is not possible in the case of a disclaimer unless the will makes specific provision.)

    (c)  The original beneficiary can control the ultimate destination of the property since it passes to whoever he specifies. The property does not have to pass under the terms of the deceased's will or the intestacy rules.

Thus, a variation may provide a solution where a person has inherited property which he does not want but which he does not wish to pass to the person next entitled under the deceased's will or the intestacy rules.

*Example*
Ann, a wealthy woman, dies leaving her residuary estate to her husband Brian. He has no need of it and wishes to give the property direct to his two grandchildren, rather than to his child Charlotte. A disclaimer will not achieve his aim since if he were to disclaim his interest under the will and his entitlement under the intestacy rules, the property would pass to Charlotte.

Brian could achieve his aim by making an ordinary *inter vivos* gift to the grandchildren without altering the disposition by the deceased at all. However, this would be a potentially exempt transfer for inheritance tax purposes and a disposal for capital gains tax purposes which might result in unnecessary payments of tax being made. If he complies with the requirements of the Inheritance Tax Act 1984, s.142, he can vary the terms of the will in favour of his grandchildren and can avoid the transaction being treated as his *inter vivos* gift.

When choosing between a variation agreement and an ordinary *inter vivos* gift, tax considerations should be uppermost in the beneficiary's mind since variation is basically a tax concept.

## 2. THE TAXATION EFFECT OF VARIATION

*The inheritance tax rules*
If an original beneficiary makes an *inter vivos* gift of all or part **19.12** of the property this is a transfer of value for inheritance tax purposes. Thus, if he dies within seven years of the gift, inheritance tax will be payable (subject to any exemptions and reliefs which may be available). However, if the conditions of Inheritance Tax Act, s.142 are complied with, a variation will not be treated as a transfer of value. Instead, inheritance tax will be payable as if the deceased had left his property to the substituted beneficiary (or beneficiaries). The first three conditions are identical with those required for a disclaimer. In addition there are two further requirements:

(a) If the original beneficiary wishes to have the variation treated as the deceased's disposition he must give a written election to this effect to the Inland Revenue within six months of the variation agreement (if no election is given the variation will be treated as an *inter vivos* gift made by the original beneficiary).

(b) If the variation results in additional tax becoming payable the personal representatives must join in the election; (additional tax would be payable where, for example, a spouse diverted property from himself to a non-exempt beneficiary). The personal representatives may only decline to join in the election if insufficient assets are held by them for discharging the tax.

As in the case of a disclaimer, any property comprised in the deceased's estate immediately before death, whether passing by will, intestacy or otherwise, can be the subject of a variation (section 142(1)).

Section 142(5) provides expressly that a variation agreement will be effective for inheritance tax purposes whether or not the administration is complete or the property concerned has already been distributed to the original beneficiary.

The legislation contains no detailed requirements as to the form of a variation or of the election to be given to the Inland Revenue. However, the Inland Revenue has its own view and has issued the following statement.' (See *The Law Society's Gazette*, May 22, 1985):

" ... [T]he following conditions must be satisfied by an instrument coming within [section 142]. 1 The instrument in writing must be made by the persons or any of the persons who benefit or would benefit under the dispositions of the property comprised in the deceased's estate immediately before his death; 2 the instrument must be made within two years after the death; 3 the instrument must clearly indicate the dispositions that are the subject of it, and vary their destination as laid down by the deceased's will, or under the law relating to intestate estates, or otherwise; 4 a notice of election must be given within six months of the date of the instrument, unless the Board see fit to accept a late election; and 5 the notice of election must refer to the appropriate statutory provisions."

The requirement that the written instrument *itself* must vary the destination of the deceased's dispositions makes it advisable to use a deed.

*Practical considerations.*

A beneficiary (B) will usually wish to make an election since this results in only one possible charge to tax, from the deceased to the new beneficiary; whereas if B makes an *inter vivos* gift there is one charge to B and a risk of a second charge if B dies within seven years of the gift. If B is the spouse of the deceased it may be beneficial not to elect since the initial transfer to B is exempt; there is still the risk of a charge if B dies within seven years but this will be at B's rates and tapering relief may be available.

*The capital gains tax rules*

**19.13** Under general principles a variation will amount to a disposal by the original beneficiaries for capital gains tax purposes. However, the Capital Gains Tax Act 1979, s.49(6) provides that if certain conditions are complied with a variation will not be treated as a disposal. Instead, the property will be treated as if the deceased had left it to the substituted beneficiary or beneficiaries. The conditions are identical to those required for inheritance tax purposes.

Although the inheritance tax and capital gains tax rules are basically the same, there is no need to elect the same way for both taxes. The original beneficiary is free to choose for each tax the method which is most beneficial in order to achieve his ends.

*Practical considerations.*

Each case depends on its own facts but three points should be borne in mind.

(a)   If a loss has arisen since the date of death the original beneficiary may wish set the loss off against his own gains and so will choose to make an *inter vivos* gift.

(b)   It is preferable to treat the gift as an *inter vivos* disposition if the property has *increased* in value by an amount not exceeding the annual exemption from capital gains tax (currently £5,000) since the beneficiary can take the benefit of the increased acquisition value.

(c)   The indexation allowance may mean that there is no chargeable gain, in which case it is immaterial whether the disposition is treated as a variation or as an *inter vivos* gift.

Apart from these circumstances, the election will probably normally be made since no capital gains tax liability arises on death.

*The income tax rules*

A variation raises problems with regard to income tax liability **19.14** since (like disclaimer) there are no statutory provisions making the variation retrospective for income tax purposes. The Revenue take the view that any income arising in the period between death and variation is to be taxed as the income of the person entitled under the terms of the will or intestacy rules irrespective of whether any income is actually paid to them. Income arising after the date of the variation is taxed as income of the substituted beneficiary.

The Inland Revenue regards a variation as a "settlement" for the purposes of section 663 of the Income and Corporation Taxes Act 1988. If a parent varies in favour of an infant, unmarried child any resulting income will, while the child remains an infant and unmarried be assessed to income tax as part of the parent's income (unless the income is lawfully accumulated under an irrevocable capital settlement). As stated earlier it is preferable for a parent, who wishes to benefit his child, to use a disclaimer rather than a variation wherever this is possible.

*The stamp duty rules*

**19.15** A variation agreement used to attract *ad valorem* stamp duty. However, the Finance Act 1985, s.84, abolished *ad valorem* stamp duty on instruments executed on or after March 26, 1985 varying any disposition whether effected by will or the intestacy rules or otherwise (unless the variation is made for consideration in money or moneys worth other than consideration consisting of the making of a variation in respect of another disposition). Fixed duty of 50p and adjudication was required. However, in respect of instruments executed after May 1, 1987 the Stamp Duty (Exempt Instruments) Regulations 1987 exempt from duty instruments certified as falling into any of the categories listed in the Schedule. Variations fall into category M. Instruments falling within the Regulations do not need to be presented to the Stamp Office.

# D. Inheritance (Provision for Family and Dependants) Act 1975

**19.16** The position in relation to orders made under this Act is governed by section 146 of the Inheritance Tax Act 1984 which provides that for inheritance tax purposes the provision ordered by the court is treated as if it were the disposition of the deceased.

The new beneficiary is liable to income tax on income arising after the date of death from property awarded to him.

# E. Settlements Without an Interest in Possession— Property Vested Within Two Years of Death

**19.17** Some testators wish to leave the ultimate destination of their property flexible so that their personal representatives can look at the circumstances existing at the date of the testators's death and made a distribution which is suitable in the light of those circumstances. This flexibility can be achieved by leaving property on discretionary trusts. It is usual for a testator to leave a letter of intent explaining the person(s) the testator would like to receive a benefit.

Where a deceased creates a settlement without an interest in possession in his will and property is vested in any person within two years of the death, the inheritance tax payable on the death estate is calculated as if the will left the property to the beneficiary who receives the property once the trustees exercise their discretion.

There are no special capital gains tax rules applicable in these circumstances so that the exercise of the trustees' discretion is a deemed disposal and re-acquisition by them (see paragraph 7.23). The recipient acquires the asset at its market value when the discretion is exercised and not the value at death. As the appointment from the trust is not a transfer chargeable to inheritance tax no holdover relief is available to the trustees under Finance Act 1989, Sched. 14.

The normal income tax rules for settlements where no beneficiary has a right to income will apply (see paragraphs 7.27 and 7.28).

## F. Precatory Words

Where a testator expresses a wish that property left in his will to **19.18** a beneficiary should be transferred by that beneficiary to someone else, and that beneficiary complies with the wish within two years of the death, inheritance tax is payable as if the deceased had left the property to the eventual recipient.

There are no special capital gains tax rules so the transfer will be treated as a disposal by the original beneficiary.

There are no special income tax rules so income receivable up to the date of transfer will be assessed to tax as part of the original beneficiary's income.

## G. Capitalisation of Life Interest by Surviving Spouse

If a surviving spouse capitalises the life interest received under **19.19** the intestacy rules (see above paragraph 3.10) this is not a transfer of value for inheritance tax purposes and the spouse is treated as entitled to the capitalised amount. The capitalisation may, however, lead to more inheritance tax being paid since the spouse exemption will be lost on that part of the capital in which the spouse no longer has any interest.

There are no special capital gains tax or income tax rules.

# 20. The Inheritance (Provision for Family and Dependants) Act 1975

## A. Introduction

A testator is free to leave his property in whatever way he **20.1** pleases; no relative has a *right* to receive property under the will. However, this principle of testamentary freedom is to some extent eroded by the Inheritance (Provision for Family and Dependants) Act 1975. This Act gives the court limited powers to order financial provision to be made from the net estate of a deceased person for the benefit of certain categories of applicant. Applications under the Act can also be made where a person dies intestate.

If an application is to be successful the following matters must be established:

(i)    that certain preliminary requirements are satisfied;

(ii)   that the application is made within the time limit;

(iii)  that the applicant falls into one of the five possible categories of applicant;

(iv)  that the will or intestacy rules have not made reasonable provision for the applicant.

If these matters are established the court must then decide whether and in what manner to order financial provision for the applicant from the net estate of the deceased (to help the court in its decision there are certain statutory guidelines to be taken into account).

The Act contains certain anti-avoidance provisions under which orders may, in limited circumstances, be made against people who have received property from the deceased before death (see below, paragraph 20.20).

## B. Preliminary Requirements

**20.2** The Act applies only in the case of a deceased who dies domiciled in England and Wales after March 31, 1976 (section 1(1)); earlier legislation (which was narrower in its scope) applies to deaths before that date.

There is no equivalent statute applying to persons who die domiciled in Scotland. (However, under Scots law if a person dies domiciled in Scotland leaving a spouse and issue the spouse is entitled to a one-third share in the whole of the moveable estate of the deceased and the children are entitled to another one-third share. If there is a spouse and no children the spouse's share is increased to one-half. The deceased is free to dispose only of the remaining portion).

## C. Time Limits

### 1. NORMAL PERIOD

**20.3** Application must normally be made within six months of the date of the first effective grant of representation (section 4). If a grant is revoked because it was wrongly made, the application must be made within six months of the subsequent valid grant (*Re Freeman* (1984)). However, where a limited grant is made time runs only from the making of a full grant. This was decided in the case of *Re Paul Anthony Johnson (Deceased)* (1987) where a grant limited to pursuing negligence claims was made in 1983. The full grant of probate was made in 1987 and it was held that time ran from the date of the full grant. The court does, however, have a discretion to extend the time limit. This discretion is unfettered and the Act itself contains no guidance as to how the court should exercise it. However in *Re Salmon (Deceased)* (1980) Megarry V.-C. suggested six guidelines. These were concisely summarised in *Re Dennis* (1981) as follows:

> "First, the discretion of the court, though judicial, is unfettered. Second, the onus is on the applicant to show special reasons for taking the matter out of the general six-month time-limit; ... this is not a mere triviality but a substantial requirement. Third, the court has to consider how promptly and in what circumstances the application has been made after the time has expired; one has to look at all the circumstances surrounding the delay. Fourth, the court

has to see whether negotiations had started within the six-months period. Fifth, one has to consider whether or not the estate has been distributed before the claim has been notified. Sixth, the court has to consider whether refusal of leave to bring proceedings out of time will leave the applicant without recourse against anyone else, ... "
(An example of such a person would be a negligent solicitor).

The list was not intended to be exhaustive and *Re Dennis* itself added a further guideline, by analogy with applications for leave to defend in Order 14 proceedings, the applicant must show that he has "an arguable case, a case fit to go to trial."

### 2. PRACTICAL CONSIDERATIONS

The reason for having such a short time limit is to enable personal representatives to distribute assets without fear of personal liability if a successful application is later made. The Act provides therefore that a personal representative can distribute after the expiry of six months from the date of grant without personal liability even if the court does later extend the time limit (section 20). Where an out of time application is allowed there is power to recover any part of the estate already distributed to the beneficiaries by the personal representatives.

**20.4**

Obviously a cautious personal representative would wait six months before distributing assets; yet in most cases such caution will be unnecessary and may even cause hardship if a beneficiary is in urgent need of finance. A personal representative must therefore carefully consider the circumstances before deciding whether or not to wait for the expiry of the six month period. The following matters are relevant:

(a)  Since an order for financial provision is made against the *net* estate of the deceased (see below, paragraph 20.18) there can be no objection to paying funeral, testamentary and administration expenses, debts and liabilities before the expiry of the six months period.

(b)  It will normally be safe to pay a legacy to a beneficiary who is intending to make an application to obtain more (unless there is a risk of applications from other people).

(c)  Since it is unlikely that the court would order provision to be financed out of a very small legacy when the estate is large such a legacy can safely be paid.

(d) Similarly it will often be safe to distribute assets to a beneficiary who has a strong moral claim particularly if in urgent need.

## D. The Categories of Applicants

### 1. SECTION 1(1)

**20.5** The following persons may apply to the court for an order in their favour on the ground that the deceased's will or the intestacy rules have not made reasonable provision for them.

(a) *The spouse of the deceased.* The applicant must show that there was a subsisting marriage at the time of the deceased's death. This category includes a judicially separated spouse and a party to a voidable marriage which has not been annulled prior to death. Unusually a person will be regarded as a surviving spouse even though the marriage was *void*, provided the applicant entered into the marriage in good faith, unless in the lifetime of the deceased:

(1) the marriage has been dissolved or annulled; or
(2) the applicant entered into a later marriage.

The Act provides that a decree of judicial separation may contain a term barring the spouses from making an application for financial provision (section 15).

(b) *A former spouse.* A former spouse is a person whose marriage with the deceased was dissolved or annulled during the deceased's lifetime by a decree made under the law of any part of the British Islands or in any country or territory outside the British Islands by a divorce or annulment "which is entitled to be recognised as valid by the law of England and Wales" (section 25). The Act provides, however, in the interests of finality that a former spouse may be barred from applying for financial provision by a court order on the granting of a decree of divorce or nullity (sections 15 and 15A). Moreover, the Court of Appeal observed in *Re Fullard* (1981) that in view of the wide powers of the court to make financial arrangements on divorce, the number of cases in which it would be appropriate for a former spouse to apply under the family provision legislation would be small; an example of such a case might be where the deceased's estate receives the proceeds of a large insurance policy on the deceased's death or where the applicant had been provided for in the divorce proceedings by means of periodical payments rather than by a lump sum.

(c) *A child of the deceased.* This category includes a child of a non-marital relationship, a legitimated or adopted child and a child *en ventre sa mere.*

There is no distinction between sons and daughters and neither age nor marriage are automatic disqualifications. However, it must be said that the court has not so far looked sympathetically at applications by adult, able-bodied sons.

In *Re Coventry* (1980) for example, an adult, able-bodied son in a poor financial position made an application for provision from his father's estate; the estate was small and had passed under the intestacy rules to the deceased's elderly wife (the deceased and his wife had long been separated). The Court of Appeal stated that in such a case it was reasonable for the applicant to receive nothing. They were influenced by the fact that the applicant, though penniless, was capable of earning his own living and took the view that some special circumstance would be required to make failure to make financial provision for such an applicant unreasonable. The court quoted with approval the statement by Oliver J. at first instance that "applications under the Act of 1975 for maintenance by able-bodied and comparatively young men in employment and able to maintain themselves must be relatively rare and need to be approached ... with a degree of circumspection."

(d) *A person (not being a child of the deceased) who is treated by the deceased as a child of the family in connection with a marriage to which the deceased was a party.* The concept of "a child of the family" is imported from family law (Matrimonial Causes Act 1973, s.52(1) although under that Act the child must have been treated as a child of the family by *both* parties to the marriage). In *Re Callaghan* (1984) and in *Re Leach (Deceased)* (1985) it was held that a person was a child of the family even though he was an adult when the deceased married his parent.

(e) *Any person (not being a person included in the foregoing paragraphs) who immediately before the death of the deceased was being maintained wholly or partly by the deceased.* It is often difficult to decide whether a person is within this category but certain points have been decided in recent cases:

(i) *The meaning of "maintained"*
The starting point is section 1(3) which provides that "a person shall be treated as being maintained by the deceased, either

wholly or partly, ... if the deceased otherwise than for full valuable consideration, was making a substantial contribution in money or money's worth towards the reasonable needs of that person." It has been held that a person is to be regarded as maintained by the deceased *only* if he can bring himself within section 1(3) (*Re Beaumont* (1980); *Jelley* v. *Iliffe* (1981)). It is obviously difficult to state definitely what amounts to "a substantial contribution" but in *Jelley* v. *Iliffe* the Court of Appeal regarded the provision of rent free accommodation as substantial.

Once it is established that the deceased was making a substantial contribution, the next problem for a would-be applicant is to show that it was not made for full valuable consideration. It is accepted that consideration may be full and valuable even though not provided under a contract (*Re Beaumont; Jelley* v. *Iliffe*).

(ii) *The provision of services can amount to valuable consideration*

The court sometimes has to balance imponderables like companionship and other services provided by an applicant against contributions of cash or accommodation provided by the deceased. The court accepts that such services are *capable* of amounting to full valuable consideration (*Re Wilkinson* (1978); *Re Beaumont; Jelley* v. *Iliffe*). However, it is a question of fact in each case. The court will normally allow an application to proceed to the later stages of trial unless it is absolutely clear that the services made by the applicant outweigh the contributions made by the deceased to the applicant's maintenance. If, however, it is *clear* that the services amounted to full valuable consideration the application should be struck out at a preliminary stage in order to avoid the costs of further proceedings.

(iii) *The meaning of "immediately before the death"*

Section 1(1)(e) expressly states that the applicant must have been maintained "immediately before the death" of the deceased. Problems have arisen in connection with this phrase. For example, in *Re Beaumont* the deceased had habitually maintained the applicant but had been unable to do so in the few weeks immediately before her death, when she was ill in hospital. Megarry V.-C. accepted that the court must look at "the settled basis or ... general arrangement between the parties" not at "the actual, perhaps fluctuating, variation of it which exists immediately before ... death."

# E. Reasonable Provision

## 1. TWO STANDARDS

The Act sets out two standards for judging whether or not **20.6** provision is reasonable, one to be applied in the case of a surviving spouse and one to be applied in other cases.

## 2. THE SURVIVING SPOUSE STANDARD

This is such financial provision as it would be reasonable in all **20.7** the circumstances for a spouse (not including a judicially separated spouse) to receive "whether or not that provision is required for his or her maintenance" (section 1(2)(*a*)). This standard was introduced so that the claim of a surviving spouse to matrimonial assets should be equal to that of a divorced spouse and the court's powers to order financial provision as extensive as in a divorce application.

The court has a discretion to apply this standard where a decree of judicial separation, nullity or divorce has been made within 12 months of death and no order for financial provision has been made (or refused) in the matrimonial proceedings (section 14). The reason is that the applicant would otherwise have no opportunity to obtain a fair share of the matrimonial assets.

## 3. THE ORDINARY STANDARD

This is "such financial provision as it would be reasonable in all **20.8** the circumstances of the case for the applicant to receive for his *maintenance*" (section 1(2)(*b*)). It is difficult to give a precise meaning to the word "maintenance" in this context. It does not mean just enough to enable a person to get by (*i.e.* mere subsistence) but on the other hand it does not extend to everything which may be regarded as reasonably desirable for their general benefit or welfare. Buckley L.J. suggested in *Re Coventry* (1980) that it could be regarded as "such financial provision as would be reasonable in all the circumstances of the case to enable the applicant to maintain himself in a manner suitable to these circumstances."

It is not the purpose of the Act to provide legacies for disappointed beneficiaries but this does not mean that provision for maintenance is limited to income payments. Provision could be by way of a lump sum, for example, to buy a house in which the applicant could be housed, thereby removing one expense from the applicant (*Re Dennis* (1981)).

### 4. AN OBJECTIVE STANDARD

**20.9** The court is to decide whether the provision made for an applicant *is* reasonable. This is an entirely objective question. The court is concerned therefore with the facts of the case rather than merely with the facts known to the deceased. If a testator has reasons for making no provision for a relative or dependant it is desirable that he should leave a record of those reasons with the will. The court will consider the reasons given by the testator and in so far as the reasons are good will take them into account; if, however, the testator was mistaken or motivated by malice the reasons will be ignored. It is not advisable to include the reasons in the will itself as a will is a document of public record.

The court will consider changes in the position of beneficiaries and applicants arising after the death of the deceased (for example, if a poor beneficiary has a large win on the football pools after the death of the deceased, a dependant of the deceased may have more chance of making a successful application). The Court will not consider facts which arise between the hearing of the application and an appeal to the Court of Appeal (*Re Coventry*), nor will it consider legally unenforceable assurances given by beneficiaries to an applicant (*Rajabally* v. *Rajabally* (1987)).

It may be reasonable for the deceased to have made no financial provision at all for an applicant; we saw earlier that this was the case in *Re Coventry* where the Court of Appeal refused to order any provision for the adult son of the deceased.

## F. The Court Must Decide Whether and in What Manner to Make an Order (Section 3(1))

### 1. THIS IS A DISCRETIONARY MATTER

**20.10** If the court decides that the provision made for the applicant is not reasonable it must then go on to consider whether to exercise its discretion to make an order (and what type of order to make). At both stages the court is directed to consider various guidelines. Some guidelines are common to all applicants while some are limited to a particular category.

## 2. THE COMMON GUIDELINES

Under section 3(1) the court will have regard to the following **20.11** matters:

(a) *The financial resources and needs of the applicant, any other applicant and any beneficiary.* Earning capacity and social security benefits would be relevant here (*Re E* (1966)). The court must balance the resources and needs of all the persons with a claim on the estate.

(b) *Any obligations and responsibilities of the deceased toward the applicant or any beneficiary.*

(c) *The size and nature of the estate.* If an estate is large it is frequently relatively easy for the court to make adequate provision for applicants; where the estate is very small, however, it is often impossible to provide adequately for all beneficiaries and applicants. Moreover since the costs of an action normally come out of the estate the action may exhaust a large part of the assets. The courts, therefore, discourage applications in such cases (*Re Coventry; Jelley* v. *Iliffe*). In *Re Fullard* (1982) Ormrod L.J. suggested that judges might reconsider the practice of ordering the costs of both sides to be paid out of the estate and look very closely indeed at the merits of an unsuccessful application before ordering the estate to bear the costs. Solicitors should always bear in mind the question of costs when advising clients who wish to make a claim, especially one against a small estate. The Court of Appeal have also exhorted practitioners to inform the legal aid authorities of the likely effects of an application and (*a fortiori*) an appeal on an estate in cases where legal aid is applied for.

(d) *Any physical or mental disability of any applicant or any beneficiary.* The availability of state aid, hospital accommodation and social security benefits may be considered (*Re Watkins* (1949)).

(e) *Any other matter,* including the conduct of the applicant or any other person which the court may consider relevant. This obviously gives the court a great deal of freedom. In *Re Snook (Deceased)* (1983) an award to a spouse was set at a much lower amount than it would otherwise have been as a result of a history of assaults and other abuses in the years before the deceased's death.

3. THE PARTICULAR GUIDELINES

**20.12** Under section 3(2) without prejudice to the common guidelines the court will also consider additional guidelines in relation to each category.

(a) *The surviving spouse*
The court will consider:

(i) the age of the applicant and the duration of the marriage; and

(ii) the contribution made by the applicant to the welfare of the family of the deceased, including any contribution made by looking after the home or caring for the family; and

(iii) the provision the applicant might reasonably have expected to receive if on the day on which the deceased died the marriage, (instead of being terminated by death) had been terminated by a decree of divorce. In *Re Besterman (Deceased)* (1984) the Court of Appeal held that this did not mean that the same provision should be made as if there were a divorce on the day of the death. The other guidelines must also be taken into account and, in any case, further applications to the court if circumstances change may be made following a divorce whereas this is not possible in the case of a family provision application.

(b) *The former spouse*
Guidelines (i) and (ii) above also apply in the case of an application by a former spouse. Guideline (iii) does not apply unless the court has exercised its limited discretion to apply the surviving spouse standard (see above, paragraph 20.7).

Unless there is some special reason an application by a former spouse who has already received financial provision on the termination of the marriage with a view to a "clean break" will rarely be successful (*Re Fullard* (1981)).

(c) *A child of the deceased*
The additional guideline here is the manner in which the applicant was being or in which he might expect to be educated or trained.

(d) *A person treated by the deceased as a child of the family*
In addition to the education guideline set out in (c) above the court is also directed to consider:

(i) whether the deceased had assumed any responsibility for the applicant's maintenance and if so the extent to which and the basis upon which the deceased assumed that responsibility and the length of time for which the deceased discharged that responsibility; and

(ii) whether in assuming and discharging that responsibility the deceased did so knowing that the applicant was not his own child; and

(iii) the liability of any other person to maintain the applicant.

(e) *A person maintained by the deceased*

The court will consider the extent to which and the basis upon which the deceased assumed responsibility for the maintenance of the applicant and to the length of time for which the deceased discharged that responsibility.

It will be noticed that while the category (d) guideline directs the court to consider *whether* the deceased assumed responsibility, the category (e) guideline directs the court to consider *the extent* to which responsibility *has been* assumed. This suggests that a category (e) application can be made only if the deceased assumed responsibility for the applicant's maintenance. In *Re Beaumont* Megarry V.-C. accepted this and said that the applicant must be able to point to "some act or acts which demonstrates an undertaking of responsibility"; without such an act an application would fail at the outset. However, in *Jelley* v. *Iliffe*, the Court of Appeal expressly disapproved of this view and stated that the mere fact of maintenance generally raises a presumption that there was an assumption of responsibility; in the absence of evidence to rebut this presumption, therefore, the application can proceed to the later stages. However, if there is no real evidence to suggest that the deceased assumed responsibility for the applicant it is unlikely that the application will be successful. There is nothing to prevent a testator leaving a statement to the effect that he assumed no responsibility for the applicant or did so only during his lifetime and not after death.

# G. Types of Orders

## 1. THE TYPES

Under section 2(1) the court may make one or more of the following orders:

20.13

(a) *Periodical payments*
Such an order may provide for:

    (i)   payments of a specified amount (for example, £25 per week); or

    (ii)  payments equal to the whole or part of the income of the net estate (for example, one-third of the income from the net estate); or

    (iii) payments equal to the whole of the income of such part of the net estate as the court may direct to be set aside or appropriated (*e.g.* the whole income from the deceased's shares in a named company); or

    (iv) payments to be determined in any other way the court thinks fit.

Section 2(3) provides that the order for periodical payments may direct that a specified part of the net estate shall be set aside or appropriated for making periodical payments from the income. However, no more may be set aside or appropriated than is sufficient to produce the income at the date of the order.

Periodical payments are for the term specified in the order. In the case of a former spouse the Act provides expressly that an order shall cease to have effect on the remarriage of the former spouse (section 19(2)). In any other case, however, the court must decide the date of termination when it makes the order. Orders for periodical payments may be varied (see below, paragraph 20.17).

(b) *Lump sum payment*
A lump sum may be made payable by instalments in which case the number, amounts and dates for payments of the instalments can be varied; apart from that a lump sum order cannot be varied (section 7).

A lump sum is obviously appropriate in the case of an application by a surviving spouse but it can also be ordered in the case of other applicants even though they are only entitled to maintenance.

Where an estate is very small a lump sum order is particularly useful; indeed it may be the only type of provision which can realistically be made.

(c) *Transfer of property*
The court may order the transfer of a particular asset to an applicant. This may be advisable where a lump sum order would require an improvident sale of assets. Such an order once made cannot be varied.

### (d) *Settlement of property*

An order for settlement of property is particularly likely in the case of a minor or a person who is in need of protection. Such a settlement must be drafted with an eye to tax and trust law so that, for example, if a settlement on a minor does not give rise to an interest in possession it should comply with the requirements of an accumulation and maintenance settlement. Such an order, once made, cannot be varied.

### (e) *Acquisition of property for transfer or settlement*

The court may order that assets from the net estate of the deceased be used to acquire a specified item (for example, a house) which will either be transferred to or settled on an applicant.

Such an order, once made, cannot be varied.

### (f) *Variation of marriage settlements*

An ante or post-nuptial settlement may be varied by the court for the benefit of the surviving spouse of the marriage or the children of the marriage or any person who was treated by the deceased as a child of that marriage.

Such an order for variation, once made, cannot be varied.

## 2. THE BURDEN OF AN ORDER

**20.14** Any order made by the court may contain such consequential and supplemental provisions as the court thinks necessary or expedient for the purpose of securing that the order operates fairly as between one beneficiary of the estate and another. For example, if the court makes a periodical payments order or a lump sum order it may direct which part of the estate is to bear the burden; if the court orders that an asset which had been specifically left to a beneficiary is to be transferred to the applicant the court may vary the disposition of the estate to make alternative provision for the disappointed beneficiary.

"Beneficiary" in this context includes the donee of a statutory nomination or a *donatio mortis causa* or a surviving joint tenant (see paragraph 20.18 below).

## 3. INHERITANCE TAX

**20.15** The court order alters the disposition of the estate of the deceased and is deemed to have done so from the date of death of the deceased for all purposes including the payment of inheritance tax. Thus, for example, if an order increases the amount passing to a surviving spouse the chargeable value of the estate for inheritance tax purposes will be reduced whereas if less property passes to a surviving spouse the chargeable value will be increased.

### 4. INTERIM PAYMENTS

**20.16** The court has power to make an interim order in favour of an applicant if it appears to the court that:

> (i) the applicant is in immediate need of financial assistance but it is not yet possible to determine what order (if any) should be made; and
>
> (ii) property forming part of the net estate of the deceased is or can be made available to meet the needs of the applicant.

### 5. VARIATION OF PERIODICAL PAYMENTS ORDER

**20.17** The court has limited power under section 6 to vary a periodical payments order. It has no power to vary other orders (apart from the number, amounts and dates for payment of instalments of a lump sum). This is in the interest of certainty.

An application for variation can be made by the original recipient and also, inter alia, by the personal representatives of the deceased, a beneficiary of the estate or a former applicant (section 6(5)). It can be made during the currency of an order or, where the order was to terminate on the occurrence of a specified event, within six months of that event.

Only property already allocated for periodical payments (called "relevant property") can be affected by a variation order. The court cannot order that relevant property be increased (section 6(6)).

The court will consider all the circumstances of the case including any change in matters it considered when making the original order (section 6(7)). It has power to order that periodical payments continue after the occurrence of a terminating event specified in the original order (other than the remarriage of a former spouse where the termination occurs automatically under section 14 and cannot be varied). It can also direct payment of a lump sum or a transfer of property to the applicant from the relevant property.

The variation order can be made in favour of any of the possible applicants. It is not limited to the original recipient (section 6(2)).

## H. Property Available for Financial Provision

### 1. THE NET ESTATE

If the court decides to order provision to be made for an applicant such an order is made against the "net estate" of the deceased.   **20.18**

The net estate is defined by section 25 as comprising:

(a) "All property of which the deceased had power to dispose by his will (otherwise than by virtue of a special power of appointment) less the amount of his funeral, testamentary and administration expenses, debts and liabilities including any inheritance tax payable out of his estate on death."

This will obviously not include insurance policies where the proceeds are payable direct to a beneficiary rather than to the estate of the policyholder as the deceased has no power to dispose of such property.

(b) "Any property in respect of which the deceased held a general power of appointment (not being a power exercisable by will) which has not been exercised."

If the power was exercisable by will the property subject to the power falls into (a) above whether or not the deceased actually exercised it.

(c) Any property nominated by the deceased to any person under a statutory nomination (see Chapter 21) or received by any person as a result of a *donatio mortis causa* (see Chapter 21) less any inheritance tax payable in respect of such property and borne by the nominee or donee (section 8).

(d) The deceased's severable share of a joint tenancy, but only if the court so orders (see section 9 and paragraph 20.19 below).

(e) Any property which the court orders shall be available as a result of its anti-avoidance powers (see paragraph 20.20 below).

## 2. JOINT PROPERTY

20.19 As a result of the right of survivorship a deceased has no power to dispose of his interest under a joint tenancy by will. However, under section 9 where the deceased was a joint tenant of any property immediately before death the court may, for the purpose of facilitating the making of financial provision, order that the deceased's severable share of the property (or the value thereof *immediately before his death*) shall to such extent as appears to the court to be just in all the circumstances (and after allowing for any inheritance tax payable) be treated as part of the net estate. The discretion only exists in respect of applications made within six months from the date of the grant; there is no power to make such an order in connection with an out-of-time application.

Section 9(4) expressly provides for the avoidance of doubt that for the purposes of this section there may be a joint tenancy of a chose in action, for example the asset represented by a credit balance in a joint bank account.

## 3. ANTI-AVOIDANCE PROVISIONS

*Introduction*

20.20 A deceased might attempt to evade the Act either by giving away property *inter vivos* so that the net estate on death is substantially reduced or by entering into a binding contract to leave property by will; the effect of such a contract would be to give the other party to the contract a right to enforce it against the personal representatives, thus reducing the net estate available for family provision. Sections 10 and 11 of the Act enable the court to prevent such evasion; they give power to order a person to satisfy a claim for family provision if he has benefited under an *inter vivos* disposition or a contract to provide money or other property.

*Inter vivos dispositions*

20.21 A disposition is covered by section 10 if it was made:

    (i)   after March 31, 1976 and less than six years before the date of death of the deceased; and

   (ii)   with the intention of defeating an application under the Act; and

  (iii)   for less than full valuable consideration.

A "disposition" for this purpose includes any payment of money (including insurance premiums) and any conveyance of property whether or not made by instrument. It does not, however, include any statutory nomination, *donatio mortis causa* or appointment of property under a special power of appointment.

### Contracts

A contract is covered by section 11 of the Act if: **20.22**

- (i) entered into after March 31, 1976; and
- (ii) the deceased agreed to leave money or other property by will or agreed that money or other property would be paid or transferred to any person from his estate; and
- (iii) the deceased made the contract with the intention of defeating an application under the Act; and
- (iv) when the contract was made full valuable consideration was not given or promised.

In the case of a contract there is no time limit as there is in the case of *inter vivos* dispositions.

### *The intention of defeating an application*

The deceased must have made a disposition or contract with the **20.23** intention of defeating an application. Section 12 provides that this requirement is satisfied if the court is of the opinion on a balance of probabilities that the deceased's intention (though not necessarily his sole intention) in making the disposition or contract was to prevent an order for financial provision being made or to reduce the amount of the provision which might otherwise be ordered.

In the case of a contract, section 12(2) provides that, if a contract is made for no valuable consideration at all (that is, by way of a deed), there will be a presumption that the deceased's intention was to defeat an application.

### *The facilitating of financial provision for the applicant*

Even if a disposition is covered by section 10 or a contract is **20.24** covered by section 11 the court will not use its anti-avoidance powers unless satisfied that to do so will facilitate the making of financial provision.

### *The powers of the court are discretionary*

If the court is satisfied of the above requirements it may make **20.25** an order against a donee. However, this is a discretionary matter and in deciding what order (if any) to make the court is directed to consider the circumstances in which the disposition or contract was made, any valuable consideration that was given, the relationship (if any) of the donee to the deceased, the conduct and financial resources of the donee and all the other circumstances of the case (section 10(6) and section 11(4)).

### Orders against a donee of a disposition

20.26 The court may order a donee to provide such sum of money or other property as it may specify (section 10(2)). However, there are two limitations:

    (a)   if the donee was given money he cannot be ordered to provide more than the money paid to him by the deceased less any inheritance tax borne by the donee in respect of the payment (section 10(3));

    (b)   if the donee was given property he cannot be ordered to provide more than the value of the property at the date of death of the deceased less any inheritance tax borne by the donee in respect of the payment (section 10(4)). (If he has disposed of the property prior to the deceased's death the limit is the value of the property at the date of disposal).

### Order against a "donee" under a contract

20.27 If the personal representatives of the deceased have not transferred money or other property to the donee in accordance with the provisions of the contract, before the date of the application, the court may order them not to make such payment or transfer, or to make no further payment or transfer or to make only a reduced payment or transfer (section 11(2)(ii)). The effect of such an order is to increase the net estate of the deceased available for financial provision.

If the personal representatives of the deceased have already transferred money or property to the donee before the date of the application in accordance with the provisions of the contract, the court may order the donee to provide such sum of money or other property as it may specify (section 11(2)(i)).

The court may only make such orders to the extent that the property transferred under the contract exceeds the value of any consideration given (the property to be valued at the date of the hearing) (section 11(3)).

### Order against donee's personal representatives

20.28 If a donee has died the court has the same powers against the donee's personal representatives under sections 10 and 11 as it would have had against the donee. However, once property has been distributed by the personal representatives the powers of the court cease with regard to that property. The personal representatives will not be liable if they distribute the donee's property without notice of the making of an application under sections 10 and 11 (section 12(4)).

*Order against a trustee of the donee*
If the deceased transferred property to a trustee or contracted to have property transferred to a trustee with the intention of defeating an application the trustee can be ordered to provide property (section 13(1) and (3)). Section 13 also provides limits on the amount that the trustee can be ordered to repay.   **20.29**

# I. The Choice of Court

## 1. THE COUNTY COURT

A county court has jurisdiction to hear and determine applications where the net estate of the deceased (meaning property of which the deceased had power to dispose by will less funeral, testamentary and administration expenses, debts and liabilities including inheritance tax payable from the estate on death together with the other property set out in section 25) does not exceed the amount of the limit for county court jurisdiction (currently £30,000).   **20.30**

## 2. THE FAMILY OR CHANCERY DIVISION OF THE HIGH COURT

An application for an order may be made either in the Chancery Division or in the Family Division. There are no rules limiting the applicant's freedom of choice and a practitioner is therefore free to choose whichever seems the more appropriate. Frequently they will be equally suitable so that the practitioner's choice may be governed by personal preference and experience; on occasion, however, one Division may have a particular advantage. For example, in a case where an order has been made under the Matrimonial Causes Act 1973 (or its predecessors) the Family Division will be the obvious forum. The Chancery Division is more suitable where there is a dispute as to the validity of a will which is alleged not to make reasonable financial provision for the applicant (in such a case the probate action can be heard immediately before the family provision application by the same judge with a consequent saving of time and expense), where the true meaning of the will must first be determined under a construction summons or where complicated accounts have to be taken.   **20.31**

# 21. Disposing of Property otherwise than by Will

## A. Introduction

It is generally considered to be a "good thing" to make a will. **21.1**
In this chapter we will consider, firstly, to what extent it is
possible to dispose of property on death without a will and,
secondly, why solicitors advise clients to make wills.

## B. Disposition of Property without a Will

It is important to remember that making a will is not the only **21.2**
means of disposing of property after death. Solicitors advising
intending testators should ensure their clients are aware of the
other possibilities.

### 1. STATUTORY NOMINATIONS

Where a person is entitled to certain types of investments he **21.3**
can nominate a third party to receive them on his death. In such
cases the property will not vest in the nominator's personal
representatives on death but will be paid directly to the
nominee. The payer will, therefore, want to see the death
certificate of the deceased but will not require production of the
grant of representation. The nominated property does, however,
form part of the deceased's estate for inheritance tax purposes.
  Nominations were originally designed to allow the poorer
members of society to dispose of small amounts of money
without the necessity of making a will or of their representatives
obtaining a grant. They can be made in respect of deposits in
certain Trustees Savings Banks, Friendly Societies and Industrial
and Provident Societies up to a limit of £5,000 each. It used to
be possible to nominate National Savings Certificates and

deposits in National Savings Banks and Trustee Savings Banks but this power was withdrawn as from May 1, 1979 in respect of the latter and May 1, 1981 in respect of the two former (nominations of such property *made* before those dates remain effective).

To be valid, a nomination must be:

(a)   in writing,
(b)   made by a person who is 16 or over; and
(c)   attested by one witness.

Since a will cannot be made by a person who is under the age of 18, a nomination is the only way in which a minor can dispose of property (unless he has privileged status) after death.

A nomination is revoked by subsequent marriage, a later nomination or the death of the nominee before the nominator but it is *not* revoked by a subsequent will. It is therefore important when drafting a will for a client to ascertain whether or not any nominations have previously been made. They are easily overlooked as the paying authority normally holds the nomination form.

## 2. DISCRETIONARY PENSION SCHEMES

**21.4**   Many pension schemes allow contributors to "nominate" a third party to receive benefits after the contributors' death either in the form of a lump sum or a pension. Where a lump sum is paid it is often the most substantial single asset passing on death and may be used to make a substantial gift to a beneficiary. However such lump sums are normally only paid when the contributor dies "in service" and therefore the provision for the beneficiary may have to be reconsidered when the contributor ceases to contribute to the scheme (whether on retirement or as a result of changing jobs).

Such a "nomination" is not binding on the trustees of the pension fund being merely an indication of the deceased's wishes, although, naturally, they will usually abide by the expressed wishes of the deceased. This procedure is sometimes referred to as a "nomination" but it is obviously different from the type of nomination referred to in paragraph 21.3 above where the deceased has an absolute right to the property and is free to deal with it as he likes whether after his death or during his lifetime.

These benefits do not form part of the deceased's estate for inheritance tax purposes.

## 3. DONATIO MORTIS CAUSA

*The requirements for a donatio mortis causa*
A *donatio mortis causa* is an *inter vivos* gift which is conditional   **21.5**
on death. It has some of the attributes of a legacy and some of
an *inter vivos* gift. There are four requirements which must be
satisfied if a *donatio mortis causa* is to be valid:

(a) *The gift must be made in contemplation of death.* The
death need not be imminent so it is, for example, sufficient that
a person knows he has a serious illness and cannot live for long.
It is irrelevant that death occurs from a supervening cause (such
as an accident or a sudden second illness—*Wilkes* v. *Allington*
(1931)) but the gift fails if the donor recovers from the
contemplated cause of death. The cause of death need not be an
illness as such, contemplation of a dangerous operation is
enough.

(b) *The gift must be conditional on death.* If the donor
recovers from the contemplated cause of death, the gift will not
take effect and the donor will be entitled to regain possession of
the property. If, however, the donor dies then the gift to the
donee becomes absolute. If there are formal requirements for
transfer which need to be complied with in order to complete
title then the donee can compel the deceased's personal
representatives to complete the transfer.

(c) *There must be delivery.* Delivery must be made to the
donee (or his agent) of the subject-matter of the gift or the
means of obtaining it. In the case of chattels it is usually readily
apparent whether or not this has taken place but in the case of
choses in action it is a little more difficult. Since choses in action
cannot be physically delivered there must be delivery of the
essential evidence of title which will entitle the possessor to the
property given (for example, delivery of National Savings
Certificates or bills of exchange).

(d) *The subject-matter of the gift must be capable of passing as
a valid donatio mortis causa.* Most personalty is so capable (for
example, chattels, bonds, insurance policies or National Savings
Certificates). Land whether freehold or leasehold is not capable
of passing by *donatio mortis causa*. A cheque drawn by a third
party can be the subject of a valid donation but a cheque drawn
by the deceased cannot since it is merely an order to the
deceased's bank to pay which will be automatically revoked by
death.

It has been suggested that shares cannot be the subject of a valid *donatio mortis causa* (*Re Weston* (1902)) but there seems to be no reason in principle why this should be so and indeed the possibility of a *donatio mortis causa* of company shares was accepted in *Staniland* v. *Willott* (1852), although on the facts it was held to have been revoked by the donor's recovery from his illness.

*Comparison with legacies*

**21.6** It is worth noting the more important similarities and differences between legacies and *donationes mortis causa*.

(a) *Similarities*

  (i) *Lapse.* A *donatio mortis causa* lapses if the donee predeceases the donor. The subject-matter will then form part of the donor's estate on death.

  (ii) *Tax.* Inheritance tax is payable on the property which is the subject-matter of the *donatio mortis causa* as it is part of the donor's estate on death.

  (iii) *Liability for debts.* If the estate of the deceased proves insufficient to pay the deceased's debts than the subject-matter of a *donatio mortis causa* may be taken (see paragraph 15.18).

(b) *Differences*

  (i) *No assent.* Normally the personal representatives of the deceased transfer title to beneficiaries by means of an assent. However, since death makes a *donatio mortis causa* absolute, the personal representatives need do nothing unless there are formal requirements which need to be complied with in order to complete the title.

  (ii) *Revocation.* A *donatio mortis causa* is revoked if the donor recovers from the contemplated cause of death or if the donor resumes possession and dominion of the property. It cannot be revoked by a subsequent will.

4. JOINT TENANCIES

**21.7** Joint tenancies are extremely important in practice since they are the most common way for property to be transferred without a will.

Where the deceased was a joint tenant in equity of any property, on his death his interest will pass automatically to the surviving joint tenant(s). It will not devolve on the deceased's personal representatives and cannot pass under the terms of his will. This is because it is not possible to sever a joint tenancy by will. However, a joint tenant is free to sever the joint tenancy *inter vivos* in which case the deceased and the co-owners will hold as tenants-in-common in equity. Such an interest *will* devolve on the deceased's personal representatives and *will* pass under the deceased's will or on intestacy.

Solicitors who are preparing wills for clients should explain to them that jointly owned property will pass to the survivor no matter how short the period of survivorship may be, despite anything said in the will. For this reason it may be appropriate for a client to sever a joint tenancy *inter vivos*.

## 5. INSURANCE POLICIES

Where a person takes out life assurance, on his death the insurance company will pay the assured amount to the deceased's personal representatives. This sum will form part of the death estate and so can potentially attract inheritance tax. **21.8**

Inheritance tax will not be payable if the death estate falls within the nil rate band or an exemption (such as the spouse exemption) applies. However, even if the property is to be paid to a spouse, the personal representatives will have to wait until a grant is obtained before the insurance company will hand over the money. This delay may be inconvenient at best or financially disastrous for the spouse, at worst.

Rather than have the money channelled through the estate (which will be ill-advised for inheritance tax purposes if the sum is large and the intended beneficiary is not a spouse or a charity), it is better to have the money paid direct to the intended beneficiary.

This can be achieved in one of two ways. First, the assured can make use of the Married Woman's Property Act 1882, s.11. Under this section a policy of life assurance effected by a person on his own life can be expressed to be for the benefit of his spouse and/or children (which includes children of a non-marital relationship). This creates a trust in their favour and on the death, the sum assured is paid direct to the trustees of the policy for the benefit of the named beneficiaries. No inheritance tax charge will arise in respect of the assured's estate where policies are written in trust in this way since he has no beneficial interest. However, provided the gift is not subject to a contingency, the named beneficiary receives an immediate absolute interest. Therefore, should the beneficiary predecease the assured, the beneficiary's estate suffers tax on the appropriate proportion of the value of the policy. Since the beneficiary has an immediate absolute interest in the policy the assured is no longer free to surrender or assign the policy.

Since section 11 permits the assured to name his children as beneficiaries it is advisable to appoint trustees to hold the money until the children reach a suitable age. If such trustees are not appointed, the assured's personal representatives will hold the money as trustees, on trust for the children. Should this situation arise, the sum is still not taxed as part of the assured's estate since the sum does not belong to the estate, it is merely administratively convenient for the personal representatives to hold the property in this way.

Secondly if the assured wants to benefit someone other than a spouse or children (such as a friend or grandchildren) the policy must be expressly written in trust for them. The trust has the same effect as a section 11 policy. The same result will be achieved by assigning the policy to the named beneficiary.

### 6. ENDURING POWERS OF ATTORNEY

**21.9**  Any person may appoint an attorney to deal with his property. However, the power of attorney will automatically end if the person who made the appointment (the donor of the power) becomes mentally incapable. However, the Enduring Powers of Attorney Act 1985 provides for the appointment of an attorney whose powers will survive the incapacity of the donor. A solicitor who is advising on the appointment of an attorney or who is advising a person whose health makes future mental incapacity likely should consider advising the appointment of an attorney with an enduring power. Where such an appointment is made the attorney may be given power to sell the donor's property, and to a limited extent to give it away, notwithstanding the donor's incapacity. A wider power to make gifts with the assent of the court may also be made available to the attorney.

## C. Inter Vivos Planning

### 1. GIFTS

**21.10**  As an alternative to leaving property to an intended beneficiary by will, a client can consider making an *inter vivos* gift.

Such a gift has the advantage of giving the beneficiary the immediate use of the asset but it has the corresponding disadvantage that the donor will lose the benefit of the property (unless, for example, the gift is to a spouse).

Therefore, it is important to ensure that the donor has no need of the property to be given away. Thus, a gift of money that will leave the donor with financial problems is pointless as is the gift of an asset that the donor still wants to use. It is quite common for testators to want to leave books, jewellery, fishing tackle, golf clubs and similar items to friends or relatives but they would obviously not wish to make such gifts *inter vivos*.

While *inter vivos* gifts should always be considered, they are usually only practicable where the donor is fairly wealthy. An additional advantage is that an *inter vivos* gift may be useful in saving tax.

### Tax considerations

Although tax should never be the first consideration, since lifetime transfers to individuals do not attract inheritance tax an *inter vivos* gift will prima facie produce a saving. There is a danger that the donor will die within seven years of the transfer in which case inheritance tax will be charged (subject to tapering relief). It may be wise to insure against the risk of death in this period. The advantage of saving inheritance tax may be outweighed by capital gains tax considerations.

**21.11**

### Inheritance tax

In deciding when an *inter vivos* gift is advantageous for inheritance tax purposes the donor should remember that because of the existence of the nil rate band, one large estate attracts a greater liability to tax than two small ones. For example, in tax year 1990/91 an estate of £258,000 will attract £52,000 in tax on death (assuming no chargeable *inter vivos* transfers have been made within seven years). However, two estates of £129,000 will attract only £400 each (again assuming nil lifetime cumulative totals).

**21.12**

Where one party to a marriage owns substantially more property than the other, it may be advisable for that party to consider making *inter vivos* gifts to the other. Then in the event of both parties to the marriage dying at or about the same time they can each leave their estates to their children obtaining the benefit of two nil rate bands. There will not be any tax saving if the spouses equalise their estates but the first to die leaves his or her entire property to the other. However, it may be that one spouse *needs* to leave his or her estate to the surviving spouse to ensure that the survivor has sufficient funds.

There is an advantage in making potentially exempt transfers of assets which are likely to increase in value over the next few years. Inheritance tax in the event of the transferor's death is calculated on the value of the property at the time the gift is made, not on its value at the time of death. Thus, the value of the property is effectively "frozen" and less inheritance tax will be payable. This value "freezing" will not occur if the donor continues to derive a benefit from the property given away. In such a case the reservation of benefit rules will apply and the property will be treated for inheritance tax purposes as part of the deceased's estate on death (see paragraph 4.9).

*Capital gains tax*

21.13   In view of the fact that capital gains tax is not paid on death and the donor acquires the property at its market value at death, *inter vivos* gifts are apparently less advantageous. However, the exemptions or reliefs (such as the annual exemption, the spouse relief, retirement relief, hold-over relief and indexation allowance) may in many circumstances mean that no capital gains tax is actually payable, so that the gift can be made if other considerations make the disposition advisable.

2. BUSINESS PROPERTY

21.14   The proprietor of a business should give careful consideration to what provisions he wishes to make for the continuation of the business after his death. It will often be necessary to make provision *inter vivos* and not by will. For example, if the business is run through a company consideration should be given to the possible alteration of the articles so as to provide for the company purchasing its own shares and/or for rights of pre-emption in respect of these shares. If the business is a partnership some provision should be made for succession to the deceased partner's interest by the remaining partners or by the deceased partner's relatives or for the realisation of the value of the interest when the partner dies or retires.

In making such arrangements taxation must be taken into account. It is important to realise, however, that a tax effective disposition should not be made if it conflicts with more general commercial considerations.

Business property is favourably treated for tax purposes. A gift of a business or an interest in a business is eligible for inheritance tax business property relief (see paragraph 4.30) which may in itself produce a large saving in the tax payable. However, planning in advance may produce further savings. Provision may be made in a partnership agreement for automatic accrual of goodwill. This means that when a partner dies his interest in the goodwill passes automatically to the other partners. Clearly this automatic accrual reduces the partner's interest in the goodwill and the value of his estate on death. To the extent that consideration in money or money's worth was given for the accrual clause, the entry into the clause will not be a transfer of value for inheritance tax purposes. There may be some difficulty in showing that consideration was given for such an accrual clause in the case of a family partnership. However, an estate duty case (*Att-Gen.* v. *Boden* (1912)) which is generally considered still to be relevant, held that an agreement to work for the business is consideration in money or money's worth.

An option granted (for money or money's worth) to purchase goodwill at a fixed price may also give rise to a tax saving. The value of the goodwill to the partner on death is the price that his estate will be paid on the exercise of the option. An agreement that a partner's share *must* be purchased on his death is not advisable as the Inland Revenue argues that this contract of sale may disentitle the deceased partner to the business property relief (Statement of Practice 12/80 October 13, 1980).

If a business is to be run as a company then, when the company is formed consideration should be given to the possibility of providing pre-emption rights. These are rights whereby when one shareholder disposes of his shares, or dies owning these shares, the other shareholders are given a right to buy at a price fixed by or to be fixed in accordance with the company's articles of association. Such a pre-emption right is an option so that the same considerations apply as in the case of a partner's option to purchase goodwill.

# D. Why Make a Will?

There are a number of reasons why solicitors often advise clients to make wills.

## 1. TO AVOID THE APPLICATION OF THE INTESTACY RULES

As was explained in Chapter 3, the property of a person who dies without making a will, passes according to a strict legal

**21.15**

order. A person who dies intestate, therefore, has no control over who are to be the recipients of his estate and so cannot benefit friends or charities without making a will. Persons who are married will usually want their property to pass to their spouses but it is only in the case of small estates that the whole of the property will pass to the surviving spouse under the intestacy rules. If the estate is larger and the deceased is survived by a spouse and issue, the intestacy rules which leave the spouse personal chattels, a statutory legacy of £75,000 and only a life interest in one half of the residue may be unacceptable. Although the spouse may be able to capitalise the life interest, a portion of the estate will still go to the children and the spouse may have insufficient funds to maintain an existing standard of living. While a variation (see Chapter 19) may in some cases provide a solution it is clearly more desirable to prevent the problem ever arising. A beneficiary who is under 18 cannot give up an interest in an estate; a parent or guardian cannot do so on behalf of a minor.

The solicitor should, therefore, suggest making a will since otherwise clients cannot ensure that their wishes as to the disposition of their property will be respected. (A solicitor should inform a client that in certain circumstances a relative or other dependant might be able to claim under the Inheritance (Provision for Family and Dependants) Act 1975).

Even though a client is satisfied with the general disposition of property under the intestacy rules, if he wants to ensure that a particular item is to pass to one of the people specified in the intestacy rules, this can be only done by will.

Furthermore, clients may wish to demonstrate expressly that they are happy for their property to pass to the persons who would be entitled under the intestacy rules by making a will in their favour.

## 2. APPOINTMENT OF PERSONAL REPRESENTATIVES AND TRUSTEES

**21.16**  In a will, a testator can make a choice of executors and trustees, whereas on intestacy the personal representatives are determined by Rule 22 of the Non-Contentious Probate Rules 1987 (see paragraph 8.16). If a will is made, it is possible for the testator to choose persons who are suitable and who are likely to be willing to act.

Since an executor's authority dates from death, whereas an administrator's dates only from the grant of representation, the appointment of an executor may facilitate the administration of the estate.

### 3. APPOINTMENT OF TESTAMENTARY GUARDIANS

Testators are often concerned to provide appropriate care for their children. A solicitor should explain that guardians can be appointed in the will. These guardians can act jointly with the surviving spouse or alone if the children are orphaned. It is advisable to include an express appointment since this will ensure that the testator gives thought to whom to appoint. A solicitor should advise a client who proposes to appoint a guardian to consult the prospective guardian as to whether or not he or she is willing to act. The question of finance for the guardian should be considered. Guardians are dealt with more fully in paragraph 22.16.

**21.17**

### 4. EXTENSION OF STATUTORY POWERS

If a will is made, additional powers can be conferred on personal representatives and trustees which will facilitate the administration. These powers are considered in Chapter 22.

**21.18**

### 5. DIRECTIONS AS TO BURIAL AND DISPOSAL OF BODY

If the testator has special wishes as to burial or cremation these can be included in the will.

**21.19**

Similarly if the testator wishes to donate any part of his body for medical purposes this can be stated in the will. However, simply including in a will a provision to this effect probably will not be effective since the organs will be of little use if there is delay. It is, however, still desirable to include such a clause in the will since it will encourage testators to discuss their wishes with their next of kin so that the next of kin become aware of them and can ensure that such wishes are put into effect without delay. The discussion may encourage the testator to carry a donor card.

### 6. "LIVING WILLS"

Some people are concerned that in old age they may be kept alive by medical intervention at a time when they have lost their mental capacity. It is becoming common for such people to leave a written statement that in the event of a loss of mental capacity they do not wish to be given medical treatment for any life-threatening illness. Such a statement should not be incorporated into a will but should be kept separately. Close relatives should be informed of the existence and whereabouts of the statement.

### 7. TAX CONSIDERATIONS

**21.20** The possible dispositions that can be made are considered in detail in Chapter 22 but the tax advantages to be gained from a carefully drafted will should be drawn to the testator's attention.

The particular circumstances and wishes of the testator must, of course, be paramount in the mind of the solicitor who must not suggest a disposition that is tax-efficient but leaves a beneficiary destitute or that is directly contrary to the desires of the testator.

Assuming the estate is large enough to make tax planning a worthwhile exercise, the solicitor should advise on matters such as the use of the inheritance tax nil rate band to give legacies to non-exempt beneficiaries and the use of survivorship clauses. A survivorship clause will only save tax where the deaths occur within a short space of time. If the survivor outlives the first to die by the period specified in the clause, the property will belong to the survivor and any tax saving may be lost.

# 22. Planning and Drafting a Will

## A. Introduction

### 1. TAKING INSTRUCTIONS

A solicitor who is asked to prepare a will for a client will usually **22.1** find that a personal interview is necessary. The object of the interview is to obtain, in as short a time as possible, all the information which the solicitor needs in order to prepare the will.

It is often helpful to have a "checklist" for taking instructions so that none of the information required is forgotten and no further correspondence or meetings are required. If the checklist is in the form of a questionnaire it may be possible for some other member of the firm to use it to draft the will if necessary.

In appropriate circumstances the solicitor should discuss with the client possible action that can be taken during the client's lifetime to arrange financial and business affairs sensibly. In order that advice can be given on taxation and on the suitability of the proposed dispositions the solicitor should find out what property the client owns and whether there is any property (such as joint property or insurance policies) which will pass independently of the will. The client should also be advised on the effect of any proposed dispositions.

If the testator is married, the solicitor should point out that it is advisable for the testator's spouse to make a will at the same time. The reason for this is that thought can then be given to the ultimate destination of their respective estates.

The solicitor who takes instructions from the client should make a written note (on the questionnaire, if used) of the details of the name and address of the testator, the executor(s), and the beneficiaries and where relevant of any testamentary guardian(s) or trustee(s). He should make sure that he has the correct names of the various people mentioned in the will—this is particularly important in the case of institutions, such as charities.

Where specific items of property are dealt with in the will, a sufficient description is required so that they can be identified. A draftsman should be careful to avoid errors in description which may cause a gift to fail.

### 2. TYPES OF DISPOSITION

**22.2**  Dispositions of property in a will are basically of three types— specific gifts, general legacies and gifts of residue. The testator should be encouraged to think carefully about the purpose of each intended gift. If he wants a particular person to have a particular asset, then a specific gift is likely to be suitable (although he should be warned that the gift will be adeemed if the property is sold or changed in nature). If he wants a particular person to have a fixed amount of money, then a general (pecuniary) legacy is suitable. A residuary gift is likely to be most suitable for the major beneficiary or beneficiaries of the estate. A residuary gift should always be included in a will so as to avoid the possibility of a partial intestacy. For the same reason the testator should consider the possibility that the residuary beneficiary may predecease him and should consider whether he wishes to include a substitutional beneficiary.

The choice of dispositions will largely depend on the testator's family circumstances. The following are among the most common dispositions where a will is made by a married person with children:

(a) *All to spouse.* A will which leaves everything to the testator's spouse will ensure that the surviving spouse is provided for as far as possible. However, the testator has no control over the ultimate destination of the property and must trust the spouse to make appropriate dispositions. There is a danger of accidental disinheritance of children where a surviving spouse remarries without realising that marriage automatically revokes an earlier will. If, because of the size of the estate, inheritance tax is a consideration the following points should be borne in mind:

(i) No tax will be payable on the testator's death (since the spouse exemption is available);

(ii) If the entire estate is given to the surviving spouse the testator will die without having made use of the nil rate band.

(iii) Inheritance tax will be payable on the surviving spouse's death on the whole of the property owned at that time (unless an exemption is available). A relatively large amount of tax may be payable on the surviving spouse's estate since it is likely to include much of the property inherited from the first spouse and yet there will be only one nil rate band available. This problem can be mitigated if the surviving spouse makes *inter vivos* gifts, taking advantage of lifetime exemptions;

(b) *Spouse for life remainder to children.* With this type of disposition the testator retains control over the ultimate destination of the property. However, since the spouse is entitled only to the income from the property, he or she may have insufficient funds available—this problem can be alleviated if the trustees are given power to advance or lend capital to the surviving spouse.

The inheritance tax consequences are virtually the same as in the case of an outright gift (since the surviving spouse has an interest in possession in the settled property and the spouse exemption is therefore available).

(c) *Legacy to spouse, residue to children.* This type of disposition may be appropriate where the testator's spouse is independently wealthy but should always be viewed with a certain amount of caution. Changed circumstances and/or inflation may make the provision for the surviving spouse by means of a legacy quite inadequate in the future. The spouse exemption for inheritance tax is lost, except to the extent of the legacy, but in the long run there may be a tax saving because of the effect of equalising estates.

(d) *Legacy to children, residue to spouse.* This type of disposition has the advantage of making some provision for the children immediately. The legacy should not, of course, be so large as to leave the surviving spouse with insufficient funds. There may be inheritance tax advantages with this type of gift. The spouse exemption is lost to the extent of the legacy. However, there will be no tax payable until the nil rate band is exhausted. Some provision can, thus, be made for the children immediately without an inheritance tax liability.

3. USE OF PRECEDENTS

Precedents are an invaluable aid to good will drafting. **22.3** Sometimes a precedent may be available which is almost exactly what is required but this is unusual. In all but the simplest cases it is likely that the precedent will have to be substantially amended. Before a precedent can be adapted for use in a particular case the draftsman must ensure that he understands what the precedent was intended to do. For example, if a precedent was designed for use where a complicated settlement is being created it is unlikely to be of much use in drafting a will which makes a straightforward absolute gift of residue. Old precedents should be viewed with some caution since they may deal with problems which are no longer relevant (such as capital transfer tax rules) and may not deal with problems resulting from new law (such as those arising from the introduction of inheritance tax). So that the terminology used in different parts of the will is consistent it is best to use precedents from one particular source as far as possible and to take care when combining two or more precedents.

Wills are traditionally drafted without punctuation. To make reading a little easier it is usual to divide the will into numbered clauses and to capitalise the words which explain what the clause is for (so that clauses making gifts usually contain words such as "I GIVE," clauses appointing an executor usually contain the words "I APPOINT" and clauses containing trusts usually contain the words "UPON TRUST"). Definitions are sometimes very helpful. In particular where several executors or executors and trustees are appointed the words "hereinafter together called 'my Executors' " (or "my Trustees") can be included so that references later in the will can be made to those persons without setting out their names again. Where there is such a definition, it is good practice to capitalise the first letter of the word defined so that the reader can see more readily that the word has been defined (for example, "my Trustee" not "my trustee").

### 4. STRUCTURE OF A WILL

**22.4**    A will usually includes the following:

1.   Words of commencement,
2.   Revocation clause,
3.   Appointment of executors (and trustees and guardians if appropriate),
4.   Specific gifts (if any),
5.   General legacies (if any),
6.   A gift of residue,
7.   Extension of executors' and trustees' powers (if appropriate),
8.   Attestation clause,
9.   A date.

In the rest of this chapter we will consider the drafting of the various parts of the will.

## B. The Formal Parts

Every professionally drafted will should have words of commencement, a revocation clause, a date clause and an attestation clause. For the sake of convenience these "formal parts" are dealt with together in this section.

### 1. COMMENCEMENT

The commencement of the will is intended to identify the person making the will. The testator's full name and address should be included. If the testator is known to own property in a name which is different from his full name or to use a name which is not his true and proper name, it is advisable to refer to this fact in the opening words of the will. The reason for this is that after the testator's death it will be clear that the grant of representation should refer to both names.

22.5

A commonly used form of wording for the commencement of the will is "This is the Last Will and Testament of me [AB] [(also known as [CD])] of [address] [occupation]." If the will is made in expectation of the testator's marriage, it is necessary to incorporate suitable words (see paragraph 2.36).

### 2. REVOCATION CLAUSE

In Chapter 2 we explained that a later will revokes an earlier will to the extent that it is inconsistent. If the later will deals with the testator's entire estate, all earlier wills and codicils are revoked. Nevertheless, for the avoidance of any possible doubt, a revocation clause should be included in all professionally drafted wills, even if the solicitor believes the present will to be the only will the testator has ever made.

22.6

The revocation clause can be included in the commencement of the will but is often set out as a separate clause. (See Wills 1, 2 and 3 in the Appendix).

An appropriate form of wording is "I hereby REVOKE all former wills and testamentary dispositions made by me."

### 3. THE DATE CLAUSE

The date can be included in the commencement of the will, or at the end immediately before the attestation clause. It is more common to include the date at the end.

22.7

The date clause may be important in identifying which of a number of wills was the last or in identifying the subject-matter of a gift. The usual form of words is "IN WITNESS whereof I have hereunto set my hand this     day of     199  ."

## 4. THE ATTESTATION CLAUSE

**22.8** The presence of a correctly drafted attestation clause will in most cases satisfy the registrar that the requirements of Wills Act 1837, s.9 as amended by the Administration of Justice Act 1982 have been complied with. (As was explained in paragraph 10.54 the absence of an attestation clause will lead the registrar to require affidavit evidence to prove due execution under the Non-Contentious Probate Rules 1987, rule 12).

The two most common forms of attestation are as follows:

    (a)   The Short Form.
           "Signed by the above [AB] in our joint presence and then by us in [his/hers]."
    (b)   The Long Form.
           "Signed by the above-named [AB] as [his/her] last will in the presence of us both present at the same time who at [his/her] request in [his/her] presence and in the presence of each other have hereunto subscribed our names as witnesses."

These clauses, implying as they do that the witnesses signed in each other's presence as well as in the presence of the testator, go beyond the strict wording of section 9 as amended but may reduce the possibility of the attestation being challenged after the death.

Where the testator suffers from some disability which would cast doubt on the validity of the will due to the suspected absence of knowledge and approval of the wording of the will, the forms of attestation clause set out above should be amended. The purpose of the amendment is to indicate that the testator did in fact know and approve of the contents of the will.

Thus, if the testator is blind or illiterate or seriously ill the attestation clause should state that the will was read over to him and that he appeared thoroughly to understand and approve its contents.

If someone signs on the testator's behalf, this fact should be stated in the clause together with a confirmation that the will was signed in the presence of, and at the direction of, the testator. The person signing may sign in his or her own name or that of the testator.

Whenever the circumstances are such that, after the testator's death, there may be doubt as to his capacity or as to his knowledge and approval of the contents of the will the solicitor should try to be present and should make a full and careful file note. It is desirable that a medical practitioner be asked to prepare a note of the testator's mental and physical state.

Illustrations of such clauses appear below.

(i) ATTESTATION CLAUSE WHERE SOMEONE SIGNS ON BEHALF OF THE TESTATOR

Signed by [AB] with the name of the above-named [testator] as [his/her] last will in [his/her] presence and by [his/her] direction in the presence of us present at the same time who at [his/her] request in [his/her] presence and in the presence of each other have hereunto subscribed our names as witnesses.

(ii) ATTESTATION CLAUSE WHERE THE TESTATOR IS BLIND (AND SOMEONE SIGNS ON BEHALF OF THE TESTATOR)

Signed by [AB] with the name of the above-named [testator] as [his/her] last will (the will having been first read over to [him/her] when the said [testator] appeared thoroughly to understand and approve the contents thereof) in [his/her] presence and by [his/her] direction in the presence of us present at the same time who at [his/her] request in [his/her] presence and in the presence of each other have hereunto subscribed our names as witnesses.

(iii) ATTESTATION CLAUSE WHERE THE TESTATOR IS ILLITERATE AND SIGNS HIS OR HER MARK

Signed by the above-named [testator] as [his/her] last will with [his/her] mark (the will having been first read over to [him/her] when the said [testator] appeared thoroughly to understand and approve the contents thereof) in [his/her] presence and by [his/her] direction in the presence of us present at the same time who at [his/her] request in [his/her] presence and in the presence of each other have hereunto subscribed our names as witnesses.

## C. Executors and Trustees

When taking instructions for the drafting of the will, the **22.9** testator's wishes must be ascertained as to the persons who will administer the estate (the executors) and who will act as trustees of any trust created under the will.

It is often administratively convenient to appoint the same people to hold both offices, a common form of wording being "I APPOINT [AB] of [address and occupation] and [CD] of [address and occupation] to be the executors and trustees of this my will (hereinafter called 'my Trustees' which expression shall where the context so admits include the trustees for the time being hereof)." The final words are required to make it clear that any powers conferred on the trustees are not personal to the original trustees.

### 1. NUMBER OF EXECUTORS AND TRUSTEES

**22.10**   Any number of executors may be appointed but no more than four may take out the grant in respect of the same property. One executor will always suffice. However, two are often appointed in case one predeceases the testator or dies before completing the administration. Moreover, if the executors are also to be trustees, it is desirable to appoint two since two trustees (or a trust corporation) are required to give a good receipt for capital money.

### 2. THE CHOICE OF APPOINTEES

**22.11**   A testator may appoint an individual, a firm of solicitors, a bank or trust corporation or the Public Trustee. The testator must consider the relative merits of such appointees.

*Individuals*

**22.12**   Testators frequently appoint friends or relatives to act as executors. Such an appointment has the advantage of ensuring the administration is completed by someone of whom the testator has personal knowledge and who will not charge for the work done. A disadvantage may be that the appointee lacks expertise but there is nothing to prevent the appointee taking professional advice. However, the need for such advice may mean that the supposed advantage of cheapness is more apparent than real.

The testator has freedom of choice and so can appoint any person to act, including a bankrupt, a criminal, an infant or a person suffering from a mental or physical disability but there are limitations on who can actually take a grant (see paragraph 8.2).

Further points must be considered when choosing individuals. The most important points are the appointee's ability to cope with the burdens of the office and his willingness to act. A commercially inexperienced person may find the problems of dealing with a complicated estate excessively onerous.

It may be appropriate to appoint a beneficiary as an executor. The beneficiary will have a personal interest in ensuring the estate is properly administered. However, the possibility of a conflict of interest may arise. If the only executor is a specific legatee, there may be a danger that the interests of the residuary beneficiary will be disregarded. Appointing several individuals may lead to disputes if they are unable to agree on the appropriate steps to be taken when dealing with the assets.

No matter how suitable the appointee may seem to be, if he is older than the testator, there is the probability of the executor predeceasing the testator. In this circumstance a substitutional appointment should be included in the will.

*Professional advisers*

The appointment of professional advisers, such as solicitors or accountants, has the advantage of ensuring that the administration is dealt with by experts who, frequently, will have a detailed knowledge of the estate and its assets. Such knowledge, together with their knowledge of estate administration and probate practice, may be invaluable when the estate is complex. The disadvantage of appointing professionals, as compared with individuals, is that the executors will have no personal interest in the estate and will charge for their services.

**22.13**

When appointing solicitors or accountants as executors, although the testator may wish to appoint a particular person to act, problems will arise if that person dies, retires or leaves the firm. For this reason it is usual (subject to the testator's wishes) to appoint the firm to act rather than named individuals.

Unless the will says otherwise, an appointment of a firm of solicitors is construed as an appointment of the partners in the firm at the date the will is made. Since partners may die, retire or leave the firm, it is advisable to provide expressly that appointment is of the partners in the firm at the date of death. It is possible that the firm may change its name or amalgamate with another firm and the testator may wish to consider making provision to cover this possibility. It is usual to express the wish that only two of the partners should take the grant but this is not essential.

A suggested wording for such an appointment is to be found in Will 2, clause 2 and Will 3, clause 2 in the Appendix.

Since executors and trustees (as holders of fiduciary positions) are unable to make a profit from their offices unless expressly authorised, a charging clause must be included in the will.

*Trust corporations—banks*

**22.14** Instead of or in addition to individuals and professional advisers it is possible to appoint corporations sole or trust corporations, such as the trustee department of one of the leading banks.

Banks generally insist that their own standard appointment clause (which incorporates a charging clause) be inserted in the will otherwise they will refuse to act. Such clauses can be readily obtained from any branch. Furthermore, where banks are appointed they often require a sight of the draft will before it is signed.

The banks have scales of charges which the testator may wish to compare with solicitors' fees. The appointment of a corporation may prove expensive since if difficulties arise the corporation may instruct solicitors to act on its behalf with the result that there may be an element of double charging.

*The Public Trustee*

**22.15** The testator can appoint the Public Trustee but the circumstances when the appointment will be appropriate may be limited.

The office was created (by the Public Trustee Act 1906) to meet the difficulty of finding someone willing and able to act as a trustee. He can refuse to accept any trust (except on the ground that it is too small) and he cannot accept the appointment if the trust is solely for religious or charitable purposes. He will not normally accept an appointment which would involve the management of a business.

The Public Trustee can act either alone or jointly with others. (If sole trustee, he is empowered to deal with land.)

The appointment has some advantages:

(1) The Public Trustee is a corporation sole and so has a permanent existence independent of the office holder.
(2) The State is liable for loss caused by breach.

A fee will be charged for the service and this will have to be compared with the fees a solicitor would charge.

The disadvantage of the appointment is that the Public Trustee will know nothing of the estate or its beneficiaries prior to the appointment and the fees may be higher than those of a solicitor.

## D. Guardians

Testators with minor children should consider who will have the    **22.16**
care of any minor children who survive them.

If the will is silent, the Guardianship of Minors Act 1971, s.3
provides that the surviving spouse will be the guardian of the
children.

This may be entirely satisfactory but in certain circumstances
(for example, where the spouse suffers from a disability) it may
be advisable to appoint, in the will, a guardian to act jointly
with the survivor after the death of the testator. The power to
do this is given by the Guardianship of Minors Act 1971, s.4.

In many cases the testator will want to appoint a guardian to
act only after the death of the surviving spouse. Strictly
speaking, the 1971 Act gives no power to appoint a guardian to
act after the surviving spouse dies but, nevertheless, this is, in
practice, frequently done. Such an appointment is a useful
indication of the wishes of the testator should the court find it
necessary to exercise its overriding jurisdiction to appoint
guardians (given by the Guardianship of Minors Act 1971,
ss.5–7). Furthermore, it may prevent a dispute with the
testator's family over who is to look after the children.

An appropriate form of words is "I APPOINT [AB] of
[address] and [CD] of [address] to be the guardians [jointly
with/after the death of] [my husband/wife] of any of my children
who may then be minors." (See Will 2, clause 3 in the
Appendix).

When a testator is considering appointing guardians, the
appointees should be consulted to ensure that they are willing to
act. He should also be made aware that the court has an
overriding jurisdiction.

Where testamentary guardians are appointed consideration
should be given to the additional expense the guardians will
incur. It is common to make them trustees (either alone or
jointly with the professional executors) of a trust fund for the
benefit of the children. In such a case the powers of trustees will
have to be amended to suit the circumstances.

Although sections 31 and 32 of the Trustee Act 1925 permit
the income and capital of a trust fund to be made available for
the benefit of the children, testators might wish to make express
provision in the will. For example, power could be given to the
trustees to allow the trust's capital to be used for the purchase
of a larger house for the guardians and the children to live in.
The capital could be lent to the guardians at a low rate of

interest, alternatively the money could be used to help fund a purchase of the property in the joint names of the guardians and the trust fund.

# E. Specific Gifts and General Legacies

### 1. INTRODUCTION

**22.17** When drafting specific gifts and general legacies, the draftsman must consider both the nature of the legacy and the status of the beneficiary (for example, particular problems may arise where the beneficiary is a charity or a minor).

### 2. SPECIFIC GIFTS

**22.18** A specific gift is one the wording of which distinguishes the gifted property from all other property belonging to the testator at the date of death.

*Section 24 of the Wills Act 1837*
**22.19** Section 24 provides that, as regards property, the will "speaks from death" unless it expresses a contrary intention. The use of the word "my" coupled with a specific item (for example "my piano") is often construed as showing such a contrary intention. However, if the word "my" is followed by a description of property capable of increase or decrease, this is not usually construed as contrary intention so that, for example, a gift of "my collection of Dresden china" would be construed as a gift of the whole collection at the date of death.

*Drafting specific gifts*
**22.20** The solicitor should take great care to ascertain the testator's wishes. The testator may wish to give a particular item owned at the date the will is made or may wish to give any item which corresponds to a particular description owned at the date of death.

If the testator wishes to give a particular item owned at the date of the will, the property must be carefully identified.

This may be relatively easy where, for example, shares are involved but difficulties can arise where the gift is of personal chattels. Thus, a gift of "my gold ring" may give rise to problems if the testator owned several gold rings. A reference to an insurance valuation may be helpful in identifying the particular ring given.

When taking instructions, the solicitor should explain to the client that a gift of a particular item owned at the date of the will suffers ademption if the item is sold, destroyed or changed in substance. The result of such ademption is that the beneficiary will get nothing. This may or may not be what the testator wishes.

If the testator wants the beneficiary to receive any item owned at the death corresponding to a particular description, suitable wording should be used. An example of such wording is "I give to [AB] any motor car which I own at the date of my death."

In some cases, the testator may wish to give a particular item with a provision for a substitutional gift if that item is sold, destroyed or changed in substance. A suggested wording is "I GIVE to [AB] absolutely my grand piano or any other piano which has replaced it and which I own at the date of my death." Such wording is not desirable where there may be several changes between the making of the will and the death (for example, where a testator makes a gift of shares) as it may prove difficult to identify the replacement assets accurately. In such a case it may be preferable for the testator to include a pecuniary legacy to be given in substitution for the original property, if that property is not owned at the date of death.

*Power to select*
Specific legacies are often made as a way of passing a **22.21**
"keepsake" to a friend or relative. An outright gift of items of property causes no difficulty but if the testator wishes property to be shared between beneficiaries as they choose various matters should be considered:

(a)   the order of selection;
(b)   the insertion of a time limit to avoid the executors' having to wait an unspecified length of time before the beneficiary or beneficiaries make up their minds;
(c)   a procedure for resolution of disputes (for example by the executors);
(d)   a gift over to a substitutional beneficiary in the event of a beneficiary pre-deceasing or the beneficiaries failing to choose all the items, as the case may be;
(e)   a limit on the value of items selected.

Selection clauses are included in Will 1, clause 6 and Will 2, clause 5 in the Appendix. The latter clause avoids problems by giving the personal representative an overriding discretion as to the distribution.

The testator may give to *one* beneficiary the right to select such items as he chooses. In this case paragraph (a) above will not be relevant.

*Mortgage, expenses and inheritance tax*

**22.22**    (a) *Mortgage.* Where a gift is made of property which was charged during the testator's lifetime with a mortgage or other debt the Administration of Estates Act 1925, s.35 provides that the property passes to the beneficiary subject to that debt unless the will provides otherwise. The effect of section 35 should, therefore, be explained to the testator so that if he wishes the beneficiary to take the property free of the debt suitable wording can be included. An example of such wording is given in Will 1, clause 4 in the Appendix. The solicitor should remember that in the case of a mortgage, a mortgage protection policy may have been taken out by the testator. The solicitor should, therefore, enquire whether or not such a policy exists so that the testator can give thought to the destination of the estate bearing in mind the existence of the policy (see paragraph 15.10).

(b) *Expenses.* Unless the will provides otherwise specific beneficiaries bear any costs of insuring, packing and transporting of property left to them in a will from the time that the assent is made in their favour. This should be explained to the testator who may not wish a specific beneficiary to bear the costs. This is especially likely where the nature of the gift or the circumstances of the beneficiary would result in high insurance or transportation costs being incurred, which the beneficiary might have difficulty meeting.

If contrary provision is made in the will the costs are borne by residue. An example of such wording is given in Will 1, clause 5 in the Appendix.

(c) *"Free of tax."* Whenever the disposition of an estate may give rise to an inheritance tax liability, the testator should consider which beneficiaries should bear the burden. Inheritance tax on U.K. free estate which vests in the personal representatives is usually a testamentary expense borne by undisposed of property or residue unless the will provides otherwise. The draftsman may consider providing expressly that non-residuary gifts are to be "free of tax" so that the question of burden is brought to the testator's attention. The testator can then consider whether the disposition of the estate is suitable having regard to the burden of inheritance tax.

## 3. GENERAL LEGACIES

A general legacy is a gift of property which is not in any way **22.23**
distinguished from property of the same kind (for example, a
gift of "100 shares in ABC Ltd"). If the testator does not own
such property at death, the personal representatives will
purchase property fulfilling the description. Unless there are
special reasons for such a gift, a gift of money is usually more
appropriate.

## 4. PARTICULAR PROBLEMS ARISING FROM PECUNIARY LEGACIES

Particular problems arise where a pecuniary legacy is given to a **22.24**
minor as, in the absence of an express direction, a minor cannot
give a good receipt. (This problem was discussed in paragraph
18.16).

Problems also arise where a pecuniary legacy is given to an
unincorporated association. Such an association has no legal
identity separate from its individual members. Therefore, a
legacy to such an association is construed as a gift to all the
individual members. In the absence of an express provision in
the will the personal representative would have to obtain a
receipt from each individual member of the association. This
would be an onerous and time consuming task and, therefore, it
is advisable to provide that the receipt of the person appearing
to be the treasurer, bursar or other appropriate officer will be
sufficient to give the personal representatives a good discharge.

The words "appearing to be" are used so that the personal
representatives do not have to enquire whether the appointment
of the treasurer etc. was properly made. (See Will 3, clause 8 in
the Appendix).

When drafting a gift to an unincorporated association, the
draftsman, having taken appropriate instructions from the
testator, should ensure that:

(a)   the association is in existence;
(b)   the association is correctly identified;
(c)   provision is included to cover a change of name,
change of objects, the amalgamation of the association
with another similar body or the dissolution of the
association prior to the testator's death.

Where a gift is left to a charity which ceases to exist during
the lifetime of the testator, the gift will not lapse but will be
applied *cy-près* provided the testator showed a general
charitable intention. If this is in accordance with the testator's

wishes it may be desirable to include words clearly showing a general charitable intent, for example, "To X association for its general charitable purposes." It is important to check whether any particular institution has charitable status.

## F. Gifts of Residue

**22.25**  Once the formal parts of the will and any specific or pecuniary legacies have been drafted, it is necessary to consider the drafting of the clause or clauses disposing of residue. The main objective of the draftsman in drafting such clauses is to ensure that the residue of the estate goes to the testator's intended beneficiaries. This will include consideration of whether substitutional beneficiaries should be included in case a primary beneficiary fails to achieve a vested interest and whether a survivorship provision is required. The draftsman should also consider how best to deal with the payment of debts and expenses (which will usually be paid out of residue).

### 1. PAYMENT OF DEBTS

**22.26**  The rules as to payment of debts of the estate were considered in Chapter 15 where we saw that, unless there is undisposed of property, unsecured debts are, in most circumstances, payable out of residue. This will usually comply with the testator's wishes but, even so, it is usual to make express provision in a professionally drawn will. One way in which this is commonly done is by making the residuary gift subject to the payment of debts and other expenses.

For example, "I GIVE all the rest and residue of my estate both real and personal SUBJECT TO the payment of my debts, funeral expenses and testamentary expenses unto [AB] of [address]."

Another way in which payment of debts can be provided for is by creating a trust for sale, the first object of which is the payment of debts (there are a number of other reasons why a trust for sale may be desirable—see below).

For example, "I GIVE all the rest and residue of my estate both real and personal unto my Trustee UPON TRUST for sale with full power to postpone sale and after payment thereout of my debts funeral expenses and testamentary expenses to hold the balance (and any parts of my estate for the time being unsold) UPON the following TRUSTS ... "

Where a debt of the estate is charged during the deceased's lifetime on specific property it will be payable out of that property unless the will shows a contrary intention (Administration of Estates Act 1925, s.35). Clauses, such as those above which deal with the payment of debts generally, are not sufficient to require charged debts to be paid out of residue. If the intention is that charged debts should be paid out of residue then words such as "including any debts charged on specific property" should be added after the word "debts" in the clauses above.

## 2. PAYMENT OF PECUNIARY LEGACIES

The rules as to property available for payment of pecuniary **22.27** legacies are considered in Chapter 16. They are complicated and, in order to avoid possible problems, it is desirable to direct that residue be held on trust for sale and proceeds used to pay debts *and legacies*. This has the effect of making realty available proportionately with personalty under the rule in *Roberts* v. *Walker*. It also ensures that, in cases where residue has been left to two or more persons equally and one has predeceased (with the result that part of the residue is undisposed of), it is clear that legacies are to be paid before the residue is divided into shares. This avoids the possibility of costly disputes between residuary beneficiaries and the persons entitled to the testator's undisposed of property.

## 3. TRUST FOR SALE

Personal representatives have power to sell the assets of the **22.28** estate both at common law and by statute (principally the Administration of Estates Act 1925, s.39) for the purposes of administration. It is not necessary to include an express trust for sale when drafting a residuary gift. It is, however, very common to include an express trust for sale because:

(i)   this is one method of providing expressly for the payment of debts;

(ii)  it is similarly one way to provide expressly for the payment of legacies; and

(iii) where a gift of residue creates successive or contingent interests a trust for sale prevents the creation of an unwanted strict settlement in relation to any land in the estate.

As with any other drafting problem the draftsman should consider carefully whether a trust for sale is necessary in each particular case. It is usually advisable to include a trust for sale where there are successive interests, where a minority may arise (whether because a primary beneficiary is a minor or because there is a substitutional gift to a minor which may come into effect) and where the draftsman wishes to avoid the creation of a strict settlement. A trust for sale is inadvisable where residue is given to one person and the testator wishes that person to enjoy the actual assets of the estate *in specie.* In other cases it does not really matter whether a trust for sale is included or not.

If a trust for sale is included a power to postpone is essential. (For an example of a gift of residue on trust for sale see Will 2, clause 7 in the Appendix).

### 4. ABSOLUTE GIFT OF RESIDUE TO ONE PERSON

**22.29**  Where the residue is to be given to one person absolutely, the drafting of the will is quite straightforward. It is usual to describe the gift as a gift of "all my real and personal property whatsoever and wheresoever not hereby or by any codicil hereto specifically disposed of" or of "all the rest and residue of my estate." The draftsman should consider whether to make a substitutional gift so as to prevent an intestacy if the intended residuary beneficiary predeceases and whether to include a survivorship clause (see paragraph 22.34 below).

### 5. ABSOLUTE GIFT OF RESIDUE TO MORE THAN ONE PERSON

*Named beneficiaries*

**22.30**  If the residue is to be divided between two or more persons in equal shares the following form may be used "My Trustee shall hold all the rest and residue of my estate UPON TRUST for [names] in equal shares." If the shares are to be unequal the simplest technique is to divide the residue into a suitable number of equal parts and to say how many parts each beneficiary is to get.

Where residue is given "equally" or "in equal shares" and any of the residuary beneficiaries predecease, there will be a partial intestacy. It is, therefore, desirable to add words giving the lapsed share to the surviving beneficiaries or words making a substitutional gift of that share (for example, to the children of the deceased beneficiary). If it is intended that the surviving beneficiaries are to take a larger share suitable wording of the whole clause would be "My Trustee shall hold all the rest and residue of my estate for such of [names] as survive me and if more than one in equal shares."

*Class gifts*

Many gifts of residue to more than one person are gifts to a class of beneficiaries rather than to several named individuals. Most class gifts are gifts to a particular class of relative. The draftsman should explain the class closing rules to the testator and explain that they may artificially exclude certain unborn persons. He should also explain that the exclusion of the class closing rules is possible but may delay final distribution of the estate.

**22.31**

A draftsman should consider carefully whether or not it is desirable to include words expressly limiting class gifts to persons *living at the testator's death*. Where there is an immediate gift to a class (for example, "to my grandchildren") the class closing rules apply (unless excluded). Their effect is that the class will close at the date of the testator's death and will include only those class members living or *en ventre sa mere* at that date (if there are no members living or *en ventre sa mere* at that date the class remains open indefinately). This is likely to accord with the wishes of most testators since, although it will exclude any later born class members, it does allow the benefits of early distribution. Many precedents state expressly that such gifts are to be limited to persons *living at the testator's death*. These words merely restate the relevant class closing rule but it is probably desirable to include them to ensure that the testator is aware of the position.

Where a gift to a class is contingent (for example, "to those of my grandchildren who reach 18") or deferred (for example, "to X for life and then to my grandchildren") the class closing rules apply (unless excluded). Their effect is, broadly speaking (but see Chapter 16 for a fuller discussion), that such a class will remain open until the first class member fulfils the contingency or until the life tenant dies and will include any persons born after the date of the testator's death and before the date of which the class closes. This is likely to accord with the wishes of most testators. Since any distribution is impossible until one person fulfils the contingency or until any life tenant dies there is no point in closing the class until distribution is possible. If the words *living at my death* are included they limit the gift to persons alive or *en ventre sa mere* at the testator's death and exclude any born thereafter. Unless this is an accurate reflection of the testator's wishes it is desirable not to include the words.

Care should also be taken with the definition of the class so as to avoid any ambiguity and so as to comply with the testator's wishes. If the testator says that he wishes to benefit his "cousins," further instructions are needed to establish what degree of relationship is intended. A reference to any class of relative is construed as a reference to the testator's blood relatives only and not to relatives by marriage. Thus, a testator who wishes to benefit "nephews and nieces" should be asked whether the nephews and nieces of his spouse are to be included or only his own nephews and nieces (if the spouse's nephews and nieces are to be included in the gift suitable words must be inserted in the will). Unless contrary provision is made a reference to any class of relative is deemed to include adopted relatives of the testator but not, for example, step-children who have not been adopted. The fact that a person's parents were not married to each other at the time of his birth is irrelevant for the purposes of succession to property unless a contrary intention is expressed in the will.

As with gifts to named beneficiaries the will should make it clear what is to happen to the share of a member of the class who predeceases. A class gift (for example, "to my nieces") is normally construed as a gift to those nieces who survive the testator. There will, therefore, be no question of lapse unless all the members of the class predecease the testator. The testator may wish to include a substitutional clause providing that, if any member of the class predeceases the testator leaving issue who survive the testator, the issue will take *per stirpes* the share which their parent would have taken. In the case of a class gift to *children or issue of a testator* section 33(2) of the Wills Act 1837, as substituted by the Administration of Justice Act 1982, s.19, provides that such a substitution shall take place unless a contrary intention appears by the will. Despite this provision, it is probably desirable to include express words of substitution so that the matter is brought to the testator's attention and so that there can be no doubt as to his wishes. Suitable wording is given in paragraph 22.35.

6. SUCCESSIVE INTERESTS IN RESIDUE

**22.32** The testator may wish to create a life or other limited interest in the residue of his estate. In such a case it is best to include an express trust for sale with power to postpone, the first object of which is to pay debts and legacies. The trustees are then directed to pay income to the life tenant and, subject thereto, to hold the balance for the remainderman. For example "UPON TRUST to pay the income thereof to [name of life tenant] during his lifetime and subject thereto UPON TRUST for [name of remainderman] absolutely."

The life tenant will frequently be the testator's spouse, in which case the testator may wish to ensure that the spouse is entitled to occupy the matrimonial home for life. This can be achieved by making a specific devise of the matrimonial home (so that it is not part of residue), by excluding it from the trust for sale of residue and creating a strict settlement, by including it in the trust for sale but requiring the spouse's consent for sale or by expressing a wish that the trustees should not sell while the spouse wishes to remain in occupation. (This last possibility does not prevent sale since the testator has merely expressed a wish but it is satisfactory where the testator has chosen trustees on whom he can rely to respect the spouse's wishes.)

A testator may wish to give the trustees power to advance or lend capital to the life tenant.

### 7. CONTINGENT INTERESTS IN RESIDUE

A gift of residue, whether to a named beneficiary, a number of named beneficiaries or a class and whether immediate or in remainder, may be contingent on the happening of some event or the satisfaction of some condition. (For example, "To such of my children as survive me and reach 18 or marry under that age"). Wherever the gift is contingent the testator should be asked to decide what is to happen to the income pending the satisfaction of the contingency and what is to happen if the contingency is never satisfied. In the absence of any direction to the contrary the provisions of the Trustee Act, s.31 (as to which see paragraphs 11.14–11.16) will apply in respect of the income. If the contingency is never satisfied the capital and any income which has been added to it will pass as on an intestacy unless there is a substitutional gift.

The effect of the rule against perpetuities should be considered whenever a contingent gift is made. A gift which would vest outside the perpetuity period (a life or lives in being plus 21 years or the statutory period of 80 years) is void. However, the Perpetuity and Accumulations Act 1964 introduced various provisions which mitigate the severity of the rule against perpetuities. Thus, a gift which *might* vest outside the

**22.33**

perpetuity period will not fail at the outset as it is possible to "wait and see"; it is possible where necessary to save a gift to reduce the age at which a gift will vest and/or to exclude members of a class from benefit where otherwise the whole gift would fail. As a result of these provisions problems of perpetuity are much less likely to lead to failure of benefit.

It is always worth remembering that a gift to the testator's *children* contingent on reaching any specified age can never present a perpetuity problem as the children are all lives in being. A gift to a testator's *grandchildren* contingent on reaching a specified age can only present a perpetuity problem if the specified age is greater than 21.

## 8. SURVIVORSHIP CLAUSES

**22.34** A beneficiary who survives a testator by a very short time or who is deemed to survive (under section 184 of the Law of Property Act 1925) will obtain a vested interest in any unconditional gift made to him. Often a testator will want to provide that a beneficiary is not to benefit unless he survives for a reasonable period. This can be achieved by means of a "survivorship clause" which provides that the beneficiary is only to take if he survives the testator for a specified period, if he does not so survive, then a substitutional gift takes effect. Such clauses are particularly common in the case of gifts to spouses (this is because the possibility of death in a common accident is greatest in the case of spouses).

The advantages of a survivorship clause in such a case are:

(i) the testator retains control of the ultimate destination of the property—if there were no such clause the property would pass on the death of the surviving spouse according to the terms of the survivor's will or of the intestacy rules;

(ii) the property of the testator passes to the other beneficiaries rather than to the surviving spouse. This means that the spouse exemption is lost but it also means that there are two estates rather than one for inheritance tax purposes. The rate of tax will, therefore, be reduced overall where each spouse owns a substantial amount of property.

A survivorship clause should never be for more than six months since, if it is for longer, a settlement will be created for inheritance tax purposes and there may as a result be an unnecessary charge to tax. However, the spouse exemption is not lost if the survivorship clause does not exceed 12 months and the spouse does in fact survive to achieve a vested interest.

If there is a survivorship clause in a will, distribution of the estate cannot begin until the primary beneficiary dies (when the substitutional gift takes effect) or until the end of the period (when the primary beneficiary achieves a vested interest). Because of the inconvenience of a long delay, it is usual for survivorship clauses to specify a period of 28 days or one month. (See Will 2, clause 7 in the Appendix).

### 9. SUBSTITUTIONAL GIFTS

When a specific or general legacy lapses the subject-matter "falls into residue" and goes to the residuary beneficiary. When a residuary gift fails, there is, prima facie, a partial intestacy. The draftsman should ascertain the testator's wishes as to the disposition of property in the event of a beneficiary predeceasing or failing to survive for a specified period. The testator may decide that he would rather make a substitutional gift than have the property pass on intestacy. A suitable clause substituting one beneficiary for another if that other predeceases or fails to survive for a specified period is "I GIVE all the rest and residue of my estate to [AB] or if [he/she] shall predecease me or fail to survive for 28 days then to [CD]". **22.35**

Where the primary beneficiary is the spouse of the testator the effect of the Administration of Justice Act 1982, s.18A, must be remembered. In the case of deaths occurring after December 31, 1982, a divorce causes a gift to a spouse to fail. If the will gives residue to the spouse, the residue will pass as undisposed of property unless a substitutional gift can take effect. Unfortunately, many precedents for substitutional gifts were prepared before the 1982 Act and are worded narrowly with the result that the substitutional gift is only to take effect if the spouse *predeceases* or *fails to survive* for a specified period. In order to take account of the effect of section 18A a draftsman can:

(1) state that the substitutional gift is to take effect if the spouse predeceases, fails to survive for a specified period *or if the gift fails for any other reason*; or

(2) include a separate clause in the will stating that in the event of divorce a spouse is to be treated as having predeceased the testator.

Often the most appropriate substitutional beneficiaries are the children of the primary beneficiary. If the gift of residue is to the *testator's* children, the testator may decide that the property be divided amongst the surviving children or he may decide that the share of a deceased child should go to that child's children or remoter issue. If the will is silent, then the Wills Act 1837, s.33 (as substituted) provides that, if a child of the testator predeceases leaving issue who survive the testator, the issue take the share that their parent would have taken.

Despite section 33 it is advisable to include an express substitutional gift so that the testator is given an opportunity to consider whether or not the clause accords with his wishes. (An *express* substitutional gift is always required if the original gift is to anyone other than a child or issue of the testator). A suitable clause for a substitution of a child by his own issue on the assumption that there is a trust for sale of residue is "My Trustee shall hold the proceeds thereof UPON TRUST for such of my children as are living at my death in equal shares PROVIDED THAT if any child of mine shall predecease me leaving issue living at my death such issue shall take by substitution and if more than one in equal shares per stirpes the share of the said proceeds which such deceased child of mine would have taken if he or she had survived me." (Note that, under this clause issue of a non-marital relationship will take. If the testator wishes to exclude them, express provision must be made). If desired a further substitution providing for the possibility of the testator dying without any living issue may be included. However, in drafting a substitutional clause unnecessary complications arising from the remote possibility of a large number of potential beneficiaries predeceasing the testator should be avoided by advising the testator of the need to make a new will if circumstances change.

## G. Administrative Powers

### 1. INTRODUCTION

**22.36**   As we saw in Chapter 11 personal representatives and trustees have various powers conferred on them by statute which can be excluded, restricted or extended by the will. It is also possible for the will to confer *additional* powers on the personal representatives. We will now list and consider some of the more common extensions and additions. The purpose of including such clauses is to facilitate the administration of the estate and of any trust that may arise under the will.

## 2. COMMON EXTENSIONS TO POWERS OF PERSONAL REPRESENTATIVES

*Power to appropriate assets without consent of beneficiary*

(a) The personal representatives have a power under section 41 of the Administration of Estates Act to appropriate assets in or towards satisfaction of a legacy bequeathed by the deceased or interest under the intestacy rules but must obtain the consent of the beneficiary (or other specified persons as set out in paragraph 11.17). **22.37**

The need for consent led the Revenue to regard such an appropriation as a contract on sale and therefore any instrument effecting the appropriation attracted *ad valorem* stamp duty (*Jopling* v. *I.R.C.* (1940)). However, as a result of the Stamp Duty (Exempt Instruments) Regulations 1987, instruments executed after May 1, 1987 giving effect to appropriations are exempt provided they are certified as falling within the appropriate category of the Schedule to the Regulations. The appropriate category for appropriations is category C or E. The instrument need not be presented to the Stamp Office. The fact that *ad valorem* stamp duty is no longer chargeable might suggest that it is no longer necessary to exclude the requirement for the consent of the beneficiary. However, cautious draftsmen may continue to exclude the requirement as it may be thought to be administratively convenient for personal representatives to be excused from the necessity of obtaining formal consent (even so they would, no doubt, informally consult with the beneficiaries and would be under an obligation to exercise their powers in good faith).

(b) Since an appropriation is in effect a sale of assets to the beneficiary any personal representative who is beneficially entitled to a part of the estate and who makes an appropriation in his own favour will be purchasing estate property. There is authority that this is permissible (*Re Richardson* (1896)) but there remains a possibility that such a purchase might be attacked subsequently as a breach of the equitable rule that a trustee must not profit from his trust. Where personal representatives are beneficially entitled it is, therefore, common to authorise such personal representatives to exercise the power to appropriate in their own favour. (See Will 1, clause 8 in the Appendix).

*Power to insure*

**22.38**    (a) The statutory power to insure assets contained in the Trustee Act, s.19 is limited. It provides that personal representatives and trustees may insure the property for up to three quarters of its value against the risk of *fire* and that premiums are to be paid from income. It is usual to give the personal representatives (and trustees) an express power to insure against all risks, to any amount and to give the trustees a discretion as to whether premiums are paid from income or capital.

(b) It is also usual to provide that the personal representatives (and trustees) are to have a discretion whether to apply any moneys received under an insurance policy in reinstatement of damaged property or as if it was the proceeds of sale of the property. This prevents any possible dispute as to whether or not a beneficiary can *require* the moneys to be used in reinstatement. (See Will 2, clause 8(3) in the Appendix).

*Power to accept the receipt of parent or guardian on behalf of a minor or of the minor at a specified age*

**22.39**    (a) An unmarried minor has no statutory power to give a good receipt for capital or income. A married minor can give a good receipt for income only. The minor's parent, guardian or spouse has no power to give a good receipt on the minor's behalf (see Chapter 18). A testator may, therefore, consider including a clause which expressly authorises the personal representatives to accept the receipt of a minor's parent or guardian (or spouse) and which discharges the personal representatives from further liability in respect of the legacy. This can only be done if the testator is content to allow the legacy to pass into the hands of the parent or guardian (or spouse). (See Will 1, clause 7 in the Appendix).

(b) There is a statutory power under section 42 of the Administration of Estates Act for the personal representatives to appoint trustees to hold a legacy for a minor who is *absolutely* entitled but this does not apply if the minor has only a contingent interest. There is no reason why the testator should not expressly authorise the personal representatives to appoint trustees in such a case.

(c) The testator may authorise the minor to give a good receipt at a specified age, for example 16.

(d) Alternatively, the will may direct the personal representatives to purchase a suitable investment (perhaps National Savings Certificates) in the name of the minor.

*Exclusion of the Apportionment Act 1870 and the common law rules on apportionment*
As we saw in Chapters 16 and 18, the Apportionment Act 1870 **22.40** requires that "rents, annuities, dividends and other periodical payments in the nature of income ... shall, like interest on money lent, be considered as accruing from day to day" and shall be apportioned accordingly. Interest has to be apportioned under the common law rules. The trouble and expense involved in the calculations is usually thought to outweigh any benefits to the beneficiaries. As a result, in cases where the apportionment of income would otherwise be necessary (that is, where a will gives an income-producing asset to one person, residue to another) the Act and the common law rules are frequently excluded. The effect of exclusion is that all income paid to the personal representatives after death is treated as income of the estate for *distribution* purposes even though some or all of it may be attributable to the period before death. (See Will 2, clause 8(5) in the Appendix).

*Power to carry on a business of the deceased*
As we saw in Chapter 11 the powers of personal representatives **22.41** to run a business carried on by the deceased as a sole trader are limited. It is, therefore, usual in cases where a testator is a sole trader to provide that personal representatives may:

(a)  continue to run the business for as long as they see fit,
(b)  use such assets of the estate as they see fit.

(A specimen clause is set out below).

"I DIRECT that my Trustees shall have power to carry on my business of [nature of business] for so long as they shall in their absolute discretion think fit and they shall have power to use any assets employed in the said business at the date of my death together with any assets comprised in my Residuary Estate I DECLARE that my Trustees shall have the same powers to carry on the said business as if they were absolute owners thereof without being personally liable for any loss that may arise I FURTHER DECLARE that in the event of my business being carried on at a loss my Trustees shall be reimbursed for any loss they suffer from my Residuary Estate."

It is most desirable that a sole trader should consider and make provision for the running of a business after his death, perhaps by taking in partners or by incorporation of the business during his lifetime. Such matters should certainly be discussed when drafting a will for a sole trader. The question of personal representatives should also be carefully considered. It is usually difficult to find a professional person who is willing to accept the office of personal representative where this would involve the running or supervision of a business. Where the business is to be transferred to a beneficiary it may be helpful to appoint that beneficiary either as a general personal representative or as a special personal representative to deal only with the business.

Where a client is a partner in a business or runs a business through the medium of a limited company it is desirable to discuss with the client what provisions if any have been included in the partnership agreement or Articles of Association to deal with death. Matters which should be considered are whether persons surviving the deceased should have options to purchase the interest of a deceased partner/shareholder and what financial arrangements should be made for the dependants of the deceased.

### 3. COMMON EXTENSIONS TO POWERS OF TRUSTEES

**22.42** These extensions should be considered where a will creates a trust initially (for example by leaving property to a spouse for life) or where a trust may arise if a beneficiary predeceases the testator (for example "to my spouse absolutely but if he does not survive me by 28 days for such of our children as may reach the age of 25"; even if all the testator's children are over 25 at the time the will is drafted a trust may still arise if a child predeceases and is replaced by issue).

*Power to invest*

**22.43** (a) We saw in Chapter 11 that the powers of investment enjoyed by trustees under the Trustees Investment Act 1961 are limited and that the administrative requirements of the Act are rather complicated. It is, therefore, common to give trustees an express power of investment. The usual type of clause authorises them to invest at their discretion in any investment as if they were sole absolute beneficial owners. (See Will 2, clause 8(1) in the Appendix). Despite the wide wording trustees are still required as a matter of general law to exercise their power with reasonable prudence and to act honestly; moreover, the

Trustee Investments Act, s.6(1) provides that trustees must when exercising a power of investment have regard to the following matters:

(i)   the need for diversification of investments; and
(ii)  the suitability of investments of the type proposed and of the particular investment as an example of the type.

(b) Even the widest *investment* clause will not authorise trustees to purchase property for purposes other than investment and if, therefore, a testator wishes to confer such a power on trustees (for example to purchase a house as a residence for a beneficiary), an express clause authorising such a purchase must be included. (See paragraph 22.44 below and Will 2, clause 8(2) in the Appendix).

*Power to purchase house as a residence for a beneficiary*
Trustees of personalty do not have any statutory power to buy land. However, capital money under the Settled Land Act 1925, s.73(1) may be applied in the purchase of land in fee simple or leaseholds with at least 60 years to run and the same powers of investment are enjoyed by trustees for sale of land (Law of Property Act 1925, s.28(1)); however, *Re Wakeman* (1945) suggests that if trustees for sale of land sell all the land they are holding, even if they intend to buy more land immediately, they will lose their statutory power to buy land. (*Re Wellsted's Will Trusts* (1949) does, however, cast some doubt on this). Thus, if a testator wishes trustees for sale to have power to purchase land *as a residence* for a beneficiary, it is advisable to include an express clause to this effect even if they are trustees for sale of land. (See Will 2, clause 8(2) in the Appendix). As explained in paragraph 22.45 it is not sufficient for this purpose to give trustees a wide power of *investment* as this will not authorise the purchase of land for other purposes such as residence.

Where trustees have exercised such a power they would normally be responsible for the burden of repairs and other outgoings. The testator may prefer to leave the question of the burden of repairs to the discretion of the trustees who can then take into account the financial position of beneficiaries after the testator's death and if they think it appropriate require the occupying beneficiary to be responsible for the repairs.

*Power to advance capital to beneficiaries with a vested or contingent interest in capital*
We saw in Chapter 11 that trustees have a statutory power under section 32 of the Trustee Act 1925 to advance capital to

**22.44**

**22.45**

beneficiaries with a vested or contingent interest *in capital,* but that it is subject to the following three limitations:

(a) No more than one half of the beneficiary's vested or presumptive interest can be advanced.

(b) Any advances must be brought into account when and if the beneficiary becomes absolutely entitled.

(c) Any person with a prior interest (for example the right to receive income from the trust property) must be in existence, of full age and must consent in writing to the advance.

It is common to give the trustees wider powers of advancement by excluding some or all of the limitations listed above and giving them power to advance in their absolute discretion. (See Will 2, clause 8(4) in the Appendix). The case of *Henley* v. *Wardell* (1989) illustrates the need for careful drafting. A will enlarged the powers conferred by section 32 "so as to permit my trustees in their absolute and uncontrolled discretion to advance ... the whole ... of any ... share. ... " The trustees made advances without the consent of the life tenant arguing that as they had an "absolute" and "uncontrolled" discretion such consent was unnecessary. It was held that the only purpose of the enlargement of trustees' powers was to permit the advancement of "the whole" of a share and that the wording was not sufficient to do away with the need for consents. It is important, therefore, in cases where there is a prior interest and reference is made to enlarging the statutory power expressly to exclude the need for consent. For example, in such a case the clause should include the words:

" ... without the need to secure the consent of any person with a prior interest."

Such an advance will not attract inheritance tax if the settlement is a qualifying accumulation and maintenance settlement under the Inheritance Tax Act 1984, s.71 although it may do so if the settlement is not. There will be a disposal for capital gains tax purposes if assets are advanced *in specie* or if assets are sold to raise cash for the advancement.

A testator may also wish to include an express power authorising trustees to *lend* money to beneficiaries on whatever terms they think fit.

*Power to advance capital and make loans to life tenants*

**22.46** The statutory power to advance capital to beneficiaries is only available where beneficiaries have an interest in capital. There is no statutory power to advance capital to a life tenant. Neither is there a statutory power to *lend* capital to a life tenant. A testator, who is proposing to leave property to a person for life, may wish to give the trustees a power to advance or lend capital to the life tenant in case the life tenant finds the income insufficient. (See Will 3, clause 7(4) in the Appendix). This is particularly likely where a testator proposes to leave a life interest to a spouse.

Advances and loans to a life tenant will have no inheritance tax effect since the life tenant is already treated as the owner of the underlying trust assets. Such payments may, however, amount to disposals for capital gains tax purposes (as in paragraph 22.45).

If advances are made regularly to a life tenant for the purposes of supplementing income there is a danger that they will be regarded as "annual payments" for the purposes of income tax and will have to be grossed up and included on the life tenant's income tax return as part of total *income*. This danger can be avoided to some extent if the advances are made irregularly. Alternatively, there will be no danger if the payments are treated as loans repayable on death.

*Power to apply income for maintenance, education or benefit of minor beneficiaries*

**22.47** We saw in Chapter 11 that trustees have power under the Trustee Act 1925, s.31 to apply available income to the maintenance, education or benefit of minor beneficiaries and that to the extent that they do not, such income must be accumulated. If the beneficiary reaches the age of 18 and his interest is still contingent the discretion ceases and the trustees must pay the income to the beneficiary until the interest vests or fails.

(a) Section 31(1) provides that the trustees may apply the whole of the income or such part as may in all the circumstances be reasonable; they are required to have regard to the age of the minor and his requirements and generally the circumstances of the case and in particular to what other income, if any, is applicable for the same purpose; where trustees have notice that the income of more than one fund is applicable for these purposes, then so far as practicable unless the entire income of the funds is paid or applied as aforesaid or the court otherwise directs, a proportionate part only of the income of each fund shall be so paid or applied. These provisions are sometimes varied to give the trustees an unfettered discretion to apply income as they see fit. A specimen clause is included in Will 3, clause 8(7) in the Appendix.

(b) The provision that a beneficiary who attains the age of 18 is to be *entitled* to income at 18 even though his interest in capital is still contingent is sometimes excluded or postponed to a later age. One reason for this is that once a beneficiary becomes entitled to income the beneficiary is treated for inheritance tax purposes as the owner of the underlying trust assets even if his interest in capital is merely contingent. Thus, should the beneficiary die after becoming entitled to income an appropriate portion of the trust assets will be included in his estate for the purposes of calculating inheritance tax. The inheritance tax attributable to the trust fund will be borne by the trust fund and will reduce the trust assets available to surviving beneficiaries of the trust; the inclusion of the trust property in the estate of the deceased beneficiary will increase the *rate* of inheritance tax payable on the deceased beneficiary's estate and will reduce the assets of the estate of the deceased beneficiary available for distribution.

When excluding the proviso to section 31 the draftsman must remember that if the trust is to be a qualifying accumulation and maintenance settlement under section 71 of the Inheritance Tax Act 1984 he must ensure that the beneficiaries will become entitled to the capital or income before reaching age 25. (A suitable specimen clause is shown below).

Section 31 Trustee Act 1925 will have effect as regards the income arising from my Residuary Estate as if:

(a) the words in subsection 1(i) "as may, in all the circumstances, be reasonable" were deleted and in their place the words "as my Trustess shall in their absolute discretion think fit" were substituted.

(b) the words from "Provided that" to the end of subsection 1 were deleted.
I FURTHER DIRECT that during the period of twenty-one years from my death the statutory powers of maintenance and accumulation shall continue to be exercisable by my Trustees in favour of any child or remoter issue of mine who has reached the age of 18 but not yet attained a vested interest in the capital of my Residuary Estate.

The draftsmen should also be aware of the capital gains tax implications of removing the right to income at 18. If the beneficiary becomes entitled to both income and capital at 25 the settlement continues as an accumulation and maintenance trust until the end of its life; thus, holdover relief will be available when the beneficiary becomes absolutely entitled to the capital assets. This would normally be regarded as an advantage. However, so far as the beneficiary has no right to receive income, the trust income will be subject to the additional rate of income tax and therefore all gains realised by the trustees will be taxed at 35 per cent., rather than 25 per cent.

*Exclusion of the Apportionment Act 1870 and the common law rules on apportionment*
We have already explained in paragraph 22.40 above that it is usual to exclude the need to apportion for the purposes of distribution of the estate on the death of a testator. However, the duty to apportion does not arise only on the death of a testator. If a trust is created in favour of a person for life, the duty arises on the death of the life tenant. Similarly, if there is a trust in favour of those members of a class who fulfil a contingency, a need to apportion arises whenever an additional member joins the class (for example, by birth or whenever an existing member leaves the class either by attaining a vested interest or by dying before reaching a specified age (*Re Joel's Will Trusts* (1967)). It is, therefore, most important that any clause intended to exclude the duty to apportion is drafted sufficiently widely to exclude it not merely on the death of the testator but on any other occasion where it would otherwise apply. The specimen clause contained in Will 2, clause 8(5) in the Appendix is intended to have this effect. **22.48**

*Exclusion of the equitable rules as to apportionment*
We saw in Chapter 18 that where residuary personalty is left to persons in succession there is an obligation under the rule in *Howe* v. *Lord Dartmouth* (1802) to sell wasting, hazardous and unauthorised assets together with reversionary interests and non-income producing assets; where such an obligation arises the personal representatives will be under a duty to apportion between life tenant and remainderman any income received pending sale from assets in the first category and to apportion the proceeds of sale of assets in the second category between life tenant and remainderman. Similarly under the rule in *Allhusen* v. *Whittell* (1867) where residue (real or personal) is left to persons in succession outgoings must be treated as paid partly from capital and partly from the income accruing from **22.49**

that portion of capital from the testator's death to the date of payment of the outgoings. It is extremely common to exclude these rules so as to avoid the need for complex calculations. The rules do not apply on the death of a life tenant and it is, therefore, unnecessary to exclude them on the death of the life tenant. No similar calculations are required for inheritance tax or income tax purposes. (See Will 3, clause 7(5) in the Appendix).

### 4. POWER TO CHARGE

**22.50**  If the personal representatives or trustees are to have power to charge for their services an express power to that effect must be included (otherwise they can only claim an indemnity for out of pocket expenses). The clause should give power to charge for everything done in connection with the estate whether or not it could be done by a lay person. In the case of a bank or trust corporation the appointment must, in practice, be made in the institution's approved form. A charging clause is a legacy and the will must, therefore, not be witnessed by any individual who is to take the benefit of it (or the spouse of such a person); if a firm is appointed no partner in the firm at the date the will is made (or the spouse of such a partner) should witness it (Wills Act 1837, s.15).

As legacies abate proportionately if there are insufficient funds to pay them in full, it is quite common to provide that the charges of personal representatives and trustees be paid in priority to other legacies. (See Will 2, clause 4 and Will 3, clause 2 in the Appendix).

### 5. INDEMNITY

**22.51**  Personal representatives and trustees have a statutory power to indemnify themselves for expenses incurred in carrying out their powers and duties (Trustee Act 1925, s.30(2)). A testator may wish to extend this to provide that they shall not be liable for any loss resulting from improper investment or from any mistake or omission made in good faith. However, it may be thought inappropriate to include such a clause particularly in the case of professional trustees.

# Appendix

## Introduction

In this appendix we have included various blank forms and specimen wills. We have prepared three relatively straightforward wills each illustrating common types of disposition. In order that the reader may consider what clauses should be included in each will we have listed full details of three imaginary testators, for example, their names, details of their property, their intended beneficiaries and their executors.

We have also used the estates of fictitious testators to illustrate the preparation of the IHT Forms 200 and 202. In order that the reader may consider the form of such documents we have indicated on the list of information provided, which documents have been prepared (in draft) and have included such additional information as is required. The draft documents assume that the application for the grant will be made within six months of the death of each testator.

Any resemblance to real persons, alive or dead, is purely accidental.

Oath for Executors

# IN THE HIGH COURT OF JUSTICE

## Family Division

Extracting Solicitor ............................................................

Address ............................................................

THE PRINCIPAL REGISTRY
IN the Estate of*

deceased.

make Oath and say,                                                              that [A]
believe the paper writing now produced to and marked by
to contain the true and original last Will and Testament
of*
of

formerly of

deceased

who died on the                                          day of                          19   ,
aged                    years      domiciled in
and that to the best of                    knowledge, information and belief there was (?) [no] [B]
land vested in the said deceased which was settled previously to h        death (and
not by h          Will                                                                          )
and which remained settled land notwithstanding h        death
And I/we further make oath and say      that notice of this application has been given to

the executor(s) to whom power is to be reserved, [save

].

And            further make Oath and say                                        [C]
that

Execut

named in the said

and that                will (i) collect, get in and administer according to the law the real and [D]
personal estate                                                          of the said
deceased; (ii) when required to do so by the Court, exhibit on oath in the Court a full inventory
of the said estate
and when so required render an account of the administration of the said estate to the Court;
and (iii) when required to do so by the High Court, deliver up the grant of probate to that Court;
and that to the best of                    knowledge, information and belief

[the gross estate passing under the grant does not exceed      £                    , [E]
and the net estate does not exceed      £                    , and that this is not a case in
which an Inland Revenue Account is required to be delivered]

[the gross estate passing under the grant amounts to £
and the net estate amounts to £                    ].

SWORN by                          the above-named
Deponent

at                                                                                          [F]

this          day of                    19   ,

Before me,

A Commissioner for Oaths/Solicitor.

Oath for Administrators with the Will

# IN THE HIGH COURT OF JUSTICE

Extracting Solicitor

Address

## Family Division

The Principal Registry

IN the Estate of*

deceased

make Oath and say                                                                that [A]
believe the paper writing       now produced to and marked by
to contain the true and original last Will and Testament

of*

of

formerly of

deceased,

who died on the                     day of                              19   .

aged           years    domiciled in

and that              minority and          life interest in the estate of the said
deceased; and that to the best of          knowledge, information and belief there was (⁸) [no]
land vested in the deceased which was settled previously to h     death (and not by [B]
h     Will                                                              ) and which
remained settled land notwithstanding h       death

and             further make Oath and say                                         [C]
that

that

; and that
will (i) collect, get in and administer according to the law the real and personal Estate [D]
of the said deceased;
(ii) when required to do so by the Court, exhibit on oath in the Court a full inventory of the said
Estate,                                    and when so required render an
account of the administration of the said Estate to the Court; and (iii) when required to do so by
the High Court, deliver up the grant of letters of administration with  Will annexed to that Court;
and that to the best of          knowledge, information and belief.

[the gross estate passing under the grant does not exceed      £                , and [E]
the net estate does not exceed      £                , and that this is not a case in which an
Inland Revenue Account is required to be delivered]

(¹⁶) [the gross estate passing under the grant amounts to £
and the net estate amounts to £                         ].
*

SWORN by                     the above-named
Deponent                                                        }
                                                                            [F]
at                                                                }
this           day of              19                             }

Before me,

A Commissioner for Oaths/Solicitor.

Oath for Administrators

# IN THE HIGH COURT OF JUSTICE

## Family Division

Extracting Solicitor ...............................................

Address ...........................................................

The Principal Registry

IN the Estate of*

deceased.

make Oath and say
that*

of

deceased,

died on the                                    day of                          19    .

aged                  years (³) domiciled in                                                      [A]
Intestate

or any other
person entitled in priority to share in h          estate by virtue of any enactment and that
minority                                life interest arises under the intestacy; and
that to the best of          knowledge, information and belief there was    [no] land  [B]
vested in the said deceased which was settled previously to h        death and which remained
settled land notwithstanding h        death

And          further make Oath and say                                                      [C]
that                          the

of the said Intestate,
and that                      will (i) collect, get in and administer according to the law the real and
personal Estate                                                              of the said  [D]
deceased; (ii) when required to do so by the Court, exhibit on oath in the Court a full inventory
of the said Estate
and when so required render an account of the administration of the said Estate to the Court;
and (iii) when required to do so by the High Court, deliver up the grant of letters of administration
to that Court; and that to the best of          knowledge, information and belief

[the gross estate passing under the grant does not exceed      £                      , and the  [E]
net estate does not exceed      £                      , and that this is not a case in which an
Inland Revenue Account is required to be delivered]

[the gross estate passing under the grant amounts to £
and the net estate amounts to £                                    ].

SWORN by                    the above-named
Deponent

at                                                                                              [F]

this          day of                    19

Before me,

A Commissioner for Oaths/Solicitor.

## A2.1   Instruction sheet for Will of Evelyn Worth (Will No. 1)

INTRODUCTION

This is the will of an unmarried person with a small to medium estate. The executors appointed are individuals. Apart from some minor gifts the estate is given to the testatrix's parents with a substitutional gift to a sister.

DETAILS OF TESTATRIX

| | |
|---|---|
| name: | Evelyn Worth |
| address: | Flat 8, |
| | 33 Woodland Gardens, |
| | London, S.W.6. |
| occupation: | Civil Servant. |
| date of birth: | 3rd March, 1959. |

INTENDED BENEFICIARIES

| | |
|---|---|
| sister: | Dr. Annabel Worth |
| | 12 Arundel Street, London, S.W.3. |
| parents: | Colonel Stephen Worth |
| | Doctor Moira Worth |
| | both of 'The Blue House', |
| | Hazlemere, Sussex. |
| godchild: | William Nicholls, |
| | Garden Cottage, Long Wootton, |
| | Lincs. |
| | (age 6). |
| friend: | Philip Markham, |
| | 16 Glebe Street, London, S.W.6. |

DETAILS OF ESTATE

| | |
|---|---|
| flat: | 33 Woodland Gardens (see above) |
| | £80,000 (less mortgage £40,000). |
| chattels: | £5,000 (includes a car (£2,000), a |
| | pair of candlesticks (worth £1,000 see |

|  | below), books (£800) and various items of furniture, other household effects and clothing (£1,200)). |
|---|---|
| money: | £13,000 (in a Building Society Account). |
| pension: | £62,000 is payable at the discretion of trustees (*i.e.* it will not form part of the deceased's estate).<br>Evelyn Worth informed the trustees that they should pay the money to her parents. |
| debts: | Mortgage (see above). Other debts—£750. |

PROPOSED TESTAMENTARY DISPOSITIONS

| minor gifts: | Flat (free of mortgage) to sister. Candlesticks (inherited from grandmother, Lorna Worth) to Philip Markham. Books—to be shared between sister and Markham as they choose. £1,000 to Godchild. |
|---|---|
| residue: | Residue to parents (or survivor if one predeceases), substitutional gift to sister. |
| direction as to body: | Deceased's body is to be available for organ transplants and/or medical research. |
| executors: | Sister and Philip Markham. |

A draft will is shown below.

**A2.2**                    WILL NO. 1

THIS IS THE LAST WILL AND TESTAMENT of me EVELYN WORTH of Flat 8 33 Woodland Gardens, London S.W.6.

1. I HEREBY REVOKE all former wills and testamentary dispositions made by me.

2. I APPOINT my sister Doctor Annabel Worth of 12 Arundel Street London S.W.3. and Philip Markham of 16 Glebe Street London S.W.6. to be my executors.

3. I REQUEST that my body or any part thereof may be used for medical purposes including corneal grafting organ transplantation and medical education or research in accordance with the provisions of the Human Tissue Act 1961.

4. I GIVE to the said Annabel Worth absolutely my leasehold property known as Flat 8 Woodland Gardens free of all taxes[1] and from any mortgage debt or other charge affecting the same which I direct shall be paid out of my residuary estate.

5. I GIVE the pair of Georgian silver candelsticks which I inherited from my grandmother Lorna Worth to the said Philip Markham free of all taxes[1] and all costs of package carriage and insurance incurred for the purposes of giving effect to this gift.

6. I GIVE all the books which I own at the date of my death free of all taxes[1] to the said Annabel Worth and the said Philip Markham equally as they shall choose within three months of my death choosing turn and turn about in the order in which their names appear in this clause each choosing five volumes on each turn.

7. I GIVE to my godchild William Nicholls of Garden Cottage Long Wooton Lincolnshire one thousand pounds (£1,000) absolutely and free of all taxes[1] and I DIRECT that if he has not attained the age of 18 years at the time when the said legacy is payable my executors may pay the said legacy to his parent or guardian whose receipt shall be a full discharge to them.

8. I GIVE my executors power to exercise the powers of appropriation conferred by section 41 of the Administration of Estates Act 1925 without obtaining any of the consents required by that section and even though one or more of them may be beneficially interested.[2]

9. I GIVE all the rest and residue of my estate both real and personal whatsoever and wheresoever SUBJECT TO the payment of my debts and funeral and testamentary expenses (hereinafter called my 'Residuary Estate') unto my parents Colonel Stephen Worth and Doctor Moira Worth of The Blue House Hazlemere Sussex in equal shares absolutely PROVIDED THAT they survive me by 28 days. In the event that either of my parents shall predecease me or fail to survive me by 28 days I GIVE the whole of my Residuary Estate to the survivor absolutely.

If both my parents predecease me or fail to survive me by 28 days but not otherwise than I GIVE my Residuary Estate to the said Annabel Worth absolutely.

IN WITNESS whereof I have hereunto set my hand this     day
of     19

Signed by the said Evelyn Worth   ⎫
in our joint presence and then by  ⎬
us in hers   ⎭

*Note:*

1  It is not necessary to provide that specific and pecuniary legacies should be free of inheritance tax since under Inheritance Tax Act 1984, s.211 inheritance tax on such gifts will be a testamentary expense (unless the will provides otherwise). However, it is desirable to state that such gifts are to be free of tax to ensure that the testator and beneficiaries are aware of the position.

2  This clause is included for administrative convenience.

**A3.1  Instruction sheet for Will of Susan Webster (Will No. 2)**

INTRODUCTION

This is the will of a married person with a medium sized estate. A firm of solicitors is appointed as executors. The estate is given to the testatrix's husband with a substitutional gift to their children.

TESTATRIX

| | |
|---|---|
| name: | Susan Ann Webster |
| address: | 13 Norwich Way, Wanstead London, E11 4PP |
| occupation: | School teacher |
| date of birth: | 14th February, 1947 |

INTENDED BENEFICIARIES

| | |
|---|---|
| husband: | Peter Webster 13 Norwich Way, Wanstead London, E11 4PP |
| children: | David Webster (aged 14) and Karen Webster (aged 12). |

DETAILS OF ESTATE

house:   13 Norwich Way, Wanstead, London, E.11., in joint names with husband. Value £165,000 (net of mortgage £29,000).

chattels:   A car (£7,200), jewellery (£800) and various items of furniture, other household effects and clothing (£1,000).

money:   £500 (approx.) in a building society.

pension:   £69,000 is payable at the discretion of trustees (*i.e.* not part of the deceased's estate).
Susan Webster has asked the trustees to pay the money to her husband.

PROPOSED TESTAMENTARY DISPOSITIONS

minor gifts:   Personal chattels to son and daughter in equal shares subject to husband's power to select such chattels as he wishes.

residue:   Residue to husband absolutely provided he survives by 28 days otherwise to be held on trust for sale for such of the children as reach the age of 21.

executors:   Green & Co., Solicitors of 13, High Street, Wanstead, London, E.11.

trustees:   Green & Co., Solicitors (as above) and Testatrix's Brother, Eric Jameson of 18, Norwich Way, Wanstead, London, E.11.

guardians:   Eric Jameson and his wife, Mary Jameson both of 18, Norwich Way, Wanstead, London, E.11.

funeral:                Cremation desired.

A draft will is shown below.

## A3.2                          WILL NO. 2

THIS IS THE LAST WILL AND TESTAMENT of me SUSAN ANN WEBSTER of 13 Norwich Way Wanstead London E.11.

1. I HEREBY REVOKE all wills and testamentary dispositions heretofore made by me.

2. (a) I APPOINT the partners at the date of my death in the firm of Green & Co. Solicitors of 13 High Street Wanstead London E11 or the firm which at that date has succeeded to and carries on its practice (hereinafter called 'my Executors') to be the executors of this my will. I express the wish that two and only two of them shall prove my will in the first instance.

(b) I APPOINT my proving Executors and my brother Eric Jameson of 18 Norwich Way Wanstead London E.11 (hereinafter together called 'my Trustees' which expression shall include my Trustees for the time being of this will) to be the trustees of this my will.

3. I APPOINT my brother Eric Jameson and his wife Mary Jameson to be the guardians after the death of my husband of any of my children who may then be minors.

4. I DECLARE that any of my Executors or Trustees who are solicitors shall be entitled to charge and be paid without abatement all usual professional or other charges for business done services rendered or time spent by them or their firm in the administration of my estate or the trusts hereof including acts which a trustee who was not a solicitor could have done personally.

5. I GIVE to my husband Peter Webster of 13 Norwich Way aforesaid absolutely such of my personal chattels as defined by section 55(1)(x) of the Administration of Estates Act 1925 as he may within three months after my death select and subject thereto I give the same to my children David and Karen to be divided between them equally as my Executors shall in their absolute discretion determine.

6. If my said husband is living at my death and survives me by 28 days (but not otherwise) I GIVE to him absolutely but subject to the payment of debts funeral and testamentary expenses all the rest and residue of my estate both real and personal whatsoever and wheresoever not hereby or by any codicil hereto

more specifically disposed of (hereinafter called my 'Residuary Estate').

7. If my husband is not living at my death or does not survive me by 28 days or if the gift to my husband fails for any other reason[1] (but not otherwise) I GIVE my Residuary Estate unto my Trustees TO HOLD the same on trust to sell and convert the same into money with power to postpone the sale and conversion thereof so long as they shall in their absolute discretion think fit without being liable for any loss UPON TRUST TO HOLD the proceeds of the said sale and conversion and any property for the time being remaining unsold and unconverted for such of my children as attain the age of 21 and if more than one in equal shares PROVIDED THAT if any of my children shall die before attaining a vested interest in my Residuary Estate leaving issue who attain the age of 21 years such issue shall take by substitution and if more than one in equal shares per stirpes the share of my Residuary Estate which such deceased child of mine would have taken if he or she had survived me to attain a vested interest.

8. I DIRECT that my Trustees shall have the following powers in addition to the powers given to them by the general law:

(1) To invest money and to vary and transpose investments from time to time with the same full and unrestricted freedom to choose investments as if they were a sole absolute beneficial owner.[2]

(2) To apply money in the purchase or improvement of land as a residence for all or any of the beneficiaries for the time being of any trust hereof on such terms as they may in their absolute discretion from time to time impose.[2]

(3) To insure against loss or damage howsoever arising any property for the time being comprised in my Residuary Estate to any amount and to pay any premiums for any such insurance at their absolute discretion out of the income or capital of my Residuary Estate and to use any money received under any such insurance at their absolute discretion either towards making good the loss or damage in respect of which it was received or as if it were proceeds of sale of the insured property.

(4) To advance any capital money from my Residuary Estate in such manner as they in their absolute discretion think fit to or for the benefit of any of the beneficiaries for the time being hereof provided that the money so advanced to or for the benefit of any beneficiary shall not exceed in amount the presumptive or vested share in my Residuary Estate of that beneficiary.[2]

(5) To treat as income all the income from my Residuary Estate whatever the period in respect of which it accrues and to disregard in this respect the legal rules of apportionment.[2]

(6) In any case where my Trustees have power to apply income or capital to or for the benefit of any person who is a minor to accept the receipt of the parent or guardian of such a person or of the minor personally if of the age of 16 years in full discharge and my Trustees shall not be required to see the application of any income or capital so paid.[2]

(7) Section 31 Trustee Act 1925 will have effect as regards the income arising from my Residuary Estate as if:

    (a)    the words in subsection 1(i) "as may, in all the circumstances, be reasonable" were deleted and in their place the words "as my Trustees shall in their absolute discretion think fit" were substituted.

    (b)    the words from "Provided that" to the end of subsection 1 were deleted.

I FURTHER DIRECT that during the period of twenty-one years from my death the statutory powers of maintenance and accumulation shall continue to be exercisable by my Trustees in favour of any child or remoter issue of mine who has reached the age of 18 but not yet attained a vested interest in the capital of my Residuary Estate.[2]

8. I DESIRE that my body shall be cremated.

IN WITNESS whereof I have hereunto set my hand this
              day of         199  .

Signed by the above named
Susan Ann Webster as her
last will in the presence of us
present at the same time who
at her request in her
presence and in the presence
of each other have hereunto
subscribed our names as
witnesses

*Note:*

    1    These words are included to cover the possibility of the gift to the spouse failing (as a result of Wills Act 1837, s.18A) on divorce.

2   These clauses are included because there is a possibility that a trust may arise in the event of the spouse predeceasing and a minor taking under the substitutional gift.

## A3.3  Additional Information required for Preparation of IHT Form 202

We have prepared the IHT Form 202 on the basis that Susan has died survived by her husband.

| | |
|---|---|
| DATE OF BIRTH: | February 14, 1947 |
| DATE OF DEATH: | July 13, 1990 |
| HOUSE: | This was purchased on June 10, 1980. The initial contribution of £38,000 was made by the Websters from joint savings. |
| DEBTS: | A joint mortgage in the names of the testatrix and her husband with the Great Northern Building Society, 35–41, Gladstone Way, Huddersfield, Yorks. The amount outstanding at the date of death is £29,000. There are no other debts. |
| MONEY OWED TO TESTATRIX: | Interest on Building Society Account accrued to date of death, £25 |
| FUNERAL: | Herbert & Co., Wanstead, £500 |
| INTER VIVOS GIFTS: | None. |
| PARTNERS IN GREEN & CO. TAKING GRANT: | Frederick Green and Sarah Lewis |

It is assumed that the Details of the Estate given on p. 467 have remained unchanged.

**Inland Revenue**
**Inheritance Tax**

**Inland Revenue Account**

**For use for an original full grant where**

- the deceased died on or after 18 March 1986 domiciled in the United Kingdom; and
- the estate comprises only property which has passed under the deceased's Will or intestacy or by nomination or beneficially by survivorship, and all that property was situate in the United Kingdom; and
- the total net value of the estate, after deducting any Exemptions and Reliefs claimed, does not exceed the threshhold above which Inheritance Tax is payable at the date of death.

If the above conditions are met, save only that the deceased died on a date between 27 March 1981 and 17 March 1986 inclusive, the appropriate form is Cap 202. In all other cases form IHT 200 or 201 or Cap 200 or 201 as appropriate must be used unless the estate is an excepted estate under the IHT (Delivery of Accounts) Regulations. For an excepted estate no account need be completed, although exceptionally one may be required.

| Name and address of person to whom any communication should be sent. | For Official use |
|---|---|
| FREDERICK GREEN<br>GREEN & CO., 13 HIGH STREET<br>WANSTEAD<br>LONDON          Postcode E11 4PP | Date of Grant<br><br>FCS _____<br><br>Review S _____<br><br>Reader _____<br><br>Stats _____ |

| Reference | Telephone No |
|---|---|
| GPP/122 | 111/2222 |

**In the High Court of Justice Family Division (Probate)**

The (a) ....PRINCIPAL................................................ **Registry**     *(a) Insert "Principal" or "District" as required; in the latter case please add the name of the district*

In the estate of ..ISUSAN ANN WEBSTER,................
*please use CAPITAL letters*

| Surname in CAPITAL letters | WEBSTER | | |
|---|---|---|---|
| Title and first names in full | SUSAN ANN | | |

| Date of birth<br>(eg 9 September 1988 = 09 SEP 1988) | 1 4 F E B 1 9 4 7 | Date of death | 1 3 J U L 1 9 9 0 |
|---|---|---|---|

| Last usual address | Marital status | *Tick as appropriate* | |
|---|---|---|---|
| 13 NORWICH WAY<br>WANSTEAD<br>LONDON | married ☑    divorced ☐<br>single ☐    widowed ☐ | | |
| | Surviving relatives | | |
| | Husband ☑    Child(ren) ☑<br>Wife ☐    Parent(s) ☐ | | |
| Postcode E11 4PP | Occupation    SCHOOL TEACHER | | |

| Country of domicile  *Tick as appropriate*  England and Wales ☐ | Scotland ☐ | N. Ireland ☐ |
|---|---|---|

Names and addresses of executors or intending administrators:

| FREDERICK GREEN<br>GREEN & CO.<br>(AS ABOVE)          Postcode | SARAH LEWIS<br>GREEN & CO.<br>(AS ABOVE)          Postcode |
|---|---|
| Postcode | Postcode |

**IHT 202**                    1

*Declaration*

1   I/we desire to obtain a grant of (b) **PROBATE**                    *(b) insert kind of grant*

***No alteration is permitted to paragraphs 2 - 8***

2   To the best of ~~my~~/our knowledge and belief all the statements and particulars furnished in this account and its accompanying schedules are true and complete.

3   The deceased made no transfers of value or potentially exempt transfers chargeable with Inheritance Tax (ie no transfers of value that were not covered by the IHT exemptions) within 7 years of the death.

4   The deceased made no gifts, subject to a reservation to the donor, on or after 18 March 1986 and within 7 years of the death.

5   Account "A" is a complete and true account of all the property in the estate at the death in respect of which the grant is to be made and of its value at that time.

6   Account "B" is a complete and true account of any nominated property, and of any property held jointly with any other person(s) the beneficial interest in which passed by survivorship, and of its value at the date of death.

7   No property situate outside the United Kingdom was comprised in the estate at the death.

8   The deceased did not have an interst in settled property at his death nor had he within 7 years of his death an interest in settled property or settled any property.

| | |
|---|---|
| Signed by the above named<br><br>**FREDERICK GREEN**<br><br>Date | Signed by the above named<br><br><br>Date |
| Signed by the above named<br>**SARAH LEWIS**<br><br>Date | Signed by the above named<br><br><br>Date |

**Warning: An executor or intending administrator who fails to make full enquiries and personally verify that the statements in this account are true may make himself liable for prosecution or penalties.**

**Account A - property of the deceased in respect of which the grant is to be made**

| **Property without the instalment option** | **Gross value at date of death (before deduction of exemption(s) or relief(s))**<br>**£** |
|---|---|
| 1   British Savings Bonds and other Government Securities, Savings Certificates and Premium Bonds. *Give description and state amount of each security held, attaching a schedule if necessary.* In the case of Savings Certificates please attach a letter from the Savings Certificates Division or a list giving details of purchase and value of each certificate at date of death. | |
| 2   Other Stocks, Shares or Investments including Unit Trusts. (Give details on form Cap 40 or similar schedule attached and state in adjoining box the total value of all investments). | |
| 3   Cash and Cash at Bank, Savings Banks or in Building, Co-operative or Friendly Societies, including interest to date of death (state each separately and attach a schedule if necessary). **AB BUILDING SOCIETY: CAPITAL**<br>**INTEREST TO DATE OF DEATH** | 500<br>25 |
| 4   Policies of Insurance<br>a   on the life of the deceased, including any bonuses thereon (state each item separately, giving names of companies).<br>b   on the life of any other person (enter surrender value and attach letter from the Company). | |

2

| 5 | Household and Personal Goods (furniture, jewellery, clothes, car, etc). | | 9,000 |
|---|---|---|---|
| 6 | Other assets not included above or as instalment option property. (If space is insufficient please give details on schedule attached and state in adjoining column total value of these assets). | | |
| | | **Total 1** | 9,525 |

**Debts due from the deceased**

Amount

1  Debts (other than mortgage and business debts)

£

| Name and address of creditor | Description of debt |
|---|---|
| | |

*If there is insufficient space to list all debts a schedule should be attached*

| 2 | Funeral expenses | | 500 |
|---|---|---|---|
| | HERBERT & CO. WANSTEAD HIGH STREET WANSTEAD | **Total 2** | 500 |

**Instalment option property**

Gross value at date of death (before deduction of exemption(s) or relief(s)) £

1  Freehold and leasehold property *(form Cap 37 should also be completed)* situated at

2  Business interests *state nature of business*
   a  Net value of deceased's interest in business, as statement of balance sheet annexed.

   b  Net value of deceased's interest as a partner in a firm of

   as statement annexed.

| | **Total 3** | NIL |
|---|---|---|

**Debts due in respect of instalment option property**

Amount

1  Mortgages on freehold and leasehold property (amount outstanding at date of death)
   Date of mortgage
   Property on which mortgage charged
   To whom owed

£

2  Other debts if space is insufficient please attach a schedule

| Name and address of creditor | Description of debt |
|---|---|
| | |

| | **Total 4** | NIL |
|---|---|---|

3

**Joint Property - Questions**

Was the deceased joint owner of any property of any description or did he hold any money on a joint account (apart from property or money of which he was merely a trustee)?

*Tick as appropriate*

Yes ☑   No ☐

If so, please give full particulars including

a   the date when the joint ownership began (or the date of opening the joint account)

b   the name(s) of the other owner(s)

c   by whom and from what source the joint property was provided and, if it or its purchase price was contributed by one or more of the joint owners, the extent of the contribution made by each

d   how the income (if any) was dealt with and enjoyed

e   what is considered to be the extent of the deceased's share of interest

(a) HOUSE PURCHASED JUNE 10, 1980

(b) PETER WEBSTER

(c) INITIAL CONTRIBUTION OF £38,000 PROVIDED FROM JOINT SAVINGS. SUBSEQUENT PAYMENTS MADE BY PETER WEBSTER

(d) ——

(e) ONE HALF

---

**Account B - Nominated and joint property**

Gross value at date of death (before deduction of exemption(s) and relief(s)

Full description of property, real and personal, being nominated property and property held jointly with any other person(s) the beneficial interest in which passed by survivorship. *Show gross value at date of death of the proportion chargeable to tax before deduction of exemption(s) and relief(s). If space is insufficient, please attach a schedule.*

£

FREEHOLD PROPERTY 13, NORWICH WAY WANSTEAD LONDON HELD AS BENEFICIAL JOINT TENANTS — **Total 5** — 82,500

Less appropriate share of debts or incumbrances thereon. *Give details. If space is insufficient please attach a schedule.* — 14,500

JOINT MORTGAGE ON ABOVE PROPERTY WITH THE GREAT NORTHERN BUILDING SOCIETY, 35–41 GLADSTONE WAY, HUDDERSFIELD, YORKS. — **Total 6** — 68,000

| Value for probate purposes | | | £ |
|---|---|---|---|
| Gross estate | as total 1 | 9,525 | 9,525 |
| | as total 3 | NIL | **Total 7** |
| Less debts | as total 2 | 500 | |
| | as total 4 | NIL | |
| | Net estate for probate purposes **Total 8** | | 9,025 |

| Value of estate for tax purposes | | £ |
|---|---|---|
| Nominated and joint property (net) | as **Total 6** | 68,000 |
| Net estate for probate purposes | as **Total 8** | 9,025 |
| | **Total 9** | 77,025 |

**Deduct Exemptions and Reliefs claimed**
1   Agricultural relief: Schedule annexed
2   Business relief: Schedule annexed
3   Spouse exemption: Schedule annexed   3.   77,025
4   Other (please specify)

Net estate for tax purposes   NIL

Prints of this form and of the instructions (IHT 210) can be obtained from the Capital Taxes Office, Inland Revenue, Rockley Road, London W14 0DF and on personal application only at the Stamps Office, Room G3, South West Wing, Bush House, Strand, WC2B 4DN, the London Chief Post Office, King Edward Street, EC1A 1AA, The Branch Post Offices at 24 Throgmorton Street, EC2N 2JF; 40 Fleet Street, EC4Y 1BT; 181 High Holborn, WC1 1AA; 2-4 Bishops Court, Chancery Lane, WC2A 1EA and from other large branch post offices in major towns and cities outside the Metropolitan Postal District as listed in form CAP 18 (which can be obtained from the Capital Taxes Office).

Printed in the UK for HMSO. Dd 8137975/80 C 1/89 C 1500 5924

## A4.1 Instruction sheet for Will of Thomas Shaw (Will No. 3)

INTRODUCTION

This will is a will of a widower with a relatively large estate. The executors appointed are the members of a firm of solicitors. Apart from some minor gifts including one to a University College the estate is given to the testator's sister for life remainder to a charity.

DETAILS OF TESTATOR

| | |
|---|---|
| name: | Thomas Shaw, |
| address: | 3, Normandy Street, Hastings, Sussex. |
| occupation: | Retired company director. |
| date of birth: | 12th May, 1912. |

INTENDED BENEFICIARIES

| | |
|---|---|
| sister: | Miss Edith Shaw,<br>16, Gray Square, Eastbourne, Sussex. |
| college: | St. Michael's, University of Camford. |
| cousin: | Frederick Roberts,<br>3, Castle View, Dorking, Surrey. |
| charity: | Hastings Society for the Relief of Poverty. |

DETAILS OF ESTATE

| | |
|---|---|
| house: | 3, Normandy Street as above value £260,000. |
| shares: | (a) Minority shareholding in Hastings Holdings (Manufacturing) Ltd. value £5,000 (20% of share capital in Company).<br>(b) Quoted shares in various companies total value £55,428. |
| money: | Building Society Account £10,527. (South Coast Building Society Ordinary A/C No. 1234567) Bank Account current (at Bartholomew's Bank Hastings) £583. |

money:                    Cash £37.

stamp collection:         Value £12,700.

household goods,
etc:                      Value £5,000.

PROPOSED TESTAMENTARY DISPOSITIONS
   minor gifts:           Stamp collection to sister
                          £1,000 to St. Michael's College
                          Camford.
                          £5,000 to Frederick Roberts

   residue:               To sister for life remainder to Hastings
                          Society for the Relief of Poverty.

   executors and          Messrs. French and Co. (Solicitors)
   trustees:              Bank Chambers, 27 South Street,
                          Hastings HA1 4SJ

A draft will is shown below.

## A4.2                    WILL NO. 3

THIS IS THE LAST WILL AND TESTAMENT of me THOMAS SHAW of
3 Normandy Street, Hastings, Sussex.
   1. I HEREBY REVOKE all former wills and testamentary
dispositions made by me.
   2. I APPOINT the partners at the date of my death in the firm
of French and Co. Solicitors or the firm which at that date has
succeeded to and carries on its practice (hereinafter called 'my
Trustees' which expression shall where the context so permits
include any trustee for the time being of this will) of Bank
Chambers 27 South Street Hastings to be the executors and
trustees of this will and I express the wish that two and only two
of them shall prove my will I DECLARE that my Trustees shall be
entitled to charge and be paid without abatement all usual
professional or other charges for services rendered and time
spent by them or their firm connected with the administration of
my estate or the trusts of this will including anything which a
trustee not engaged in any profession could have done
personally.
   3. I GIVE to my sister Edith Shaw of 16 Gray Square
Eastbourne Sussex absolutely and free of all taxes[1] and all costs

of package carriage and insurance incurred for the purposes of giving effect to this gift, my collection of postage stamps together with all albums catalogues and other materials relating thereto.

4. I GIVE to the Master Fellows and Scholars of the College of St. Michael in the University of Camford the sum of £1,000.

5. I GIVE to my cousin Frederick Roberts of 3 Castle View Dorking Surrey the sum of £5,000 absolutely and free of all taxes.

6. I GIVE all the rest and residue of my estate both real and personal whatsoever and wheresoever not more specifically disposed of hereby or by any codicil hereto to my Trustees TO HOLD the same on trust for sale with full power to postpone the sale thereof without being liable for loss and after payment thereout of all my debts and funeral and testamentary expenses and all legacies given hereby or by any codicil hereto TO HOLD the balance and any property for the time being remaining unsold (hereinafter called my 'Residuary Estate') UPON TRUST to pay the income therefrom to my said sister Edith Shaw during her lifetime and subject thereto UPON TRUST after the death of my said sister to pay and transfer the same to the Hastings Society for the Relief of Poverty for its general purposes.

7. I DIRECT that my Trustees shall have the following powers in addition to the powers given to them by the general law:

(1)   [Power of investment as in clause 8(1) of Will No. 2]

(2)   [Power of insurance as in clause 8(3) of Will No. 2]

(3)   Power to exercise the power of appropriation conferred by section 41 of the Administration of Estates Act 1925 without obtaining any of the consents required by that section.

(4)   Power in their absolute discretion to pay to my sister for her sole benefit or to lend to my sister with or without security and on such terms as to repayment and as to the payment of interest as they see fit the whole or any part or parts of the capital of my Residuary Estate.

(5)   Power to treat as income all the income from my Residuary Estate whatever the period in respect of which it accrues and to disregard in this respect the rules of equity known as the rules in Howe v. Lord Dartmouth and Allhusen v. Whittell in all their branches and the legal rules of apportionment.

8. I DIRECT that if before my Trustees have given effect to any gift contained herein any charitable or other body to which such gift is made has changed its name or has amalgamated with or transferred its assets to any other body my Trustees shall give effect to such gift as if it had been made as a gift to the body in its changed name or to the body with which it had amalgamated or to which it had transferred its assets as the case may be and I FURTHER DIRECT that the receipt of the person who appears to my Trustees to be the bursar treasurer or other proper officer for the time being of any charitable or other body to which any gift contained herein is made shall be a sufficient discharge to my Trustees.

IN WITNESS whereof (etc. as in Will No. 1 or 2).

## A4.3 Additional information required for Preparation of IHT Form 200

| | | |
|---|---|---|
| DATE OF BIRTH: | 12th May 1912 | |
| DATE OF DEATH: | 15th August 1990 | |
| DEBTS: | Owed to Conqueror | |
| | Auctions Ltd. | £454 |
| | " "  British Telecom | £27 |
| | " "  Council (Community | |
| | Charge) | £52 |
| MONEY OWED | Dividends on quoted shares | |
| TO TESTATOR: | attributable to period before death | £680 |
| | Building Society Interest accrued | |
| | to date of death | £400 |
| | Pension | £326 |
| | Income tax repayment | £469 |
| FUNERAL: | Peters & Co. Ltd. | £437 |
| INTER VIVOS | A car worth £10,000 to sister | |
| GIFTS: | 1st January, 1988. | |
| PARTNERS IN | George Albert French    } to take | |
| FRENCH & CO.: | Alice Emily Brown        } grant | |
| TAKING GRANT: | Michael French—power reserved to | |
| | prove at later stage. | |

It is assumed that the Details of the Estate given on p. 476 have remained unchanged.

A draft IHT Form 200 is shown below, pages 480–491.

**Inland Revenue**
Inheritance Tax *

**Inland Revenue Account**

- For use where the deceased died on or after 18 March 1986 domiciled in the United Kingdom
- Please see IHT 210 for instructions on how to complete this form

* Capital Transfer Tax in the case of a death before 25 July 1986

| For Official Use |
| --- |

| Your reference | Name and address of solicitors ∅ |
| --- | --- |
| GAF1211 | FRENCH & CO. BANK CHAMBERS 27 SOUTH STREET HASTINGS SUSSEX  Postcode HA1 4SJ |
| **Your telephone number** | |
| 001–45–273–265 | |

∅ All communications concerning Inheritance Tax will be sent to the Solicitors unless the executors or administrators request otherwise.

**In the High Court of Justice Family Division (Probate)**

**The PRINCIPAL Registry**

**In the estate of** THOMAS SHAW

| Date of Grant |
| --- |

Please use CAPITAL letters

| Surname | Date of birth |
| --- | --- |
| SHAW | 1 2 M A Y 1 9 1 2 |

| Title and Forenames | Date of death |
| --- | --- |
| MR THOMAS | 1 5 A U G 1 9 9 0 |

| Marital Status | Please tick as appropriate | Last usual address |
| --- | --- | --- |
| Married ☐  Single ☐  Divorced ✓  Widowed ☐ | | 3 NORMANDY STREET HASTINGS SUSSEX |
| **Surviving Relatives** | | |
| Husband ☐  Wife ☐  Child(ren) ☐  Parent(s) ☐ | | Postcode   111 |
| **Domicile** | | |
| England and Wales ☐  Scotland ☐  N.Ireland ☐ | Occupation | RETIRED COMPANY DIRECTOR |

| Please state the Tax District at which the tax affairs of the deceased were handled | HASTINGS | Tax District Reference 000/111/222 |
| --- | --- | --- |

Please give the names and permanent addresses of the executors or intending administrators:

| GEORGE ALBERT FRENCH FRENCH & CO. (AS ABOVE)  Postcode | ALICE EMILY BROWN FRENCH & CO. (AS ABOVE)  Postcode |
| --- | --- |
| Postcode | Postcode |

IHT200

1

## Declaration

1. I/We desire to obtain a grant of PROBATE OF THE WILL of the aforenamed deceased.

2. To the best of my/our knowledge and belief all the statements and particulars furnished in this account and its accompanying schedules are true and complete.

*Delete paragraph if inappropriate*

3. I/We have made the fullest enquiries that are reasonably practicable in the circumstances but have not been able to ascertain the exact value of the property referred to in Exhibit                    to section            So far as the value can now be estimated, it is stated in section            . I/We undertake, as soon as the value is ascertained, to deliver a further account, and to pay both any additional tax payable for which I/We may be liable, and any further tax payable, for which I/We may be liable on the other property mentioned in this account.

*Delete what is inappropriate*

4. So far as the tax on the property disclosed in sections 1B, 2B and 3 may be paid by instalments, I/We elect to pay/not to pay by instalments as indicated in these sections.

Signed by the above-named

### GEORGE ALBERT FRENCH

date

Signed by the above-named

### ALICE EMILY BROWN

date

Signed by the above-named

date

Signed by the above-named

date

### Warning

An executor or intending administrator who fails to make the fullest enquiries that are reasonably practicable in the circumstances may be liable to penalties.

He or she may be liable to penalties or prosecution if he or she fails to disclose in Section 1A, 1B, 2A, 2B and 3 (as appropriate) and in his or her answers to the questions on page 3 and at the foot of page 9 all the property to the best of his or her knowledge and belief in respect of which tax may be payable on the death of the deceased.

Transfers of value which need not be reported are

a. gifts or other transfers of value made to the deceased's spouse unless at the time of transfer the deceased was domiciled in the United Kingdom and the spouse was not

b. gifts of money not exceeding £3,000 in any one year, where the executors or intending administrators are satisfied that they are wholly exempt as normal gifts out of income

c. outright gifts to one individual which are clearly exempt as not exceeding £250 in any one year (to 5 April): (for gifts before 6 April 1980 the exemption is restricted to £100 in any one year)

d. other gifts of money, or of shares or securities quoted on the Stock Exchange, where these, together with any other gifts not within (b) or (c) above, do not in total exceed the exemption for gifts of £3,000 in any one year (to 5 April)

- Any property mentioned on this page which is subject to Inheritance Tax, whether or nor tax is actually payable, **must** also be included in sections 1A, 1B, 2A, 2B, or 3 of this account as appropriate. If it is claimed that the property is not subject to Inheritance Tax, reasons should be given.
- Even if a full report has been made or any other information relevant to the answers to any of the questions below has been given to an Inland Revenue Office, affirmative answers must nonetheless be given to the appropriate questions. Please also identify the office and quote any relevant official reference.
- Where necessary schedules may be attached.

### 1. Gifts etc.

For official use only

**Did the deceased, within 7 years of his/her death**

Please tick yes or no
| | yes | no |
|---|---|---|
| make any gift, settlement or other transfer of value other than a transfer mentioned in the notes on page 2. | ✓ | |
| make any disposition for the maintenance of a relative | | ✓ |
| pay any premium on a policy of life assurance not included in Section 1 of this form? | | ✓ |

**Did the deceased at any time on or after 18 March 1986 dispose of any property by way of gift where either**

- possession and enjoyment of the property was not bona fide assumed by the donee, or
- the property was not enjoyed to the entire exclusion of the donor and of any benefit to him/her by contract or otherwise?

If the reply to any of the questions above is "yes", please give full particulars including dates, details of any property affected and the names and addresses of the other parties concerned, on a separate sheet of paper.

### 2. Settled property

- Was the deceased, at the time of his/her death, entitled to a life interest, annuity or other interest in possession in settled property whether as beneficiary under the settlement or otherwise? ✓
- Did the deceased cease to be entitled to any such interest in settled property within 7 years of his/her death? ✓

If the reply to either question is "yes", please give full particulars of the title (including, in the case of a Will/intestacy, the name and date of death of the testator/intestate and date and place of grant). Where the interest was under a settlement and no previous report has been made, kindly forward a copy of the settlement.

### 3. Nominations

Did the deceased in his lifetime nominate any Savings Bank Account, Savings Certificates or other assets in favour of any person? ✓

If you have answered "yes", please give full particulars in section 2 on page 8.

### 4. Joint property

Was the deceased joint owner of any property of any description or did he/she hold any money on a joint account (apart from property or money of which he/she was merely a trustee)? ✓

**If you have answered "yes" please give the following details on a separate sheet of paper**

- the date when the joint ownership began (or the date of opening the joint account)
- The name(s) of the other joint owner(s)
- By whom and from what source the joint property was provided and, if it or its purchase price was contributed by one or more of the joint owners, the extent ot the contribution made by each
- how the income (if any) was dealt with and enjoyed
- whether the deceased's interest passed under his/her will or intestacy or by survivorship.

## Section 1

**A schedule of all the property of the deceased** within the United Kingdom to which the deceased was beneficially entitled and **in respect of which the grant is made,** excluding property over which the deceased had and exercised by will a general power of appointment. The appointed property should be included in Section 3. Property gifted by the deceased subject to a reservation retained by the deceased should also be included in Section 3 rather than here.

| Section 1A Property without the Instalment Option | Gross value at date of death* | For official use only |
|---|---|---|
| Stocks, shares, debentures and other securities as set out in CAP 40: | | |
| ● Quoted in the Stock Exchange daily official list except so far as included in Section 1B | 55,428 | |
| ● Others, except so far as included in Section 1B | | |
| National Savings Certificates and interest to the date of death | | |
| Uncashed dividends and interest received, dividends declared, and interest accrued due, in respect of the above investments, to the date of death, as statement annexed | 680 | |
| Cash at the bank: | | |
| ● On current account and interest (if any) to the date of death at | | |
| BARTHOLOMEW'S BANK HASTINGS | 583 | |
| ● On deposit and interest to the date of death at | | |
| Cash (other than cash at banks) | | |
| Money at a National or Trustee Savings Bank and interest to the date of death, as statement annexed | 37 | |
| Money out on Mortgage, and interest to the date of death, as statement annexed | | |
| Money with a building society, co-operative or friendly society, and interest to the date of death, as statement annexed    SOUTH COAST BUILDING SOCIETY ORDINARY SHARE ACCOUNT NO. 1234567 | 10,927 | |
| Money out on promissary notes, bonds and other securities, and interest to the date of death, as statement annexed | | |
| Other debts due to the deceased and interest to the date of death, except book debts included in Section 1B, as statement annexed | | |
| Unpaid purchase money of real and leasehold property contracted in the lifetime of the deceased to be sold, as statement annexed | | |
| Rents of the deceased's own real and leasehold property to the date of death | | |
| Apportionment of the rents of the deceased's real and leasehold property to the date of death | | |
| Income accrued due, but not received before the death, arising from real and personal property, in which the deceased had a life or other limited interest, viz:- | | |
| Apportionment of Income from that source to the date of death | | |
| Any other income, apportioned where necessary, to which the deceased was entitled at his death (eg pensions, annuities, director's fees, etc) as statement annexed                     PENSION | 326 | |
| Policies of insurance and bonuses (if any) thereon, on the life of the deceased, as statement annexed | | |
| Saleable value of policies of insurance and bonuses (if any) not payable on the death of the deceased, as statement annexed | | |
| * All claims for exemptions or reliefs should be made in the Summary on page 10                         **To be carried forward** | 67,981 | |

4

## 484 APPENDIX

| Section 1A | Continued | | | For official use only |
|---|---|---|---|---|

| | | | Gross value at date of death* | |
|---|---|---|---|---|
| | | Brought forward | 67,981 | |

**Household and personal goods,** including pictures, china, linen, clothes, books plate, jewels, motor cars, boats, etc.

| | | |
|---|---|---|
| Sold, realised gross | £ | |
| Unsold, estimated | £ | 5,000 |

**The deceased's interest expectant upon death of**

aged          years, under the will/intestacy of

who died on the
or under a settlement dated the
and made between

(setting out the parties to the deed), in the property set out in the statement annexed, of which fund the present trustees are

Tick as appropriate

Was the interest at any time acquired for value whether by the deceased or a predecessor in title?          Yes ☐          No ☐

**Income tax payable**

469

**Other personal property not comprised under the preceding heads**
*Please give details*

STAMP COLLECTION
(AS PER VALUATION ATTACHED)

12,700

**Gross property not subject to the instalment option to be carried to page 6 and to the Probate Summary on page 12**

86,150

* All claims for exemptions or reliefs should be made in the Summary on page 10

5

**Section 1A    continued**

**Schedule of liabilities and funeral expenses.** Particulars of the funeral expenses of the deceased and the liabilities due and owing from him at the time of his death to persons resident within the United Kingdom or to persons resident out of the United Kingdom but contracted to be paid in the United Kingdom, or charged on property situated within the United Kingdom (other than liabilities deducted in Section 1B or section 2 under footnote (b) on page 8).

| Name and address of creditor | Description of liability | Amount | For official use only |
|---|---|---|---|
| HASTINGS BOROUGH COUNCIL TOWN HALL HIGH STREET HASTINGS | COMMUNITY CHARGE | 52 | |
| BRITISH TELECOM TELECOM HOUSE SIDE STREET HASTINGS | TELEPHONE BILL | 27 | |
| CONQUEROR AUCTIONS LTD. 33 LOWER STREET HASTINGS | OUTSTANDING ACCOUNT | 454 | |
| **Funeral expenses** PETERS & CO. LTD. HASTINGS | | 437 | |
| **Total to be carried to the Summary below and to the Probate Summary on page 12** | | 970 | |

**Summary**

| | |
|---|---|
| Gross property (from page 5) not subject to the instalment option | 86,150 |
| Less total of liabilities and funeral expenses from above | 970 |
| Net property in the United Kingdom not subject to the instalment option to be carried to page 11 (Section 1A, net total before relief(s) | 85,180 |

Section 4 on page 9 must be completed in respect of all liabilities listed in the above schedule.

6

| Section 1B | Property with the Instalment Option | For official use only |
|---|---|---|

*Tick as appropriate*

- Is the tax on this property to be paid on delivery of this account?  Yes ☐  No ☑
- Is payment to be made in yearly instalments?  Yes ☑  No ☐

| | Value at date of death |
|---|---|
| **Land etc.** owned by the deceased in the United Kingdom (not being settled land) whether or not subject to a trust for sale as described on Cap 37 annexed. | 260,000 |
| **Business interests** | |
| • Net value of deceased's interest in the business(es), as statement or balance sheet annexed. | |
| • Net value of deceased's interest as partner in the firm of | |
| as statement or balance sheet annexed | |
| **Stocks, shares, debentures and other securities,** as set out on Cap 40. | |
| • Shares or securities etc within Section 228(1) (a) Inheritance Tax Act 1984 which gave the deceased control of the company immediately before his death *see Section 269 Inheritance Tax Act 1984.* | |
| • Other unquoted shares or securities etc. within Section 228(1) (b) or (c) or (d) Inheritance Tax Act 1984 (all other unquoted shares to be included in Section 1A). | 5,000 |
| Value of property within the instalment option to be carried to the Probate Summary on Page 12. | 265,000 |

**Liabilities charged at the date of the deceased's death on the property included above other than those already taken into account above**

| Particulars of liability | Property on which charged | Amount |
|---|---|---|
| | | |
| Total liabilities to be carried to the Probate Summary on page 12. | | NIL |

| Value of property with the instalment option less liabilities to be carried to page 11 (Section 1B, net total before reliefs). | 265,000 |
|---|---|

*\* All claims for exemptions and reliefs should be made in the Summary on page 10.*

**Section 4 on page 9 must be completed in respect of all liabilities listed above**

7

**Section 2**

**All other property on which the personal representatives are liable to pay the tax** (or would be liable if any tax were payable) including:-

- all nominated property and property passing by survivorship

- all property situated outside the UK

---

**Section 2A - Property without the Instalment Option**

**Particulars of the property, local situation and details of disposition if nominated or in joint names**

**Value at date of death**

Gross Value

**Liabilities* in respect of the property above**

**Amount**

| Name and Address of Creditor | Description of liability |
|---|---|
| | |

Total liabilities

Net value to be carried to page 11 (Section 2A, net total before reliefs) | **NIL**

For official use only

---

**Section 2B - Property with the Instalment Option**

*Tick as appropriate*

- Is the tax on this property to be paid on delivery of this account?  Yes [ ]  No [ ]

- Is payment to be made by yearly instalments?  Yes [ ]  No [ ]

**Particulars of the property, local situation and details of disposition if nominated or in joint names**

**Value at date of death**

Gross Value

**Liabilities* In respect of the property above**

**Amount**

| Name and Address of Creditor | Description of Liability |
|---|---|
| | |

Total liabilities

Net value to be carried to page 11 (Section 2B, net total before reliefs) | **NIL**

* All claims for exemptions or reliefs should be made in the Summary on page 10
+ Liabilities    (a) due from the deceased at the time of his death to persons resident outside the United Kingdom (other than liabilities contracted to be paid in the United Kingdom, or charged on property within the United Kingdom which have been deducted in Sections 1A and 1B) or
   (b) (so far as not included in (a) charged upon incurred in connection with or otherwise affecting the property included in this Section

**Section 4 on page 9 must be completed in respect of all liabilities listed above.**

8

**Section 3**

**Any other property in the UK and elsewhere** in which the deceased had or is treated as having had a beneficial interest in possession immediately before his death including:-

- property over which the deceased had and exercised by will a general power of appointment.

- property outside the UK comprised in a settlement made by a UK domiciled person.

- property gifted by the deceased subject to a reservation retained by the deceased.

---

**Part 1 Property on which tax is elected to be paid on delivery of this account** should be listed below and headed "Part 1"

- Is the tax on any property with the Instalment Option to be paid by yearly    *Tick as appropriate*
  instalments?

  [ ] Yes          [ ] No

- Separate net totals for Part 1 (property without the instalment option) and Part 1 (property with the instalment option) should be carried to page 11 (Sections 1a (non-instalment option property) and 1b (instalment option property) net totals before reliefs).

**Part 2 Property on which tax is not to be paid on delivery of this account** should be listed below and headed "Part 2" and its net value carried to page 11 (Section 1c, net total before reliefs).

---

| Separate consecutive numbering for part 1 and part 2 | Particulars of the property | Net value at date of death * | | For official use only |
|---|---|---|---|---|
| | | **Property without the instalment option £** | **Property with the instalment option £** | |
| | | | | |

\* *All claims for exemptions or reliefs should be made in the Summary on page 10*

**Section 4**

**Deductions of liabilities listed in this account**

|  | *Tick as appropriate* | |
|---|---|---|
| | Yes | No |

In the case of any liability for which a decuction has been taken in either section 1A, 1B, 2A, 2B or 3 of this account did the consideration for any such debt or incumbrance incurred or created on or after 18 March 1986 consist of property derived from the deceased or was the consideration given by any person who was at any time entitled to, or amongst whose resources there was at any time included any property derived from the deceased?                                          [ ] Yes   [✓] No

If "Yes", please give full particulars, including the liabilities in question, the consideration given and the derivation of that consideration from the deceased.

*Please attach schedules as necessary.*

**Summary of exemptions and reliefs against capital**

- please see instruction booklet IHT 210 as to how this page should be completed

- Schedules should be attached as necessary

| Property in respect of which exemption or relief is claimed. The description should not be more detailed than is necessary to identify the property | Nature of exemption or relief claimed | Net value of property £ | Amounts exemption or relief claimed £ | For official use only |
|---|---|---|---|---|
| **Property included in Section 1A**<br><br>LEGACY TO ST MICHAEL'S COLLEGE CAMFORD OF £1,000 CASH | NATIONAL PURPOSES<br><br>(IHTA 1984, S.25) | 1,000 | 1,000 | |
| Total of exemptions and reliefs Section 1A to be carried to page 11 (reliefs column) | | | 1,000 | |
| **Property included in Section 1B**<br><br>SHARES IN HASTINGS HOLDINGS (MANUFACTURING) LTD. | BUSINESS PROPERTY<br><br>(IHTA 1984, S.104) | 5,000 | 1,500 | |
| Total of exemptions and reliefs Section 1B to be carried to page 11 (reliefs column) | | | 1,500 | |
| **Property included in other sections - state and show separately which section (sections 2A and B and 3 (Part 1) and 3 (Part 2)** A separate total of exemptions and reliefs for each of these sections should be carried to page 11 (reliefs column) | | | | |
| | | | | |

## Assessment of Inheritance Tax

**Summary for determining chargeable rates**

**Calculation of tax**

| Section of accounts | Net total £ | Reliefs £ | Value of property after reliefs £ |
|---|---|---|---|
| 1(a) Property without the instalment option | | | |
| 1A | 85,180 | 1,000 | 84,180 |
| 2A | NIL | | NIL |
| 3, Part 1 | NIL | | NIL |
| Total 1(a) | | | 84,180 |
| 1(b) Property with the instalment option | | | |
| 1B | 265,000 | 1,500 | 263,500 |
| 2B | NIL | | NIL |
| 3, Part 1 | NIL | | NIL |
| Total 1(b) | | | 263,500 |
| 1(c) Other property on which tax is not being paid on this account | | | |
| 3, Part 2 | NIL | | |
| Total 1(c) | NIL | | NIL |
| Total 1 (a) to (c) | | A | 347,680 |
| Cumulative total of chargeable transfers made prior to the deceased's death | | B | 4,000 |
| Aggregate chargeable transfers (A + B) | | C | 351,680 |

| | £ | p |
|---|---|---|
| Tax on **C** on first £ 128,000 | NIL | |
| plus on balance of £ 223,680 @ 40% | 89,472 | 00 |
| Total | 89,472 | 00 |
| Less tax on **B** at death rate on first £ 4,000 | NIL | |
| plus on balance of £ NIL @ % | NIL | |
| Total | NIL | |
| Less QSR (as attached schedule) | NIL | |
| Total tax chargeable on **A**    **D** | 89,472 | 00 |

Any capital figure multiplied by **D** gives the
$$\frac{D}{A}$$
proportion of tax assessable on that capital

**Value on which tax is now being paid**

| | Value of property | |
|---|---|---|
| | non-instalment £ | Instalment option £ |
| Total value at 1(a) | 84,180 | |
| That part of 1(b) on which tax now to be paid | | NIL |

**Amount payable on this account**

| Non instalment property | £ | p |
|---|---|---|
| Total value at 1(a) £ 84,180 × $\frac{D}{A}$ = | 21,662 | 88 |
| *Less* reliefs against tax other than QSR | NIL | |
| Net tax | 21,662 | 88 |
| *add interest on net tax from 19 to 19 ( years days at %) | NIL | |
| Total tax and interest on non-instalment property (carried to page 12) | 21,662 | 88 |
| Additional tax and interest due under S7 IHTA 1984-as attached schedule (carried to page 12) | NIL | |

| Instalment option property | £ | p |
|---|---|---|
| That part of 1(b) on which tax now to be paid £ × $\frac{D}{A}$ = | NIL | |
| *Less* reliefs against tax other than QSR    Net tax | | |
| *add interest on net tax from 19 to 19 ( years days at %) | | |
| **Instalments** - tenths of net tax | | |
| add interest on instalments now assessed from 19 (date last instalment due) to 19 ( days at %) | | |
| †add interest on whole of net tax on instalment property from 19 to 19 ( years days at %) | | |
| Total tax and interest on instalment option property (carried to page 12) | | |

**Interest**

Tax becomes due 6 months after the end of the month in which the death occurred. Unpaid tax carries interest from and including the day after the due date, irrespective of the reason for the late payment.
† Only if the due date for the second or subsequent instalment has now passed and interest relief (see IHT 210) is not in point, add here interest on the whole of the net tax on the instalment option property up to the due date of the last instalment.

Interest on overpaid tax: please note that, where tax or interest is paid in excess of the amount found to be due, interest is allowed on the amount overpaid.

## Probate Summary

| | | £ |
|---|---|---|
| Aggregate Gross Value which in law devolves on and vests in the personal representatives of the deceased, for and in respect of which the Grant is to be made | Section 1A | 86,150 |
| | Section 1B | 265,000 |
| | Section 3* | NIL |

*\* absolute power property only*

| | £ |
|---|---|
| **Total to be carried to the probate papers** | 351,150 |

**Deduct**

| | £ |
|---|---|
| Section 1A, total of liabilities and funeral expenses | 970 |
| Section 1B, total of liabilities | NIL |
| **Net value for probate purposes** | 350,180 |

**For official use only**

| | £ |
|---|---|
| Total of Tax and Interest from page 11 | |
| Total Tax and Interest - Non-Instalment Property | 21,662.88 |
| Total Tax and Interest - Instalment Option Property | NIL |
| Additional Tax and Interest due under S7 Inheritance Tax Act 1984 | NIL |
| **Total tax and interest payable now on this account** | 21,662.88 |

**EDP**

| | £ |
|---|---|
| On the basis of this Account the tax (and interest) payable now is | 21,662.88 |

FRENCH & CO.

_____ 19____

Solicitor(s) for the applicant(s)

**This receipt and stamp do not imply that the assessment is not subject to rectification: the account will be fully examined after the issue of the grant.**

Prints of this form and of the instructions (IHT 210) can be obtained from the Capital Taxes Office, Inland Revenue, Rockley Road, London W14 0DF and on personal application only at the Stamps Office, Room G3, South West Wing, Bush House, Strand, WC2B 4QN the London Chief Post Office, King Edward Street, EC1A 1AA, the Branch Post Offices at 24 Throgmorton Street, EC2N 2JE; 40 Fleet Street, EC4Y 1BT; 181 High Holborn, WC1 1AA; 2-4 Bishops Court, Chancery Lane, WC2A 1EA and from other large branch post offices in major towns and cities outside the Metropolitan Postal District as listed in form CAP 18 (which can be obtained from the Capital Taxes Office).

Printed in the UK for HMSO 1/89 Dd 8137979 250M 25038

## A5.1 Wills Instructions Checklist

1. *Details of testator*
    (a) Testator's full name
    (b) Any former name(s) or alias(es)
    (c) Address/occupation
    (d) Age (for purposes of tax advice)

2. *Value of estate*
    (a) Property owned in testator's sole name
    (b) Property owned with another as beneficial tenants in common
    (c) Property owned with another as beneficial joint tenants
    (d) Nominations
    (e) Superannuation benefits—nominated?
    (f) Insurance policies—MWPA
                    written in trust
                    payable to estate
    (g) Trust property
    (h) Foreign property
    (i) Inter vivos gifts to date
    (j) Property likely to be inherited
    (k) Debts charged on property?
    (l) Mortgage protection policy
    (m) Business and Agricultural property

3. *Intended beneficiaries*
    (a) Spouse—full name/size of spouse's personal estate
    (b) Children—names/ages
    (c) Others—names/addresses
  N.B. Explain Family Provision legislation particularly if disposition is away from immediate family.

4. *Disposition of property*
    (a) Legacies
        (i) specific
        (ii) general
        (iii) free of tax/expenses/mortgage?
  N.B. Explain possibility of ademption of specific gifts.
    (b) Residue
    (c) Trust for sale
    (d) Directions as to substitutional gift where beneficiary predeceases.
        In case of gift to institution directions as to possible change of name, amalgamation, dissolution.
    (e) Provision for payment of debts? Secured debts?

6. *Extension of statutory powers*
   (a) No trust created (remember that a trust may arise where minor beneficiaries take by substitution the share of a deceased parent)
       (i) insurance
       (ii) appropriation
       (iii) receipt clause—infant—unincorporated association
       (iv) exclude Apportionment Act
   (b) Trust created
       as above *plus*
       (i) investment
       (ii) power to buy land
       (iii) maintenance
       (iv) advancement
       (v) loans to beneficiaries
       (vi) exclude legal and equitable apportionments if appropriate

7. *Executors/Trustees*
   (a) Choice—explain merits of individuals, solicitors' firms, banks
   (b) Charging clause if appropriate
   (c) Special PR's to deal with special parts of estate e.g. literary executors.

8. *Guardians*
   (a) Names and addresses
   (b) Willing to act?
   (c) Finance?

9. *Special problems*
   (a) Testator suffering from disability—capacity? Special attestation clause?
   (b) Testator sole trader—special provisions to deal with business?

10. *Directions as to body, funeral etc.*

# Index